A
BOOK OF LIGHT VERSE

Herrick
1591–1674

Jonson
1573–1637

Prior
1664–1721

Praed
1802–1839

Landor
1775–1864

A BOOK OF
LIGHT VERSE

EDITED BY

R. M. LEONARD

From witty men and mad,
All poetry conception had.
Randolph

HENRY FROWDE
OXFORD UNIVERSITY PRESS
LONDON, NEW YORK, TORONTO AND MELBOURNE
1910

PREFACE

MR. SWINBURNE, in his essay on 'Social Verse', declared
that there was no better or completer anthology than
Mr. F. Locker-Lampson's *Lyra Elegantiarum*; 'a collection of
some of the best specimens of *vers de société* and *vers d'occasion*
in the English language by deceased authors' which was
indeed incomparable, and has been heavily laid under contribution for the present volume. If Mr. Locker-Lampson were
alive to bring out a twentieth-century edition of his collection,
he would, as a matter of course, make many additions and
omissions, especially if space had to be studied. In his 1867
edition there are 24 authors and 52 poems which find no
place in that published nearly a quarter of a century later,
and the latter contains 38 authors and 130 poems which the
earlier volume lacks. Mr. Locker-Lampson expresses regret
that he was prevented by his rule from giving specimens of the
writings of living poets; the Fates have so willed that the
present editor is able to include poems by Robert Browning, Lord
Tennyson, Lord Houghton, Sir Theodore Martin, C. S. Calverley,
Lewis Carroll, O. W. Holmes, J. R. Lowell, and others, English
and American, particularly mentioned in the prefaces to *Lyra
Elegantiarum*, as well as examples of Mr. Locker-Lampson's own
delightful compositions. There are in the present collection
upwards of 60 poets, contributing between them 120 poems,
whose names will not be found in the last edition of the older
anthology. The newer poetry has necessitated omissions, but
some would have been made in any case, for canons of taste
are not fixed once for all, and an editor to-day would be foolish
who did not seek to profit by the criticism of Mr. Swinburne
and other fine judges of poetry. The scope of this volume,
too, is not quite so restricted in intention as was that of *Lyra*

Elegantiarum.   But neither Mr. Locker-Lampson, nor his chief critic, Mr. Swinburne, was able to keep within the limits which the former laid down.   Mr. Locker-Lampson, for example, omits Waller's ' Go Lovely Rose ' as ' too highly poetical ', and Herrick's ' To Blossoms ' and ' To Daffodils ' as ' too elevated ', but he gives Mrs. Barbauld's lyric on death, ' Life ! I know not what thou art ' ; he stipulates that ' brevity and buoyancy are absolutely essential ', and yet gives Swift's ' The Grand Question Debated '.   For Mr. Swinburne's departures from the narrow path his essay may be consulted.   Generally, however, the present editor has kept Mr. Locker-Lampson's touchstone before him, and has availed himself freely of the admirable editing, the almost invariably sound choice, and the interesting notes in *Lyra Elegantiarum*.   In that volume (to quote from the original preface) and in this :—

' Fables, prologues, rhymed anecdotes, and pieces of purely ephemeral interest, such as satirical or political squibs, have been generally avoided, as well as those specimens which expand into real song or crystallize into mere epigram, though in these cases, as already observed, the border line is often extremely difficult of definition.   Riddles, paradoxes, and punning couplets are for the most part omitted ; not, as some readers may suppose, because they are contemptible, for nothing is contemptible that is really good of its kind ; but because they do not, strictly speaking, come within the scope of this work.'

It would be difficult to find a better judge than Mr. Locker-Lampson, though, as already said, he found it impossible to maintain an exact line of demarcation, and his definitions are worth giving again.

' It may be as well to observe, that *vers de société* need by no means be confined to topics of artificial life.   Subjects of the most exalted, and of the most trivial, character, may be treated with equal success, provided the manner of their treatment is in accordance with the following characteristics, which the Editor ventures to submit as expressive of his own ideas on this subject.   In his judgement genuine *vers de société* and *vers d'occasion* should be short, elegant, refined, and fanciful, not seldom distinguished by chastened sentiment, and often playful. The tone should not be pitched high ; it should be idiomatic, and rather in the conversational key ; the rhythm should be crisp and sparkling, and the rhyme frequent and never forced, while the entire poem should be marked by tasteful moderation, high finish, and completeness : for, however trivial the subject-matter may be, indeed rather in proportion to its triviality, subordination to the rules of composition and perfection of execution should be strictly enforced. . . . The two qualities of brevity and buoyancy are absolutely essential. The poem may be tinctured with a well-bred philosophy, it may be gay and gallant, it may be playfully malicious or tenderly ironical, it may display lively banter, and it may be satirically facetious ; it may even, considering it merely as a work of art, be pagan in its philosophy, or trifling in its tone, but it must never be ponderous or common-place. . . . The chief merit of *vers de société* is, that it should seem to be entirely spontaneous : when the reader says to himself, " I could have written that, and easily too," he pays the poet the highest possible compliment. At the same time it is right to observe that this absence of effort, as recognized in most works of real excellence, is only apparent ; the writing of *vers de société* is a difficult accomplishment, and no one has fully succeeded in it without possessing a certain gift of irony, which is not only a much rarer quality than humour, or even wit, but is altogether less commonly met with than is sometimes imagined. At the same time this description of poetry seems so easy to write that a long catalogue of authors, both famous and obscure, have attempted it, but in the great majority of cases with very indifferent success. This frequent liability to failure will excite less surprise if it be borne in mind that the possession of the true poetic faculty is not sufficient of itself to guarantee capacity for this inferior branch of the art of versification. The writer of *vers de société*, in order to be genuinely successful, must not only be more or less of a poet, but he must also be a man of the world, in the most liberal sense of the expression ; he must have mixed throughout his life with the most refined and cultivated members of his species, not merely as an idle bystander, but as a busy actor in the throng. A professed poet, however exalted his faculty, will seldom write the best *vers de société*, just because writing is the business of his life ; for it appears to be an essential characteristic of these brilliant trifles, that they should be thrown off in the leisure moments of men whose lives are devoted to graver pursuits. Swift was an ardent politician ; Prior a zealous ambassador ; Suckling, Praed, and Landor were essentially men of action ; even Cowper was no recluse, but a man of the world, forced by mental suffering into a state of modified seclusion. Indeed, it may be affirmed of most of the authors quoted in this volume—and it is curious to see what a large proportion of them are men of a certain social position—that they submitted their intellects to the monotonous grindstone of worldly business, and that their poetical compositions were like the sparks which fly off and prove the generous quality of the metal thus applied ; and it must be remembered, to pursue the simile, that but for the dull grindstone, however finely tempered the metal might be, there would be no sparks at all : in other words, the writer of *vers de société* needs perpetual contact with the world.'

When *Lyra Elegantiarum* first appeared, the art of writing light verse—' where a boudoir decorum is, or ought to be, preserved ; where sentiment never surges into passion, and where humour never overflows into boisterous merriment '— had fallen upon evil days. Now, happily, there are several living poets who have revived, or who now cultivate, the art, and no invidious comparisons need be provoked by the mention of Mr. Austin Dobson, Mr. Andrew Lang, Sir W. S. Gilbert, Sir Arthur Quiller-Couch, Mr. A. D. Godley, and Mr. Owen Seaman. The work of living authors is, however, necessarily excluded from this volume.

No one who reads through the following pages carefully can fail to be struck with the modern characteristics of much old poetry which age cannot wither. It is often impossible to realize, for instance, that Prior has been dead for nearly two centuries. Not only may the reader say ' I could have written that ', but also ' It might have been written yesterday '. Sir Arthur Quiller-Couch has noted ' how constantly and curiously Jonson, especially in the *Underwoods*, seems to anticipate the best and something more than the best, manner of Browning ' ; especially mentioning ' The Triumph of Charis ' as a case in point.

A slight modification here and there, or an occasional

omission, has enabled the present editor, as it enabled
Mr. Locker-Lampson, to include poems which would be
otherwise unsuitable for a popular anthology. If justifica-
tion be required for changing, by the substitution of one
word for another, what some might regard as blasphemy
into a classical allusion, or what all must regard as indecency
into innocent merriment, Mr. Swinburne himself may be
pressed into service. ' That to enact the part of Bowdler,'
Mr. Swinburne says, ' should ever be a thankless part to
play in any case of obvious or apparent necessity reflects
little credit on the taste and judgement of those whose
objections or whose ridicule would make it so. More nauseous
and more foolish cant was never chattered than that which
would deride the memory or depreciate the merits of Bowdler.'
Mr. Swinburne's tribute to Mr. Locker-Lampson's skill in the
case of Swift will be found in the notes at the end of this
volume. It may be explained that orthography has been
modernized, and that the poems have been grouped according
to their subject, and printed as a general rule in chronological
order of the authors within the groups.

No compiler of an anthology can expect to please everybody,
for the personal equation is ineradicable, but none can dispute that in light verse there is an extraordinary amount
of imperishable poetry which glorifies the English language.
The editor is grateful to those who have enabled him to make
the collection as complete and representative as it is : to
Lord Tennyson for permission to include Charles Tennyson
Turner's sonnet ; to Sir Herbert Stephen, Bart., for poems by
his brother, J. K. Stephen ; to Mr. Theodore Watts-Dunton,
for various poems by Swinburne, whose essay has also been
indispensable ; to Mr. Edward Garnett, for Richard Garnett's
poem ; to Messrs. George Bell & Sons, Ltd., for the copyright
poems of C. S. Calverley reprinted from *Fly Leaves*, and for
Coventry Patmore's honeymoon lines ; to Messrs. William
Blackwood & Sons, for the Earl of Rosslyn's poem, Sir

Theodore Martin's parody of Tennyson (from the *Bon Gaultier Ballads*), and H. D. Traill's verses; to Messrs. Chatto & Windus, for R. L. Stevenson's lines to Mr. Andrew Lang; to Messrs. Ellis for Dante Gabriel Rossetti's sonnet; to the Houghton Mifflin Co., for the poems by Bret Harte, J. G. Saxe, and Whittier, and for O. W. Holmes's copyright poem *L'Inconnue*; to Messrs. Macmillan & Co., for Charles Kingsley's 'Invitation' (to Tom Hughes); to Messrs. Metcalfe & Co., for A. C. Hilton's parody; to Messrs. Charles Scribner's Sons, for a poem by H. C. Bunner; and to Messrs. Smith, Elder & Co., for Robert Browning's ' The Pope and the Net '.

R. M. L.

ALPHABETICAL LIST OF AUTHORS WITH THE TITLES OF THEIR POEMS

A BOOK

OF

LIGHT VERSE

1. TO A CHILD OF QUALITY, FIVE YEARS OLD, 1704,
    THE AUTHOR THEN FORTY

LORDS, knights and squires, the numerous band
  That wear the fair Miss Mary's fetters,
Were summoned by her high command
  To show their passions by their letters.

My pen amongst the rest I took,
  Lest those bright eyes that cannot read
Should dart their kindling fires, and look
  The power they have to be obeyed.

Nor quality, nor reputation,
  Forbids me yet my flame to tell;
Dear five-years-old befriends my passion,
  And I may write till she can spell.

For, while she makes her silkworms' beds
  With all the tender things I swear;
Whilst all the house my passion reads
  In papers round her baby's hair;

She may receive and own my flame,
  For, though the strictest prudes should know it,
She'll pass for a most virtuous dame,
  And I for an unhappy poet.

Then too, alas! when she shall tear
  The lines some younger rival sends;
She'll give me leave to write, I fear,
  And we shall still continue friends.

For, as our different ages move,
  'Tis so ordained (would Fate but mend it!)
That I shall be past making love,
  When she begins to comprehend it.

                                        M. PRIOR.

2. TO THE YOUNGER LADY LUCY SYDNEY

WHY came I so untimely forth
Into a world which, wanting thee,
Could entertain us with no worth,
Or shadow of felicity ?
That time should me so far remove
From that which I was born to love.

Yet, fairest Blossom ! do not slight
That eye which you may know so soon ;
The rosy morn resigns her light
And milder splendours to the noon :
If such thy dawning beauty's power
Who shall abide its noon-tide hour ?

Hope waits upon the flowery prime ;
And summer though it be less gay,
Yet is not looked on as a time
Of declination or decay ;
For with a full hand she doth bring
All that was promised by the spring.

E. WALLER.

3. CHILD AND MAIDEN

AH, Chloris ! that I now could sit
　　As unconcerned as when
Your infant beauty could beget
　　No pleasure, nor no pain !

When I the dawn used to admire
　　And praised the coming day
I little thought the growing fire
　　Must take my rest away.

Your charms in harmless childhood lay,
　　Like metals in the mine ;
Age from no face took more away
　　Than youth concealed in thine

But as your charms insensibly
　　To their perfection pressed,
Fond love as unperceived did fly,
　　And in my bosom rest.

My passion with your beauty grew ;
　And Cupid at my heart
Still, as his mother favoured you,
　Threw a new flaming dart :

Each gloried in their wanton part ;
　To make a lover, he
Employed the utmost of his art—
　To make a beauty, she.

SIR C. SEDLEY.

4. THE FAIR THIEF

BEFORE the urchin well could go,
She stole the whiteness of the snow ;
And more, that whiteness to adorn,
She stole the blushes of the morn ;
Stole all the sweetness ether sheds
On primrose buds or violet beds.

Still to reveal her artful wiles
She stole the Graces' silken smiles :
She stole Aurora's balmy breath ;
And pilfered orient pearl for teeth :
The cherry, dipped in morning dew,
Gave moisture to her lips, and hue.

These were her infant spoils, a store ;
And she in time still pilfered more !
At twelve, she stole from Cyprus' queen
Her air and love-commanding mien ;
Stole Juno's dignity ;　and stole
From Pallas sense to charm the soul.

Apollo's wit was next her prey ;
Her next the beam that lights the day ;
She sang　amazed the Sirens heard ;
And to assert their voice appeared :
She played ; the Muses from the hill
Wondered who thus had stole their skill.

Great Jove approved her crimes and art ;
And, t'other day, she stole my heart !
If lovers, Cupid, are thy care,
Exert thy vengeance on this Fair ;
To trial bring her stolen charms,
And let her prison be my arms.

C. WYNDHAM, EARL OF EGREMONT.

5. A RHYME

Babe, if rhyme be none
　For that sweet small word
Babe, the sweetest one
　Ever heard,

Right it is and meet
　Rhyme should keep not true
Time with such a sweet
　Thing as you.

Meet it is that rhyme
　Should not gain such grace :
What is April's prime
　To your face ?

What to yours is May's
　Rosiest smile ? what sound
Like your laughter sways
　All hearts round ?

None can tell in metre
　Fit for ears on earth
What sweet star grew sweeter
　At your birth.

Wisdom doubts what may be :
　Hope, with smile sublime,
Trusts : but neither, baby,
　Knows the rhyme.

Wisdom lies down lonely ;
　Hope keeps watch from far ;
None but one seer only
　Sees the star.

Love alone, with yearning
　Heart for astrolabe,
Takes the star's height, burning
　O'er the babe.

A. C. Swinburne.

6. ON PARENT KNEES, A NAKED NEW-BORN CHILD

On parent knees, a naked new-born child,
Weeping thou sat'st while all around thee smiled :
So live, that sinking to thy life's last sleep,
Calm thou mayest smile, whilst all around thee weep.

Sir W. Jones.

7. TO CHARLOTTE PULTENEY

TIMELY blossom, infant fair,
Fondling of a happy pair,
Every morn and every night
Their solicitous delight,
Sleeping, waking, still at ease,
Pleasing, without skill to please;
Little gossip, blithe and hale,
Tattling many a broken tale,
Singing many a tuneless song,
Lavish of a heedless tongue;
Simple maiden, void of art,
Babbling out the very heart,
Yet abandoned to thy will,
Yet imagining no ill,
Yet too innocent to blush;
Like the linnet in the bush
To the mother-linnet's note
Moduling her slender throat;
Chirping forth thy petty joys,
Wanton in the change of toys,
Like the linnet green, in May
Flitting to each bloomy spray;
Wearied then and glad of rest,
Like the linnet in the nest:—
This thy present happy lot,
This in time will be forgot:
Other pleasures, other cares,
Ever-busy Time prepares;
And thou shalt in thy daughter see,
This picture, once, resembled thee.

A. PHILIPS.

8. A LETTER

TO THE HONOURABLE LADY MARGARET CAVENDISH HARLEY, WHEN A CHILD

MY noble, lovely, little Peggy,
Let this my first epistle beg ye,
At dawn of morn, and close of even,
To lift your heart and hands to Heaven.
In double beauty say your prayer:
Our Father first,—then *Notre Père*:

And, dearest child, along the day,
In everything you do and say,
Obey and please my lord and lady,
So God shall love, and angels aid ye.
   If to these precepts you attend,
   No second letter need I send,
   And so I rest your constant friend.

M. PRIOR.

9. BEDTIME

'TIS bedtime ; say your hymn, and bid ' Good-night,
' God bless Mamma, Papa, and dear ones all,'
Your half-shut eyes beneath your eyelids fall,
Another minute you will shut them quite.
Yes, I will carry you, put out the light,
And tuck you up, although you are so tall !
What will you give me, Sleepy One, and call
My wages, if I settle you all right ?
I laid her golden curls upon my arm,
I drew her little feet within my hand,
Her rosy palms were joined in trustful bliss,
Her heart next mine beat gently, soft and warm ;
She nestled to me, and, by Love's command,
Paid me my precious wages—' Baby's kiss.'

F. ERSKINE, EARL OF ROSSLYN.

10. LETTY'S GLOBE

WHEN Letty had scarce passed her third glad year,
And her young, artless words began to flow,
One day we gave the child a coloured sphere
Of the wide earth, that she might mark and know,
By tint and outline, all its sea and land.
She patted all the world ; old empires peeped
Between her baby fingers ; her soft hand
Was welcome at all frontiers. How she leaped,
And laughed, and prattled in her world-wide bliss ;
But when we turned her sweet unlearnèd eye
On our own isle, she raised a joyous cry,
' Oh ! yes, I see it, Letty's home is there ! '
And, while she hid all England with a kiss,
Bright over Europe fell her golden hair.

C. TENNYSON TURNER.

11. PARENTAL RECOLLECTIONS

A CHILD's a plaything for an hour ;
    Its pretty tricks we try
For that or for a longer space ;
    Then tire, and lay it by.

But I knew one, that to itself
    All seasons could control ;
That would have mocked the sense of pain
    Out of a grievèd soul.

Thou straggler into loving arms,
    Young climber up of knees,
When I forget thy thousand ways,
    Then life and all shall cease.

C. LAMB.

12. VALENTINE

To THE HONBLE. M. C. STANHOPE

HAIL, day of Music, day of Love,
On earth below, in air above.
In air the turtle fondly moans,
The linnet pipes in joyous tones ;
On earth the postman toils along,
Bent double by huge bales of song,
Where, rich with many a gorgeous dye,
Blazes all Cupid's heraldry—
Myrtles and roses, doves and sparrows,
Love-knots and altars, lamps and arrows.
What nymph without wild hopes and fears
The double rap this morning hears !
Unnumbered lasses, young and fair,
From Bethnal Green to Belgrave Square,
With cheeks high flushed, and hearts loud-beating,
Await the tender annual greeting.
The loveliest lass of all is mine—
Good morrow to my Valentine !
GOOD morrow, gentle child ! and then
Again good morrow, and again,
Good morrow following still good morrow,
Without one cloud of strife or sorrow.
And when the god to whom we pay
In jest our homages to-day
Shall come to claim, no more in jest,
His rightful empire o'er thy breast,

Benignant may his aspect be,
His yoke the truest liberty :
And if a tear his power confess,
Be it a tear of happiness.
It shall be so. The Muse displays
The future to her votary's gaze ;
Prophetic rage my bosom swells—
I taste the cake—I hear the bells !
From Conduit Street the close array
Of chariots barricades the way
To where I see, with outstretched hand,
Majestic, thy great kinsman stand,
And half unbend his brow of pride,
As welcoming so fair a bride.
Gay favours, thick as flakes of snow,
Brighten St. George's portico :
Within I see the chancel's pale,
The orange flowers, the Brussels veil,
The page on which those fingers white,
Still trembling from the awful rite,
For the last time shall faintly trace
The name of Stanhope's noble race,
I see kind faces round thee pressing,
I hear kind voices whisper blessing ;
And with those voices mingles mine—
All good attend my Valentine !

THOMAS, LORD MACAULAY.

13. TO MY COUSIN ANNE BODHAM, ON RECEIVING FROM HER A PURSE

MY gentle Anne, whom heretofore,
When I was young, and thou no more
    Than plaything for a nurse,
I danced and fondled on my knee,
A kitten both in size and glee !
    I thank thee for my purse.

Gold pays the worth of all things here ;
But not of love :—that gem 's too dear
    For richest rogues to win it ;
I, therefore, as a proof of love,
Esteem thy present far above
    The best things kept within it.

W. COWPER.

14.   TO A PROUD KINSWOMAN

FAIR maid, had I not heard thy baby cries,
Nor seen thy girlish sweet vicissitude,
Thy mazy motions, striving to elude,
Yet wooing still a parent's watchful eyes,—
Thy humours, many as the opal's dyes,
And lovely all ; methinks thy scornful mood
And bearing high of stately womanhood,
Thy brow where Beauty sits to tyrannize
O'er humble love, had made me sadly fear thee ;
For never sure was seen a Royal Bride,
Whose gentleness gave grace to so much pride.
My very thoughts would tremble to be near thee :
But when I see thee at thy father's side,
Old times unqueen thee, and old loves endear thee.

HARTLEY COLERIDGE.

15.   IANTHE'S SHELL

DARLING shell, where hast thou been,
West or East ? or heard or seen ?
From what pastimes art thou come ?
Can we make amends at home ?

Whether thou hast tuned the dance
　　To the maids of ocean
Know I not ; but Ignorance
　　Never hurts Devotion.

This I know, Ianthe's shell,
I must ever love thee well,
Though too little to resound
While the Nereids dance around ;

For, of all the shells that are,
　　Thou art sure the brightest ;
Thou, Ianthe's infant care,
　　Most these eyes delightest.

To thy early aid she owes
Teeth like budding snowdrop rows :
And what other shell can say
On her bosom once it lay ?

That which into Cyprus bore
　　Venus from her native sea,
(Pride of shells !) was never more
　　Dear to her than thou to me.

W. S. LANDOR.

16. IN CLEMENTINA'S ARTLESS MIEN

IN Clementina's artless mien
  Lucilla asks me what I see,
And are the roses of sixteen
    Enough for me ?

Lucilla asks, if that be all,
  Have I not culled as sweet before :
Ah yes, Lucilla ! and their fall
    I still deplore.

I now behold another scene,
  Where Pleasure beams with heaven's own light,
More pure, more constant, more serene,
    And not less bright :

Faith, on whose breast the Loves repose,
  Whose chain of flowers no force can sever,
And Modesty who, when she goes,
    Is gone for ever.

                                        W. S. LANDOR.

17. HOUSEHOLD GODS

YE little household gods, that make
  My heart leap lighter with your play,
And never let it sink or ache,
  Unless you are too far away ;

Eight years have flown, and never yet
  One day has risen up between
The kisses of my earlier pet,
  And few the hours he was not seen.

How can I call to you from Rome ?
  Will *mamma* teach what *babbo* said ?
Have ye not heard him talk at home
  About the city of the dead ?

Marvellous tales will *babbo* tell,
  If you don't clasp his throat too tight,
Tales which you, Arnold, will love well,
  Though Julia's cheek turns pale with fright.

How, swimming o'er the Tiber, Clelia
 Headed the rescued virgin train ;
And, loftier virtue ! how Cornelia
 Lived when her two brave sons were slain.

This is my birthday : may ye waltze
 Till mamma cracks her best guitar !
Yours are true pleasures ; those are false
 We wise ones follow from afar.

What shall I bring you ? would you like
 Urn, image, glass, red, yellow, blue,
Stricken by Time, who soon must strike
 As deep the heart that beats for you.

W. S. LANDOR.

18. MY LITTLE COUSINS

LAUGH on, fair Cousins, for to you
 All life is joyous yet ;
Your hearts have all things to pursue,
 And nothing to regret ;
And every flower to you is fair,
 And every month is May :
You've not been introduced to Care,—
 Laugh on, laugh on to-day !

Old Time will fling his clouds ere long
 Upon those sunny eyes;
The voice whose every word is song
 Will set itself to sighs ;
Your quiet slumbers,—hopes and fears
 Will chase their rest away :
To-morrow you'll be shedding tears,—
 Laugh on, laugh on to-day.

Oh yes, if any truth is found
 In the dull schoolman's theme,
If friendship is an empty sound,
 And love an idle dream,
If mirth, youth's playmate, feels fatigue
 Too soon on life's long way,
At least he'll run with you a league ;—
 Laugh on, laugh on to-day !

Perhaps your eyes may grow more bright
  As childhood's hues depart ;
You may be lovelier to the sight
  And dearer to the heart ;
You may be sinless still, and see
  This earth still green and gay ;
But what you are you will not be :
  Laugh on, laugh on to-day !

O'er me have many winters crept
  With less of grief than joy ;
But I have learned, and toiled, and wept ;
  I am no more a boy !
I've never had the gout, 'tis true ;
  My hair is hardly grey ;
But now I cannot laugh like you :
  Laugh on, laugh on to-day !

I used to have as glad a face,
  As shadowless a brow ;
I once could run as blithe a race
  As you are running now ;
But never mind how I behave !
  Don't interrupt your play ;
And though I look so very grave,
  Laugh on, laugh on to-day !

                              W. M. Praed.

19. MY LITTLE DOLL

I once had a sweet little doll, dears,
  The prettiest doll in the world ;
Her cheeks were so red and so white, dears,
  And her hair was so charmingly curled.
But I lost my poor little doll, dears,
  As I played in the heath one day ;
And I cried for her more than a week, dears,
  But I never could find where she lay.

I found my poor little doll, dears,
  As I played in the heath one day ;
Folks say she is terribly changed, dears,
  For her paint is all washed away,
And her arm trodden off by the cows, dears,
  And her hair not the least bit curled :
Yet, for old sakes' sake she is still, dears,
  The prettiest doll in the world.

                              C. Kingsley.

20. TO VINCENT CORBET, HIS SON

WHAT I shall leave thee, none can tell,
But all shall say I wish thee well :
I wish thee, Vin, before all wealth,
Both bodily and ghostly health ;
Nor too much wealth nor wit come to thee,
So much of either may undo thee.
I wish thee learning not for show,
Enough for to instruct and know ;
Not such as gentlemen require
To prate at table or at fire.

I wish thee all thy mother's graces,
Thy father's fortunes and his places.
I wish thee friends, and one at court,
Not to build on, but support ;
To keep thee not in doing many
Oppressions, but from suffering any.
I wish thee peace in all thy ways,
Nor lazy nor contentious days ;
And, when thy soul and body part,
As innocent as now thou art.

R. CORBET.

21. A FABLE FOR FIVE YEARS OLD

THE BOY AND HIS TOP

A LITTLE boy had bought a top,
The best in all the toyman's shop ;
He made a whip with good eel's skin,
He lashed the top and made it spin ;
All the children within call,
And the servants, one and all,
Stood round to see it and admire.
At last the top began to tire ;
He cried out, ' Pray, don't whip me, master,
You whip too hard ; I can't spin faster ;
I can spin quite as well without it.'
The little boy replied, ' I doubt it ;
I only whip you for your good.
You were a foolish lump of wood ;
By dint of whipping you were raised
To see yourself admired and praised,
And if I left you, you'd remain
A foolish lump of wood again.'

Whipping sounds a little odd,
It don't mean whipping with a rod.
It means to teach a boy incessantly,
Whether by lessons or more pleasantly,
Every hour and every day,
By every means, in every way,
By reading, writing, rhyming, talking,
By riding to see sights, and walking:
If you leave off he drops at once,
A lumpish, wooden-headed dunce.

J. H. FRERE.

22.   ODE ON A DISTANT PROSPECT OF CLAPHAM ACADEMY

AH me ! those old familiar bounds !
That classic house, those classic grounds,
    My pensive thought recalls !
What tender urchins now confine,
What little captives now repine,
    Within yon irksome walls ?

Aye, that 's the very house ! I know
Its ugly windows, ten a-row !
    Its chimneys in the rear !
And there 's the iron rod so high,
That drew the thunder from the sky,
    And turned our table-beer !

There I was birched ! there I was bred !
There like a little Adam fed
    From Learning's woeful tree !
The weary tasks I used to con !—
The hopeless leaves I wept upon !—
    Most fruitless leaves to me !—

The summoned class !—the awful bow !—
I wonder who is master now
    And wholesome anguish sheds !
How many ushers now employs,
How many maids to see the boys
    Have nothing in their heads !

And Mrs. S—— ?—Doth she abet
(Like Pallas in the parlour) yet
    Some favoured two or three,—
The little Crichtons of the hour,
Her muffin-medals that devour,
    And swill her prize—bohea ?

Aye, there's the play-ground ! there's the lime
Beneath whose shade in summer's prime
    So wildly I have read !—
Who sits there *now*, and skims the cream
Of young Romance, and weaves a dream
    Of Love and Cottage-bread ?

Who struts the Randall of the walk ?
Who models tiny heads in chalk ?
    Who scoops the light canoe ?
What early genius buds apace ?
Where's Poynter ? Harris ? Bowers ? Chase ?
    Hal Baylis ? blithe Carew ?

Alack ! they're gone—a thousand ways !
And some are serving in 'the Greys',
    And some have perished young !—
Jack Harris weds his second wife ;
Hal Baylis drives the *wane* of life ;
    And blithe Carew—is hung !

Grave Bowers teaches A B C
To savages at Owhyee ;
    Poor Chase is with the worms !—
All, all are gone—the olden breed !—
New crops of mushroom boys succeed,
    'And push us from our *forms !*'

Lo ! where they scramble forth, and shout,
And leap, and skip, and mob about,
    At play where we have played !
Some hop, some run (some fall), some twine
Their crony arms ; some in the shine,—
    And some are in the shade !

Lo there what mixed conditions run !
The orphan lad ; the widow's son ;
    And Fortune's favoured care—
The wealthy-born, for whom she hath
Mac-Adamized the future path—
    The Nabob's pampered heir !

Some brightly starred—some evil born,—
For honour some, and some for scorn,—
    For fair or foul renown !
Good, bad, indifferent—none may lack !
Look, here's a White, and there's a Black !
    And there's a Creole brown !

Some laugh and sing, some mope and weep,
And wish *their* frugal sires would keep
   Their only sons at home ;—
Some tease the future tense, and plan
The full-grown doings of the man,
   And pant for years to come !

A foolish wish ! There 's one at hoop ;
And four at *fives !* and five who stoop
   The marble taw to speed !
And one that curvets in and out,
Reining his fellow Cob about,—
   Would I were in his *stead !*

Yet he would gladly halt and drop
That boyish harness off, to swop
   With this world's heavy van—
To toil, to tug. O little fool !
While thou canst be a horse at school,
   To wish to be a man !

Perchance thou deem'st it were a thing
To wear a crown,—to be a king !
   And sleep on regal down !
Alas ! thou know'st not kingly cares ;
Far happier is thy head that wears
   That hat without a crown !

And dost thou think that years acquire
New added joys ? Dost think thy sire
   More happy than his son ?
That manhood's mirth ?—Oh, go thy ways
To Drury Lane when —— *plays,*
   And see how *forced* our fun !

Thy taws are brave !—thy tops are rare !—
Our tops are spun with coils of care,
   Our *dumps* are no delight !—
The Elgin marbles are but tame,
And 'tis at best a sorry game
   To fly the Muse's kite !

Our hearts are dough, our heels are lead,
Our topmost joys fall dull and dead
   Like balls with no rebound !
And often with a faded eye
We look behind, and send a sigh
   Towards that merry ground !

Then be contented.   Thou hast got
The most of heaven in thy young lot;
   There 's sky-blue in thy cup!
Thou'lt find thy Manhood all too fast—
Soon come, soon gone! and Age at last
   A sorry *breaking-up!*

T. HOOD.

23. SCHOOL AND SCHOOLFELLOWS

' Floreat Etona '

TWELVE years ago I made a mock
   Of filthy trades and traffics:
I wondered what they meant by stock;
   I wrote delightful sapphics;
I knew the streets of Rome and Troy;
   I supped with Fates and Furies,—
Twelve years ago I was a boy,
   A happy boy, at Drury's.

Twelve years ago!—how many a thought
   Of faded pains and pleasures
Those whispered syllables have brought
   From Memory's hoarded treasures!
The fields, the farms, the bats, the books,
   The glories and disgraces,
The voices of dear friends, the looks
   Of old familiar faces!

Kind Mater smiles again to me,
   As bright as when we parted;
I seem again the frank, the free,
   Stout-limbed and simple-hearted!
Pursuing every idle dream,
   And shunning every warning;
With no hard work but Bovney stream,
   No chill except Long Morning:

Now stopping Harry Vernon's ball
   That rattled like a rocket;
Now hearing Wentworth's ' Fourteen all!
   And striking for the pocket;
Now feasting on a cheese and flitch,—
   Now drinking from the pewter;
Now leaping over Chalvey ditch,
   Now laughing at my tutor.

Where are my friends ?   I am alone ;
   No playmate shares my beaker :
Some lie beneath the churchyard stone,
   And some—before the Speaker ;
And some compose a tragedy,
   And some compose a rondeau ;
And some draw sword for liberty,
   And some draw pleas for John Doe.

Tom Mill was used to blacken eyes
   Without the fear of sessions ;
Charles Medlar loathed false quantities,
   As much as false professions ;
Now Mill keeps order in the land,
   A magistrate pedantic ;
And Medlar's feet repose unscanned
   Beneath the wide Atlantic.

Wild Nick, whose oaths made such a din,
   Does Dr. Martext's duty ;
And Mullion, with that monstrous chin,
   Is married to a Beauty ;
And Darrell studies, week by week,
   His Mant, and not his Manton ;
And Ball, who was but poor at Greek,
   Is very rich at Canton.

And I am eight-and-twenty now ;—
   The world's cold chains have bound me ;
And darker shades are on my brow,
   And sadder scenes around me :
In Parliament I fill my seat,
   With many other noodles ;
And lay my head in Jermyn Street,
   And sip my hock at Boodle's.

But often when the cares of life
   Have set my temples aching,
When visions haunt me of a wife,
   When duns await my waking,
When Lady Jane is in a pet,
   Or Hoby in a hurry,
When Captain Hazard wins a bet,
   Or Beaulieu spoils a curry,—

For hours and hours I think and talk
   Of each remembered hobby ;
I long to lounge in Poets' Walk,
   To shiver in the lobby ;

I wish that I could run away
    From House and Court and Levee,
Where bearded men appear to-day
    Just Eton boys grown heavy,—

That I could bask in childhood's sun
    And dance o'er childhood's roses,
And find huge wealth in one pound one,
    Vast wit in broken noses,
And play Sir Giles at Datchet Lane,
    And call the milk-maids Houris,—
That I could be a boy again,—
    A happy boy,—at Drury's.

                        W. M. Praed.

24. IN SCHOOL-DAYS

Still sits the school-house by the road,
    A ragged beggar sleeping ;
Around it still the sumachs grow,
    And blackberry-vines are creeping.

Within, the master's desk is seen,
    Deep scarred by raps official ;
The warping floor, the battered seats,
    The jack-knife's carved initial ;

The charcoal frescoes on its wall ;
    Its door's worn sill, betraying
The feet that, creeping slow to school,
    Went storming out to playing !

Long years ago a winter sun
    Shone over it at setting ;
Lit up its western window-panes,
    And low eaves' icy fretting.

It touched the tangled golden curls,
    And brown eyes full of grieving,
Of one who still her steps delayed
    When all the school were leaving.

For near her stood the little boy
    Her childish favour singled :
His cap pulled low upon a face
    Where pride and shame were mingled.

Pushing with restless feet the snow
    To right and left, he lingered ;—
As restlessly her tiny hands
    The blue-checked apron fingered.

He saw her lift her eyes ; he felt
   The soft hand's light caressing,
And heard the tremble of her voice,
   As if a fault confessing.

' I'm sorry that I spelt the word :
   I hate to go above you,
Because,'—the brown eyes lower fell,—
   ' Because, you see, I love you ! '

Still memory to a grey-haired man
   That sweet child-face is showing.
Dear girl ! the grasses on her grave
   Have forty years been growing !

He lives to learn, in life's hard school
   How few who pass above him
Lament their triumph and his loss,
   Like her,—because they love him.

J. G. WHITTIER.

25. 'HIC *VIR*, HIC EST'

OFTEN, when o'er tree and turret,
   Eve a dying radiance flings,
By that ancient pile I linger
   Known familiarly as ' King's '.
And the ghosts of days departed
   Rise, and in my burning breast
All the undergraduate wakens,
   And my spirit is at rest.

What, but a revolting fiction,
   Seems the actual result
Of the Census's inquiries
   Made upon the 15th ult. ?
Still my soul is in its boyhood ;
   Nor of year or changes recks,
Though my scalp is almost hairless,
   And my figure grows convex.

Backward moves the kindly dial ;
   And I'm numbered once again
With those noblest of their species
   Called emphatically ' Men ' :
Loaf, as I have loafed aforetime,
   Through the streets, with tranquil mind,
And a long-backed fancy-mongrel
   Trailing casually behind :

Past the Senate-house I saunter,
    Whistling with an easy grace ;
Past the cabbage-stalks that carpet
    Still the beefy market-place ;
Poising evermore the eye-glass
    In the light sarcastic eye,
Lest, by chance, some breezy nurse-maid
    Pass, without a tribute, by.

Once, an unassuming Freshman,
    Through these wilds I wandered on,
Seeing in each house a College,
    Under every cap a Don :
Each perambulating infant
    Had a magic in its squall,
For my eager eye detected
    Senior Wranglers in them all.

By degrees my education
    Grew, and I became as others ;
Learned to blunt my moral feelings
    By the aid of Bacon Brothers ;
Bought me tiny boots of Mortlock,
    And colossal prints of Roe ;
And ignored the proposition
    That both time and money go.

Learned to work the wary dogcart
    Artfully through King's Parade ;
Dress, and steer a boat, and sport with
    Amaryllis in the shade :
Struck, at Brown's, the dashing hazard ;
    Or (more curious sport than that)
Dropped, at Callaby's, the terrier
    Down upon the prisoned rat.

I have stood serene on Fenner's
    Ground, indifferent to blisters,
While the Buttress of the period
    Bowled me his peculiar twisters :
Sung ' We won't go home till morning ' ;
    Striven to part my backhair straight ;
Drunk (not lavishly) of Miller's
    Old dry wines at 78/- :—

When within my veins the blood ran,
  And the curls were on my brow,
I did, oh ye undergraduates,
  Much as ye are doing now.
Wherefore bless ye, O beloved ones :—
  Now unto mine inn must I,
Your ' poor moralist ', betake me,
  In my ' solitary fly '.

C. S. CALVERLEY.

26. THE HEATHEN PASS-EE

BEING THE STORY OF A PASS EXAMINATION. BY BRED HARD

WHICH I wish to remark,
  And my language is plain,
That for plots that are dark
  And not always in vain,
The heathen Pass-ee is peculiar,
  And the same I would rise to explain.

I would also premise
  That the term of Pass-ee
Most fitly applies,
  As you probably see,
To one whose vocation is passing
  The ' ordinary B.A. degree '.

Tom Crib was his name,
  And I shall not deny
In regard to the same
  What that name might imply,
But his face it was trustful and childlike,
  And he had the most innocent eye.

Upon April the First
  The Little-Go fell,
And that was the worst
  Of the gentleman's sell,
For he fooled the Examining Body
  In a way I'm reluctant to tell.

The candidates came
  And Tom Crib soon appeared ;
It was Euclid. The same
  Was ' the subject he feared ',
But he smiled as he sat by the table
  With a smile that was wary and weird.

Yet he did what he could
   And the papers he showed
Were remarkably good,
   And his countenance glowed
With pride when I met him soon after
   As he walked down the Trumpington Road.

We did not find him out,
   Which I bitterly grieve,
For I've not the least doubt
   That he'd placed up his sleeve
Mr. Todhunter's excellent Euclid,
   The same with intent to deceive.

But I shall not forget
   How the next day at two
A stiff paper was set
   By Examiner U . . .
On Euripides' tragedy, Bacchae.
   A subject Tom ' partially knew '.

But the knowledge displayed
   By that heathen Pass-ee,
And the answers he made
   Were quite frightful to see,
For he rapidly floored the whole paper
   By about twenty minutes to three.

Then I looked up at U . . .
   And he gazed upon me.
I observed, ' This won't do.'
   He replied, ' Goodness me !
We are fooled by this artful young person,'
   And he sent for that heathen Pass-ee.

The scene that ensued
   Was disgraceful to view,
For the floor it was strewed
   With a tolerable few
Of the ' tips ' that Tom Crib had been hiding
   For the ' subject he partially knew '.

On the cuff of his shirt
   He had managed to get
What we hoped had been dirt,
   But which proved, I regret,
To be notes on the rise of the Drama,
   A question invariably set.

In his various coats
    We proceeded to seek,
Where we found sundry notes
    And—with sorrow I speak—
One of Bohn's publications, so useful
    To the student of Latin or Greek.

In the crown of his cap
    Were the Furies and Fates,
And a delicate map
    Of the Dorian States,
And we found in his palms which were hollow,
    What are frequent in palms,—that is dates.

Which is why I remark,
    And my language is plain,
That for plots that are dark
    And not always in vain,
The heathen Pass-ee is peculiar,
    Which the same I am free to maintain.

                                A. C. HILTON.

27. TO —— ——

NEVER mind how the pedagogue proses,
    You want not antiquity's stamp;
The lip that such fragrance discloses,
    Oh! never should smell of the lamp.

Old Cloe, whose withering kiss
    Hath long set the Loves at defiance,
Now, done with the science of bliss,
    May take to the blisses of science.

Young Sappho, for want of employments,
    Alone o'er her Ovid may melt,
Condemned but to read of enjoyments
    Which wiser Corinna had felt.

But for *you* to be buried in books—
    Ah, Fanny, they're pitiful sages,
Who could not in *one* of your looks
    Read more than in millions of pages.

Astronomy finds in those eyes
    Better light than she studies above,
And Music would borrow your sighs
    As the melody fittest for Love.

In Ethics—'tis you that can check,
  In a minute, their doubts and their quarrels ;
Oh ! show but that mole on your neck,
  And 'twill soon put an end to their morals:

Your Arithmetic only can trip
  If to count your own charms you endeavour ;
And Eloquence glows on your lip
  When you swear, that you'll love me for ever.

Thus you see, what a brilliant alliance
  Of arts is assembled in you;—
A course of more exquisite science
  Man never need wish to pursue !

And, oh !—if a Fellow like me
  May confer a diploma of hearts,
With my lip thus I seal your degree,
  My divine little Mistress of Arts !

T. MOORE.

28. AD CHLOEN, M.A.

(FRESH FROM HER CAMBRIDGE EXAMINATION)

LADY, very fair are you,
And your eyes are very blue,
  And your hose ;
And your brow is like the snow,
And the various things you know
  Goodness knows.

And the rose-flush on your cheek,
And your algebra and Greek
  Perfect are ;
And that loving lustrous eye
Recognizes in the sky
  Every star.

You have pouting piquant lips,
You can doubtless an eclipse
  Calculate ;
But for your caerulean hue,
I had certainly from you
  Met my fate.

If by an arrangement dual
I were Adams mixed with Whewell,
  Then some day
I, as wooer, perhaps might come
To so sweet an Artium
  Magistra.

M. COLLINS.

29. ONE-AND-TWENTY

LONG-EXPECTED One-and-twenty,
  Lingering year, at length is flown :
Pride and pleasure, pomp and plenty,
  Great *** ****, are now your own.

Loosened from the minor's tether,
  Free to mortgage or to sell,
Wild as wind and light as feather,
  Bid the sons of thrift farewell.

Call the Betsies, Kates, and Jennies,
  All the names that banish care ;
Lavish of your grandsire's guineas,
  Show the spirit of an heir.

All that prey on vice and folly
  Joy to see their quarry fly :
There the gamester, light and jolly,
  There the lender, grave and sly.

Wealth, my lad, was made to wander,
  Let it wander as it will ;
Call the jockey, call the pander,
  Bid them come and take their fill.

When the bonny blade carouses,
  Pockets full, and spirits high—
What are acres ?   What are houses ?
  Only dirt, or wet or dry.

Should the guardian friend or mother
  Tell the woes of wilful waste,
Scorn their counsel, scorn their pother ;—
  You can hang or drown at last !

S. JOHNSON.

30. OH, TALK NOT TO ME OF A NAME GREAT IN STORY

OH, talk not to me of a name great in story ;
The days of our youth are the days of our glory ;
And the myrtle and ivy of sweet two-and-twenty
Are worth all your laurels, though ever so plenty.

What are garlands and crowns to the brow that is wrinkled ?
'Tis but as a dead-flower with May-dew besprinkled.
Then away with all such from the head that is hoary !
What care I for the wreaths that can *only* give glory ?

Oh Fame !—if I e'er took delight in thy praises,
'Twas less for the sake of thy high-sounding phrases,
Than to see the bright eyes of the dear one discover,
She thought that I was not unworthy to love her.

There chiefly I sought thee, *there* only I found thee ;
Her glance was the best of the rays that surround thee ;
When it sparkled o'er aught that was bright in my story,
I knew it was love, and I felt it was glory.

G. GORDON, LORD BYRON.

31. YOUTH

THE days of our youth are not over while sadness
  Chills never, and seldom o'ershadows, the heart ;
While Friendship is crowning the banquet of Gladness
  And bids us be seated and offers us part ;
While the swift-spoken *when ?* and the slowly-breathed *hush !*
  Make us half-love the maiden and half-hate the lover,
And feel too what is or what should be a blush . . .
  Believe me, the days of our youth are not over.

W. S. LANDOR.

32. NOW THE LUSTY SPRING IS SEEN

Now the lusty Spring is seen ;
  Golden yellow, gaudy blue,
  Daintily invite the view.
Everywhere, on every green,
Roses blushing as they blow,
  And enticing men to pull !
Lilies whiter than the snow,
  Woodbines, of sweet honey full :
    All Love's emblems ! and all cry,
    ' Ladies, if not plucked, we die ! '

Yet the lusty Spring hath stayed ;
  Blushing red and purest white
  Daintily to Love invite
Every woman, every maid !
Cherries kissing, as they grow ;
  And inviting men to taste !
Apples even ripe below,
  Winding gently to the waist !
    All Love's emblems, and all cry,
    ' Ladies, if not plucked, we die ! '

J. FLETCHER.

33. HEAR YE, LADIES, THAT DESPISE

HEAR ye, ladies, that despise,
  What the mighty love has done ;
Fear examples, and be wise :
  Fair Callisto was a nun ;
Leda, sailing on the stream
  To deceive the hopes of man,
Love accounting but a dream,
  Doted on a silver swan ;
    Danaë, in a brazen tower,
    Where no love was, loved a shower.

Hear, ye ladies that are coy,
  What the mighty love can do ;
Fear the fierceness of the boy :
  The chaste moon he makes to woo ;
Vesta, kindling holy fires,
  Circled round about with spies,
Never dreaming loose desires,
  Doting at the altar dies ;
    Ilion, in a short hour, higher
    He can build, and once more fire.

J. FLETCHER.

34. MY SWEETEST LESBIA

MY sweetest Lesbia, let us live and love,
And though the sager sort our deeds reprove,
Let us not weigh them ; heaven's great lamps do dive
Into their west, and straight again revive ;
But, soon as once is set our little light,
Then must we sleep one ever-during night.

If all would lead their lives in love like me,
Then bloody swords and armour should not be,
No drum nor trumpet peaceful sleeps should move,
Unless alarm came from the camp of love.
But fools do live, and waste their little light,
And seek with pain their ever-during night.

When timely death my life and fortune ends,
Let not my hearse be vexed with mourning friends ;
But let all lovers rich in triumph come,
And with sweet pastimes grace my happy tomb ;
And, Lesbia, close up thou my little light,
And crown with love my ever-during night.

T. CAMPION.

35. VIVAMUS

Come, my Celia, let us prove,
While we can, the sports of love ;
Time will not be ours for ever,
He, at length, our good will sever ;
Spend not then his gifts in vain ;
Suns that set may rise again ;
But if once we lose this light,
'Tis with us perpetual night.

Why should we defer our joys ?
Fame and rumour are but toys.
Cannot we delude the eyes
Of a few poor household spies ?

Or his easier ears beguile,
Thus removèd by our wile ?—
'Tis no sin love's fruits to steal,
But the sweet thefts to reveal,
　　To be taken, to be seen,
　　These have crimes accounted been.

BEN. JONSON.

36. NOW THAT THE APRIL OF YOUR YOUTH ADORNS

Now that the April of your youth adorns
　　The garden of your face,
Now that for you each knowing lover mourns,
　　And all seek to your grace,
Do not repay affection with scorns.

What though you may a matchless beauty vaunt,
　　And that all hearts can move,
By such a power, as seemeth to enchant ?
　　Yet, without help of love,
Beauty no pleasure to itself can grant.

Then think each minute that you lose, a day ;
　　The longest youth is short,
The shortest age is long ; Time flies away,
　　And makes us but his sport,
And that which is not Youth's, is Age's prey.

EDWARD, LORD HERBERT OF CHERBURY.

37. LOVE IN THY YOUTH, FAIR MAID

Love in thy youth, fair maid, be wise,
  Old Time will make thee colder,
And though each morning new arise,
  Yet we each day grow older.

Thou as heaven art fair and young,
  Thine eyes like twin stars shining ;
But ere another day be sprung,
  All these will be declining ;

Then winter comes with all his fears,
  And all thy sweets shall borrow ;
Too late then wilt thou shower thy tears,
  And I, too late, shall sorrow.

UNKNOWN.

38. O MISTRESS MINE, WHERE ARE YOU ROAMING

O Mistress mine, where are you roaming ?
O ! stay and hear ! your true-love 's coming,
  That can sing both high and low ;
Trip no further, pretty sweeting ;
Journeys end in lovers meeting,
  Every wise man's son doth know.

What is love ? 'tis not hereafter ;
Present mirth hath present laughter ;
  What 's to come is still unsure :
In delay there lies no plenty ;
Then come kiss me, Sweet-and-twenty,
  Youth 's a stuff will not endure.

W. SHAKESPEARE.

39. THE ADVICE

Phyllis, for shame, let us improve
  A thousand several ways,
These few short minutes stolen by love
  From many tedious days.

Whilst you want courage to despise
  The censure of the grave,
For all the tyrants in your eyes,
  Your heart is but a slave.

My love is full of noble pride,
  And never will submit
To let that fop, Discretion, ride
  In triumph over wit.

False friends I have, as well as you,
  That daily counsel me
Vain frivolous trifles to pursue,
  And leave off loving thee.

When I the least belief bestow
  On what such fools advise,
May I be dull enough to grow
  Most miserably wise.

C. SACKVILLE, EARL OF DORSET.

40. TO VIRGINS

HEAR, ye virgins, and I'll teach
What the times of old did preach.
Rosamond was in a bower
Kept, as Danaë, in a tower ;
But yet Love, who subtle is,
Crept to that, and came to this.
Be ye locked up like to these,
Or the rich Hesperides :
Or those babies in your eyes,
In their crystal nunneries ;
Notwithstanding, love will win,
Or else force a passage in ;
And as coy be as you can,
Gifts will get ye, or the man.

R. HERRICK.

41. TO THE VIRGINS TO MAKE MUCH OF TIME

GATHER ye rose-buds while ye may,
  Old Time is still a-flying ;
And this same flower that smiles to-day,
  To-morrow will be dying.

The glorious lamp of heaven, the Sun,
  The higher he's a-getting,
The sooner will his race be run,
  And nearer he's to setting.

That age is best which is the first,
  When youth and blood are warmer ;
But being spent the worse and worst
  Times still succeed the former.

Then be not coy, but use your time,
  And while ye may, go marry ;
For having lost but once your prime,
  You may for ever tarry.

R. HERRICK.

42. TO DIANEME

Sweet, be not proud of those two eyes
Which, starlike, sparkle in their skies
Nor be you proud, that you can see
All hearts your captives, yours yet free ;
Be you not proud of that rich hair,
Which wantons with the lovesick air ;
Whenas that ruby, which you wear
Sunk from the tip of your soft ear,
Will last to be a precious stone
When all your world of beauty 's gone.

R. Herrick.

43. DISDAIN RETURNED

He that loves a rosy cheek,
    Or a coral lip admires,
Or from star-like eyes doth seek
    Fuel to maintain his fires ;
As old Time makes these decay,
So his flames must waste away.

But a smooth and stedfast mind,
    Gentle thoughts, and calm desires.—
Hearts with equal love combined,
    Kindle never-dying fires :—
Where these are not, I despise
Lovely cheeks or lips or eyes.

T. Carew.

44. BLUSH NOT REDDER THAN THE MORNING

Blush not redder than the morning,
Though the virgins gave you warning ;
Sigh not at the chance befell ye,
Though they smile and dare not tell ye.

Maids, like turtles, love the cooing,
Bill and murmur in their wooing.
Thus like you, they start and tremble
And their troubled joys dissemble.

Grasp the pleasure while 'tis coming,
Though your beauties now are blooming ;
Time at last your joys will sever,
And they'll part, they'll part for ever.

N. Lee.

45. YOUTH AND ART

IT once might have been, once only:
  We lodged in a street together,
You, a sparrow on the housetop lonely,
  I, a lone she-bird of his feather.

Your trade was with sticks and clay,
  You thumbed, thrust, patted and polished,
Then laughed ' They will see some day
  Smith made, and Gibson demolished.'

My business was song, song, song;
  I chirped, cheeped, trilled and twittered,
' Kate Brown 's on the boards ere long,
  And Grisi's existence embittered ! '

I earned no more by a warble
  Than you by a sketch in plaster ;
You wanted a piece of marble,
  I needed a music-master.

We studied hard in our styles,
  Chipped each at a crust like Hindoos,
For air, looked out on the tiles,
  For fun, watched each other's windows.

You lounged, like a boy of the South,
  Cap and blouse—nay, a bit of beard too ;
Or you got it, rubbing your mouth
  With fingers the clay adhered to.

And I—soon managed to find
  Weak points in the flower-fence facing,
Was forced to put up a blind
  And be safe in my corset-lacing.

No harm ! It was not my fault
  If you never turned your eye's tail up,
As I shook upon E *in alt*,
  Or ran the chromatic scale up :

For spring bade the sparrows pair,
  And the boys and girls gave guesses,
And stalls in our street looked rare
  With bulrush and watercresses.

Why did not you pinch a flower
  In a pellet of clay and fling it ?
Why did not I put a power
  Of thanks in a look, or sing it ?

I did look, sharp as a lynx,
  (And yet the memory rankles)
When models arrived, some minx
  Tripped up-stairs, she and her ankles.

But I think I gave you as good !
  ' That foreign fellow,—who can know
How she pays, in a playful mood,
  For his tuning her that piano ? '

Could you say so, and never say
  ' Suppose we join hands and fortunes,
And I fetch her from over the way,
  Her, piano, and long tunes and short tunes ? '

No, no : you would not be rash,
  Nor I rasher and something over :
You've to settle yet Gibson's hash,
  And Grisi yet lives in clover.

But you meet the Prince at the Board,
  I'm queen myself at *bals-paré*,
I've married a rich old lord,
  And you're dubbed knight and an R.A.

Each life unfulfilled, you see ;
  It hangs still, patchy and scrappy:
We have not sighed deep, laughed free,
  Starved, feasted, despaired,—been happy.

And nobody calls you a dunce,
  And people suppose me clever :
This could but have happened once,
  And we missed it, lost it for ever.

              R. BROWNING.

46. HOW MANY VOICES GAILY SING

How many voices gaily sing,
' O happy morn, O happy spring
Of life ! ' Meanwhile there comes o'er me
A softer voice from Memory,
And says, ' If loves and hopes have flown
With years, think too what griefs are gone ! '

              W. S. LANDOR.

47. SHADOWS

THEY seemed, to those who saw them meet,
  The casual friends of every day ;
Her smile was undisturbed and sweet,
  His courtesy was free and gay.

But yet if one the other's name
  In some unguarded moment heard,
The heart you thought so calm and tame
  Would struggle like a captured bird :

And letters of mere formal phrase
  Were blistered with repeated tears,—
And this was not the work of days,
  But had gone on for years and years !

Alas, that love was not too strong
  For maiden shame and manly pride !
Alas, that they delayed so long
  The goal of mutual bliss beside !

Yet what no chance could then reveal,
  And neither would be first to own,
Let fate and courage now conceal,
  When truth could bring remorse alone.

R. M. MILNES, LORD HOUGHTON.

48. LOVE AND REASON

'TWAS in the summer-time so sweet,
  When hearts and flowers are both in season,
That—who, of all the world, should meet,
  One early dawn, but Love and Reason !

Love told his dream of yesternight,
  While Reason talked about the weather ;
The morn, in sooth, was fair and bright,
  And on they took their way together.

The boy in many a gambol flew,
  While Reason, like a Juno, stalked,
And from her portly figure threw
  A lengthened shadow, as she walked.

No wonder Love, as on they passed,
  Should find the sunny morning chill,
For still the shadow Reason cast
  Fell o'er the boy, and cooled him still.

In vain he tried his wings to warm,
   Or find a pathway not so dim,
For still the maid's gigantic form
   Would stalk between the sun and him.

' This must not be,' said little Love—
   ' The sun was made for more than you.'
So, turning through a myrtle grove,
   He bid the portly nymph adieu.

Now gaily roves the laughing boy
   O'er many a mead, by many a stream ;
In every breeze inhaling joy,
   And drinking bliss in every beam.

From all the gardens, all the bowers,
   He culled the many sweets they shaded,
And ate the fruits and smelled the flowers,
   Till taste was gone and odour faded !

But now the sun, in pomp of noon,
   Looked blazing o'er the sultry plains ;
Alas ! the boy grew languid soon,
   And fever thrilled through all his veins.

The dew forsook his baby brow,
   No more with healthy bloom he smiled—
Oh ! where was tranquil Reason now,
   To cast her shadow o'er the child ?

Beneath a green and agèd palm,
   His foot at length for shelter turning,
He saw the nymph reclining calm,
   With brow as cool as his was burning.

' Oh ! take me to that bosom cold,'
   In murmurs at her feet he said ;
And Reason oped her garment's fold,
   And flung it round his fevered head.

He felt her bosom's icy touch,
   And soon it lulled his pulse to rest ;
For, ah ! the chill was quite too much,
   And Love expired on Reason's breast !

                        T. MOORE.

49. JE NE SAIS QUOI

Yes, I'm in love, I feel it now,
  And Celia has undone me !
And yet I'll swear I can't tell how
  The pleasing plague stole on me.

'Tis not her face that love creates,
  For there no graces revel ;
'Tis not her shape, for there the Fates
  Have rather been uncivil.

'Tis not her air, for, sure, in that
  There 's nothing more than common ;
And all her sense is only chat,
  Like any other woman.

Her voice, her touch, might give the alarm,
  'Twas both, perhaps, or neither !
In short, 'twas that provoking charm
  Of Celia all together.

W. Whitehead.

50. LOVE UNACCOUNTABLE

'Tis not her birth, her friends, nor yet her treasure,
Nor do I covet her for sensual pleasure,
Nor for that old morality
Do I love her, 'cause she loves me.
Sure he that loves his lady 'cause she 's fair,
Delights his eye, so loves himself, not her.
Something there is moves me to love, and I
Do know I love, but know not how, nor why.

A. Brome.

51. LOVE NOT ME FOR COMELY GRACE

Love not me for comely grace,
For my pleasing eye or face ;
Nor for any outward part,
No, nor for my constant heart :
    For those may fail or turn to ill,
      So thou and I shall sever.
Keep therefore a true woman's eye,
And love me still, but know not why ;
    So hast thou the same reason still
      To doat upon me ever.

Unknown.

52. I DO NOT LOVE THEE

I DO not love thee !—no ! I do not love thee !
And yet when thou art absent I am sad ;
  And envy even the bright blue sky above thee,
Whose quiet stars may see thee and be glad.

I do not love thee !—yet, I know not why,
Whate'er thou dost seems still well done, to me :
  And often in my solitude I sigh
That those I do love are not more like thee !

I do not love thee !—yet, when thou art gone,
I hate the sound (though those who speak be dear)
  Which breaks the lingering echo of the tone
Thy voice of music leaves upon my ear.

I do not love thee !—yet thy speaking eyes,
With their deep, bright, and most expressive blue,
  Between me and the midnight heaven arise,
Oftener than any eyes I ever knew.

I know I do not love thee ! yet, alas !
Others will scarcely trust my candid heart ;
  And oft I catch them smiling as they pass,
Because they see me gazing where thou art.

THE HON. MRS. C. E. S. NORTON.

53. LOVE IS A SICKNESS

LOVE is a sickness full of woes,
  All remedies refusing ;
A plant that with most cutting grows,
  Most barren with best using.
      Why so ?
More we enjoy it, more it dies ;
If not enjoyed, it sighing cries
      Heigh-ho !

Love is a torment of the mind,
  A tempest everlasting ;
And Jove hath made it of a kind
  Not well, nor full, nor fasting.
      Why so ?
More we enjoy it, more it dies ;
If not enjoyed, it sighing cries
      Heigh-ho !

S. DANIEL.

54. FIRST LOVE

'Tis sweet to hear the watch-dog's honest bark
   Bay deep-mouthed welcome as we draw near home ;
'Tis sweet to know there is an eye will mark
   Our coming, and look brighter when we come ;
'Tis sweet to be awakened by the lark,
   Or lulled by falling waters ; sweet the hum
Of bees, the voice of girls, the song of birds,
The lisp of children, and their earliest words.

Sweet is the vintage, when the showering grapes
   In Bacchanal profusion reel to earth,
Purple and gushing ; sweet are our escapes
   From civic revelry to rural mirth ;
Sweet to the miser are his glittering heaps,
   Sweet to the father is his first-born's birth,
Sweet is revenge—especially to women,
Pillage to soldiers, prize-money to seamen.

Sweet is a legacy, and passing sweet
   The unexpected death of some old lady
Or gentleman of seventy years complete,
   Who've made ' us youth ' wait too—too long already
For an estate, or cash, or country seat,
   Still breaking, but with stamina so steady
That all the Israelites are fit to mob its
Next owner for their double-damned post-obits.

'Tis sweet to win, no matter how, one's laurels,
   By blood or ink ; 'tis sweet to put an end
To strife ; 'tis sometimes sweet to have our quarrels,
   Particularly with a tiresome friend :
Sweet is old wine in bottles, ale in barrels ;
   Dear is the helpless creature we defend
Against the world ; and dear the schoolboy spot
We ne'er forget, though there we are forgot.

But sweeter still than this, than these, than all,
   Is first and passionate love—it stands alone,
Like Adam's recollection of his fall ;
   The tree of knowledge has been plucked—all 's known—
And life yields nothing further to recall
   Worthy of this ambrosial sin, so shown,
No doubt in fable, as the unforgiven
Fire which Prometheus filched for us from heaven.

                G. GORDON, LORD BYRON.

55. THE CRIER

Good folk, for gold or hire,
　　But help me to a crier ;
For my poor heart is run astray
After two eyes, that passed this way.
　　O yes, O yes, O yes,
　　If there be any man,
　　In town or country, can
　　Bring me my heart again,
　　I'll please him for his pain ;
And by these marks I will you show
That only I this heart do owe.

　　It is a wounded heart,
　　Wherein yet sticks the dart,
Every piece sore hurt throughout it,
　Faith and troth writ round about it :
It was a tame heart and a dear,
　　And never used to roam ;
But having got this haunt, I fear,
　　'Twill hardly stay at home.
For God's sake, walking by the way,
　　If you my heart do see,
Either impound it for a stray,
　　Or send it back to me.

M. DRAYTON.

56. TO OENONE

What conscience, say, is it in thee,
　　When I a heart had one,
To take away that heart from me,
　　And to retain thy own ?

For shame or pity now incline
　　To play a loving part ;
Either to send me kindly thine,
　　Or give me back my heart.

Covet not both ; but if thou dost
　　Resolve to part with neither,
Why, yet to show that thou art just,
　　Take me and mine together !

R. HERRICK.

57. I PRITHEE SEND ME BACK MY HEART

I PRITHEE send me back my heart,
  Since I cannot have thine ;
For if from yours you will not part,
  Why, then, shouldst thou have mine ?

Yet now I think on't, let it lie,
  To find it were in vain ;
For thou hast a thief in either eye
  Would steal it back again.

Why should two hearts in one breast lie,
  And yet not lodge together ?
O Love ! where is thy sympathy,
  If thus our breasts thou sever ?

But love is such a mystery,
  I cannot find it out ;
For when I think I'm best resolved,
  I then am in most doubt.

Then farewell care, and farewell woe ;
  I will no longer pine ;
For I'll believe I have her heart,
  As much as she hath mine.

Sir J. Suckling.

58. LOVE IN FANTASTIC TRIUMPH SATE

Love in fantastic triumph sate,
  Whilst bleeding hearts around him flowed :
For whom fresh pains he did create,
  And strange tyrannic power he showed.
From thy bright eyes he took his fires,
  Which round about in sport he hurled ;
But 'twas from mine he took desires
  Enough to undo the amorous world.

From me he took his sighs and tears,
  From thee his pride and cruelty ;
From me his languishments and fears,
  And every killing dart from thee.
Thus thou and I the God have armed,
  And set him up a deity,
But my poor heart alone is harmed,
  Whilst thine the victor is, and free.

Aphra Behn.

59.   THE ENCHANTMENT

I DID but look and love awhile—
　'Twas but for one half-hour ;
Then to resist I had no will,
　And now I have no power.

To sigh, and wish, is all my ease,
　Sighs which do heat impart
Enough to melt the coldest ice,
　Yet cannot warm your heart.

Oh, would your pity give my heart
　One corner of your breast,
'Twould learn of yours the winning art,
　And quickly steal the rest.

T. OTWAY.

60.   THE EXCHANGE

WE pledged our hearts, my love and I,—
　I in my arms the maiden clasping ;
I could not tell the reason why,
　But, oh ! I trembled like an aspen.

Her father's love she bade me gain ;
　I went, and shook like any reed !
I strove to act the man—in vain !
　We had exchanged our hearts indeed.

S. T. COLERIDGE.

61.   INSPIRATION

I NEVER drank of Aganippe well,
Nor ever did in shade of Tempe sit,
And Muses scorn with vulgar brains to dwell ;
Poor layman I, for sacred rites unfit,
Some do I hear of poets' fury tell,
But, God wot, wot not what they mean by it ;
And this I swear by blackest brook of hell,
I am no pick-purse of another's wit.
How falls it then, that with so smooth an ease
My thoughts I speak ; and what I speak doth flow
In verse, and that my verse best wits doth please ?
Guess we the cause ?   What, is it this : Fie, no.
Or so ?   Much less.   How then ?   Sure thus it is,
My lips are sweet, inspired with Stella's kiss.

SIR P. SIDNEY.

62.   LOOK IN THY HEART AND WRITE

Loving in truth, and fain in verse my love to show,
That she, dear she, might take some pleasure of my pain—
Pleasure might cause her read, reading might make her know,
Knowledge might pity win, and pity grace obtain—
I sought fit words to paint the blackest face of woe,
Studying inventions fine, her wits to entertain ;
Oft turning others' leaves, to see if thence would flow
Some fresh and fruitful showers upon my sunburned brain.
But words came halting forth, wanting Invention's stay ;
Invention, Nature's child, fled step-dame Study's blows ;
And others' feet still seemed but strangers in my way.
Thus, great with child to speak, and helpless in my throes,
  Biting my truant pen, beating myself for spite,
  ' Fool,' said my Muse to me, ' look in thy heart and write ! '

                             Sir P. Sidney.

63.   IMMORTALITY IN SONG

How many paltry, foolish, painted things,
That now in coaches trouble every street,
Shall be forgotten, whom no poet sings,
Ere they be well wrapped in their winding-sheet ?
Where I to thee eternity shall give,
When nothing else remaineth of these days,
And queens hereafter shall be glad to live
Upon the alms of thy superfluous praise ;
Virgins and matrons reading these my rhymes,
Shall be so much delighted with thy story,
That they shall grieve they lived not in these times,
To have seen thee, their sex's only glory :
    So shalt thou fly above the vulgar throng,
    Still to survive in my immortal song.

                             M. Drayton.

64.   UNGRATEFUL BEAUTY THREATENED

Know, Celia, since thou art so proud,
  'Twas I that gave thee thy renown ;
Thou hadst in the forgotten crowd
  Of common beauties lived unknown,
Had not my verse exhaled thy name,
And with it imped the wings of Fame.

That killing power is none of thine :
  I gave it to thy voice and eyes ;
Thy sweets, thy graces, all are mine ;
  Thou art my star, shin'st in my skies ;
Then dart not from thy borrowed sphere
Lightning on him that fixed thee there.

Tempt me with such affrights no more,
  Lest what I made I uncreate ;
Let fools thy mystic forms adore,
  I know thee in thy mortal state :
Wise poets, that wrapped Truth in tales,
Knew her themselves through all her veils.

T. CAREW.

65. WHO WILL BELIEVE MY VERSE

WHO will believe my verse in time to come,
If it were filled with your most high deserts ?
Though yet, heaven knows, it is but as a tomb
Which hides your life and shows not half your parts.
If I could write the beauty of your eyes
And in fresh numbers number all your graces,
The age to come would say, ' This poet lies ;
Such heavenly touches ne'er touched earthly faces.'
So should my papers, yellowed with their age,
Be scorned, like old men of less truth than tongue,
And your true rights be termed a poet's rage
And stretchèd metre of an antique song :
    But were some child of yours alive that time,
    You should live twice,—in it and in my rhyme.

W. SHAKESPEARE.

66. ONE DAY I WROTE HER NAME

ONE day I wrote her name upon the strand,
But came the waves and washèd it away :
Again I wrote it with a second hand,
But came the tide and made my pains his prey.
' Vain man,' said she, ' that dost in vain essay
A mortal thing so to immortalize ;
For I myself shall like to this decay,
And eke my name be wipèd out likewise.'
' Not so,' quoth I ; ' let baser things devise
To die in dust, but you shall live by fame ;
My verse your virtues rare shall eternize,
And in the heavens write your glorious name :
    Where, whenas Death shall all the world subdue,
    Our love shall live, and later life renew.'

E. SPENSER.

67. WELL I REMEMBER HOW YOU SMILED

Well I remember how you smiled
  To see me write your name upon
The soft sea-sand—'*O ! what a child !*
  You think you're writing upon stone ! '

I have since written what no tide
  Shall ever wash away, what men
Unborn shall read o'er ocean wide
  And find Ianthe's name again.

W. S. Landor.

68. HER RIGHT NAME

As Nancy at her toilet sat,
Admiring this and blaming that ;
' Tell me,' she said ; ' but tell me true ;
The nymph who could your heart subdue.
What sort of charms does she possess ? '
' Absolve me, fair one : I'll confess
With pleasure,' I replied. ' Her hair,
In ringlets rather dark than fair,
Does down her ivory bosom roll,
And, hiding half, adorns the whole.
In her high forehead's fair half-round
Love sits in open triumph crowned :
He in the dimple of her chin,
In private state, by friends is seen.
Her eyes are neither black nor grey ;
Nor fierce nor feeble is their ray ;
Their dubious lustre seems to show
Something that speaks nor Yes, nor No.
Her lips no living bard, I weet,
May say, how red, how round, how sweet :
Old Homer only could indite
Their vagrant grace and soft delight :
They stand recorded in his book,
When Helen smiled, and Hebe spoke '—
  The gipsy, turning to her glass,
Too plainly showed she knew the face :
' And which am I most like,' she said,
' Your Chloe, or your nut-brown maid ? '

M. Prior.

69. THE MERCHANT, TO SECURE HIS TREASURE

THE merchant, to secure his treasure,
    Conveys it in a borrowed name :
Euphelia serves to grace my measure,
    But Chloe is my real flame.

My softest verse, my darling lyre,
    Upon Euphelia's toilet lay—
When Chloe noted her desire
    That I should sing, that I should play.

My lyre I tune, my voice I raise,
    But with my numbers mix my sighs ;
And whilst I sing Euphelia's praise,
    I fix my soul on Chloe's eyes.

Fair Chloe blushed : Euphelia frowned :
    I sung, and gazed ; I played, and trembled :
And Venus to the Loves around
    Remarked how ill we all dissembled.

M. PRIOR.

70. A SONNET ON CHRISTIAN NAMES

(Written in the album of Edith Southey)

IN Christian world Mary the garland wears !
Rebecca sweetens on a Hebrew's ear ;
Quakers for pure Priscilla are more clear ;
And the light Gaul by amorous Ninon swears.
Among the lesser lights how Lucy shines !
What air of fragrance Rosamond throws round !
How like a hymn doth sweet Cecilia sound !
Of Marthas, and of Abigails, few lines
Have bragged in verse.   Of coarsest household stuff
Should homely Joan be fashionèd.   But can
You Barbara resist, or Marian ?
And is not Clare for love excuse enough ?
Yet, by my faith in numbers, I profess,
These all, than Saxon Edith, please me less.

C. LAMB.

71. NAMES

I ASKED my fair one happy day,
What I should call her in my lay ;
    By what sweet name from Rome or Greece ;
Lalage, Neaera, Chloris,
Sappho, Lesbia, or Doris,
    Arethusa or Lucrece.

74. A STOLEN KISS

Now gentle sleep hath closèd up those eyes
  Which, waking, kept my boldest thoughts in awe ;
And free access unto that sweet lip lies,
  From whence I long the rosy breath to draw.
Methinks no wrong it were, if I should steal
  From those two melting rubies one poor kiss ;
None sees the theft that would the theft reveal,
  Nor rob I her of aught that she can miss ;
Nay, should I twenty kisses take away,
  There would be little sign I would do so ;
Why then should I this robbery delay ?
  O she may wake, and therewith angry grow !
Well, if she do, I'll back restore that one,
And twenty hundred thousand more for loan.

G. WITHER.

75. TO ELECTRA

I DARE not ask a kiss,
  I dare not beg a smile ;
Lest having that, or this,
  I might grow proud the while.

No, no, the utmost share
  Of my desire, shall be,
Only to kiss that air
  That lately kissèd thee.

R. HERRICK.

76. COME, CHLOE, AND GIVE ME SWEET KISSES

Come, Chloe, and give me sweet kisses,
  For sweeter sure never girl gave ;
But why, in the midst of my blisses,
  Do you ask me how many I'd have ?
I'm not to be stinted in pleasure,
  Then, prithee, my charmer, be kind,
For whilst I love thee above measure,
  To numbers I'll ne'er be confined.
Count the bees that on Hybla are playing,
  Count the flowers that enamel its fields,
Count the flocks that on Tempe are straying,
  Or the grain that rich Sicily yields,
Go number the stars in the heaven,
  Count how many sands on the shore,

When so many kisses you've given,
   I still shall be craving for more.
To a heart full of love, let me hold thee,
   To a heart that, dear Chloe, is thine ;
In my arms I'll for ever enfold thee,
   And twist round thy limbs like a vine.
What joy can be greater than this is ?
   My life on thy lips shall be spent !
But the wretch that can number his kisses,
   With few will be ever content.

Sir C. Hanbury Williams.

77.   TO A KISS

Soft child of love, thou balmy bliss,
Inform me, O delicious kiss,
Why thou so suddenly art gone,
Lost in the moment thou art won ?

Yet go !   For wherefore should I sigh ?
On Delia's lips, with raptured eye,
On Delia's blushing lips I see
A thousand full as sweet as thee.

J. Wolcot.

78.   THE MAID I LOVE NE'ER THOUGHT OF ME

The maid I love ne'er thought of me
Amid the scenes of gaiety ;
But when her heart or mine sank low,
Ah, then it was no longer so.
From the slant palm she raised her head,
And kissed the cheek whence youth had fled.
Angels ! some future day for this,
Give her as sweet and pure a kiss.

W. S. Landor.

79.   JENNY KISSED ME WHEN WE MET

Jenny kissed me when we met,
   Jumping from the chair she sat in ;
Time, you thief ! who love to get
   Sweets into your list, put that in.
Say I'm weary, say I'm sad ;
   Say that health and wealth have missed me ;
Say I'm growing old, but add—
     Jenny kissed me !

J. H. Leigh Hunt.

80. LOVE'S PHILOSOPHY

THE fountains mingle with the river
　　And the rivers with the Ocean,
The winds of Heaven mix for ever
　　With a sweet emotion ;
Nothing in the world is single ;
　　All things by a law divine
In one spirit meet and mingle.
　　Why not I with thine ?—

See the mountains kiss high Heaven
　　And the waves clasp one another ;
No sister-flower would be forgiven
　　If it disdained its brother ;
And the sunlight clasps the earth
　　And the moonbeams kiss the sea :
What is all this sweet work worth,
　　If thou kiss not me ?

　　　　　　　　　P. B. SHELLEY.

81. A MATCH WITH THE MOON

WEARY already, weary miles to-night
　　I walked for bed : and so, to get some ease,
　　I dogged the flying moon with similes.
And like a wisp she doubled on my sight
In ponds ; and caught in tree-tops like a kite ;
　　And in a globe of film all liquorish
　　Swam full-faced like a silly silver fish ;—
Last, like a bubble shot the welkin's height
Where my road turned and got behind me, and sent
　　My wizened shadow craning round at me,
　　And jeered, ' So, step the measure,—one, two, three ! '—
And if I faced on her, looked innocent.
　　But just at parting, halfway down a dell,
　　She kissed me for good-night.　So you'll not tell.

　　　　　　　　　D. G. ROSSETTI.

82. THE KISS

' I SAW you take his kiss ! '　　' 'Tis true.'
　　' O, modesty ! '　　' 'Twas strictly kept :
' He thought me asleep ; at least, I knew
　　He thought I thought he thought I slept.'

　　　　　　　　　COVENTRY PATMORE.

83. STILL TO BE NEAT

STILL to be neat, still to be dressed
As you were going to a feast ;
Still to be powdered, still perfumed :
Lady, it is to be presumed,
Though art's hid causes are not found,
All is not sweet, all is not sound.

Give me a look, give me a face,
That makes simplicity a grace ;
Robes loosely flowing, hair as free :
Such sweet neglect more taketh me,
Than all the adulteries of art ;
They strike mine eyes, but not my heart.

BEN. JONSON.

84. MY LOVE IN HER ATTIRE DOTH SHOW HER WIT

MY Love in her attire doth show her wit,
It doth so well become her ;
For every season she hath dressings fit,
For winter, spring, and summer.
No beauty she doth miss
When all her robes are on ;
But Beauty's self she is
When all her robes are gone.

UNKNOWN.

85. DELIGHT IN DISORDER

A SWEET disorder in the dress
Kindles in clothes a wantonness ;
A lawn about the shoulders thrown
Into a fine distraction ;
An erring lace, which here and there
Enthrals a crimson stomacher ;
A cuff neglectful, and thereby
Ribands to flow confusedly ;
A winning wave, deserving note,
In the tempestuous petticoat ;
A careless shoe-string, in whose tie
I see a wild civility ;
Do more bewitch me, than when art
Is too precise in every part.

R. HERRICK.

86. UPON JULIA'S CLOTHES

WHENAS in silks my Julia goes,
Then, then, methinks, how sweetly flows
That liquefaction of her clothes.

Next, when I cast mine eyes and see
That brave vibration each way free ;
O how that glittering taketh me !

R. HERRICK.

87. A RING PRESENTED TO JULIA

JULIA, I bring
To thee this ring,
Made for thy finger fit ;
To show by this,
That our love is,
Or should be, like to it.

Close though it be,
The joint is free :
So when Love's yoke is on,
It must not gall,
Or fret at all
With hard oppression.

But it must play
Still either way,
And be, too, such a yoke,
As not too wide,
To over-slide ;
Or be so strait to choke.

So we, who bear
This beam, must rear
Ourselves to such a height :
As that the stay
Of either may
Create the burden light.

And as this round
Is nowhere found
To flaw, or else to sever :
So let our love
As endless prove,
And pure as gold for ever.

R. HERRICK.

88. THE BRACELET TO JULIA

WHY I tie about thy wrist
Julia, this my silken twist ;
For what other reason is 't,
But to show thee how in part,
Thou my pretty captive art ?
But thy bondslave is my heart :
'Tis but silk that bindeth thee,
Snap the thread, and thou art free :
But 'tis otherwise with me ;
I am bound, and fast bound so,
That from thee I cannot go,
If I could, I would not so.

R. HERRICK.

89. ON A GIRDLE

THAT which her slender waist confined
Shall now my joyful temples bind :
No monarch but would give his crown
His arms might do what this has done.

It was my heaven's extremest sphere,
The pale which held that lovely dear :
My joy, my grief, my hope, my love
Did all within this circle move.

A narrow compass ! and yet there
Dwelt all that 's good, and all that 's fair :
Give me but what this riband bound,
Take all the rest the sun goes round.

E. WALLER.

90. THE NATIONS

THE Spaniard loves his ancient slop,
  A Lombard the Venetian :
And some like breechless women go,
  The Russ, Turk, Jew, and Grecian.
The thrifty Frenchman wears small waist,
  The Dutch his belly boasteth,
The Englishman is for them all,
  And for each fashion coasteth.
The Turk in linen wraps his head,
  The Persian his in lawn too,
The Russ with sables furs his cap
  And change will not be drawn to.
The Spaniard 's constant to his block,
  The French inconstant ever ;

But of all felts that may be felt
  Give me your English beaver.
The German loves his coney-wool,
  The Irishman his shag too,
The Welsh his Monmouth loves to wear,
  And of the same will brag too.
Some love the rough, and some the smooth,
  Some great, and others small things,
But O your liquorish Englishman,
  He loves to deal in all things.
The Russ drinks quasse ; Dutch, Lubeck's beer,
  And that is strong and mighty;
The Briton he metheglin quaffs,
  The Irish aqua-vitae.
The French affects the Orleans grape,
  The Spaniard sips his sherry,
The English none of these can 'scape,
  But he with all makes merry.
The Italian in her high chioppine,
  Scotch lass, and lovely Erse too,
The Spanish donna, French madame,
  He doth not fear to go to.
Nothing so full of hazard, dread,
  Naught lies above the centre,
No health, no fashion, wine or wench,
  On which he dare not venture.

               T. HEYWOOD.

91. TO AMARANTHA

THAT SHE WOULD DISHEVEL HER HAIR

AMARANTHA, sweet and fair,
Ah, braid no more that shining hair !
As my curious hand or eye
Hovering round thee, let it fly.

Let it fly as unconfined
As its calm ravisher the wind,
Who hath left his darling, the east !
To wanton o'er that spicy nest.

Every tress must be confessed ;
But neatly tangled at the best ;
Like a clue of golden thread
Most excellently ravellèd.

Do not, then, wind up that light
In ribands, and o'ercloud in night,
Like the sun in 's early ray ;
But shake your head and scatter day.

               R. LOVELACE.

92. TO HIS MISTRESS

Tyrian dye why do you wear,
You whose cheeks best scarlet are ?
  Why do you fondly pin
  Pure linens o'er your skin,
    Your skin that 's whiter far ?—
Casting a dusky cloud before a star.

Why bears your neck a golden chain ?
Did Nature make your hair in vain,
  Of gold most pure and fine ?
  With gems why do you shine ?
    They, neighbours to your eyes,
Show but like Phosphor when the sun doth rise.

I would have all my mistress' parts
Owe more to Nature than the arts ;
  I would not woo the dress,
  Or one whose nights give less
    Contentment than the day ;
She 's fair whose beauty only makes her gay.

A. Cowley.

93. THE MILLER'S DAUGHTER

It is the miller's daughter,
  And she is grown so dear, so dear,
That I would be the jewel
  That trembles at her ear :
For hid in ringlets day and night,
I'd touch her neck so warm and white.

And I would be the girdle
  About her dainty dainty waist
And her heart would beat against me,
  In sorrow and in rest :
And I should know if it beat right,
I'd clasp it round so close and tight.

And I would be the necklace,
  And all day long to fall and rise
Upon her balmy bosom,
  With her laughter or her sighs,
And I would lie so light, so light,
I scarce should be unclasped at night.

Alfred, Lord Tennyson.

94.   TO MY MISTRESS'S BOOTS

THEY nearly strike me dumb,
And I tremble when they come
          Pit-a-pat :
This palpitation means
That these boots are Geraldine's—
          Think of that !

Oh, where did hunter win
So delicate a skin
          For her feet ?
You lucky little kid,
You perished, so you did,
          For my sweet.

The faery stitching gleams
On the toes, and in the seams,
          And reveals
That Pixies were the wags
Who tipped these funny tags,
          And these heels.

What soles ! so little worn !
Had Crusoe—soul forlorn !—
          Chanced to view
One printed near the tide,
How hard he would have tried
          For the two !

For Gerry's debonair,
And innocent, and fair
          As a rose :
She's an angel in a frock,
With a fascinating cock
          To her nose.

Those simpletons who squeeze
Their extremities to please
          Mandarins,
Would positively flinch
From venturing to pinch
          Geraldine's.

Cinderella's *lefts and rights*
To Geraldine's were frights :
          And, in truth,
The damsel, deftly shod,
Has dutifully trod
          From her youth.

The mansion—aye, and more,
The cottage of the poor,
      Where there's grief,
Or sickness, are her choice—
And the music of her voice
      Brings relief.

Come, Gerry, since it suits
Such a pretty Puss-in-Boots
      These to don,
Set your little hand awhile
On my shoulder, dear, and I'll
      Put them on.

                  F. LOCKER-LAMPSON.

95.   ON AN OLD MUFF

TIME has a magic wand !
What is this meets my hand,
Moth-eaten, mouldy, and
      Covered with fluff ?
Faded, and stiff, and scant ;
Can it be ? no, it can't—
Yes,—I declare 'tis Aunt
      Prudence's muff !

Years ago—twenty-three—
Old Uncle Barnaby
Gave it to Aunty P.—
      Laughing and teasing—
' Pru., of the breezy curls,
Whisper these solemn churls,
What holds a pretty girl's
      Hand without squeezing ? '

Uncle was then a lad
Gay, but, I grieve to add,
Sinful ; if smoking bad
      Baccy's a vice :
Glossy was then this mink
Muff, lined with pretty pink
Satin, which maidens think
      ' Awfully nice ! '

I see, in retrospect,
Aunt, in her best bedecked,
Gliding, with mien erect,
      Gravely to Meeting :

Psalm-book, and kerchief new,
Peeped from the muff of Pru.—
Young men—and pious too—
      Giving her greeting.

Pure was the life she led
Then—from this Muff, 'tis said,
Tracts she distributed :—
      Scapegraces many,
Seeing the grace they lacked,
Followed her—one, in fact,
Asked for—and got his tract
      Oftener than any.

Love has a potent spell !
Soon this bold Ne'er-do-well,
Aunt's sweet susceptible
      Heart undermining,
Slipped, so the scandal runs,
Notes in the pretty nun's
Muff—triple-cornered ones—
      Pink as its lining !

Worse even, soon the jade
Fled (to oblige her blade !)
Whilst her friends thought that they'd
      Locked her up tightly :
After such shocking games
Aunt is of wedded dames
Gayest—and now her name 's
      Mrs. Golightly.

In female conduct flaw
Sadder I never saw,
Still I've faith in the law
      Of compensation.
Once Uncle went astray—
Smoked, joked, and swore away—
Sworn by, he's now, by a
      Large congregation !

Changed is the Child of Sin,
Now he's (he once was thin)
Grave, with a double chin,—
      Blest be his fat form !
Changed is the garb he wore,—
Preacher was never more
Prized than is Uncle for
      Pulpit or platform.

If all 's as best befits
Mortals of slender wits,
Then beg this Muff, and its
      Fair Owner pardon :
All 's for the best,—indeed
Such is *my* simple creed—
Still I must go and weed
      Hard in my garden.

F. Locker-Lampson.

96. THE LAY OF THE LEVITE

There is a sound that 's dear to me,
    It haunts me in my sleep ;
I wake, and, if I hear it not,
    I cannot choose but weep.
Above the roaring of the wind,
    Above the river's flow,
Methinks I hear the mystic cry
    Of ' Clo !—Old Clo ! '

The exile's song, it thrills among
    The dwellings of the free,
Its sound is strange to English ears,
    But 'tis not strange to me ;
For it hath shook the tented field
    In ages long ago,
And hosts have quailed before the cry
    Of ' Clo !—Old Clo ! '

O lose it not ! forsake it not !
    And let no time efface
The memory of that solemn sound,
    The watchword of our race ;
For not by dark and eagle eye
    The Hebrew shall you know,
So well as by the plaintive cry
    Of ' Clo !—Old Clo ! '

Even now, perchance, by Jordan's banks,
    Or Sidon's sunny walls,
Where, dial-like, to portion time,
    The palm-tree's shadow falls,
The pilgrims, wending on their way,
    Will linger as they go,
And listen to the distant cry
    Of ' Clo !—Old Clo ! '

W. E. Aytoun.

97.   JULIA'S BED

See'st thou that cloud as silver clear,
Plump, soft, and swelling everywhere ?
'Tis Julia's bed, and she sleeps there.

R. Herrick.

98. A TERNARY OF LITTLES, UPON A PIPKIN OF JELLY SENT TO A LADY

A little Saint best fits a little shrine,
A little prop best fits a little vine,
As my small cruse best fits my little wine.

A little seed best fits a little soil,
A little trade best fits a little toil :
As my small jar best fits my little oil.

A little bin best fits a little bread,
A little garland fits a little head :
As my small stuff best fits my little shed.

A little hearth best fits a little fire,
A little chapel fits a little choir,
As my small bell best fits my little spire.

A little stream best fits a little boat ;
A little lead best fits a little float ;
As my small pipe best fits my little note.

A little meat best fits a little belly,
As sweetly, Lady, give me leave to tell ye,
This little pipkin fits this little jelly.

R. Herrick.

99.   GRATITUDE

This cap, that so stately appears,
   With ribbon-bound tassel on high,
Which seems, by the crest that it rears,
   Ambitious of brushing the sky :
This cap to my cousin I owe,
   She gave it, and gave me beside,
Wreathed into an elegant bow,
   The ribbon with which it is tied.

This wheel-footed studying chair,
   Contrived both for toil and repose,
Wide-elbowed, and wadded with hair,
   In which I both scribble and doze,

Bright-studded to dazzle the eyes,
    And rival in lustre of that,
In which, or astronomy lies,
    Fair Cassiopeia sat :

These carpets, so soft to the foot,
    Caledonia's traffic and pride !
Oh spare them, ye Knights of the Boot !
    Escaped from a cross-country ride !
This table and mirror within,
    Secure from collision and dust,
At which I oft shave cheek and chin,
    And periwig nicely adjust :

This movable structure of shelves,
    For its beauty admired and its use,
And charged with octavos and twelves,
    The gayest I had to produce,
Where, flaming in scarlet and gold,
    My Poems enchanted I view,
And hope, in due time, to behold
    My Iliad and Odyssey too :

This china, that decks the alcove,
    Which here people call a beaufette,
But what the Gods call it above,
    Has ne'er been revealed to us yet :
These curtains, that keep the room warm
    Or cool, as the season demands,
These stoves, that for pattern and form
    Seem the labour of Mulciber's hands :

All these are not half that I owe
    To one, from our earliest youth
To me ever ready to show
    Benignity, friendship, and truth,
For Time, the destroyer declared
    And foe of our perishing kind,
If even her face he has spared,
    Much less could he alter her mind.

Thus compassed about with the goods
    And chattels of leisure and ease,
I indulge my poetical moods
    In many such fancies as these ;
And fancies I fear they will seem,
    Poets' goods are not often so fine ;
The poets will swear that I dream,
    When I sing of the splendour of mine.

W. COWPER.

100. THE CANE-BOTTOMED CHAIR

In tattered old slippers that toast at the bars,
And a ragged old jacket perfumed with cigars,
Away from the world and its toils and its cares,
I've a snug little kingdom up four pair of stairs.

To mount to this realm is a toil, to be sure,
But the fire there is bright and the air rather pure ;
And the view I behold on a sunshiny day
Is grand through the chimney-pots over the way.

This snug little chamber is crammed in all nooks,
With worthless old knicknacks and silly old books,
And foolish old odds and foolish old ends,
Cracked bargains from brokers, cheap keepsakes from friends.

Old armour, prints, pictures, pipes, china (all cracked),
Old rickety tables, and chairs broken-backed ;
A twopenny treasury, wondrous to see ;
What matter ? 'tis pleasant to you, friend, and me.

No better divan need the Sultan require,
Than the creaking old sofa that basks by the fire ;
And 'tis wonderful, surely, what music you get
From the rickety, ramshackle, wheezy spinet.

That praying-rug came from a Turcoman's camp ;
By Tiber once twinkled that brazen old lamp ;
A Mameluke fierce yonder dagger has drawn :
'Tis a murderous knife to toast muffins upon.

Long, long through the hours, and the night, and the chimes,
Here we talk of old books, and old friends, and old times ;
As we sit in a fog made of rich Latakie
This chamber is pleasant to you, friend, and me.

But of all the cheap treasures that garnish my nest,
There's one that I love and I cherish the best ;
For the finest of couches that's padded with hair
I never would change thee, my cane-bottomed chair.

'Tis a bandy-legged, high-shouldered, worm-eaten seat
With a creaking old back, and twisted old feet ;
But since the fair morning when Fanny sat there,
I bless thee and love thee, old cane-bottomed chair.

If chairs have but feeling in holding such charms,
A thrill must have passed through your withered old arms !
I looked, and I longed, and I wished in despair—
I wished myself turned to a cane-bottomed chair.

It was but a moment she sat in this place,
She'd a scarf on her neck, and a smile on her face !
A smile on her face, and a rose in her hair,
And she sat there, and bloomed in my cane-bottomed chair.

And so I have valued my chair ever since,
Like the shrine of a saint, or the throne of a prince ;
Saint Fanny, my patroness sweet I declare,
The queen of my heart and my cane-bottomed chair.

When the candles burn low, and the company 's gone,
In the silence of night as I sit here alone—
I sit here alone, but we yet are a pair—
My Fanny I see in my cane-bottomed chair.

She comes from the past and revisits my room ;
She looks as she then did, all beauty and bloom ;
So smiling and tender, so fresh and so fair,
And yonder she sits in my cane-bottomed chair.

W. M. THACKERAY.

101. WHY WAS CUPID A BOY

WHY was Cupid a boy,
    And why a boy was he ?
He should have been a girl,
    For aught that I can see.

For he shoots with his bow,
    And the girl shoots with her eye,
And they both are merry and glad,
    And laugh when we do cry.

Then to make Cupid a boy
    Was surely a woman's plan,
For a boy ne'er learns so much
    Till he is become a man.

And then he 's so pierced with cares,
    And wounded with arrowy smarts,
That the whole business of his life
    Is to pick out the heads of the darts.

'Twas the Greeks' love of war
    Turned love into a boy,
And woman into a statue of stone—
    And away fled every joy.

W. BLAKE.

102. VENUS, BY ADONIS' SIDE

Venus, by Adonis' side,
Crying kissed, and kissing cried,
Wrung her hands and tore her hair,
For Adonis dying there.

' Stay,' quoth she, ' Oh, stay and live !
Nature, surely, doth not give
To the earth her sweetest flowers,
To be seen but some few hours.'

On his face, still as he bled,
For each drop a tear she shed,
Which she kissed or wiped away,
Else had drowned him where he lay.

' Fair Proserpina,' quoth she,
' Shall not have thee yet from me ;
Nor thy soul, to fly begin ;
While my lips can keep it in ! '

Here she ceased again.   And some
Say, Apollo would have come
To have cured his wounded limb,
But that she had smothered him.

W. Browne.

103. CUPID MISTAKEN

As after noon, one summer's day,
   Venus stood bathing in a river ;
Cupid a-shooting went that way,
   New strung his bow, new filled his quiver.

With skill he chose his sharpest dart :
   With all his might his bow he drew :
Swift to his beauteous parent's heart
   The too-well-guided arrow flew.

' I faint ! I die !' the goddess cried :
   ' O cruel, could'st thou find none other
To wreck thy spleen on : Parricide !
   Like Nero, thou hast slain thy mother.'

Poor Cupid sobbing scarce could speak ;
   ' Indeed, mama, I did not know ye :
Alas ! how easy my mistake ?
   I took you for your likeness, Chloe.

M. Prior.

104. APELLES' SONG

Cupid and my Campaspe played
At cards for kisses, Cupid paid ;
He stakes his quiver, bow, and arrows,
His mother's doves, and team of sparrows ;
Loses them too ; then, down he throws
The coral of his lip, the rose
Growing on 's cheek (but none knows how),
With these, the crystal of his brow,
And then the dimple of his chin :
All these did my Campaspe win.
At last he set her both his eyes ;
She won, and Cupid blind did rise.
    O Love ! has she done this to thee ?
    What shall (alas !) become of me ?

J. Lyly.

105. DORINDA

Dorinda's sparkling wit and eyes
    United, cast too fierce a light,
Which blazes high, but quickly dies ;
    Pains not the heart, but hurts the sight.

Love is a calmer, gentler joy ;
    Smooth are his looks, and soft his pace ;
Her Cupid is a blackguard boy,
    That runs his link full in your face.

C. Sackville, Earl of Dorset.

106. WHEN LOVE, WHO RULED

When Love, who ruled as Admiral o'er
    His rosy mother's isles of light,
Was cruising off the Paphian shore,
    A sail at sunset hove in sight.
' A chase, a chase ! my Cupids all,'
Said Love, the little Admiral.

Aloft the wingèd sailors sprung,
    And, swarming up the mast like bees,
The snow-white sails expanding flung,
    Like broad magnolias to the breeze.
' Yo ho, yo ho, my Cupids all ! '
Said Love, the little Admiral.

The chase was o'er—the bark was caught,
    The wingèd crew her freight explored ;
And found 'twas just as Love had thought,
    For all was contraband aboard.

' A prize, a prize, my Cupids all !'
Said Love, the little Admiral.

Safe stowed in many a package there,
    And labelled slyly o'er, as ' Glass,'
Were lots of all the illegal ware,
    Love's Custom-House forbids to pass.
' O'erhaul, o'erhaul, my Cupids all,'
Said Love, the little Admiral.

False curls they found, of every hue,
    With rosy blushes ready made ;
And teeth of ivory, good as new,
    For veterans in the smiling trade.
' Ho ho, ho ho, my Cupids all,'
Said Love, the little Admiral.

Mock sighs, too,—kept in bags for use,
    Like breezes bought of Lapland seers,—
Lay ready here to be let loose,
    When wanted, in young spinsters' ears.
' Ha ha, ha ha, my Cupids all,'
Said Love, the little Admiral.

False papers next on board were found,
    Sham invoices of flames and darts,
Professedly for Paphos bound,
    But meant for Hymen's golden marts.
' For shame, for shame, my Cupids all !'
Said Love, the little Admiral.

Nay, still to every fraud awake,
    Those pirates all Love's signals knew,
And hoisted oft his flag, to make
    Rich wards and heiresses bring-to.
' A foe, a foe, my Cupids all !'
Said Love, the little Admiral.

' This must not be,' the boy exclaims,
    ' In vain I rule the Paphian seas,
If Love's and Beauty's sovereign names
    Are lent to cover frauds like these.
Prepare, prepare, my Cupids all !'
Said Love, the little Admiral.

Each Cupid stood with lighted match—
    A broadside struck the smuggling foe,
And swept the whole unhallowed batch
    Of falsehood to the depths below.
' Huzza, huzza ! my Cupids all !'
Said Love, the little Admiral.

T. MOORE.

107. TO ROSEMOUNDE. A BALADE

MADAME, ye ben of al beautè shryne
As fer as cercled is the mappemounde ;
For as the cristal glorious ye shyne,
And lyke ruby ben your chekes rounde.
Therwith ye ben so mery and so iocounde,
That at a revel whan that I see you daunce,
It is an oynement unto my wounde,
Thogh ye to me ne do no daliaunce.

For thogh I wepe of teres ful a tyne,
Yet may that wo myn herte nat confounde ;
Your seemly voys that ye so smal out-twyne
Maketh my thoght in Ioye and blis habounde.
So curteisly I go, with lovë bounde,
That to my-self I sey, in my penaunce,
Suffyseth me to love you, Rosemounde,
Thogh ye to me ne do no daliaunce.

Nas never pyk walwed in galauntyne
As I in love am walwed and y-wounde ;
For which ful ofte I of my-self divyne
That I am trewe Tristam the secounde.
My love may not refreyd be nor afounde ;
I brenne ay in an amorous plesaunce.
Do what you list, I wil your thral be founde,
Thogh ye to me ne do no daliaunce.

G. CHAUCER.

108. APOLLO'S SONG

MY Daphne's hair is twisted gold,
Bright stars apiece her eyes do hold,
My Daphne's brow enthrones the Graces,
My Daphne's beauty stains all faces,
On Daphne's cheek grow rose and cherry,
On Daphne's lip a sweeter berry,
Daphne's snowy hand but touched does melt,
And then no heavenlier warmth is felt,
My Daphne's voice tunes all the spheres,
My Daphne's music charms all ears.
Fond am I thus to sing her praise ;
These glories now are turned to bays.

J. LYLY.

109. THE TRIUMPH OF CHARIS

SEE the chariot at hand here of Love,
    Wherein my Lady rideth !
Each that draws is a swan or a dove,
    And well the car Love guideth.
As she goes, all hearts do duty
    Unto her beauty ;
And enamoured, do wish, so they might
    But enjoy such a sight,
That they still were to run by her side,
Through sands, through seas, whither she would ride.

Do but look on her eyes, they do light
    All that Love's world compriseth !
Do but look on her hair, it is bright
    As Love's star when it riseth !
Do but mark, her forehead's smoother
    Than words that soothe her !
And from her arched brows such a grace
    Sheds itself through the face,
As alone there triumphs to the life
All the gain, all the good of the elements' strife.

Have you seen but a bright lily grow,
    Before rude hands have touched it ?
Have you marked but the fall o' the snow
    Before the soil hath smutched it ?
Have you felt the wool of the beaver,
    Or swan's down ever ?
Or have smelled o' the bud of the briar,
    Or the 'nard in the fire ?
Or have tasted the bag of the bee ?
O so white ! O so soft ! O so sweet is she !

                BEN. JONSON.

110. ON HIS MISTRESS, THE QUEEN OF BOHEMIA

You meaner beauties of the night,
    That poorly satisfy our eyes
More by your number than your light,
    You common people of the skies ;
What are you, when the Moon shall rise ?

You curious chanters of the wood
    That warble forth Dame Nature's lays,
Thinking your passions understood
    By your weak accents ; what's your praise
When Philomel her voice shall raise ?

You violets that first appear,
  By your pure purple mantles known
Like the proud virgins of the year,
  As if the spring were all your own,
What are you, when the Rose is blown ?

So, when my Mistress shall be seen
  In form and beauty of her mind,
By virtue first, then choice, a Queen,
  Tell me, if she were not designed
The eclipse and glory of her kind ?

Sir H. Wotton.

111.   A PRAISE OF HIS LADY

Give place, you ladies, and be gone !
  Boast not yourselves at all,
For here at hand approacheth one
  Whose face will stain you all.

The virtue of her lively looks
  Excels the precious stone ;
I wish to have none other books
  To read or look upon.

In each of her two crystal eyes
  Smileth a naked boy ;
It would you all in heart suffice
  To see that lamp of joy.

I think Nature hath lost the mould
  Where she her shape did take ;
Or else I doubt if Nature could
  So fair a creature make.

She may be well compared
  Unto the Phoenix kind,
Whose like was never seen or heard,
  That any man can find.

In life she is Diana chaste;
  In truth Penelope ;
In word and eke in deed steadfast;
  —What will you more say we ?

If all the world were sought so far,
  Who could find such a wight ?
Her beauty twinkleth like a star
  Within the frosty night.

Her rosial colour comes and goes
  With such a comely grace,
More ruddier, too, than doth the rose,
  Within her lively face.

At Bacchus' feast none shall her meet,
  Nor at no wanton play,
Nor gazing in an open street,
  Nor gadding as a stray.

The modest mirth that she doth use
  Is mixed with shamefastness ;
All vice she doth wholly refuse,
  And hateth idleness.

O Lord ! it is a world to see
  How virtue can repair,
And deck in her such honesty,
  Whom Nature made so fair.

Truly she doth so far exceed
  Our women nowadays,
As doth the gillyflower a weed ;
  And more a thousand ways.

How might I do to get a graff
  Of this unspotted tree ?
—For all the rest are plain but chaff,
  Which seem good corn to be.

This gift alone I shall her give ;
  When death doth what he can,
Her honest fame shall ever live
  Within the mouth of man.

                              J. Heywood.

112. A SONG

In Imitation of Sir John Eaton

Too late, alas ! I must confess,
  You need not arts to move me ;
Such charms by nature you possess,
  'Twere madness not to love ye.

Then spare a heart you may surprise,
  And give my tongue the glory
To boast, though my ungrateful eyes
  Betray a tender story.

              J. Wilmot, Earl of Rochester.

113. MAY THE AMBITIOUS EVER FIND

MAY the ambitious ever find
  Success in crowds and noise,
While gentle love does fill my mind
  With silent real joys.

May knaves and fools grow rich and great,
  And the world think them wise,
While I lie dying at her feet,
  And all that world despise !

Let conquering kings new triumphs raise,
  And melt in court delights ;
Her eyes can give much brighter days,
  Her arms much softer nights.

C. SACKVILLE, EARL OF DORSET.

114. WHEN THY BEAUTY APPEARS

WHEN thy beauty appears
  In its graces and airs
All bright as an angel new dropped from the sky,
At distance I gaze, and am awed by my fears,
  So strangely you dazzle my eye !

But when without art,
  Your kind thoughts you impart,
When your love runs in blushes through every vein ;
When it darts from your eyes, when it pants in your heart,
  Then I know you're a woman again.

There 's a passion and pride
  In our sex (she replied),
And thus, might I gratify both, I would do ;
Still an angel appear to each lover beside,
  But still be a woman to you !

T. PARNELL.

115. WHEN SAPPHO TUNED THE RAPTURED STRAIN

WHEN Sappho tuned the raptured strain,
The listening wretch forgot his pain ;
With art divine the lyre she strung,
Like thee she played, like thee she sung.

For while she struck the quivering wire,
The eager breast was all on fire ;
And when she joined the vocal lay,
The captive soul was charmed away.

But had she added still to these
Thy softer, chaster power to please,
Thy beauteous air of sprightly youth,
Thy native smiles of artless truth :

She ne'er had pined beneath disdain,
She ne'er had played and sung in vain,
Despair had ne'er her soul possessed
To dash on rocks the tender breast.

T. G. SMOLLETT.

116.   FAIR HEBE AND REASON

FAIR Hebe I left, with a cautious design,
To escape from her charms, and to drown Love in wine ;
I tried it, but found, when I came to depart,
The wine in my head, but still Love in my heart.

I repaired to my Reason, entreating her aid,
Who paused on my case, and each circumstance weighed :
Then gravely pronounced, in return to my prayer,
That Hebe was fairest of all that were fair.

That's a truth, replied I, I've no need to be taught,
I came for your counsel to find out a fault ;
If that's all, quoth Reason, return as you came,
For to find fault with Hebe would forfeit my name.

J. WEST, EARL DE LA WARR.

117.   TO LADY ANNE HAMILTON

Too late I stayed—forgive the crime ;
  Unheeded flew the hours ;
How noiseless falls the foot of Time,
  That only treads on flowers !

What eye with clear account remarks
  The ebbing of the glass,
When all its sands are diamond sparks,
  That dazzle as they pass !

Oh, who to sober measurement
  Time's happy swiftness brings,
When birds of Paradise have lent
  Their plumage for his wings !

W. R. SPENCER.

118. AMO, AMAS

Amo, amas,
I love a lass
As a cedar tall, and slender.
Sweet cowslip's grace
Is her Nominative Case,
And she's of the Feminine Gender.
　　Rorum corum, sunt Divorum !
　　　Harum, scarum, Divo !
　　Tag rag, merry derry, periwig and hatband !
　　　Hic hoc horum Genitivo !

Can I decline
A nymph divine ?
Her voice as a flute is *dulcis ;*
Her *oculi* bright,
Her *manus* white,
And soft, when I *tacto,* her pulse is.
　　Rorum corum, sunt Divorum !
　　　Harum, scarum, Divo !
　　Tag rag, merry derry, periwig and hatband !
　　　Hic hoc horum Genitivo !

O, how *bella*
Is my *puella* !
I'll kiss *saecula saeculorum.*
If I've luck, sir,
She's my *uxor.*
O dies benedictorum !
　　Rorum corum, sunt Divorum !
　　　Harum, scarum, Divo !
　　Tag rag, merry derry, periwig and hatband !
　　　Hic hoc horum Genitivo !

　　　　　　　　　　　　J. O'KEEFFE.

119. BONNIE LESLEY

O SAW ye bonnie Lesley
　As she gaed o'er the border ?
She's gane, like Alexander,
　To spread her conquests farther.

To see her is to love her,
　And love but her for ever ;
For Nature made her what she is,
　And never made anither !

Thou art a queen, fair Lesley,
  Thy subjects we, before thee :
Thou art divine, fair Lesley,
  The hearts o' men adore thee.

The Deil he could na scaith thee,
  Or aught that wad belang thee ;
He'd look into thy bonnie face,
  And say, ' I canna wrang thee.'

The Powers aboon will tent thee ;
  Misfortune sha'na steer thee ;
Thou'rt like themselves sae lovely,
  That ill they'll ne'er let near thee.

Return again, fair Lesley,
  Return to Caledonie !
That we may brag we hae a lass
  There 's nane again sae bonnie.

R. BURNS.

120. SHE IS NOT FAIR TO OUTWARD VIEW

SHE is not fair to outward view
  As many maidens be,
Her loveliness I never knew
  Until she smiled on me.
O then I saw her eye was bright,
A well of love, a spring of light.

But now her looks are coy and cold,
  To mine they ne'er reply,
And yet I cease not to behold
  The love-light in her eye :
Her very frowns are fairer far
Than smiles of other maidens are.

HARTLEY COLERIDGE.

121. WITH LEADEN FOOT TIME CREEPS ALONG

WITH leaden foot time creeps along,
  While Delia is away ;
With her, nor plaintive was the song,
  Nor tedious was the day.
Ah ! envious power, reverse my doom ;
  Now double thy career ;
Strain every nerve, stretch every plume,
  And rest them when she 's here.

R. JAGO.

122. THE MISTRESS

An age, in her embraces passed,
  Would seem a winter's day ;
Where life and light, with envious haste,
  Are torn and snatched away.

But oh ! how slowly minutes roll,
  When absent from her eyes,
That fed my love, which is my soul ;
  It languishes and dies.

For then, no more a soul but shade,
  It mournfully does move ;
And haunts my breast, by absence made
  The living tomb of love.

You wiser men despise me not,
  Whose love-sick fancy raves,
On shades of souls and Heaven knows what ;
  Short ages live in graves.

Whene'er those wounding eyes so full
  Of sweetness you did see,
Had you not been profoundly dull,
  You had gone mad like me.

Nor censure us, you who perceive
  My best-beloved and me,
Sigh and lament, complain and grieve ;
  You think we disagree.

Alas ! 'tis sacred jealousy,
  Love raised to an extreme ;
The only proof, 'twixt them and me,
  We love, and do not dream.

Fantastic fancies fondly move,
  And in frail joy believe :
Taking false pleasure for true love ;
  But pain can ne'er deceive.

Kind jealous doubts, tormenting fears,
  And anxious cares, when past,
Prove our heart's treasure fixed and dear,
  And make us blessed at last.

                    J. WILMOT, EARL OF ROCHESTER

123. AMARYLLIS I DID WOO

AMARYLLIS I did woo ;
And I courted Phillis too ;
Daphne for her love I chose ;
Chloris, for that damask rose
In her cheek I held as dear ;
Yea, a thousand liked, well near ;
And, in love with all together,
Fearèd the enjoying either,
'Cause to be of one possessed,
Barred the hope of all the rest.

G. WITHER.

124. IF I FREELY MAY DISCOVER

IF I freely may discover
What would please me in my lover,
I would have her fair and witty,
Savouring more of court than city ;
A little proud, but full of pity :
Light and humorous in her toying ;
Oft building hopes, and soon destroying ;
Long, but sweet, in the enjoying ;
Neither too easy, nor too hard :
All extremes I would have barred.

She should be allowed her passions,
So they were but used as fashions ;
Sometimes froward, and then frowning,
Sometimes sickish and then swooning,
Every fit with change still crowning.
Purely jealous I would have her,
Then only constant when I crave her :
'Tis a virtue should not save her.
Thus, nor her delicates would cloy me,
Neither her peevishness annoy me.

BEN. JONSON.

125. WHAT WIGHT HE LOVED

SHALL I tell you whom I love ?
  Hearken then awhile to me,
And if such a woman move,
  As I now shall versify,
Be assured 'tis she or none
That I love and love alone.

Nature did her so much right,
   That she scorns the help of art,
In as many virtues dight
   As ere yet embraced a heart,
So much good as truly tried,
Some for less were deified.

Wit she hath without desire
   To make known how much she hath ;
And her anger flames no higher
   Than may fitly sweeten wrath.
Full of pity as may be,
Though perhaps not so to me !

Reason masters every sense,
   And her virtues grace her birth ;
Lovely as all excellence,
   Modest in her most of mirth :
Likelihood enough to prove
Only worth could kindle love.

Such she is, and if you know
   Such a one as I have sung,
Be she brown or fair or so
   That she be but somewhile young,
Be assured 'tis she or none
That I love and love alone.

                                   W. BROWNE.

126.   WISHES FOR THE SUPPOSED MISTRESS

WHOE'ER she be,
That not impossible She
That shall command my heart and me :

Where'er she lie,
Locked up from mortal eye
In shady leaves of destiny :

Till that ripe birth
Of studied fate stand forth,
And teach her fair steps to our earth :

Till that divine
Idea take a shrine
Of crystal flesh, through which to shine :

—Meet you her, my Wishes,
Bespeak her to my blisses,
And be ye called my absent kisses.

I wish her Beauty
That owes not all his duty
To gaudy tire, or glistering shoe-tie;

Something more than
Taffata or tissue can,
Or rampant feather, or rich fan.

More than the spoil
Of shop or silkworm's toil,
Or a bought blush, or a set smile.

A face that's best
By its own beauty dressed,
And can, alone, command the rest.

A face, made up
Out of no other shop
Than what Nature's white hand sets ope.

A cheek where youth
And blood, with pen of truth,
Write what the reader sweetly rueth.

A cheek where grows
More than a morning rose;
Which to no box his being owes.

Lips where all day
A lover's kiss may play
Yet carry nothing thence away.

Looks that oppress
Their richest tires, but dress
And clothe their simplest nakedness.

Eyes that displace
The neighbour diamond, and out-face
That sunshine by their own sweet grace.

Tresses that wear
Jewels but to declare
How much themselves more precious are,

Whose native ray
Can tame the wanton day
Of gems, that in their bright shades play.

Each ruby there
Or pearl, that dare appear,
Be its own blush, be its own tear!

A well-tamed heart,
For whose more noble smart
Love may be long choosing a dart.

Eyes that bestow
Full quivers on Love's bow,
Yet pay less arrows than they owe.

Smiles that can warm
The blood, yet teach a charm
That chastity shall take no harm.

Blushes, that bin
The burnish of no sin,
Nor flames of aught too hot within.

Joys that confess
Virtue their mistress,
And have no other head to dress.

Fears, fond and slight
As the coy bride's, when night
First does the longing lover right.

Days that need borrow
No part of their ' Good morrow '
From a forespent night of sorrow:

Days that in spite
Of darkness, by the light
Of a clear mind are day all night.

Nights, sweet as they
Made short by lovers' play,
Yet long by the absence of the day.

Life that dares send
A challenge to his end,
And, when it comes, say ' Welcome, friend ! '

Sidneian showers
Of sweet discourse, whose powers
Can crown old Winter's head with flowers.

Soft, silken hours,
Open suns, shady bowers,
'Bove all, nothing within that lowers.

Whate'er delight
Can make Day's forehead bright,
Or give down to the wings of Night.

In her whole frame
Have Nature all the name ;
Art and ornament, the shame.

Her flattery,
Picture and Poesy ;
Her counsel her own virtue be.

I wish her store
Of worth may leave her poor
Of wishes.   And I wish—No more !

Now, if Time knows
That her, whose radiant brows
Weave them a garland of my vows ;

Her, whose just bays
My future hopes can raise,
A trophy to her present praise ;

Her, that dares be
What these lines wish to see,
I seek no further : it is she !

'Tis she, and here,
Lo, I unclothe and clear
My wishes' cloudy character.

May she enjoy it,
Whose merit dare apply it
But modesty dares still deny it.

Such worth as this is
Shall fix my flying wishes,
And determine them to kisses.

Let her full glory,
My fancies, fly before ye ;
Be ye my fictions, but her story.

R. CRASHAW.

127.   CLORIS AND FANNY

CLORIS ! if I were Persia's king,
    I'd make my graceful queen of thee ;
While Fanny, wild and artless thing,
    Should but thy humble handmaid be.

There is but *one* objection in it—
    That, verily, I'm much afraid
I should, in some unlucky minute,
    Forsake the mistress for the maid !

T. MOORE.

128. THE CHRONICLE

MARGARITA first possessed,
If I remember well, my breast ;
   Margarita first of all !
      But when a while the wanton maid
      With my restless heart had played,
   Martha took the flying ball.

Martha soon did it resign
To the beauteous Catharine.
   Beauteous Catharine gave place
      (Though loath and angry she to part
      With the possession of my heart)
   To Eliza's conquering face.

Eliza till this hour might reign,
Had not she evil counsels ta'en.
   Fundamental laws she broke ;
      And still new favourites she chose,
      Till up in arms my passions rose,
   And cast away her yoke.

Mary then and gentle Anne
Both to reign at once began.
   Alternately they swayed ;
      And sometimes Mary was the fair,
      And sometimes Anne the crown did wear ;
   And sometimes both I obeyed.

Another Mary then arose
And did rigorous laws impose ;
   A mighty tyrant she !
      Long, alas, should I have been
      Under that iron-sceptred Queen,
   Had not Rebecca set me free.

When fair Rebecca set me free,
'Twas then a golden time with me.
   But soon those pleasures fled,
      For the gracious Princess died
      In her youth and beauty's pride,
   And Judith reigned in her stead.

One month, three days, and half an hour,
Judith held the sovereign power.
   Wondrous beautiful her face ;
      But so weak and small her wit
      That she to govern was unfit,
   And so Susanna took her place.

But when Isabella came,
Armed with a resistless flame
  And the artillery of her eye,
    Whilst she proudly marched about
    Greater conquests to find out,
  She beat out Susan by the by.

But in her place I then obeyed
Black Bess, her viceroy maid,
  To whom ensued a vacancy.
    Thousand worse passions then possessed
    The Interregnum of my breast ;
  Bless me from such an anarchy !

Gentle Henrietta then,
And a third Mary next began ;
  Then Joan and Jane and Audria,
    And then a pretty Thomasine,
    And then another Katharine,
  And then a long *et caetera*.

But should I now to you relate
The strength and riches of their state,
  The powder, patches, and the pins,
    The ribands, jewels, and the rings,
    The lace, the paint and warlike things
  That make up all their magazines ;

If I should tell the politic arts
To take and keep men's hearts,
  The letters, embassies, and spies,
    The frowns and smiles and flatteries,
    The quarrels, tears, and perjuries.
  Numberless, nameless mysteries ;

And all the little lime-twigs laid
By Machiavel, the waiting-maid,
  I more voluminous should grow
    (Chiefly if I, like them, should tell
    All change of weathers that befell)
  Than Holinshed or Stow.

But I will briefer with them be,
Since few of them were long with me.
  A higher and a nobler strain
    My present Emperess does claim :
    Heleonora, first o' th' name,
  Whom God grant long to reign !

A. COWLEY.

129.   MARGARET AND DORA

MARGARET 's beauteous.   Grecian arts
Ne'er drew form completer ;
Yet why, in my heart of hearts,
Hold I Dora's sweeter ?

Dora's eyes of heavenly blue
Pass all painting's reach ;
Ringdoves' notes are discord to
The music of her speech.

Artists ! Margaret's smile receive,
And on canvas show it ;
But for perfect worship leave
Dora to her poet.

T. CAMPBELL.

130.   LESBIA HATH A BEAMING EYE

LESBIA hath a beaming eye,
　　But no one knows for whom it beameth ;
Right and left its arrows fly,
　　But what they aim at no one dreameth.
Sweeter 'tis to gaze upon
　　My Nora's lid that seldom rises ;
Few its looks, but every one,
　　Like unexpected light, surprises.
　　　　Oh, my Nora Creina, dear,
　　My gentle, bashful Nora Creina,
　　　　　　Beauty lies
　　　　　　In many eyes,
　　But Love in yours, my Nora Creina !

Lesbia wears a robe of gold,
　　But all so close the nymph hath laced it,
Not a charm of beauty's mould
　　Presumes to stay where nature placed it.
Oh ! my Nora's gown for me,
　　That floats as wild as mountain breezes,
Leaving every beauty free
　　To sink or swell as Heaven pleases.
　　　　Yes, my Nora Creina, dear,
　　My simple, graceful Nora Creina,
　　　　　　Nature's dress
　　　　　　Is loveliness—
　　The dress *you* wear, my Nora Creina.

Lesbia hath a wit refined,
  But when its points are gleaming round us,
Who can tell if they're designed
  To dazzle merely, or to wound us ?
Pillowed on my Nora's heart
  In safer slumber Love reposes—
Bed of peace ! whose roughest part
  Is but the crumpling of the roses.
    Oh ! my Nora Creina, dear,
    My mild, my artless Nora Creina !
        Wit, though bright,
        Hath no such light,
    As warms your eyes, my Nora Creina.

T. Moore.

131. PHILLIDA AND CORYDON

In the merry month of May,
In a morn by break of day,
Forth I walked by the wood-side,
Whenas May was in his pride :
There I spièd all alone
Phillida and Corydon.
Much ado there was, God wot !
He would love and she would not.
She said, Never man was true ;
He said, None was false to you.
He said, He had loved her long ;
She said, Love should have no wrong.
Corydon would kiss her then ;
She said, Maids must kiss no men
Till they did for good and all ;
Then she made the shepherd call
All the heavens to witness truth
Never loved a truer youth.
Thus with many a pretty oath,
Yea and nay, faith and troth,
Such as silly shepherds use
When they will not love abuse,
Love, which had been long deluded,
Was with kisses sweet concluded ;
And Phillida with garlands gay
Was made the Lady of the May.

N. Breton.

132. SALLY IN OUR ALLEY

Of all the girls that are so smart
   There's none like pretty Sally ;
She is the darling of my heart,
   And she lives in our alley.
There is no lady in the land
   Is half so sweet as Sally ;
She is the darling of my heart,
   And she lives in our alley.

Her father he makes cabbage-nets
   And through the streets does cry them ;
Her mother she sells laces long
   To such as please to buy them :
But sure such folks could ne'er beget
   So sweet a girl as Sally !
She is the darling of my heart,
   And she lives in our alley.

When she is by, I leave my work,
   I love her so sincerely ;
My master comes like any Turk,
   And bangs me most severely—
But let him bang his bellyful,
   I'll bear it all for Sally ;
She is the darling of my heart,
   And she lives in our alley.

Of all the days that's in the week
   I dearly love but one day—
And that's the day that comes betwixt
   A Saturday and Monday ;
For then I'm dressed all in my best
   To walk abroad with Sally ;
She is the darling of my heart,
   And she lives in our alley.

My master carries me to church,
   And often am I blamed
Because I leave him in the lurch
   As soon as text is named ;
I leave the church in sermon-time
   And slink away to Sally ;
She is the darling of my heart,
   And she lives in our alley.

When Christmas comes about again
   O then I shall have money ;
I'll hoard it up, and box and all
   I'll give it to my honey :

And would it were ten thousand pounds,
  I'd give it all to Sally ;
She is the darling of my heart.
  And she lives in our alley.

My master and the neighbours all
  Make game of me and Sally,
And, but for her, I'd better be
  A slave and row a galley ;
But when my seven long years are out
  O then I'll marry Sally,—
O then we'll wed, and then we'll bed,
  But not in our alley !

H. CAREY.

133. THE COURTIN'

GOD makes sech nights, all white an' still
  Fur 'z you can look or listen,
Moonshine an' snow on field an' hill,
  All silence an' all glisten.

Zekle crep' up quite unbeknown
  An' peeked in thru' the winder,
An' there sot Huldy all alone,
  'Ith no one nigh to hender.

A fireplace filled the room's one side
  With half a cord o' wood in—
There warn't no stoves (tell comfort died)
  To bake ye to a puddin'.

The wa'nut logs shot sparkles out
  Towards the pootiest, bless her,
An' leetle flames danced all about
  The chiny on the dresser.

Agin the chimbley crook-necks hung,
  An' in amongst 'em rusted
The ole queen's-arm that gran'ther Young
  Fetched back f'om Concord busted.

The very room, coz she was in,
  Seemed warm f'om floor to ceilin',
An' she looked full ez rosy agin
  Ez the apples she was peelin'.

'Twas kin' o' kingdom-come to look
  On sech a blessed cretur,
A dogrose blushin' to a brook
  Ain't modester nor sweeter.

He was six foot o' man, A 1,
   Clear grit an' human natur',
None couldn't quicker pitch a ton
   Nor dror a furrer straighter.

He'd sparked it with full twenty gals,
   Hed squired 'em, danced 'em, druv 'em,
Fust this one, an' then thet, by spells—
   All is, he couldn't love 'em.

But long o' her his veins 'ould run
   All crinkly like curled maple,
The side she breshed felt full o' sun
   Ez a south slope in Ap'il.

She thought no v'ice hed sech a swing
   Ez hisn in the choir ;
My ! when he made Ole Hunderd ring,
   She *knowed* the Lord was nigher.

An' she'd blush scarlit, right in prayer,
   When her new meetin'-bunnet
Felt somehow thru' its crown a pair
   O' blue eyes sot upun it.

That night, I tell ye, she looked *some !*
   She seemed to 've got a new soul,
For she felt sartin-sure he'd come,
   Down to her very shoe-sole.

She heered a foot, an' knowed it tu,
   A-raspin' on the scraper,—
All ways to once her feelins flew
   Like sparks in burnt-up paper.

He kin' o' l'itered on the mat,
   Some doubtfle o' the sekle,
His heart kep' goin' pity-pat,
   But hern went pity Zekle.

An' yit she gin her cheer a jerk
   Ez though she wished him furder,
An' on her apples kep' to work,
   Parin' away like murder.

' You want to see my Pa, I s'pose ? '
   ' Wal—no—I come dasignin' '—
' To see my Ma ?   She 's sprinklin' clo'es
   Agin to-morrer's i'nin'.'

To say why gals act so or so,
  Or don't, 'ould be presumin';
Mebbe to mean *yes* an' say *no*
  Comes nateral to women.

He stood a spell on one foot fust,
  Then stood a spell on t'other,
An' on which one he felt the wust
  He couldn't ha' told ye nuther.

Says he, 'I'd better call agin;'
  Says she, 'Think likely, Mister:'
Thet last word pricked him like a pin,
  An'—Wal, he up an' kissed her.

When Ma bimeby upon 'em slips,
  Huldy sot pale ez ashes,
All kin' o' smily roun' the lips
  An' teary roun' the lashes.

For she was jes' the quiet kind
  Whose naturs never vary,
Like streams that keep a summer mind
  Snow-hid in Jenooary.

The blood clost roun' her heart felt glued
  Too tight for all expressin',
Tell mother see how metters stood,
  An' gin 'em both her blessin'.

Then her red come back like the tide
  Down to the Bay o' Fundy
An' all I know is they was cried
  In meetin' come nex' Sunday.

                              J. R. LOWELL.

134. WOOING STUFF

FAINT Amorist! what, dost thou think
To taste Love's honey, and not drink
One dram of gall? or to devour
A world of sweet, and taste no sour?
Dost thou ever think to enter
The Elysian fields, that dar'st not venture
In Charon's barge? A lover's mind
Must use to sail with every wind.
He that loves, and fears to try,
Learns his mistress to deny.
  Doth she chide thee? 'Tis to show it,
That thy coldness makes her do it.

Is she silent ?   Is she mute ?
Silence fully grants thy suit.
   Doth she pout and leave the room ?
Then she goes, to bid thee come.
   Is she sick ?   Why then, be sure
She invites thee to the cure.
   Doth she cross thy suit with 'No' ?
Tush !   She loves to hear thee woo.
   Doth she call the faith of man
In question ?   Nay, she loves thee then.
And if e'er she makes a blot,
She's lost if that thou hitt'st her not.
   He that after ten denials
Dares attempt no further trials,
Hath no warrant to acquire
The dainties of his chaste desire.

Sir P. Sidney.

135. GRAMMAR-RULES

O GRAMMAR-RULES, O now your virtues show ;
So children still read you with awful eyes,
As my young dove may, in your precepts wise,
Her grant to me by her own virtue know :
For late, with heart most high, with eyes most low,
I craved the thing which ever she denies ;
She, lightning love, displaying Venus' skies,
Lest once should not be heard, twice said No, No.
Sing then, my Muse, now *Io Paean* sing ;
Heavens, envy not at my high triumphing,
But grammar's force with sweet success confirm :
For grammar says,—O this, dear Stella, say,—
For grammar says,—to grammar who says nay ?—
That in one speech two negatives affirm !

Sir P. Sidney.

136. TO HIS MISTRESS OBJECTING TO HIM NEITHER TOYING OR TALKING

You say I love not, 'cause I do not play
Still with your curls, and kiss the time away.
You blame me, too, because I can't devise
Some sport, to please those babies in your eyes ;
By Love's religion, I must here confess it,
The most I love, when I the least express it.

Small griefs find tongues : full casks are ever found
To give, if any, yet but little sound.
Deep waters noiseless are ; and this we know,
That chiding streams betray small depth below.
So when Love speechless is, she doth express
A depth in love, and that depth bottomless.
Now since my love is tongueless, know me such,
Who speak but little, 'cause I love so much.

R. HERRICK.

137. THE NIGHT-PIECE, TO JULIA

HER eyes the glow-worm lend thee,
The shooting stars attend thee ;
  And the elves also,
  Whose little eyes glow
Like the sparks of fire, befriend thee.

No will-o'-th'-wisp mis-light thee ;
Nor snake, or slow-worm bite thee :
  But on, on thy way
  Not making a stay,
Since ghost there 's none to affright thee.

Let not the dark thee cumber ;
What though the moon does slumber ?
  The stars of the night
  Will lend thee their light,
Like tapers clear without number.

Then Julia let me woo thee,
Thus, thus to come unto me :
  And when I shall meet
  Thy silvery feet,
My soul I'll pour into thee.

R. HERRICK.

138. THE TIME I'VE LOST IN WOOING

THE time I've lost in wooing,
In watching and pursuing
  The light that lies
  In woman's eyes,
Has been my heart's undoing.
Though Wisdom oft has sought me,
I scorned the lore she brought me,
  My only books
  Were woman's looks,
And folly 's all they taught me.

Her smile when Beauty granted,
I hung with gaze enchanted,
    Like him the sprite
    Whom maids by night
Oft met in glen that's haunted.
But while her eyes were on me,
Like him, too, Beauty won me,
    If once their ray
    Was turned away,
O ! winds could not outrun me.

And are those follies going ?
And is my proud heart growing
    Too cold or wise
    For brilliant eyes
Again to set it glowing ?
No, vain, alas ! the endeavour
From bonds so sweet to sever ;
    Poor Wisdom's chance
    Against a glance
Is now as weak as ever.

                    T. MOORE.

139. NEVER SEEK TO TELL THY LOVE

NEVER seek to tell thy love,
    Love that never told can be ;
For the gentle wind does move
    Silently, invisibly.

I told my love, I told my love,
    I told her all my heart ;
Trembling, cold, in ghastly fears,
    Ah ! she doth depart.

Soon as she was gone from me,
    A traveller came by,
Silently, invisibly—
    O ! was no deny.

                    W. BLAKE.

140. AN EXPOSTULATION

WHEN late I attempted your pity to move,
    What made you so deaf to my prayers ?
Perhaps it was right to dissemble your love,
    But—why did you kick me downstairs ?

                    I. BICKERSTAFFE.

141. HIS LOVE ADMITS NO RIVAL

SHALL I, like a hermit, dwell
On a rock, or in a cell,
Calling home the smallest part
That is missing of my heart,
To bestow it where I may
Meet a rival every day ?
If she undervalue me,
What care I how fair she be ?

Were her tresses angel gold,
If a stranger may be bold,
Unrebukèd, unafraid,
To convert them to a braid,
And with little more ado
Work them into bracelets too ;
If the mine be grown so free,
What care I how rich it be ?

SIR W. RALEGH.

142. SHALL I, WASTING IN DESPAIR

SHALL I, wasting in despair,
Die because a woman 's fair ?
Or make pale my cheeks with care
'Cause another's rosy are ?
Be she fairer than the day,
Or the flowery meads in May,
  If she be not so to me
  What care I how fair she be ?

Should my heart be grieved or pined
'Cause I see a woman kind ?
Or a well-disposèd nature
Joinèd with a lovely feature ?
Be she meeker, kinder than
Turtle-dove, or pelican,
  If she be not so to me,
  What care I how kind she be ?

Shall a woman's virtues move
Me to perish for her love ?
Or her well-deserving, known,
Make me quite forget my own ?
Be she with that goodness blessed
Which may gain her name of best,
  If she be not such to me
  What care I how good she be ?

'Cause her fortune seems too high,
Shall I play the fool, and die ?
Those that bear a noble mind,
Where they want of riches find,
Think what with them they would do
That without them dare to woo ;
    And unless that mind I see,
    What care I though great she be ?

Great, or good, or kind, or fair,
I will ne'er the more despair :
If she love me, this believe
I will die ere she shall grieve :
If she slight me when I woo,
I can scorn and let her go ;
    For if she be not for me,
    What care I for whom she be ?

G. WITHER.

143.   WHY SO PALE AND WAN, FOND LOVER

WHY so pale and wan, fond lover ?
    Prithee, why so pale ?
Will, when looking well can't move her,
    Looking ill prevail ?
    Prithee, why so pale ?

Why so dull and mute, young sinner ?
    Prithee, why so mute ?
Will, when speaking well can't win her,
    Saying nothing do't ?
    Prithee, why so mute ?

Quit, quit, for shame ! this will not move,
    This cannot take her ;
If of herself she will not love,
    Nothing can make her :
    The Devil take her !

SIR J. SUCKLING.

144.   VALOUR MISDIRECTED

' I'LL hunt for dangers North and South,
    To prove my love, which sloth maligns ! '
What seems to say her rosy mouth ?
    ' I'm not convinced by proofs but signs.'

COVENTRY PATMORE.

145. I NE'ER COULD ANY LUSTRE SEE

I NE'ER could any lustre see
In eyes that would not look on me ;
I ne'er saw nectar on a lip,
But where my own did hope to sip.
Has the maid who seeks my heart
Cheeks of rose, untouched by art ?
I will own the colour true
When yielding blushes aid their hue.

Is her hand so soft and pure ?
I must press it, to be sure ;
Nor can I be certain then,
Till it, grateful, press again.
Must I, with attentive eye,
Watch her heaving bosom sigh ?
I will do so, when I see
That heaving bosom sigh for me.

R. B. SHERIDAN.

146. THE LARK NOW LEAVES HIS WATERY NEST

THE lark now leaves his watery nest
And climbing shakes his dewy wings.
He takes this window for the East,
And to implore your light he sings—
Awake, awake ! the morn will never rise
Till she can dress her beauty at your eyes.

The merchant bows unto the seaman's star,
The ploughman from the sun his season takes ;
But still the lover wonders what they are
Who look for day before his mistress wakes.
Awake, awake ! break through your veils of lawn !
Then draw your curtains, and begin the dawn !

SIR W. DAVENANT.

147. SABINA WAKES

SEE ! see, she wakes ! Sabina wakes !
And now the sun begins to rise !
Less glorious is the morn that breaks
From his bright beams than her fair eyes.

With light united, day they give ;
But different fates ere night fulfil ;
How many by his warmth will live !
How many will her coldness kill !

W. CONGREVE.

148. WITHOUT AND WITHIN

Love in her sunny eyes doth basking play ;
  Love walks the pleasant mazes of her hair ;
Love does on both her lips for ever stray,
  And sows and reaps a thousand kisses there :
In all her outward parts Love 's always seen ;
But oh ! he never went within.

A. Cowley.

149. I LOVED A LASS, A FAIR ONE

I loved a lass, a fair one,
  As fair as e'er was seen ;
She was indeed a rare one,
  Another Sheba Queen !
But, fool as then I was,
  I thought she loved me too :
But now, alas ! she 's left me,
  Falero, lero, loo.

Her hair like gold did glister,
  Each eye was like a star,
She did surpass her sister,
  Which passed all others far ;
She would me honey call,
  She'd,—oh she'd kiss me too :
But now, alas ! she 's left me,
  Falero, lero, loo.

Many a merry meeting
  My love and I have had ;
She was my only sweeting,
  She made my heart full glad ;
The tears stood in her eyes
  Like to the morning dew :
But now, alas ! she 's left me,
  Falero, lero, loo.

Her cheeks were like the cherry,
  Her skin as white as snow ;
When she was blithe and merry,
  She angel-like did show ;
Her waist exceeding small,
  The fives did fit her shoe :
But now, alas ! she 's left me,
  Falero, lero, loo.

In summer time or winter
   She had her heart's desire ;
I still did scorn to stint her
   From sugar, sack, or fire ;
The world went round about,
   No cares we ever knew :
But now, alas ! she 's left me,
   Falero, lero, loo.

As we walked home together
   At midnight through the town,
To keep away the weather
   O'er her I'd cast my gown.
No cold my love should feel,
   Whate'er the heavens could do ;
But now, alas ! she 's left me,
   Falero, lero, loo.

Like doves we should be billing,
   And clip and kiss so fast ;
Yet she would be unwilling
   That I should kiss the last.
They're Judas-kisses now,
   Since that they proved untrue ;
For now, alas ! she 's left me,
   Falero, lero, loo.

To maidens' vows and swearing
   Henceforth no credit give
You may give them the hearing
   But never them believe ;
They are as false as fair,
   Unconstant, frail, untrue :
For mine, alas ! hath left me,
   Falero, lero, loo.

G. WITHER.

150.   TO HIS COY LOVE

I PRAY thee leave, love me no more,
   Call home the heart you gave me,
I but in vain that saint adore,
   That can, but will not save me :
These poor half-kisses kill me quite
   Was ever man thus servèd ?
Amidst an ocean of delight,
   For pleasure to be starvèd.

Show me no more those snowy breasts,
  With azure riverets branchèd,
Where whilst my eye with plenty feasts,
  Yet is my thirst not stanchèd.
O Tantalus, thy pains ne'er tell,
  By me thou art prevented ;
'Tis nothing to be plagued in hell,
  But thus in heaven tormented.

Clip me no more in those dear arms,
  Nor thy life's comfort call me ;
Oh, these are but too powerful charms,
  And do but more enthral me.
But see, how patient I am grown,
  In all this coil about thee ;
Come, nice thing, let my heart alone,
  I cannot live without thee.

                  M. DRAYTON.

151. THOU ART NOT FAIR

THOU art not fair for all thy red and white,
  For all those rosy ornaments in thee,
Thou art not sweet, though made of mere delight,
  Nor fair nor sweet, unless thou pity me.
I will not soothe thy fancies : thou shalt prove
That beauty is no beauty without love.

Yet love not me, nor seek thou to allure
  My thoughts with beauty, were it more divine,
Thy smiles and kisses I cannot endure,
  I'll not be wrapped up in those arms of thine,
Now show it, if thou be a woman right,—
Embrace, and kiss, and love me, in despite !

                  T. CAMPION.

152. THE LOST MISTRESS

ALL'S over, then : does truth sound bitter
  As one at first believes ?
Hark, 'tis the sparrows' good-night twitter
  About your cottage eaves !

And the leaf-buds on the vine are woolly,
  I noticed that, to-day ;
One day more bursts them open fully
  —You know the red turns grey.

To-morrow we meet the same then, dearest ?
  May I take your hand in mine ?
Mere friends are we,—well, friends the merest
  Keep much that I'll resign :

For each glance of that eye so bright and black,
  Though I keep with heart's endeavour,—
Your voice, when you wish the snowdrops back,
  Though it stay in my soul for ever !—

Yet I will but say what mere friends say,
  Or only a thought stronger ;
I will hold your hand but as long as all may,
  Or so very little longer !

R. BROWNING.

153.   THE SIEGE

'Tis now, since I sat down before
  That foolish fort, a heart,
(Time strangely spent !) a year, and more ;
  And still I did my part.

Made my approaches, from her hand
  Unto her lip did rise ;
And did already understand
  The language of her eyes.

Proceeding on with no less art,
  My tongue was engineer ;
I thought to undermine the heart
  By whispering in the ear.

When this did nothing, I brought down
  Great canon-oaths, and shot
A thousand thousand to the town,
  And still it yielded not.

I then resolved to starve the place,
  By cutting off all kisses,
Praising and gazing on her face,
  And all such little blisses.

To draw her out, and from her strength,
  I drew all batteries in :
And brought myself to lie at length,
  As if no siege had been.

When I had done what man could do,
  And thought the place my own,
The enemy lay quiet too,
  And smiled at all was done.

I sent to know from whence, and where,
   These hopes, and this relief ?
A spy informed, Honour was there,
   And did command in chief.

March, march (quoth I), the word straight give,
   Let 's lose no time, but leave her :
That giant upon air will live,
   And hold it out for ever.

To such a place our camp remove
   As will no siege abide ;
I hate a fool that starves her love,
   Only to feed her pride.

SIR J. SUCKLING.

154. WOMAN'S HONOUR

LOVE bade me hope, and I obeyed ;
   Phyllis continued still unkind ;
' Then you may e'en despair,' he said,
   ' In vain I strive to change her mind.

' Honour 's got in, and keeps her heart ;
   Durst he but venture once abroad,
In my own right I'd take your part,
   And show myself the mightier god.'

This huffing Honour domineers
   In breasts where he alone has place ;
But if true generous Love appears,
   The hector dares not show his face.

Let me still languish and complain,
   Be most inhumanly denied ;
I have some pleasure in my pain,
   She can have none with all her pride.

I fall a sacrifice to Love,
   She lives a wretch for Honour's sake !
Whose tyrant does most cruel prove,
   The difference is not hard to make.

Consider real Honour then,
   You'll find hers cannot be the same.
'Tis noble confidence in men ;
   In women, mean distrustful shame.

J. WILMOT, EARL OF ROCHESTER.

155.   A DUTCH PROVERB

'FIRE, Water, Woman, are Man's ruin !'
Says wise Professor Van der Bruin.
By flames, a house I hired was lost
Last year ; and I must pay the cost.
This spring, the rains o'erflowed my ground,
And my best Flanders mare was drowned.
A slave am I to Clara's eyes ;
The gipsy knows her power, and flies !
Fire, Water, Woman, are my ruin ;
And great thy wisdom, Van der Bruin !

M. PRIOR.

156.   NEVER LOVE UNLESS —

NEVER love unless you can
Bear with all the faults of man :
Men sometimes will jealous be,
Though but little cause they see,
   And hang the head as discontent,
   And speak what, straight, they will repent.

Men that but one saint adore
Make a show of love to more :
Beauty must be scorned in none,
Though but truly served in one :
   For what is courtship, but disguise ?
   True hearts may have dissembling eyes.

Men when their affairs require,
Must a while themselves retire :
Sometimes hunt, and sometimes hawk,
And not ever sit and talk.
   If these, and such like you can bear,
   Then like, and love, and never fear.

T. CAMPION.

157.   RIVALS IN LOVE

OF all the torments, all the cares,
   With which our lives are cursed ;
Of all the plagues a lover bears,
   Sure, rivals are the worst !
By partners in each other kind,
   Afflictions easier grow ;
In love alone we hate to find
   Companions of our woe.

Sylvia, for all the pangs you see
    Are labouring in my breast,
I beg not you would favour me,
    Would you but slight the rest.
How great soe'er your rigours are
    With them alone I'll cope :—
I can endure my own despair,
    But not another's hope.

W. WALSH.

158. ANSWER TO CHLOE JEALOUS

DEAR Chloe, how blubbered is that pretty face !
    Thy cheek all on fire, and thy hair all uncurled :
Prithee quit this caprice ; and, as old Falstaff says,
    Let us e'en talk a little like folks of this world.

How canst thou presume, thou hadst leave to destroy
    The beauties which Venus but lent to thy keeping ?
Those looks were designed to inspire love and joy :
    More ordinary eyes may serve people for weeping.

To be vexed at a trifle or two that I writ,
    Your judgement at once, and my passion, you wrong :
You take that for fact, which will scarce be found wit ;
    Ods life ! must one swear to the truth of a song ?

What I speak, my fair Chloe, and what I write, shows
    The difference there is betwixt nature and art :
I court others in verse—but I love thee in prose ;
    And they have my whimsies—but thou hast my heart.

The God of us verse-men (you know, child) the Sun,
    How after his journeys he sets up his rest :
If at morning o'er Earth 'tis his fancy to run ;
    At night he declines on his Thetis's breast.

So when I am wearied with wandering all day ;
    To thee, my delight, in the evening I come :
No matter what beauties I saw in my way :
    They were but my visits, but thou art my home.

Then finish, dear Chloe, this pastoral war ;
    And let us like Horace and Lydia agree ;
For thou art a girl as much brighter than her,
    As he was a poet sublimer than me.

M. PRIOR.

159. THE WHEEDLER

IN vain, dear Chloe, you suggest
That I, inconstant, have possessed
 Or loved a fairer she ;
Would you with ease at once be cured
Of all the ills you've long endured,
 Consult your glass and me !

If then you think that I can find
A nymph more fair, or one more kind,
 You've reason for your fears ;
But if impartial you will prove
To your own beauty and my love,
 How needless are your tears !

If, in my way, I should by chance
Receive, or give, a wanton glance,
 I like but while I view ;
How slight the glance, how faint the kiss,
Compared to that substantial bliss
 Which I receive from you !

With wanton flight the curious bee
From flower to flower still wanders free ;
 And where each blossom blows,
Extracts the juice of all he meets,
But for his quintessence of sweets,
 He ravishes the rose.

So, my fond fancy to employ
On each variety of joy
 From nymph to nymph I roam ;
Perhaps see fifty in a day !
Those are but visits which I pay—
 For Chloe is my home !

SIR W. YONGE.

160. THE NYMPH'S REPLY TO THE PASSIONATE SHEPHERD

IF all the world and love were young,
And truth in every shepherd's tongue,
These pretty pleasures might me move
To live with thee, and be thy love.

But Time drives flocks from field to fold
When rivers rage and rocks grow cold,
And Philomel becometh dumb ;
The rest complain of cares to come.

The flowers do fade; and wanton fields
To wayward winter reckoning yields:
A honey tongue, a heart of gall,
Is fancy's spring, but sorrow's fall.

Thy gowns, thy shoes, thy beds of roses,
Thy cap, thy kirtle, and thy posies
Soon break, soon wither, soon forgotten,
In folly ripe, in reason rotten.

Thy belt of straw and ivy buds,
Thy coral clasps and amber studs,
All these in me no means can move
To come to thee, and be thy love.

But could youth last, and love still breed,
Had joys no date, nor age no need;
Then these delights my mind might move
To live with thee, and be thy love.

SIR W. RALEGH.

161. THINK'ST THOU TO SEDUCE ME

THINK'ST thou to seduce me then with words that have no meaning?
Parrots so can learn to prate, our speech by pieces gleaning:
Nurses teach their children so about the time of weaning.

Learn to speak first, then to woo: to wooing much pertaineth:
He that courts us, wanting art, soon falters when he feigneth,
Looks asquint on his discourse and smiles when he complaineth.

Skilful anglers hide their hooks, fit baits for every season;
But with crooked pins fish thou, as babes do that want reason;
Gudgeons only can be caught with such poor tricks of treason.

Ruth forgive me, if I erred, from human heart compassion,
When I laughed sometimes too much to see thy foolish fashion:
But alas! who less could do that found so good occasion!

T. CAMPION.

162. THE QUESTION TO LISETTA

WHAT nymph should I admire or trust,
But Chloe beauteous, Chloe just?
What nymph should I desire to see,
But her who leaves the plain for me?
To whom should I compose the lay,
But her who listens when I play?
To whom in song repeat my cares,
But her who in my sorrow shares?

For whom should I the garland make,
But her who joys the gift to take,
And boasts she wears it for my sake ?
In love am I not fully blest ?
Lisetta, prithee tell the rest.

LISETTA'S REPLY

Sure Chloe just, and Chloe fair,
Deserves to be your only care ;
But, when she and you to-day
Far into the wood did stray,
And I happened to pass by ;
Which way did you cast your eye ?
But, when your cares to her you sing,
You dare not tell her whence they spring ;
Does it not more afflict your heart,
That in those cares she bears a part ?
When you the flowers for Chloe twine,
Why do you to her garland join
The meanest bud that falls from mine ?
Simplest of swains ! the world may see,
Whom Chloe loves, and who loves me.

                                        M. PRIOR.

163. THE LOVER

ADDRESSED TO CONGREVE

AT length, by so much importunity pressed,
Take, Congreve, at once the inside of my breast.
The stupid indifference so often you blame,
Is not owing to nature, to fear, or to shame ;
I am not as cold as a virgin in lead,
Nor is Sunday's sermon so strong in my head ;
I know but too well how old Time flies along,
That we live but few years, and yet fewer are young.

But I hate to be cheated, and never will buy
Long years of repentance for moments of joy.
O ! was there a man—but where shall I find
Good sense and good nature so equally joined ?—
Would value his pleasures, contribute to mine ;
Not meanly would boast, and not grossly design ;
Not over severe, yet not stupidly vain.
For I would have the power, but not give the pain.

No pedant, yet learned ; no rakey-hell gay,
Or laughing, because he has nothing to say ;
To all my whole sex obliging and free,
Yet never be loving to any but me ;

In public preserve the decorum that 's just,
And show in his eye he is true to his trust ;
Then rarely approach, and respectfully bow,
But not fulsomely forward, or foppishly low.

But when the long hours of public are past,
And we meet with champagne and a chicken at last,
May every fond pleasure the moment endear ;
Be banished afar both discretion and fear !
Forgetting or scorning the aim of the crowd,
He may cease to be formal, and I to be proud,
Till, lost in the joy, we confess that we live,
And he may be rude, and yet I may forgive.

And that my delight may be solidly fixed,
Let the friend and the lover be handsomely mixed,
In whose tender bosom my soul may confide,
Whose kindness can soothe me, whose counsel can guide.
For such a dear lover as here I describe,
No danger should fright me, no millions should bribe ;
But till this astonishing creature I know,
As I long have lived chaste, I will keep myself so.

I never will share with the wanton coquet,
Or be caught by a vain affectation of wit,
The toasters and songsters may try all their art,
But never shall enter the pass of my heart.
I loathe the mere rake, the dressed fopling despise :
Before such pursuers the chaste virgin flies :
And as Ovid so sweetly in parable told,
We harden like trees, and like rivers grow cold.

                              LADY M. WORTLEY MONTAGU.

164. AMY'S CRUELTY

FAIR Amy of the terraced house,
    Assist me to discover
Why you who would not hurt a mouse
    Can torture so your lover.

You give your coffee to the cat,
    You stroke the dog for coming,
And all your face grows kinder at
    The little brown bee's humming.

But when *he* haunts your door . . . the town
    Marks coming and marks going . . .
You seem to have stitched your eyelids down
    To that long piece of sewing !

You never give a look, not you,
   Nor drop him a ' Good morning ',
To keep his long day warm and blue,
   So fretted by your scorning.

She shook her head—' The mouse and bee
   For crumb or flower will linger :
The dog is happy at my knee,
   The cat purrs at my finger.

'But *he* . . . to *him*, the least thing given
   Means great things at a distance ;
He wants my world, my sun, my heaven,
   Soul, body, whole existence.

' They say love gives as well as takes ;
   But I'm a simple maiden,—
My mother's first smile when she wakes
   I still have smiled and prayed in.

' I only know my mother's love
   Which gives all and asks nothing ;
And this new loving sets the groove
   Too much the way of loathing.

' Unless he gives me all in change,
   I forfeit all things by him :
The risk is terrible and strange—
   I tremble, doubt, . . . deny him.

' He 's sweetest friend, or hardest foe,
   Best angel or worst devil ;
I either hate or . . . love him so,
   I can't be merely civil !

' You trust a woman who puts forth,
   Her blossoms thick as summer's ?
You think she dreams what love is worth,
   Who casts it to new-comers ?

' Such love 's a cowslip-ball to fling,
   A moment's pretty pastime ;
I give . . . all me, if anything,
   The first time and the last time.

' Dear neighbour of the trellised house,
   A man should murmur never,
Though treated worse than dog and mouse,
   Till doted on for ever ! '

                              E. B. BROWNING.

165. 'NO, THANK YOU, JOHN'

I NEVER said I loved you, John :
    Why will you teaze me day by day,
And wax a weariness to think upon
    With always ' do ' and ' pray ' ?

You know I never loved you, John ;
    No fault of mine made me your toast :
Why will you haunt me with a face as wan
    As shows an hour-old ghost ?

I dare say Meg or Moll would take
    Pity upon you, if you'd ask :
And pray don't remain single for my sake
    Who can't perform that task.

I have no heart ?—Perhaps I have not ;
    But then you're mad to take offence
That I don't give you what I have not got :
    Use your own common sense.

Let bygones be bygones :
    Don't call me false, who owed not to be true :
I'd rather answer ' No ' to fifty Johns
    Than answer ' Yes ' to you.

Let 's mar our pleasant days no more,
    Song-birds of passage, days of youth :
Catch at to-day, forget the days before :
    I'll wink at your untruth.

Let us strike hands as hearty friends ;
    No more, no less ; and friendship 's good :
Only don't keep in view ulterior ends,
    And points not understood

In open treaty.   Rise above
    Quibbles and shuffling off and on :
Here 's friendship for you if you like ; but love,—
    No, thank you, John.

C. G. ROSSETTI.

166. A MAN'S REQUIREMENTS

LOVE me, sweet, with all thou art,
    Feeling, thinking, seeing,—
Love me in the lightest part,
    Love me in full being.

Love me with thine open youth
  In its frank surrender ;
With the vowing of thy mouth,
  With its silence tender.

Love me with thine azure eyes,
  Made for earnest granting !
Taking colour from the skies,
  Can Heaven's truth be wanting ?

Love me with their lids, that fall
  Snow-like at first meeting ;
Love me with thine heart, that all
  The neighbours then see beating.

Love me with thine hand stretched out
  Freely—open-minded ;
Love me with thy loitering foot,—
  Hearing one behind it.

Love me with thy voice, that turns
  Sudden faint above me ;
Love me with thy blush that burns
  While I murmur, *Love me* !

Love me with thy thinking soul—
  Break it to love-sighing ;
Love me with thy thoughts that roll
  On through living—dying.

Love me in thy gorgeous airs,
  When the world has crowned thee !
Love me, kneeling at thy prayers,
  With the angels round thee.

Love me pure, as musers do,
  Up the woodlands shady ;
Love me gaily, fast, and true,
  As a winsome lady.

Through all hopes that keep us brave,
  Further off or nigher,
Love me for the house and grave,—
  And for something higher.

Thus, if thou wilt prove me, dear,
  Woman's love no fable,
I will love *thee*—half-a-year—
  As a man is able.

E. B. BROWNING.

167. A RENUNCIATION

If women could be fair, and yet not fond,
  Or that their love were firm, not fickle still,
I would not marvel that they make men bond
  By service long to purchase their good will ;
But when I see how frail those creatures are,
I laugh that men forget themselves so far.

To mark the choice they make, and how they change,
  How oft from Phoebus they do flee to Pan ;
Unsettled still, like haggards wild they range,
  These gentle birds that fly from man to man ;
Who would not scorn and shake them from the fist,
And let them fly, fair fools, which way they list ?

Yet for our sport we fawn and flatter both,
  To pass the time when nothing else can please,
And train them to our lure with subtle oath,
  Till, weary of our wiles, ourselves we ease ;
And then we say when we their fancy try,
To play with fools, Oh what a fool was I.

E. Vere, Earl of Oxford.

168. WOMAN'S INCONSTANCY

I loved thee once, I'll love no more,
  Thine be the grief as is the blame ;
Thou art not what thou wast before,
  What reason I should be the same ?
    He that can love unloved again,
      Hath better store of love than brain :
  God send me love my debts to pay,
  While unthrifts fool their love away !

Nothing could have my love o'erthrown,
  If thou hadst still continued mine ;
Yea, if thou hadst remained thy own,
  I might perchance have yet been thine.
    But thou thy freedom didst recall,
      That, if thou might, elsewhere inthrall :
  And then how could I but disdain
  A captive's captive to remain ?

When new desires had conquered thee,
  And changed the object of thy will,

It had been lethargy in me,
  Not constancy to love thee still.
    Yea, it had been a sin to go
    And prostitute affection so,
  Since we are taught no prayers to say
  To such as must to others pray.

Yet do thou glory in thy choice,—
  Thy choice of his good fortune boast ;
I'll neither grieve nor yet rejoice
  To see him gain what I have lost ;
    The height of my disdain shall be
    To laugh at him, to blush for thee ;
  To love thee still, but go no more
  A-begging to a beggar's door.

Sir R. Ayton.

169. I DO CONFESS THOU'RT SMOOTH AND FAIR

I do confess thou'rt smooth and fair,
  And I might have gone near to love thee ;
Had I not found the slightest prayer
  That lips could speak had power to move thee :
But I can let thee now alone,
As worthy to be loved by none.

I do confess thou'rt sweet, yet find
  Thee such an unthrift of thy sweets,
Thy favours are but like the wind,
  That kisses everything it meets :
And since thou canst with more than one,
Thou'rt worthy to be kissed by none.

The morning rose, that untouched stands,
  Armed with her briers, how sweet her smell !
But plucked, and strained through ruder hands,
  Her sweets no longer with her dwell ;
But scent and beauty both are gone,
And leaves fall from her, one by one.

Such fate, ere long, will thee betide,
  When thou hast handled been awhile,
Like sere flowers to be thrown aside ;
  And I will sigh, while some will smile,
To see thy love for more than one
Hath brought thee to be loved by none.

Sir R. Ayton.

170.   GO AND CATCH A FALLING STAR

Go and catch a falling star,
  Get with child a mandrake root,
Tell me where all past years are,
  Or who cleft the Devil's foot ;
Teach me to hear mermaids singing,
Or to keep off envy's stinging,
          And find
          What wind
Serves to advance an honest mind.

If thou beest born to strange sights,
  Things invisible to see,
Ride ten thousand days and nights
  Till age snow white hairs on thee ;
Thou, when thou return'st, wilt tell me
All strange wonders that befell thee,
          And swear,
          No where
Lives a woman true and fair.

If thou find'st one, let me know ;
  Such a pilgrimage were sweet.
Yet do not ; I would not go,
  Though at next door we might meet.
Though she were true when you met her,
And last till you write your letter,
          Yet she
          Will be
False, ere I come, to two or three.

                              J. DONNE.

171.   A DEPOSITION FROM BEAUTY

THOUGH when I loved thee thou wert fair,
  Thou art no longer so ;
These glories all the pride they wear
  Unto opinion owe.
Beauties, like stars, in borrowed lustre shine ;
And 'twas my love that gave thee thine.

The flames that dwelt within thine eye
  Do now with mine expire ;
Thy brightest graces fade and die
  At once with my desire.
Love's fires thus mutual influence return ;
Thine cease to shine, when mine to burn.

Then, proud Celinda, hope no more
  To be implored or wooed,
Since by thy scorn thou dost restore
  The wealth my love bestowed ;
And thy despised disdain too late shall find
That none are fair but who are kind.

T. STANLEY.

172. INSULTING BEAUTY

INSULTING Beauty ! you misspend
  Those frowns upon your slave.
Your scorn against such rebels bend
Who dare with confidence pretend
That other eyes their hearts defend
  From all the charms you have.

Your conquering eyes so partial are,
  Or mankind is so dull,
That while I languish in despair
Many proud senseless hearts declare
They find you not so killing fair,
  To wish you merciful.

They an inglorious freedom boast,
  I triumph in my chain ;
Nor am I unrevenged though lost,
Nor you unpunished though unjust,
When I alone, who love you most,
  Am killed by your disdain.

J. WILMOT, EARL OF ROCHESTER.

173. MEDIOCRITY IN LOVE REJECTED

GIVE me more love, or more disdain ;
  The torrid or the frozen zone
Bring equal ease unto my pain ;
  The temperate affords me none :
Either extreme, of love or hate,
Is sweeter than a calm estate.

Give me a storm ; if it be love—
  Like Danaë in that golden shower,
I'll swim in pleasure ; if it prove
  Disdain, that torrent will devour
My vulture hopes ; and he 's possessed
Of heaven, that 's from hell released.
Then crown my joys, or cure my pain ;
Give me more love, or more disdain.

T. CAREW.

174. MAY'S LOVE

You love all, you say,
  Round, beneath, above me :
Find me then some way
  Better than to love me,
Me, too, dearest May !

O world-kissing eyes
  Which the blue heavens melt to !
I, sad, overwise,
  Loathe the sweet looks dealt to
All things—men and flies.

You love all, you say :
  Therefore, Dear, abate me
Just your love, I pray !
  Shut your eyes and hate me—
Only *me*—fair May !

E. B. BROWNING.

175. TO ——

WHEN I loved you, I can't but allow
  I had many an exquisite minute ;
But the scorn that I feel for you now
  Hath even more luxury in it.

Thus, whether we're on or we're off,
  Some witchery seems to await you ;
To love you was pleasant enough,
  And, oh ! 'tis delicious to hate you !

T. MOORE.

176. THAT WOMEN ARE BUT MEN'S SHADOWS

FOLLOW a shadow, it still flies you ;
  Seem to fly it, it will pursue :
So court a mistress, she denies you ;
  Let her alone, she will court you.
Say are not women truly, then,
Styled but the shadows of us men ?

At morn and even, shades are longest ;
  At noon they are or short or none :
So men at weakest, they are strongest,
  But grant us perfect, they're not known.
Say are not women truly, then,
Styled but the shadows of us men ?

BEN. JONSON.

177. A PAIR WELL MATCHED

FAIR Iris I love and hourly I die,
But not for a lip, nor a languishing eye ;
She 's fickle and false, and there I agree,
For I am as false and as fickle as she ;
We neither believe what either can say,
And neither believing, we neither betray.

'Tis civil to swear, and to say things of course ;
We mean not the taking for better or worse.
When present we love, when absent agree ;
I think not of Iris, nor Iris of me :
The legend of Love no couple can find
So easy to part, or so equally joined.

J. DRYDEN.

178. A MATCH

IF love were what the rose is,
　　And I were like the leaf,
Our lives would grow together
In sad or singing weather,
Blown fields or flowerful closes,
　　Green pleasure or grey grief ;
If love were what the rose is,
　　And I were like the leaf.

If I were what the words are,
　　And love were like the tune,
With double sound and single
Delight our lips would mingle,
With kisses glad as birds are
　　That get sweet rain at noon ;
If I were what the words are,
　　And love were like the tune.

If you were life, my darling,
　　And I your love were death,
We'd shine and snow together
Ere March made sweet the weather
With daffodil and starling
　　And hours of fruitful breath ;
If you were life, my darling,
　　And I your love were death.

If you were thrall to sorrow,
    And I were page to joy,
We'd play for lives and seasons
With loving looks and treasons
And tears of night and morrow
    And laughs of maid and boy;
If you were thrall to sorrow,
    And I were page to joy.

If you were April's lady,
    And I were lord in May,
We'd throw with leaves for hours
And draw for day with flowers,
Till day like night were shady
    And night were bright like day;
If you were April's lady,
    And I were lord in May.

If you were queen of pleasure,
    And I were king of pain,
We'd hunt down love together,
Pluck out his flying-feather,
And teach his feet a measure,
    And find his mouth a rein;
If you were queen of pleasure,
    And I were king of pain.

A. C. SWINBURNE.

179.   NOT, CELIA, THAT I JUSTER AM

NOT, Celia, that I juster am
    Or better than the rest;
For I would change each hour, like them,
    Were not my heart at rest.

But I am tied to very thee
    By every thought I have
Thy face I only care to see
    Thy heart I only crave.

All that in woman is adored
    In thy dear self I find—
For the whole sex can but afford
    The handsome and the kind.

Why then should I seek further store,
    And still make love anew?
When change itself can give no more,
    'Tis easy to be true.

SIR C. SEDLEY.

180. PHILLIS, MEN SAY THAT ALL MY VOWS

PHILLIS, men say that all my vows
    Are to thy fortune paid ;
Alas ! my heart he little knows,
    Who thinks my love a trade.

Were I of all these woods the lord,
    One berry from thy hand
More real pleasure would afford
    Than all my large command.

My humble love has learned to live
    On what the nicest maid,
Without a conscious blush, may give
    Beneath the myrtle shade.

SIR C. SEDLEY.

181. OUT UPON IT, I HAVE LOVED

OUT upon it, I have loved
    Three whole days together !
And am like to love three more,
    If it prove fair weather.

Time shall moult away his wings
    Ere he shall discover
In the whole wide world again
    Such a constant lover.

But the spite on't is, no praise
    Is due at all to me :
Love with me had made no stays,
    Had it any been but she.

Had it any been but she,
    And that very face,
There had been at least ere this
    A dozen dozen in her place.

SIR J. SUCKLING.

182. PERJURY

I LOVED thee, beautiful and kind,
    And plighted an eternal vow ;
So altered are thy face and mind,
    'Twere perjury to love thee now.

R. NUGENT, EARL NUGENT.

183.　THE MERIT OF INCONSTANCY

Why dost thou say I am forsworn,
　Since thine I vowed to be ?
Lady, it is already morn ;
　It was last night I swore to thee
　That fond impossibility.

Yet have I loved thee well, and long ;
　A tedious twelve-hours' space !
I should all other beauties wrong,
　And rob thee of a new embrace,
　Did I still doat upon that face.

R. Lovelace.

184.　CARPE DIEM

It is not, Celia, in your power
　To say how long our love will last ;
It may be we, within this hour,
　May lose those joys we now do taste :
The blessed, who immortal be,
From change of love are only free.

Then, since we mortal lovers are,
　Ask not how long our love will last ;
But, while it does, let us take care
　Each minute be with pleasure passed.
Were it not madness to deny
To live, because we're sure to die ?

Fear not, though love and beauty fail,
　My reason shall my heart direct :
Your kindness now shall then prevail,
　And passion turn into respect.
Celia, at worst, you'll in the end
But change a lover for a friend.

Sir G. Etherege.

185.　I PROMISED SYLVIA

I promised Sylvia to be true,
Nay, out of zeal I swore it too ;
And that she might believe me more
Gave her in writing what I swore.

Not vows nor oaths can lovers bind ;
So long as blessed so long they're kind.
'Twas in a leaf !　The wind but blew ;
Away both leaf and promise flew.

J. Wilmot, Earl of Rochester.

186. LOVE AND LIFE

ALL my past life is mine no more ;
　The flying hours are gone,
Like transitory dreams given o'er,
Whose images are kept in store
　By memory alone.

The time that is to come, is not ;
　How can it then be mine ?
The present moment 's all my lot ;
And that, as fast as it is got,
　Phillis, is only thine.

Then talk not of inconstancy,
　False hearts, and broken vows !
If I by miracle can be
This live-long minute true to thee,
　'Tis all that Heaven allows.

　　　　　　　J. WILMOT, EARL OF ROCHESTER.

187. A HUE AND CRY AFTER FAIR AMORET

FAIR Amoret is gone astray !
　Pursue and seek her, every lover !
I'll tell the signs by which you may
　The wandering shepherdess discover.

Coquet and coy at once her air,
　Both studied, though both seem neglected :
Careless she is, with artful care ;
　Affecting to seem unaffected.

With skill, her eyes dart every glance ;
　Yet change so soon, you'd ne'er suspect them :
For she'd persuade, they wound by chance ;
　Though certain aim and art direct them.

She likes herself, yet others hates
　For that which in herself she prizes,
And, while she laughs at them, forgets
　She is the thing that she despises.

　　　　　　　W. CONGREVE.

188. I LATELY VOWED, BUT 'TWAS IN HASTE

I LATELY vowed, but 'twas in haste,
　That I no more would court
The joys which seem when they are past
　As dull as they are short.

I oft to hate my mistress swear,
  But soon my weakness find :
I make my oaths when she 's severe,
  But break them when she 's kind.

J. OLDMIXON.

189.   ONE YEAR AGO

ONE year ago my path was green,
My footstep light, my brow serene ;
Alas ! and could it have been so
          One year ago ?

There is a love that is to last
When the hot days of youth are past :
Such love did a sweet maid bestow
          One year ago.

I took a leaflet from her braid
And gave it to another maid.
Love ! broken should have been thy bow
          One year ago.

W. S. LANDOR.

190.   THE STORY OF PHOEBUS AND DAPHNE APPLIED

THYRSIS, a youth of the inspirèd train,
Fair Sacharissa loved, but loved in vain :
Like Phoebus sung the no less amorous boy ;
Like Daphne she, as lovely, and as coy !
With numbers he the flying nymph pursues ;
With numbers, such as Phoebus' self might use !
Such is the chase, when Love and Fancy leads,
O'er craggy mountains, and through flowery meads
Invoked to testify the lover's care,
Or form some image of his cruel fair.
Urged with his fury, like a wounded deer,
O'er these he fled ; and now approaching near,
Had reached the nymph with his harmonious lay,
Whom all his charms could not incline to stay.
Yet, what he sung in his immortal strain,
Though unsuccessful, was not sung in vain :
All, but the nymph who should redress his wrong,
Attend his passion, and approve his song ;
Like Phoebus thus, acquiring unsought praise,
He catched at love, and filled his arms with bays.

E. WALLER.

191. POETRY AND LOVE

CADENUS many things had writ :
Vanessa much esteemed his wit,
And called for his Poetic Works :
Meantime the boy in secret lurks ;
And while the book was in her hand,
The urchin from his private stand
Took aim, and shot with all his strength
A dart of such prodigious length,
It pierced the feeble volume through,
And deep transfixed her bosom too.
Some lines, more moving than the rest,
Stuck to the point that pierced her breast,
And, borne directly to her heart,
With pains unknown increased her smart.

J. SWIFT.

192. PROUD WORD YOU NEVER SPOKE

PROUD word you never spoke, but you will speak
  Four not exempt from pride some future day.
Resting on one white hand a warm wet cheek
  Over my open volume you will say,
' This man loved *me !* ' then rise and trip away.

W. S. LANDOR.

193. THE POET

FROM witty men and mad
All poetry conception had.

No sires but these will poetry admit :
Madness or wit.

This definition poetry doth fit :
It is witty madness, or mad wit.

Only these two poetic heat admits :
A witty man, or one that 's out of 's wits.

T. RANDOLPH.

194. THE FEMALE PHAETON

Thus Kitty, beautiful and young,
  And wild as colt untamed,
Bespoke the fair from whence she sprung,
  With little rage inflamed :

Inflamed with rage at sad restraint,
  Which wise mamma ordained,
And sorely vexed to play the saint,
  Whilst wit and beauty reigned.

' Shall I thumb holy books, confined
  With Abigails, forsaken ?
Kitty 's for other things designed,
  Or I am much mistaken.

' Must Lady Jenny frisk about,
  And visit with her cousins ?
At balls must she make all the rout,
  And bring home hearts by dozens ?

' What has she better, pray, than I ?
  What hidden charms to boast,
That all mankind for her should die,
  Whilst I am scarce a toast ?

' Dearest mamma, for once let me,
  Unchained, my fortune try ;
I'll have my Earl as well as she,
  Or know the reason why.

' I'll soon with Jenny's pride quit score,
  Make all her lovers fall :
They'll grieve I was not loosed before ;
  She, I was loosed at all ! '

Fondness prevailed,—mamma gave way :
  Kitty, at heart's desire,
Obtained the chariot for a day,
  And set the world on fire.

M. PRIOR.

195. ARCADIA

The sun was now withdrawn,
  The shepherds home were sped ;
The moon wide o'er the lawn
  Her silver mantle spread ;

When Damon stayed behind,
   And sauntered in the grove.
' Will ne'er a nymph be kind,
   And give me love for love ?

' O ! those were golden hours,
   When Love, devoid of cares,
In all Arcadia's bowers
   Lodged nymphs and swains by pairs ;
But now from wood and plain
   Flies every sprightly lass ;
No joys for me remain,
   In shades, or on the grass.'

The wingèd boy draws near,
   And thus the swain reproves :
' While Beauty revelled here,
   My game lay in the groves ;
At Court I never fail
   To scatter round my arrows ;
Men fall as thick as hail,
   And maidens love like sparrows.

' Then, swain, if me you need,
   Straight lay your sheep-hook down ;
Throw by your oaten reed,
   And haste away to town.
So well I'm known at Court,
   None ask where Cupid dwells ;
But readily resort
   To Bellendens or Lepels.'

                    J. GAY.

196. PRUDERY

ANSWER TO THE FOLLOWING QUESTION OF MRS. HOWE

WHAT is Prudery ?   'Tis a beldam,
Seen with wit and beauty seldom.
'Tis a fear that starts at shadows.
'Tis (no 'tisn't) like Miss Meadows.
'Tis a virgin hard of feature,
Old, and void of all good-nature ;
Lean and fretful ; would seem wise ;
Yet plays the fool before she dies :
'Tis an ugly envious shrew
That rails at dear Lepel and you.

                    A. POPE.

197. ON A CERTAIN LADY AT COURT

[HENRIETTA HOWARD, COUNTESS OF SUFFOLK]

I KNOW the thing that 's most uncommon
    (Envy, be silent, and attend) ;
I know a reasonable woman,
    Handsome and witty, yet a friend.

Not warped by passion, awed by rumour,
    Not grave through pride, or gay through folly ;
An equal mixture of good humour,
    And sensible soft melancholy.

' Has she no faults then,' Envy says, ' Sir ? '
    Yes, she has one, I must aver ;
When all the world conspires to praise her,
    The woman 's deaf, and does not hear !

A. POPE.

198. A LONG STORY

IN Britain's isle, no matter where,
    An ancient pile of buildings stands :
The Huntingdons and Hattons there
    Employed the power of fairy hands

To raise the ceiling's fretted height,
    Each panel in achievements clothing,
Rich windows that exclude the light,
    And passages, that lead to nothing.

Full oft within the spacious walls,
    When he had fifty winters o'er him,
My grave Lord-Keeper led the brawls :
    The Seal and Maces danced before him.

His bushy beard, and shoe-strings green,
    His high-crowned hat, and satin-doublet,
Moved the stout heart of England's Queen,
    Though Pope and Spaniard could not trouble it.

What, in the very first beginning !
    Shame of the versifying tribe !
Your History whither are you spinning ?
    Can you do nothing but describe ?

A house there is (and that 's enough),
    From whence one fatal morning issues
A brace of warriors, not in buff,
    But rustling in their silks and tissues.

The first came cap-a-pie from France,
    Her conquering destiny fulfilling,
Whom meaner beauties eye askance,
    And vainly ape her art of killing.

The other Amazon kind Heaven
    Had armed with spirit, wit, and satire:
But Cobham had the polish given,
    And tipped her arrows with good-nature.

To celebrate her eyes, her air—
    Coarse panegyrics would but teaze her.
Melissa is her *nom de guerre*.
    Alas, who would not wish to please her !

With bonnet blue and capucine,
    And aprons long they hid their armour,
And veiled their weapons bright and keen
    In pity to the country-farmer.

Fame in the shape of Mr. P——t
    (By this time all the Parish know it)
Had told that thereabouts there lurked
    A wicked imp they call a Poet,

Who prowled the country far and near,
    Bewitched the children of the peasants,
Dried up the cows, and lamed the deer,
    And sucked the eggs, and killed the pheasants.

My lady heard their joint petition,
    Swore by her coronet and ermine,
She'd issue out her high commission
    To rid the manor of such vermin.

The heroines undertook the task,
    Through lanes unknown, o'er stiles they ventured,
Rapped at the door, nor stayed to ask,
    But bounce into the parlour entered.

The trembling family they daunt,
    They flirt, they sing, they laugh, they tattle,
Rummage his mother, pinch his aunt,
    And up stairs in a whirlwind rattle.

Each hole and cupboard they explore,
    Each creek and cranny of his chamber,
Run hurry-skurry round the floor,
    And o'er the bed and tester clamber,

Into the drawers and china pry,
  Papers and books, a huge imbroglio !
Under a tea-cup he might lie,
  Or creased, like dogs-ears, in a folio.

On the first marching of the troops
  The Muses, hopeless of his pardon,
Conveyed him underneath their hoops
  To a small closet in the garden.

So Rumour says.   (Who will, believe.)
  But that they left the door a-jar,
Where, safe and laughing in his sleeve,
  He heard the distant din of war.

Short was his joy.   He little knew
  The power of magic was no fable.
Out of the window, whisk, they flew,
  But left a spell upon the table.

The words too eager to unriddle
  The Poet felt a strange disorder :
Transparent birdlime formed the middle,
  And chains invisible the border.

So cunning was the apparatus,
  The powerful pothooks did so move him,
That will he, nill he, to the great house
  He went, as if the Devil drove him.

Yet on his way (no sign of grace,
  For folks in fear are apt to pray)
To Phoebus he preferred his case,
  And begged his aid that dreadful day.

The Godhead would have backed his quarrel,
  But with a blush on recollection
Owned, that his quiver and his laurel
  'Gainst four such eyes were no protection.

The court was sat, the culprit there ;
  Forth from their gloomy mansions creeping
The Lady Janes and Joans repair,
  And from the gallery stand peeping :

Such as in silence of the night
  Come (sweep) along some winding entry
(Styack has often seen the sight)
  Or at the chapel-door stand sentry ;

In peaked hoods and mantles tarnished,
  Sour visages, enough to scare ye,
High dames of honour once, that garnished
  The drawing-room of fierce Queen Mary !

The peeress comes. The audience stare,
  And doff their hats with due submission :
She curtsies, as she takes her chair,
  To all the people of condition.

The bard with many an artful fib
  Had in imagination fenced him,
Disproved the arguments of Squib
  And all that Groom could urge against him.

But soon his rhetoric forsook him,
  When he the solemn hall had seen ;
A sudden fit of ague shook him,
  He stood as mute as poor Macleane.

Yet something he was heard to mutter,
  ' How in the park beneath an old-tree
(Without design to hurt the butter,
  Or any malice to the poultry),

' He once or twice had penned a sonnet ;
  Yet hoped that he might save his bacon :
Numbers would give their oaths upon it,
  He ne'er was for a conjurer taken.'

The ghostly prudes with haggard face
  Already had condemned the sinner.
My Lady rose, and with a grace . . .
  She smiled, and bid him come to dinner.

' Jesu-Maria ! Madam Bridget,
  Why, what can the Viscountess mean ? '
(Cried the square hoods in woful fidget)
  ' The times are altered quite and clean !

' Decorum 's turned to mere civility ;
  Her air and all her manners show it.
Commend me to her affability !
  Speak to a Commoner and Poet ! '

        [*Here* 500 *Stanzas are lost.*]

And so God save our noble King,
  And guard us from long-winded lubbers,
That to Eternity would sing,
  And keep my Lady from her rubbers.

                                    T. GRAY.

199. GOOD-NIGHT TO THE SEASON

So runs the world away.—Hamlet.

GOOD-NIGHT to the Season !   'Tis over !
　　Gay dwellings no longer are gay ;
The courtier, the gambler, the lover,
　　Are scattered like swallows away :
There 's nobody left to invite one
　　Except my good uncle and spouse
My mistress is bathing at Brighton,
　　My patron is sailing at Cowes :
For want of a better enjoyment,
　　Till Ponto and Don can get out,
I'll cultivate rural enjoyment,
　　And angle immensely for trout.

Good-night to the Season ! the lobbies,
　　Their changes, and rumours of change,
Which startled the rustic Sir Bobbies,
　　And made all the Bishops look strange ;
The breaches, and battles, and blunders,
　　Performed by the Commons and Peers ;
The Marquis's eloquent blunders,
　　The Baronet's eloquent ears ;
Denouncings of Papists and treasons,
　　Of foreign dominion and oats ;
Misrepresentations of reasons,
　　And misunderstandings of notes.

Good-night to the Season !—the buildings
　　Enough to make Inigo sick ;
The paintings, and plasterings, and gildings
　　Of stucco, and marble, and brick ;
The orders deliciously blended,
　　From love of effect, into one ;
The club-houses only intended,
　　The palaces only begun ;
The hell, where the fiend in his glory
　　Sits staring at putty and stones,
And scrambles from story to story,
　　To rattle at midnight his bones.

Good-night to the Season !—the dances,
　　The fillings of hot little rooms,
The glancings of rapturous glances,
　　The fancyings of fancy costumes ;
The pleasures which fashion makes duties,
　　The praisings of fiddles and flutes,
The luxury of looking at Beauties,
　　The tedium of talking to mutes ;

The female diplomatists, planners
  Of matches for Laura and Jane ;
The ice of her Ladyship's manners,
  The ice of his Lordship's champagne.

Good-night to the Season !—the rages
  Led off by the chiefs of the throng,
The Lady Matilda's new pages,
  The Lady Eliza's new song ;
Miss Fennel's macaw, which at Boodle's
  Was held to have something to say ;
Miss Splenetic's musical poodles,
  Which bark ' *Batti Batti* ' all day ;
The pony Sir Araby sported,
  As hot and as black as a coal,
And the Lion his mother imported,
  In bearskins and grease from the Pole.

Good-night to the Season !—the Toso,
  So very majestic and tall ;
Miss Ayton, whose singing was so-so,
  And Pasta, divinest of all ;
The labour in vain of the ballet,
  So sadly deficient in stars ;
The foreigners thronging the Alley,
  Exhaling the breath of cigars ;
The *loge* where some heiress (how killing !)
  Environed with exquisites sits,
The lovely one out of her drilling,
  The silly ones out of their wits.

Good-night to the Season !—the splendour
  That beamed in the Spanish Bazaar ;
Where I purchased—my heart was so tender—
  A card-case, a pasteboard guitar,
A bottle of perfume, a girdle,
  A lithographed Riego, full-grown,
Whom bigotry drew on a hurdle
  That artists might draw him on stone ;
A small panorama of Seville,
  A trap for demolishing flies,
A caricature of the Devil,
  And a look from Miss Sheridan's eyes.

Good-night to the Season !—the flowers
  Of the grand horticultural fête,
When boudoirs were quitted for bowers,
  And the fashion was—not to be late ;
When all who had money and leisure
  Grew rural o'er ices and wines,

All pleasantly toiling for pleasure,
   All hungrily pining for pines,
And making of beautiful speeches,
   And marring of beautiful shows,
And feeding on delicate peaches,
   And treading on delicate toes.

Good-night to the Season !—Another
   Will come, with its trifles and toys,
And hurry away, like its brother,
   In sunshine, and odour, and noise.
Will it come with a rose or a brier ?
   Will it come with a blessing or curse ?
Will its bonnets be lower or higher ?
   Will its morals be better or worse ?
Will it find me grown thinner or fatter,
   Or fonder of wrong or of right,
Or married—or buried ?—no matter :
   Good-night to the Season—good-night !

W. M. PRAED.

200.   VERS DE SOCIÉTÉ

THERE, pay it, James ! 'tis cheaply earned ;
   My conscience ! how one's cabman charges !
But never mind, so I'm returned
   Safe to my native street of Clarges.
I've just an hour for one cigar
   (What style these Reinas have, and *what* ash !)
One hour to watch the evening star
   With just one Curaçao-and-potash.

Ah me ! that face beneath the leaves
   And blossoms of its piquant bonnet !
Who would have thought that forty thieves
   Of years had laid their fingers on it !
Could you have managed to enchant
   At Lord's to-day old lovers simple,
Had Robber Time not played gallant,
   And spared you every youthful dimple !

That Robber bold, like courtier Claude,
   Who danced the gay coranto jesting,
By your bright beauty charmed and awed,
   Has bowed and passed you unmolesting.
No feet of many-wintered crows
   Have traced about your eyes a wrinkle ;
Your sunny hair has thawed the snows
   That other heads with silver sprinkle.

I wonder if that pair of gloves
   I won of you you'll ever pay me !
I wonder if our early loves
   Were wise or foolish, cousin Amy ?
I wonder if our childish tiff
   Now seems to you, like me, a blunder !
I wonder if you wonder if
   I ever wonder if you wonder.

I wonder if you'd think it bliss
   Once more to be the fashion's leader !
I wonder if the trick of this
   Escapes the unsuspecting reader !
And as for him who does or can
   Delight in it, I wonder whether
He knows that almost any man
   Could reel it off by yards together !

I wonder if—   What 's that ? a knock ?
   Is that you, James ? Eh ? What ? God bless me !
How time has flown !   It 's eight o'clock,
   And here's my fellow come to dress me.
Be quick, or I shall be the guest
   Whom Lady Mary never pardons ;
I trust you, James, to do your best
   To save the soup at Grosvenor Gardens.

H. D. TRAILL.

201. THE ARCHERY MEETING

THE Archery meeting is fixed for the third ;
The fuss that it causes is truly absurd ;
I've bought summer bonnets for Rosa and Bess,
And now I must buy each an archery dress !
Without a green suit they would blush to be seen,
And poor little Rosa looks horrid in green !

Poor fat little Rosa ! she 's shooting all day !
She sends forth an arrow expertly, they say ;
But 'tis terrible when with exertion she warms,
And she seems to me getting such muscular arms ;
And if she should hit, 'twere as well if she missed,
Prize bracelets could never be clasped on her wrist !

Dear Bess with her elegant figure and face,
Looks quite a Diana, the queen of the place ;
But as for the shooting—she never takes aim ;
She talks so and laughs so ! the beaux are to blame
She doats on flirtation—but oh ! by the by,
'Twas awkward her shooting out Mrs. Flint's eye !

They've made my poor husband an archer elect;
He dresses the part with prodigious effect;
A pair of nankeens, with a belt round his waist,
And a quiver of course in which arrows are placed;
And a bow in his hand—oh! he looks of all things
Like a corpulent Cupid bereft of his wings!

They dance on the lawn, and we mothers, alas!
Must sit on camp stools with our feet in the grass;
My Rosa and Bessy no partners attract!
The Archery men are all *cross Beaux* in fact!
Among the young ladies some *hits* there may be,
But still at my elbow two *misses* I see.

T. H. Bayly.

202. DIXIT, ET IN MENSAM —

(The Scene is a Picnic, and Mr. Joseph de Clapham ventures t
think that his Fiancée, the lovely Belgravinia, is a littl
too fast)

Now don't look so glum and so sanctified, please,
For folks, *comme il faut*, sir, are always at ease;
How dare you suggest that my talk is too free?
Il n'est jamais de mal en bon compagnie.

Must I shut up my eyes when I ride in the Park;
Or pray would you like me to ride after dark?
If not, Mr. Prim, I shall say what I see,
Il n'est jamais de mal en bon compagnie.

What harm am I speaking, you stupid old Nurse?
I'm sure Papa's newspaper tells us much worse,
He's a clergyman, too, are you stricter than he?
Il n'est jamais de mal en bon compagnie.

I knew who it was, and I said so, that's all;
I said who went round to her box from his stall,
Pray what is your next prohibition to be?
Il n'est jamais de mal en bon compagnie.

'My grandmother would not'—Oh, would not, indeed?
Just read Horace Walpole—Yes, sir, I *do* read.
Besides, what's my grandmother's buckram to me?
Il n'est jamais de mal en bon compagnie.

'I said it before that old *roué*, Lord Gadde;'
That's a story, he'd gone; and what harm if I had?
He has known me for years—from a baby of three.
Il n'est jamais de mal en bon compagnie.

You go to your Club (and this makes me so wild),
There you smoke and you slander, man, woman, and child ;
But *I*'m not to know there 's such people as she—
Il n'est jamais de mal en bon compagnie.

It 's all your own fault : the Academy, sir,
You whispered to Philip, ' No, no, it 's not *her*,—
Sir Edwin would hardly '—I heard, *mon ami ;*
Il n'est jamais de mal en bon compagnie.

Well there, I'm quite sorry ; now, stop looking haughty,
Or must I kneel down on my knees and say ' naughty ' ?
There ! Get me a peach, and I wish you'd agree
Il n'est jamais de mal en bon compagnie.

C. W. SHIRLEY BROOKS.

203. THE CHAPERON

TAKE my chaperon to the play—
　　She thinks she 's taking me—
And the gilded youth who owns the box,
　　A proud young man is he.
But how would his young heart be hurt
　　If he could only know
　　That not for his sweet sake I go,
　　Nor yet to see the trifling show ;
But to see my chaperon flirt.

Her eyes beneath her snowy hair
　　They sparkle young as mine ;
There 's scarce a wrinkle in her hand
　　So delicate and fine.
And when my chaperon is seen,
　　They come from everywhere—
　　The dear old boys with silvery hair,
　　With old-time grace and old-time air,
To greet their old-time queen.

They bow as my young Midas here
　　Will never learn to bow
(The dancing-masters do not teach
　　That gracious reverence now) ;
With voices quavering just a bit,
　　They play their old parts through,
　　They talk of folk who used to woo,
　　Of hearts that broke in 'fifty-two—
Now none the worse for it.

From *Poems of H. C. Bunner.*   Copyright 1884, 1889, by Charles Scribner's Sons.

†

And as those agèd crickets chirp
  I watch my chaperon's face,
And see the dear old features take
  A new and tender grace—
And in her happy eyes I see
  Her youth awakening bright,
    With all its hope, desire, delight—
  Ah, me ! I wish that I were quite
As young—as young as she !

H. C. BUNNER.

204.   WITHOUT AND WITHIN

My coachman in the moonlight there,
  Looks through the side-light of the door ;
I hear him with his brethren swear,
  As I could do,—but only more.

Flattening his nose against the pane,
  He envies me my brilliant lot,
Breathes on his aching fists in vain,
  And dooms me to a place more hot.

He sees me in to supper go,
  A silken wonder by my side,
Bare arms, bare shoulders, and a row
  Of flounces, for the door too wide.

He thinks how happy is my arm
  'Neath its white-gloved and jewelled load ;
And wishes me some dreadful harm,
  Hearing the merry corks explode.

Meanwhile I inly curse the bore
  Of hunting still the same old coon,
And envy him, outside the door,
  In golden quiets of the moon.

The winter wind is not so cold
  As the bright smile he sees me win,
Nor the host's oldest wine so old
  As our poor gabble sour and thin

I envy him the ungyved prance
  With which his freezing feet he warms,
And drag my lady's-chains and dance
  The galley-slave of dreary forms.

O, could he have my share of din,
  And I his quiet !—past a doubt
'Twould still be one man bored within,
  And just another bored without.

J. R. LOWELL.

205. GRATIANA DANCING, AND SINGING

SEE, with what constant motion,
Even, and glorious as the sun,
   Gratiana steers that noble frame,
     Soft as her breast, sweet as her voice,
     That gave each winding law and poise,
And swifter than the wings of Fame.

She beat the happy pavèment—
By such a star made firmament,
   Which now no more the roof envies !
     But swells up high, with Atlas even,
     Bearing the brighter, nobler heaven,
And, in her, all the deities.

Each step trod out a lover's thought,
And the ambitious hopes he brought
   Chained to her brave feet with such arts,
     Such sweet command and gentle awe,
     As, when she ceased, we sighing saw
The floor lay paved with broken hearts.

So did she move, so did she sing,
Like the harmonious spheres that bring
   Unto their rounds their music's aid ;
     Which she performèd such a way
     As all the enamoured world will say,
' The Graces danced, and Apollo played ! '
                  R. LOVELACE.

206. YES ; I WRITE VERSES

YES ; I write verses now and then,
But blunt and flaccid is my pen,
No longer talked of by young men
     As rather clever :

In the last quarter are my eyes,
You see it by their form and size ;
Is it not time then to be wise ?
     Or now or never.

Fairest that ever sprang from Eve !
While Time allows the short reprieve,
Just look at me ! would you believe
     'Twas once a lover ?

I cannot clear the five-bar gate,
But, trying first its timber's state,
Climb stiffly up, take breath, and wait
    To trundle over.

Through gallopade I cannot swing
The entangling blooms of Beauty's spring:
I cannot say the tender thing,
    Be 't true or false,

And am beginning to opine
Those girls are only half-divine
Whose waists yon wicked boys entwine
    In giddy waltz.

I fear that arm above that shoulder,
I wish them wiser, graver, older,
Sedater, and no harm if colder
    And panting less.

Ah ! people were not half so wild
In former days, when, starchly mild,
Upon her high-heeled Essex smiled
    The brave Queen Bess.

                  W. S. LANDOR.

207. THE WALTZ

BEHOLD with downcast eyes and modest glance,
In measured step, a well-dressed pair advance,
One hand on hers, the other on her hip,
For thus the law's ordained by Baron Trip.
'Twas in such posture our first parents moved,
When hand in hand through Eden's bowers they roved,
Ere yet the devil with practice foul and false
Turned their poor heads and taught them how to waltz.

                  R. B. SHERIDAN.

208. AN EPITAPH

A LOVELY young lady I mourn in my rhymes,
She was pleasant, good-natured, and civil (sometimes),
Her figure was good, she had very fine eyes,
And her talk was a mixture of foolish and wise.
Her adorers were many, and one of them said,
' She waltzed rather well—it 's a pity she 's dead.'

                  G. J. CAYLEY.

209. THE BELLE OF THE BALL-ROOM

YEARS—years ago—ere yet my dreams
  Had been of being wise or witty,—
Ere I had done with writing themes,
  Or yawned o'er this infernal Chitty ;—
Years,—years ago,—while all my joy
  Was in my fowling-piece and filly,—
In short, while I was yet a boy,
  I fell in love with Laura Lily.

I saw her at the County Ball :
  There, when the sounds of flute and fiddle
Gave signal sweet in that old hall
  Of hands across and down the middle,
Hers was the subtlest spell by far
  Of all that set young hearts romancing ;
She was our queen, our rose, our star ;
  And then she danced—O Heaven, her dancing !

Dark was her hair, her hand was white ;
  Her voice was exquisitely tender ;
Her eyes were full of liquid light ;
  I never saw a waist more slender !
Her every look, her every smile,
  Shot right and left a score of arrows ;
I thought 'twas Venus from her isle,
  And wondered where she'd left her sparrows.

She talked,—of politics or prayers,—
  Of Southey's prose or Wordsworth's sonnets,—
Of danglers—or of dancing bears,
  Of battles—or the last new bonnets,
By candlelight, at twelve o'clock,
  To me it mattered not a tittle ;
If those bright lips had quoted Locke,
  I might have thought they murmured Little.

Through sunny May, through sultry June,
  I loved her with a love eternal ;
I spoke her praises to the moon,
  I wrote them to the Sunday Journal:
My mother laughed ; I soon found out
  That ancient ladies have no feeling :
My father frowned ; but how should gout
  See any happiness in kneeling ?

She was the daughter of a Dean,
  Rich, fat, and rather apoplectic ;
She had one brother, just thirteen,
  Whose colour was extremely hectic ;
F 3

Her grandmother for many a year
   Had fed the parish with her bounty ;
Her second cousin was a peer,
   And Lord Lieutenant of the County.

But titles, and the three per cents,
   And mortgages, and great relations,
And India bonds, and tithes, and rents,
   Oh what are they to love's sensations ?
Black eyes, fair forehead, clustering locks—
   Such wealth, such honours, Cupid chooses ;
He cares as little for the Stocks,
   As Baron Rothschild for the Muses.

She sketched ; the vale, the wood, the beach,
   Grew lovelier from her pencil's shading :
She botanized ; I envied each
   Young blossom in her boudoir fading :
She warbled Handel ; it was grand ;
   She made the Catalani jealous :
She touched the organ ; I could stand
   For hours and hours to blow the bellows.

She kept an album, too, at home,
   Well filled with all an album's glories ;
Paintings of butterflies, and Rome,
   Patterns for trimmings, Persian stories ;
Soft songs to Julia's cockatoo,
   Fierce odes to Famine and to Slaughter,
And autographs of Prince Leboo,
   And recipes for elder-water.

And she was flattered, worshipped, bored ;
   Her steps were watched, her dress was noted ;
Her poodle dog was quite adored,
   Her sayings were extremely quoted ;
She laughed, and every heart was glad,
   As if the taxes were abolished ;
She frowned, and every look was sad,
   As if the Opera were demolished.

She smiled on many, just for fun,—
   I knew that there was nothing in it ;
I was the first—the only one
   Her heart had thought of for a minute.—
I knew it, for she told me so,
   In phrase which was divinely moulded ;
She wrote a charming hand,—and oh !
   How sweetly all her notes were folded

Our love was like most other loves ;—
   A little glow, a little shiver,
A rose-bud, and a pair of gloves,
   And ' Fly not yet '—upon the river ;
Some jealousy of some one's heir,
   Some hopes of dying broken-hearted,
A miniature, a lock of hair,
   The usual vows,—and then we parted.

We parted ; months and years rolled by ;
   We met again four summers after :
Our parting was all sob and sigh ;
   Our meeting was all mirth and laughter :
For in my heart's most secret cell
   There had been many other lodgers ;
And she was not the ball-room's Belle,
   But only—Mrs. Something Rogers !

                          W. M. PRAED.

210.   ONE MORE QUADRILLE

NOT yet, not yet ; it 's hardly four ;
   Not yet ; we'll send the chair away ;
Mirth still has many smiles in store,
   And love has fifty things to say.
Long leagues the weary Sun must drive,
   Ere pant his hot steeds o'er the hill ;
The merry stars will dance till five ;
   One more quadrille,—one more quadrille !

'Tis only thus, 'tis only here
   That maids and minstrels may forget
The myriad ills they feel or fear,
   Ennui, taxation, cholera, debt ;
With daylight busy cares and schemes
   Will come again to chafe or chill ;
This is the fairy land of dreams ;
   One more quadrille,—one more quadrille !

What tricks the French in Paris play,
   And what the Austrians are about,
And whether that tall knave, Lord Grey,
   Is staying in, or going out ;
And what the House of Lords will do,
   At last, with that eternal Bill,
I do not care a rush,—do you ?
   One more quadrille,—one more quadrille !

My book don't sell, my play don't draw,
    My garden gives me only weeds ;
And Mr. Quirk has found a flaw—
    Deuce take him—in my title-deeds ;
My Aunt has scratched her nephew's name
    From that sweet corner in her will ;
My dog is dead, my horse is lame ;
    One more quadrille,—one more quadrille !

Not yet, not yet ; it is not late ;
    Don't whisper it to sister Jane ;
Your brother, I am sure, will wait ;
    Papa will go to cards again.
Not yet, not yet. Your eyes are bright,
    Your step is like a wood-nymph's, still.
Oh no, you can't be tired, to-night !
    One more quadrille,—one more quadrille !

                                        W. M. PRAED.

211. A, B, C

A is an Angel of blushing eighteen :
B is the Ball where the Angel was seen :
C is the Chaperon, who cheated at cards :
D is the Deuxtemps, with Frank of the Guards :
E is the Eye, which those dark lashes cover :
F is the Fan, it peeped wickedly over :
G is the Glove of superlative kid :
H is the Hand which it spitefully hid ;
I is the Ice which the fair one demanded :
J is the Juvenile, who hurried to hand it :
K is the Kerchief, a rare work of art :
L is the Lace which composed the chief part :
M is the old Maid who watched the girls dance :
N is the Nose she turned up at each glance :
O is the Olga (just then in its prime) :
P is the Partner who wouldn't keep time :
Q 's a Quadrille, put instead of the Lancers :
R the Remonstrances made by the dancers :
S is the Supper, where all went in pairs :
T is the Twaddle they talked on the stairs :
U is the Uncle who ' thought we'd be going ' :
V is the Voice which his niece replied ' No ' in :
W is the Waiter, who sat up till eight :
X is his Exit, not rigidly straight :
Y is a Yawning fit caused by the Ball :
Z stands for Zero, or nothing at all.
                                    C. S. CALVERLEY.

212. OUR BALL

You'll come to our Ball ;—since we parted,
  I've thought of you more than I'll say ;
Indeed, I was half broken-hearted
  For a week, when they took you away.
Fond fancy brought back to my slumbers
  Our walks on the Ness and the Den,
And echoed the musical numbers
  Which you used to sing to me then.
I know the romance, since it 's over,
  'Twere idle, or worse, to recall ;
I know you're a terrible rover ;
  But Clarence, you'll come to our Ball !

It 's only a year, since, at College,
  You put on your cap and your gown ;
But, Clarence, you're grown out of knowledge,
  And changed from the spur to the crown :
The voice that was best when it faltered
  Is fuller and firmer in tone,
And the smile that should never have altered—
  Dear Clarence—it is not your own :
Your cravat was badly selected ;
  Your coat don't become you at all ;
And why is your hair so neglected ?
  You must have it curled for our Ball.

I've often been out upon Haldon
  To look for a covey with pup ;
I've often been over to Shaldon,
  To see how your boat is laid up :
In spite of the terrors of Aunty
  I've ridden the filly you broke ;
And I've studied your sweet little Dante
  In the shade of your favourite oak :
When I sat in July to Sir Lawrence,
  I sat in your love of a shawl ;
And I'll wear what you brought me from Florence,
  Perhaps, if you'll come to our Ball.

You'll find us all changed since you vanished ;
  We've set up a National School ;
And waltzing is utterly banished,
  And Ellen has married a fool ;
The Major is going to travel,
  Miss Hyacinth threatens a rout,
The walk is laid down with fresh gravel,
  Papa is laid up with the gout ;

And Jane has gone on with her easels,
    And Anne has gone off with Sir Paul ;
And Fanny is sick with the measles,—
    And I'll tell you the rest at the Ball.

You'll meet all your Beauties ; the Lily,
    And the Fairy of Willowbrook Farm,
And Lucy, who made me so silly
    At Dawlish, by taking your arm ;
Miss Manners, who always abused you
    For talking so much about Hock,
And her sister who often amused you
    By raving of rebels and Rock ;
And something which surely would answer,
    An heiress quite fresh from Bengal ;
So, though you were seldom a dancer,
    You'll dance, just for once, at our Ball.

But out on the World ! from the flowers
    It shuts out the sunshine of truth :
It blights the green leaves in the bowers,
    It makes an old age of our youth ;
And the flow of our feeling, once in it,
    Like a streamlet beginning to freeze,
Though it cannot turn ice in a minute,
    Grows harder by sudden degrees :
Time treads o'er the graves of affection ;
    Sweet honey is turned into gall ;
Perhaps you have no recollection
    That ever you danced at our Ball !

You once could be pleased with our ballads,—
    To-day you have critical ears ;
You once could be charmed with our salads—
    Alas ! you've been dining with Peers ;
You trifled and flirted with many,—
    You've forgotten the when and the how ;
There was one you liked better than any,—
    Perhaps you've forgotten her now.
But of those you remember most newly,
    Of those who delight or enthrall,
None love you a quarter so truly
    As some you will find at our Ball.

They tell me you've many who flatter,
    Because of your wit and your song :
They tell me—and what does it matter ?—
    You like to be praised by the throng :

They tell me you're shadowed with laurel :
   They tell me you're loved by a Blue :
They tell me you're sadly immoral—
   Dear Clarence, that cannot be true !
But to me, you are still what I found you,
   Before you grew clever and tall ;
And you'll think of the spell that once bound you;
     And you'll come—won't you come ?—to our Ball !

                       W. M. PRAED.

213.   A BALLAD ON QUADRILLE

WHEN as corruption hence did go,
   And left the nation free ;
When Aye said aye, and No said no,
   Without or place or fee ;
Then Satan, thinking things went ill
Sent forth his spirit called Quadrille.
                 Quadrille, Quadrille, &c.

Kings, queens, and knaves, made up his pack,
   And four fair suits he wore ;
His troops they were with red and black
   All blotched and spotted o'er ;
And every house, go where you will,
Is haunted by this imp Quadrille.

Sure cards he has for everything,
   Which well court-cards they name,
And, statesman-like, calls in the king,
   To help out a bad game ;
But, if the parties manage ill,
The king is forced to lose codille.

When two and two were met of old,
   Though they ne'er meant to marry,
They were in Cupid's books enrolled,
   And called a partie quarrée ;
But now, meet when and where you will,
A partie quarrée is quadrille.

The commoner and knight and peer,
   Men of all ranks and fame,
Leave to their wives the only care
   To propagate their name ;
And well that duty they fulfil,
When the good husband's at quadrille.

When patients lie in piteous case,
  In comes the apothecary ;
And to the doctor cries, Alas !
  Non debes quadrillare :
The patient dies without a pill :
For why ? the doctor 's at quadrille.

Should France and Spain again grow loud,
  The Muscovite grow louder,
Britain, to curb her neighbours proud,
  Would want both ball and powder ;
Must want both sword and gun to kill :
For why ? the general 's at quadrille.

The king of late drew forth his sword
  (Thank God 'twas not in wrath),
And made, of many a 'squire and lord,
  An unwashed Knight of Bath :
What are their feats of arms and skill ?
They're but nine parties at quadrille.

A party late at Cambray met,
  Which drew all Europe's eyes ;
'Twas called in Post-Boy and Gazette
  The Quadruple Allies ,
But somebody took something ill,
So broke this party at quadrille.

And now God save this noble realm,
  And God save eke Hanóver ,
And God save those who hold the helm,
  When as the king goes over :
But let the king go where he will,
His subjects must play at quadrille.
                    Quadrille, Quadrille, &c.
                              J. GAY.

214. THE LADY'S LAMENTATION

  PHYLLIDA, that loved to dream
  In the grove or by the stream,
    Sighed on velvet pillow.
  What, alas ! should fill her head,
  But a fountain, or a mead,
    Water and a willow ?

  ' Love in cities never dwells,
  He delights in rural cells
    Which sweet woodbine covers.
  What are your assemblies then ?
  There, 'tis true, we see more men ;
    But much fewer lovers.

' Oh, how changed the prospect grows !
Flocks and herds to fops and beaux,
   Coxcombs without number !
Moon and stars that shone so bright,
To the torch and waxen light,
   And whole nights at ombre.

' Pleasant as it is, to hear
Scandal tickling in our ear,
   Even of our own mothers ;
In the chit-chat of the day,
To us is paid, when we're away,
   What we lent to others.

' Though the favourite toast I reign,
Wine, they say, that prompts the vain,
   Heightens defamation.
Must I live 'twixt spite and fear,
Every day grow handsomer,
   And lose my reputation ? '

Thus the fair to sighs gave way,
Her empty purse beside her lay.
   Nymph, ah ! cease thy sorrow.
Though curst fortune frown to-night,
This odious town can give delight,
   If you win to-morrow.

J. GAY.

215. PLAIN LANGUAGE FROM TRUTHFUL JAMES
TABLE MOUNTAIN, 1870

WHICH I wish to remark,—
   And my language is plain,
That for ways that are dark,
   And for tricks that are vain,
The heathen Chinee is peculiar,—
   Which the same I would rise to explain.

Ah Sin was his name.
   And I shall not deny
In regard to the same
   What that name might imply ;
But his smile it was pensive and childlike,
   As I frequent remarked to Bill Nye.

It was August the third ;
   And quite soft was the skies :
Which it might be inferred
   That Ah Sin was likewise ;
Yet he played it that day upon William
   And me in a way I despise.

Which we had a small game,
  And Ah Sin took a hand :
It was euchre.   The same
  He did not understand ;
But he smiled as he sat by the table,
  With the smile that was childlike and bland.

Yet the cards they were stocked
  In a way that I grieve.
And my feelings were shocked
  At the state of Nye's sleeve :
Which was stuffed full of aces and bowers,
  And the same with intent to deceive.

But the hands that were played
  By that heathen Chinee,
And the points that he made,
  Were quite frightful to see.—
Till at last he put down a right bower,
  Which the same Nye had dealt unto me.

Then I looked up at Nye,
  And he gazed upon me ;
And he rose with a sigh,
  And said, ' Can this be ?
We are ruined by Chinese cheap labour ' ;
  And he went for that heathen Chinee.

In the scene that ensued
  I did not take a hand ;
But the floor it was strewed
  Like the leaves on the strand
With the cards that Ah Sin had been hiding,
  In the game ' he did not understand '.

In his sleeves, which were long,
  He had twenty-four packs,—
Which was coming it strong,
  Yet I state but the facts ;
And we found on his nails, which were taper,
  What is frequent in tapers,—that 's wax.

Which is why I remark,
  And my language is plain,
That for ways that are dark,
  And for tricks that are vain,
The heathen Chinee is peculiar,—
  Which the same I am free to maintain.

F. Bret Harte.

216. THE CHESS BOARD

IRENE, do you yet remember,
  Ere we were grown so sadly wise,
Those evenings in the bleak December,
Curtained warm from the snowy weather,
When you and I played chess together,
  Checkmated by each other's eyes ?
  Ah, still I see your soft white hand
Hovering warm o'er Queen and Knight.

  Brave Pawns in valiant battle stand :
The double Castles guard the wings :
The Bishop, bent on distant things,
Moves, sidling, through the fight.
  Our fingers touch : our glances meet,
  And falter ; falls your golden hair
  Against my cheek ; your bosom sweet
Is heaving.   Down the field, your Queen
Rides slow her soldiery all between,
  And checks me unaware.

  Ah me ! the little battle 's done,
Dispersed is all its chivalry ;
Full many a move, since then, have we
'Mid Life's perplexing chequers made,
And many a game with Fortune played,—
  What is it we have won ?
  This, this at least—if this alone ;—
That never, never, never more,
As in those old still nights of yore
  (Ere we were grown so sadly wise)
  Can you and I shut out the skies,
Shut out the world, and wintry weather,
  And, eyes exchanging warmth with eyes,
Play chess, as then we played, together !

        E. R. BULWER LYTTON, EARL OF LYTTON.

217. MELANCHOLY

  Go—you may call it madness, folly ;
    You shall not chase my gloom away.
  There 's such a charm in melancholy,
    I would not, if I could, be gay.

  Oh, if you knew the pensive pleasure
    That fills my bosom when I sigh,
  You would not rob me of a treasure
    Monarchs are too poor to buy !

                    S. ROGERS.

218. FORTUNE

A FRAGMENT

FORTUNE, that, with malicious joy,
    Does man her slave oppress,
Proud of her office to destroy,
    Is seldom pleased to bless :
Still various and unconstant still,
But with an inclination to be ill,
    Promotes, degrades, delights in strife,
    And makes a lottery of life.
I can enjoy her while she's kind ;
But when she dances in the wind,
    And shakes her wings and will not stay,
    I puff the prostitute away :
The little or the much she gave, is quietly resigned :
    Content with poverty, my soul I arm ;
    And virtue, though in rags, will keep me warm.

                      J. DRYDEN.

219. WHAT MAN HAD NOT RATHER BE POOR

WHAT man in his wits had not rather be poor,
    Than for lucre his freedom to give,
Ever busy the means of his life to secure,
    And so ever neglecting to live ?

Environed from morning to night in a crowd,
    Not a moment unbent, or alone ;
Constrained to be abject, though never so proud,
    And at every one's call but his own.

Still repining, and longing for quiet, each hour,
    Yet studiously flying it still ;
With the means of enjoying his wish, in his power ;
    But accursed with his wanting the will.

For a year must be past, or a day must be come,
    Before he has leisure to rest ;
He must add to his store this or that pretty sum,
    And then he will have time to be blessed.

But his gains more bewitching the more they increase,
    Only swell the desire of his eye :
Such a wretch, let mine enemy live if he please,
    Let not even mine enemy die.

                      S. WESLEY.

220. TO ALTHEA FROM PRISON

WHEN Love with unconfinèd wings
   Hovers within my gates,
And my divine Althea brings
   To whisper at the grates ;
When I lie tangled in her hair
   And fettered to her eye,
The birds that wanton in the air
   Know no such liberty.

When flowing cups run swiftly round
   With no allaying Thames,
Our careless heads with roses bound,
   Our hearts with loyal flames ;
When thirsty grief in wine we steep,
   When healths and draughts go free—
Fishes that tipple in the deep
   Know no such liberty.

When (like committed linnets) I
   With shriller throat shall sing
The sweetness, mercy, majesty
   And glories of my King ;
When I shall voice aloud how good
   He is, how great should be,
Enlargèd winds, that curl the flood
   Know no such liberty.

Stone walls do not a prison make,
   Nor iron bars a cage ;
Minds innocent and quiet take
   That for an hermitage :
If I have freedom in my love
   And in my soul am free,
Angels alone, that soar above,
   Enjoy such liberty.

            R. LOVELACE.

221. EPITAPH ON CHARLES II

HERE lies our Sovereign Lord the King,
   Whose word no man relies on,
Who never said a foolish thing,
   Nor ever did a wise one.

       J. WILMOT, EARL OF ROCHESTER.

222. THE DEVIL'S THOUGHTS

FROM his brimstone bed at break of day
A walking the Devil is gone,
To visit his little snug farm the earth
And see how his stock goes on.

Over the hill and over the dale,
And he went over the plain,
And backward and forward he switched his long tail
As a gentleman switches his cane.

And how then was the Devil dressed ?
Oh ! he was in his Sunday's best :
His jacket was red and his breeches were blue,
And there was a hole where the tail came through.

He saw a Lawyer killing a Viper
On a dunghill hard by his own stable ;
And the Devil smiled, for it put him in mind
Of Cain and his brother, Abel.

He saw an Apothecary on a white horse
   Ride by on his vocations,
And the Devil thought of his old Friend
   Death in the Revelations.

He saw a cottage with a double coach-house,
   A cottage of gentility !
And the Devil did grin, for his darling sin
   Is pride that apes humility.

He peeped into a rich bookseller's shop,
   Quoth he ! we are both of one college,
For I sate myself like a cormorant once
   Hard by the tree of knowledge.

Down the river did glide, with wind and tide,
   A pig, with vast celerity,
And the Devil looked wise as he saw how the while,
It cut its own throat. 'There!' quoth he with a smile,
   'Goes "England's commercial prosperity." '

As he went through Cold-Bath Fields he saw
   A solitary cell ;
And the Devil was pleased, for it gave him a hint
   For improving his prisons in Hell.

General ——————'s burning face
  He saw with consternation,
And back to hell his way did he take,
For the Devil thought by a slight mistake
  It was general conflagration.

S. T. COLERIDGE.

223. RICH AND POOR; OR, SAINT AND SINNER

THE poor man's sins are glaring;
In the face of ghostly warning
    He is caught in the fact
    Of an overt act—
Buying greens on Sunday morning.

The rich man's sins are hidden
In the pomp of wealth and station;
    And escape the sight
    Of the children of light
Who are wise in their generation.

The rich man has a kitchen
And cooks to dress his dinner;
    The poor who would roast
    To the baker's must post,
And thus becomes a sinner.

The rich man has a cellar,
And a ready butler by him;
    The poor must steer
    For his pint of beer
Where the saint can't choose but spy him.

The rich man's painted windows
Hide the concerts of the quality;
    The poor can but share
    A cracked fiddle in the air,
Which offends all sound morality.

The rich man is invisible
In the crowd of his gay society;
    But the poor man's delight
    Is a sore in the sight,
And a stench in the nose of piety.

T. L. PEACOCK.

224. THE CHAUNT OF THE BRAZEN HEAD

I THINK, whatever mortals crave
  With impotent endeavour,—
A wreath, a rank, a throne, a grave,—
  The world goes round for ever :
I think that life is not too long ;
  And therefore I determine,
That many people read a song
  Who will not read a sermon.

I think you've looked through many hearts,
  And mused on many actions,
And studied Man's component parts,
  And Nature's compound fractions :
I think you've picked up truth by bits
  From foreigner and neighbour ;
I think the world has lost its wits,
  And you have lost your labour.

I think the studies of the wise,
  The hero's noisy quarrel,
The majesty of Woman's eyes,
  The poet's cherished laurel,
And all that makes us lean or fat,
  And all that charms or troubles,—
This bubble is more bright than that,
  But still they all are bubbles.

I think the thing you call Renown,
  The unsubstantial vapour
For which the soldier burns a town,
  The sonnetteer a taper,
Is like the mist which, as he flies,
  The horseman leaves behind him ;
He cannot mark its wreaths arise,
  Or if he does they blind him.

I think one nod of Mistress Chance
  Makes creditors of debtors,
And shifts the funeral for the dance,
  The sceptre for the fetters :
I think that Fortune's favoured guest
  May live to gnaw the platters,
And he that wears the purple vest
  May wear the rags and tatters.

I think the Tories love to buy
  ' Your Lordship's ' and ' your Grace's ',
By loathing common honesty,
  And lauding commonplaces :

I think that some are very wise,
  And some are very funny,
And some grow rich by telling lies,
  And some by telling money.

I think the Whigs are wicked knaves—
  (And very like the Tories)—
Who doubt that Britain rules the waves,
  And ask the price of glories :
I think that many fret and fume
  At what their friends are planning,
And Mr. Hume hates Mr. Brougham
  As much as Mr. Canning.

I think that friars and their hoods,
  Their doctrines and their maggots,
Have lighted up too many feuds,
  And far too many faggots :
I think, while zealots fast and frown,
  And fight for two or seven,
That there are fifty roads to Town,
  And rather more to Heaven.

I think that, thanks to Paget's lance,
  And thanks to Chester's learning,
The hearts that burned for fame in France
  At home are safe from burning :
I think the Pope is on his back ;
  And, though 'tis fun to shake him,
I think the Devil not so black
  As many people make him.

I think that Love is like a play,
  Where tears and smiles are blended,
Or like a faithless April day,
  Whose shine with shower is ended:
Like Colnbrook pavement, rather rough,
  Like trade, exposed to losses,
And like a Highland plaid,—all stuff,
  And very full of crosses.

I think the world, though dark it be,
  Has aye one rapturous pleasure
Concealed in life's monotony,
  For those who seek the treasure ;
One planet in a starless night,
  One blossom on a brier,
One friend not quite a hypocrite,
  One woman not a liar !

I think poor beggars court St. Giles,
  Rich beggars court St. Stephen ;
And Death looks down with nods and smiles,
  And makes the odds all even :
I think some die upon the field,
  And some upon the billow,
And some are laid beneath a shield,
  And some beneath a willow.

I think that very few have sighed
  When Fate at last has found them,
Though bitter foes were by their side,
  And barren moss around them :
I think that some have died of drought,
  And some have died of drinking ;
I think that naught is worth a thought,—
  And I'm a fool for thinking !

W. M. PRAED.

225. THE JESTER'S PLEA

THE World ! Was jester ever in
  A viler than the present ?
Yet if it ugly be—as sin,
  It almost is—as pleasant !
The world 's a merry world (*pro tem.*),
  And some are gay, and therefore
It pleases them—but some condemn
  The fun they do not care for.

It is an ugly world. Offend
  Good people—how they wrangle !
Their manners that they never mend !
  The characters they mangle !
They eat, and drink, and scheme, and plod,
  And go to church on Sunday ;
And many are afraid of God—
  And more of *Mrs. Grundy*.

The time for pen and sword was when
  ' My ladye fayre ' for pity
Could tend her wounded knight, and then
  Grow tender to his ditty.
Some ladies now make pretty songs,
  And some make pretty nurses :
Some men are good for righting wrongs,—
  And some for writing verses.

I wish we better understood
   The tax that poets levy ;
I know the Muse is very good,
   I think she 's rather heavy :
She now compounds for winning ways
   By morals of the sternest ;
Methinks the lays of nowadays
   Are painfully in earnest.

When wisdom halts, I humbly try
   To make the most of folly :
If Pallas be unwilling, I
   Prefer to flirt with Polly ;
To quit the goddess for the maid
   Seems low in lofty musers ;
But Pallas is a haughty jade —
   And beggars can't be choosers.

I do not wish to see the slaves
   Of party stirring passion,
Or psalms quite superseding staves,
   Or piety ' the fashion '.
I bless the Hearts where pity glows,
   Who, here together banded,
Are holding out a hand to those
   That wait so empty-handed !

A righteous work ! My masters, may
   A jester by confession,
Scarce noticed join, half sad, half gay,
   The close of your procession ?
The motley here seems out of place
   With graver robes to mingle,
But if one tear bedews his face,
   Forgive the bells their jingle.

F. LOCKER-LAMPSON.

226. LOVE AND DEBT ALIKE TROUBLESOME

THIS one request I make to him that sits the clouds above ;
That I were freely out of debt, as I am out of love.
Then for to dance, to drink, and sing, I should be very willing ;
I should not owe one lass a kiss, nor ne'er a knave a shilling.

'Tis only being in love and debt, that breaks us of our rest ;
And he that is quite out of both, of all the world is blessed.
He sees the golden age, wherein all things were free and common ;
He eats, he drinks, he takes his rest, he fears no man nor woman.

SIR J. SUCKLING.

227. THE RELIGION OF HUDIBRAS

For his Religion, it was fit
To match his learning and his wit ;
'Twas Presbyterian true blue ;
For he was of that stubborn crew
Of errant saints, whom all men grant
To be the true Church Militant ;
Such as do build their faith upon
The holy text of pike and gun ;
Decide all controversies by
Infallible artillery ;
And prove their doctrine orthodox
By apostolic blows and knocks ;
Call fire and sword and desolation,
A godly, thorough Reformation,
Which always must be carried on,
And still be doing, never done ;
As if Religion were intended
For nothing else but to be mended.
A sect, whose chief devotion lies
In odd perverse antipathies ;
In falling out with that or this,
And finding somewhat still amiss ;
More peevish, cross, and splenetic,
Than dog distract or monkey sick ;
That with more care keep holy-day
The wrong, than others the right way ;
Compound for sins they are inclined to,
By damning those they have no mind to :
Still so perverse and opposite,
As if they worshipped God for spite.
The self-same thing they will abhor
One way, and long another for.
Free-will they one way disavow,
Another, nothing else allow.
All piety consists therein
In them, in other men all sin.
Rather than fail, they will defy
That which they love most tenderly,
Quarrel with minced-pies, and disparage
Their best and dearest friend—plum porridge ;
Fat pig and goose itself oppose,
And blaspheme custard through the nose.

S. Butler.

228. FAREWELL, REWARDS AND FAIRIES

Farewell, rewards and fairies,
　　Good housewives now may say,
For now foul sluts in dairies
　　Do fare as well as they.
And though they sweep their hearths no less
　　Than maids were wont to do,
Yet who of late for cleanliness
　　Finds sixpence in her shoe ?

Lament, lament, old Abbeys,
　　The Fairies' lost command !
They did but change Priests' babies,
　　But some have changed your land.
And all your children, sprung from thence,
　　Are now grown Puritans,
Who live as Changelings ever since
　　For love of your demains.

At morning and at evening both
　　You merry were and glad,
So little care of sleep or sloth
　　These pretty ladies had ;
When Tom came home from labour,
　　Or Cis to milking rose,
Then merrily went their tabor,
　　And nimbly went their toes.

Witness those rings and roundelays
　　Of theirs, which yet remain,
Were footed in Queen Mary's days
　　On many a grassy plain ;
But since of late, Elizabeth,
　　And, later, James came in,
They never danced on any heath
　　As when the time hath been.

By which we note the Fairies
　　Were of the old Profession.
Their songs were ' Ave Mary's ',
　　Their dances were Procession.
But now, alas, they all are dead ;
　　Or gone beyond the seas ;
Or farther for Religion fled ;
　　Or else they take their ease.

A tell-tale in their company
  They never could endure !
And whoso kept not secretly
  Their mirth, was punished, sure ;
It was a just and Christian deed
  To pinch such black and blue.
Oh how the commonwealth doth want
  Such Justices as you !

R. CORBET.

229. PIOUS SELINDA

PIOUS Selinda goes to prayers,
  If I but ask her favour ;
And yet the silly fool 's in tears,
  If she believes I'll leave her.
Would I were free from this restraint,
  Or else had hopes to win her :
Would she could make of me a saint,
  Or I of her a sinner.

W. CONGREVE.

230. REPENTANCE

LAST Sunday at St. James's prayers,
  The prince and princess by,
I, dressed in all my whale-bone airs,
  Sat in a closet nigh.
I bowed my knees, I held my book,
  Read all the answers o'er ;
But was perverted by a look,
  Which pierced me from the door.
High thoughts of Heaven I came to use,
  With the devoutest care ;
Which gay young Strephon made me lose,
  And all the raptures there.
He stood to hand me to my chair,
  And bowed with courtly grace ;
But whispered love into my ear
  Too warm for that grave place.
' Love, love,' said he, ' by all adored,
  My tender heart has won.'
But I grew peevish at the word,
  And bade he would be gone.
He went quite out of sight, while I
  A kinder answer meant ;
Nor did I for my sins that day
  By half so much repent.

UNKNOWN.

231. WHEN MOLLY SMILES

WHEN Molly smiles beneath her cow,
I feel my heart—I can't tell how ;
When Molly is on Sunday dressed,
On Sundays I can take no rest.

What can I do ? on worky days
I leave my work on her to gaze.
What shall I say ?   At sermons, I
Forget the text when Molly 's by.

Good master curate, teach me how
To mind your preaching and my plough :
And if for this you'll raise a spell,
A good fat goose shall thank you well.

UNKNOWN.

232. THE HAPPY LIFE OF A COUNTRY PARSON

(IMITATION OF DR. SWIFT)

PARSON, these things in thy possessing
Are better than the bishop's blessing,
A wife that makes conserves ; a steed
That carries double when there 's need ;
October store, and best Virginia,
Tythe pig, and mortuary guinea ;
Gazettes sent gratis down, and franked,
For which thy patron 's weekly thanked ;
A large concordance bound long since ;
Sermons to Charles the First, when prince ;
A chronicle of ancient standing ;
A Chrysostom to smooth thy band in ;
The polyglot—three parts—my text,
Howbeit—likewise—now to my next.
Lo here the Septuagint, and Paul,
To sum the whole, the close of all.

He that has these may pass his life,
Drink with the 'squire and kiss his wife ;
On Sundays preach, and eat his fill ;
And fast on Fridays—if he will ;
Toast church and queen, explain the news,
Talk with church-wardens about pews ;
Pray heartily for some new gift,
And shake his head at Doctor Swift.

A. POPE.

233. LLYN-Y-DREIDDIAD-VRAWD

The Pool of the Diving Friar

Gwenwynwyn withdrew from the feasts of his hall :
He slept very little, he prayed not at all :
He pondered, and wandered, and studied alone ;
And sought, night and day, the philosopher's stone.

He found it at length, and he made its first proof
By turning to gold all the lead of his roof :
Then he bought some magnanimous heroes, all fire,
Who lived but to smite and be smitten for hire.

With these on the plains like a torrent he broke ;
He filled the whole country with flame and with smoke ;
He killed all the swine, and he broached all the wine ;
He drove off the sheep, and the beeves, and the kine ;

He took castles and towns ; he cut short limbs and lives ;
He made orphans and widows of children and wives :
This course many years he triumphantly ran,
And did mischief enough to be called a great man.

When, at last, he had gained all for which he had striven,
He bethought him of buying a passport to heaven ;
Good and great as he was, yet he did not well know,
How soon, or which way, his great spirit might go.

He sought the grey friars, who beside a wild stream,
Refected their frames on a primitive scheme ;
The gravest and wisest Gwenwynwyn found out,
All lonely and ghostly, and angling for trout.

Below the white dash of a mighty cascade,
Where a pool of the stream a deep resting-place made,
And rock-rooted oaks stretched their branches on high,
The friar stood musing, and throwing his fly.

To him said Gwenwynwyn, ' Hold, father, here 's store,
For the good of the church, and the good of the poor ' ;
Then he gave him the stone ; but, ere more he could speak,
Wrath came on the friar, so holy and meek.

He had stretched forth his hand to receive the red gold,
And he thought himself mocked by Gwenwynwyn the Bold ;
And in scorn of the gift, and in rage at the giver,
He jerked it immediately into the river.

Gwenwynwyn, aghast, not a syllable spake ;
The philosopher's stone made a duck and a drake ;
Two systems of circles a moment were seen,
And the stream smoothed them off, as they never had been.

Gwenwynwyn regained, and uplifted his voice,
' Oh friar, grey friar, full rash was thy choice ;
The stone, the good stone, which away thou hast thrown,
Was the stone of all stones, the philosopher's stone.'

The friar looked pale, when his error he knew ;
The friar looked red, and the friar looked blue ;
And heels over head, from the point of a rock,
He plunged, without stopping to pull off his frock.

He dived very deep, but he dived all in vain,
The prize he had slighted he found not again ;
Many times did the friar his diving renew,
And deeper and deeper the river still grew.

Gwenwynwyn gazed long, of his senses in doubt,
To see the grey friar a diver so stout ;
Then sadly and slowly his castle he sought,
And left the friar diving, like dabchick distraught.

Gwenwynwyn fell sick with alarm and despite,
Died, and went to the devil, the very same night ;
The magnanimous heroes he held in his pay
Sacked his castle, and marched with the plunder away.

No knell on the silence of midnight was rolled
For the flight of the soul of Gwenwynwyn the Bold.
The brethren, unfeed, let the mighty ghost pass,
Without praying a prayer, or intoning a mass.

The friar haunted ever beside the dark stream ;
The philosopher's stone was his thought and his dream :
And day after day, ever head under heels
He dived all the time he could spare from his meals.

He dived, and he dived, to the end of his days,
As the peasants oft witnessed with fear and amaze.
The mad friar's diving-place long was their theme,
And no plummet can fathom that pool of the stream.

And still, when light clouds on the midnight winds ride,
If by moonlight you stray on the lone river-side,
The ghost of the friar may be seen diving there,
With head in the water, and heels in the air.

T. L. PEACOCK.

234. THE VICAR

SOME years ago, ere time and taste
  Had turned our parish topsy-turvy,
When Darnel Park was Darnel Waste,
  And roads as little known as scurvy,
The man who lost his way, between
  St. Mary's Hill and Sandy Thicket,
Was always shown across the green,
  And guided to the Parson's wicket.

Back flew the bolt of lissom lath;
  Fair Margaret, in her tidy kirtle,
Led the lorn traveller up the path,
  Through clean-clipt rows of box and myrtle;
And Don and Sancho, Tramp and Tray,
  Upon the parlour steps collected,
Wagged all their tails, and seemed to say—
  ' Our master knows you—you're expected.'

Uprose the Reverend Dr. Brown,
  Uprose the Doctor's winsome marrow;
The lady laid her knitting down,
  Her husband clasped his ponderous Barrow;
Whate'er the stranger's caste or creed,
  Pundit or Papist, saint or sinner,
He found a stable for his steed,
  And welcome for himself, and dinner.

If, when he reached his journey's end,
  And warmed himself in Court or College,
He had not gained an honest friend
  And twenty curious scraps of knowledge,—
If he departed as he came,
  With no new light on love or liquor,—
Good sooth, the traveller was to blame,
  And not the Vicarage, nor the Vicar.

His talk was like a spring, which runs
  With rapid change from rocks to roses:
It slipped from politics to puns,
  It passed from Mahomet to Moses;

Beginning with the laws which keep
   The planets in their radiant courses,
And ending with some precept deep
   For dressing eels, or shoeing horses.

He was a shrewd and sound Divine,
   Of loud Dissent the mortal terror ;
And when, by dint of page and line,
   He 'stablished Truth, or startled Error,
The Baptist found him far too deep ;
   The Deist sighed with saving sorrow ;
And the lean Levite went to sleep,
   And dreamed of tasting pork to-morrow.

His sermons never said or showed
   That Earth is foul, that Heaven is gracious,
Without refreshment on the road
   From Jerome or from Athanasius :
And sure a righteous zeal inspired
   The hand and head that penned and planned them,
For all who understood admired,
   And some who did not understand them.

He wrote, too, in a quiet way,
   Small treatises, and smaller verses,
And sage remarks on chalk and clay,
   And hints to noble Lords—and nurses ;
True histories of last year's ghost,
   Lines to a ringlet, or a turban,
And trifles for the *Morning Post*,
   And nothings for Sylvanus Urban.

He did not think all mischief fair,
   Although he had a knack of joking ;
He did not make himself a bear,
   Although he had a taste for smoking ;
And when religious sects ran mad,
   He held, in spite of all his learning,
That if a man's belief is bad,
   It will not be improved by burning.

And he was kind, and loved to sit
   In the low hut or garnished cottage,
And praise the farmer's homely wit,
   And share the widow's homelier pottage :
At his approach complaint grew mild ;
   And when his hand unbarred the shutter,
The clammy lips of fever smiled
   The welcome which they could not utter.

He always had a tale for me
  Of Julius Caesar, or of Venus ;
From him I learnt the rule of three,
  Cat's cradle, leap-frog, and *Quae genus :*
I used to singe his powdered wig,
  To steal the staff he put such trust in,
And make the puppy dance a jig,
  When he began to quote Augustine.

Alack the change ! in vain I look
  For haunts in which my boyhood trifled,—
The level lawn, the trickling brook,
  The trees I climbed, the beds I rifled :
The church is larger than before ;
  You reach it by a carriage entry ;
It holds three hundred people more,
  And pews are fitted up for gentry.

Sit in the Vicar's seat : you'll hear
  The doctrine of a gentle Johnian,
Whose hand is white, whose tone is clear,
  Whose phrase is very Ciceronian.
Where is the old man laid ?—look down,
  And construe on the slab before you,
  Hic jacet Gvlielmvs Brown,
  Vir nullâ non donandus lauru.'

                                    W. M. Praed.

235. THE COUNTRY CLERGYMAN'S TRIP
TO CAMBRIDGE

An Election Ballad, 1827

As I sat down to breakfast in state,
  At my living of Tithing-cum-Boring,
With Betty beside me to wait,
  Came a rap that almost beat the door in.
I laid down my basin of tea,
  And Betty ceased spreading the toast,
' As sure as a gun, sir,' said she,
  ' That must be the knock of the post.'

A letter—and free—bring it here—
  I have no correspondent who franks.
No ! yes ! can it be ? Why, my dear,
  'Tis our glorious, our Protestant Bankes.

' Dear sir, as I know you desire
    That the Church should receive due protection,
I humbly presume to require
    Your aid at the Cambridge election.

' It has lately been brought to my knowledge,
    That the Ministers fully design
To suppress each cathedral and college,
    And eject every learned divine.
To assist this detestable scheme
    Three nuncios from Rome are come over ;
They left Calais on Monday by steam,
    And landed to dinner at Dover.

' An army of grim Cordeliers,
    Well furnished with relics and vermin,
Will follow, Lord Westmoreland fears,
    To effect what their chiefs may determine.
Lollards' Tower, good authorities say,
    Is again fitting up as a prison ;
And a wood-merchant told me to-day
    'Tis a wonder how faggots have risen.

' The finance scheme of Canning contains
    A new Easter-offering tax ;
And he means to devote all the gains
    To a bounty on thumb-screws and racks.
Your living, so neat and compact—
    Pray, don't let the news give you pain !—
Is promised, I know for a fact,
    To an olive-faced Padre from Spain.'

I read, and I felt my heart bleed,
    Sore wounded with horror and pity ;
So I flew, with all possible speed,
    To our Protestant champion's committee.
True gentlemen, kind and well-bred !
    No fleering ! no distance ! no scorn !
They asked after my wife, who is dead,
    And my children who never were born.

They then, like high-principled Tories,
    Called our Sovereign unjust and unsteady,
And assailed him with scandalous stories,
    Till the coach for the voters was ready.
That coach might be well called a casket
    Of learning and brotherly love :
There were parsons in boot and in basket ;
    There were parsons below and above.

There were Sneaker and Griper, a pair
    Who stick to Lord Mulesby like leeches ;
A smug chaplain of plausible air,
    Who writes my Lord Goslingham's speeches ;
Dr. Buzz, who alone is a host,
    Who, with arguments weighty as lead,
Proves six times a week in the *Post*
    That flesh somehow differs from bread ;

Dr. Nimrod, whose orthodox toes
    Are seldom withdrawn from the stirrup ;
Dr. Humdrum, whose eloquence flows,
    Like droppings of sweet poppy syrup ;
Dr. Rosygill puffing and fanning,
    And wiping away perspiration ;
Dr. Humbug, who proved Mr. Canning
    The beast in St. John's Revelation.

A layman can scarce form a notion
    Of our wonderful talk on the road ;
Of the learning, the wit, and devotion,
    Which almost each syllable showed :
Why divided allegiance agrees
    So ill with our free constitution ;
How Catholics swear as they please,
    In hope of the priest's absolution ;

How the Bishop of Norwich had bartered
    His faith for a legate's commission ;
How Lyndhurst, afraid to be martyred,
    Had stooped to a base coalition ;
How Papists are cased from compassion
    By bigotry, stronger than steel ;
How burning would soon come in fashion,
    And how very bad it must feel.

We were all so much touched and excited
    By a subject so direly sublime,
That the rules of politeness were slighted,
    And we all of us talked at a time ;
And in tones, which each moment grew louder,
    Told how we should dress for the show,
And where we should fasten the powder,
    And if we should bellow or no.

Thus from subject to subject we ran,
  And the journey passed pleasantly o'er,
Till at last Dr. Humdrum began ;
  From that time I remember no more.
At Ware he commenced his prelection,
  In the dullest of clerical drones :
And when next I regained recollection
  We were rumbling o'er Trumpington stones.

THOMAS, LORD MACAULAY.

236. AT THE CHURCH GATE

ALTHOUGH I enter not,
  Yet round about the spot
    Oft-times I hover ;
And near the sacred gate,
With longing eyes I wait,
    Expectant of her.

The Minster bell tolls out
Above the city's rout
    And noise and humming :
They've hushed the Minster bell :
The organ 'gins to swell :
    She's coming, she's coming !

My lady comes at last,
Timid, and stepping fast,
    And hastening hither,
With modest eyes downcast :
She comes—she's here—she's passed—
    May Heaven go with her !

Kneel, undisturbed, fair Saint !
Pour out your praise or plaint
    Meekly and duly ;
I will not enter there,
To sully your pure prayer
    With thoughts unruly.

But suffer me to pace
Round the forbidden place,
    Lingering a minute,
Like outcast spirits who wait
And see through heaven's gate
    Angels within it.

W. M. THACKERAY.

†

237. THE POPE AND THE NET

WHAT, he on whom our voices unanimously ran,
Made Pope at our last Conclave ?   Full low his life began :
His father earned the daily bread as just a fisherman.

So much the more his boy minds book, gives proof of mother-wit,
Becomes first Deacon, and then Priest, then Bishop : see him sit
No less than Cardinal ere long, while no one cries ' Unfit ! '

But some one smirks, some other smiles, jogs elbow and nods head :
Each winks at each : ' 'I-faith, a rise ! Saint Peter's net, instead
Of sword and keys, is come in vogue ! '   You think he blushes red ?

Not he, of humble holy heart ! ' Unworthy me ! ' he sighs :
' From fisher's drudge to Church's prince—it is indeed a rise :
So, here 's the way to keep the fact for ever in my eyes ! '

And straightway in his palace-hall, where commonly is set
Some coat-of-arms, some portraiture ancestral, lo, we met
His mean estate's reminder in his fisher-father's net !

Which step conciliates all and some, stops cavil in a trice :
' The humble holy heart that holds of new-born pride no spice !
He 's just the saint to choose for Pope ! '   Each adds ' 'Tis my advice'

So, Pope he was : and when we flocked—its sacred slipper on—
To kiss his foot, we lifted eyes, alack the thing was gone—
That guarantee of lowlihead,—eclipsed that star which shone !

Each eyed his fellow, one and all kept silence.   I cried ' Pish !
I'll make me spokesman for the rest, express the common wish.
Why, Father, is the net removed ? '   ' Son, it hath caught the fish.'

R. BROWNING.

From *Asolando*.   By permission of Messrs. Smith, Elder & Co.

238. THE LATEST DECALOGUE

THOU shalt have one God only ; who
Would be at the expense of two ?
No graven images may be
Worshipped, except the currency :
Swear not at all ; for, for thy curse
Thine enemy is none the worse :
At church on Sunday to attend
Will serve to keep the world thy friend :
Honour thy parents ; that is, all
From whom advancement may befall :
Thou shalt not kill ; but need'st not strive
Officiously to keep alive :

Do not adultery commit ;
Advantage rarely comes of it :
Thou shalt not steal ; an empty feat,
When it's so lucrative to cheat :
Bear not false witness ; let the lie
Have time on its own wings to fly :
Thou shalt not covet, but tradition
Approves all forms of competition.

A. H. CLOUGH.

239. HYPOCRISY

HYPOCRISY will serve as well
To propagate a church, as zeal ;
As persecution and promotion
Do equally advance devotion ;
So round white stones will serve, they say,
As well as eggs to make hens lay.

S. BUTLER.

240. SAPPHICS
THE FRIEND OF HUMANITY AND THE KNIFE-GRINDER

Friend of Humanity

NEEDY Knife-grinder ! whither are you going ?
Rough is the road, your wheel is out of order—
Bleak blows the blast ;—your hat has got a hole in't,
            So have your breeches.

Weary Knife-grinder ! little think the proud ones
Who in their coaches roll along the turnpike-
Road, what hard work 'tis crying all day, ' Knives and
            Scissors to grind O ! '

Tell me, Knife-grinder, how you came to grind knives :
Did some rich man tyrannically use you ?
Was it the 'Squire ? or Parson of the Parish ?
            Or the Attorney ?

Was it the 'Squire, for killing of his game ? or
Covetous Parson, for his tithes distraining ?
Or roguish Lawyer, made you lose your little
            All in a lawsuit ?

(Have you not read the Rights of Man, by Tom Paine ?)
Drops of compassion tremble on my eyelids,
Ready to fall, as soon as you have told your
            Pitiful story.

Knife-grinder

Story ! God bless you ! I have none to tell, Sir,
Only last night a-drinking at the ' Chequers ',
This poor old hat and breeches, as you see, were
        Torn in a scuffle.

Constables came up for to take me into
Custody ; they took me before the justice ;
Justice Oldmixon put me in the parish-
        Stocks for a vagrant.

I should be glad to drink your Honour's health in
A Pot of Beer, if you will give me Sixpence ;
But for my part, I never love to meddle
        With politics, Sir.

Friend of Humanity

I give thee Sixpence !   I will see thee damned first—
Wretch ! whom no sense of wrongs can rouse to vengeance—
Sordid, unfeeling, reprobate, degraded,
        Spiritless outcast !

(*Kicks the Knife-grinder, overturns his wheel, and exit in a transport*
of Republican Enthusiasm and Universal Philanthropy.)
        G. CANNING AND J. H. FRERE.

241. A POLITICAL DISPATCH

IN matters of commerce the fault of the Dutch
Is offering too little and asking too much.
The French are with equal advantage content,
So we clap on Dutch bottoms just 20 per cent.
    20 per cent, 20 per cent,
We clap on Dutch bottoms just 20 per cent.
Vous frapperez Falck avec 20 per cent.
        G. CANNING.

242. PADDY'S METAMORPHOSIS

ABOUT fifty years since, in the days of our daddies,
   That plan was commenced which the wise now applaud,
Of shipping off Ireland's most turbulent Paddies,
   As good raw material for *settlers*, abroad.

Some West Indian Island, whose name I forget,
   Was the reason then chosen for this scheme so romantic ;
And such the success the first colony met,
   That a second, soon after, set sail o'er the Atlantic.

Behold them now safe at the long looked-for shore,
  Sailing in between banks that the Shannon might greet,
And thinking of friends whom, but two years before,
  They had sorrowed to lose, but would soon again meet.

And, hark ! from the shore a glad welcome there came—
  ' Arrah, Paddy from Cork, is it you, my sweet boy ? '
While Pat stood astounded to hear his own name
  Thus hailed by black devils, who capered for joy !

Can it possibly be ?—half amazement—half doubt,
  Pat listens again—rubs his eyes and looks steady ;
Then heaves a deep sigh, and in horror yells out,
  ' Good Lord ! only think—black and curly already !

Deceived by the well-mimicked brogue in his ears,
  Pat read his own doom in these wool-headed figures,
And thought, what a climate, in less than two years,
  To turn a whole cargo of Pats into niggers !

MORAL

'Tis thus,—but alas !—by a moral more true
  Than is told in this rival of Ovid's best stories,—
Your Whigs, when in office a short year or two,
  By a *lusus naturae*, all turn into Tories.

And thus, when I hear them ' strong measures ' advise,
  Ere the seats that they sit on have time to get steady,
I say, while I listen, with tears in my eyes,
  ' Good Lord !—only think—black and curly already ! '

T. MOORE.

243. STANZAS TO THE SPEAKER ASLEEP

SLEEP, Mr. Speaker ; it 's surely fair
If you don't in your bed, that you should in your chair.
Longer and longer still they grow,
Tory and Radical, Aye and No ;
Talking by night, and talking by day ;—
Sleep, Mr. Speaker ; sleep, sleep while you may !

Sleep, Mr. Speaker ; slumber lies
Light and brief on a Speaker's eyes ;
Fielden or Finn, in a minute or two,
Some disorderly thing will do ;
Riot will chase repose away ;—
Sleep, Mr. Speaker ; sleep, sleep while you may !

Sleep, Mr. Speaker ; Cobbett will soon
Move to abolish the sun and moon ;
Hume, no doubt, will be taking the sense
Of the House on a saving of thirteen pence ;
Grattan will growl, or Baldwin bray ;—
Sleep, Mr. Speaker ; sleep, sleep while you may !

Sleep, Mr. Speaker ; dream of the time
When loyalty was not quite a crime ;
When Grant was a pupil in Canning's school,
When Palmerston fancied Wood a fool ;
Lord, how principles pass away !
Sleep, Mr. Speaker ; sleep, sleep while you may !

Sleep, Mr. Speaker ; sweet to men
Is the sleep that cometh but now and then ;
Sweet to the sorrowful, sweet to the ill,
Sweet to the children that work in a mill,
You have more need of sleep than they ;—
Sleep, Mr. Speaker ; sleep, sleep while you may !

W. M. PRAED.

244. A POLITICAL ALLEGORY

ONCE there was a famous nation
    With a long and glorious past :
Very splendid was its station,
    And its territory vast ;
It had won the approbation,
The applause and admiration,
Of the states who'd had occasion,
In a time of tribulation,
And of disorganization,
Not to mention degradation,
And profound humiliation,
    To observe it standing fast
Without any trepidation,
Or a sign of vacillation,
    Firm and faithful to the last.

Came a time of dire distraction,
    Full of terror and despair,
When a delicate transaction
    Called for unexampled care ;
But the people were directed,
Both the well and ill-affected,
To a wholly unexpected
And surprising course of action,
    Based on motives new and rare
(Being governed by a faction,
    As they generally were).

In a little time the nation
   Had a chance of saying whether
It and its administration
   Seemed inclined to pull together :
And it spoke its mind with vigour :—
   ' Such disgraceful conduct must
Everlastingly disfigure
   Future annals, and disgust
Evermore the candid student :
You have been unwise, imprudent,
   Pusillanimous, unjust,
And neglectful of the glory
   Appertaining to our name
Till this melancholy story
   Put a period to our fame.'

So this faction, disappointed,
   Lost the national good graces,
And their rivals were anointed,
   And were set in the high places.

Pretty soon arose conditions
   Most embarrassing and hard,
And the party politicians
   Had to be upon their guard.
Illegitimate ambitions,
Democratic rhetoricians,
Persons prone to base submissions,
Men of warlike dispositions,
Wild and wicked statisticians,
Metaphysical magicians,
People apt to sign petitions,
Men inclined to make conditions,
   And a host of wary foes,
Compassed round the ruling faction :
But a certain line of action
   They incontinently chose :
And with great determination,
And extreme discrimination,
Not untouched by exaltation,
After proper preparation,
And profound examination,
Wrought it out with acclamation,
And each other's approbation,
Till the national taxation
   Not unnaturally rose.

To the nation now occurred an
   Opportunity of saying
What they thought about the burden
   Which the government was laying

On their shoulders : and they said it
  In uncompromising terms :—
' Your behaviour would discredit
  Tigers, crocodiles, or worms :
You have ruined and disgraced us,
And successfully effaced us
From the proud commanding station
Where the zeal and penetration
  Of our ancestors had placed us.
Go ! we are a ruined nation ;
  But before our dissolution
We pronounce your condemnation—
  Sappers of our constitution,
Slayers of our reputation ! '

But the nation—mark the moral,
  For its value is untold—
During each successive quarrel
  Grew and prospered as of old.

J. K. STEPHEN.

245. TO LUCASTA, ON GOING TO THE WARS

TELL me not, Sweet, I am unkind
  That from the nunnery
Of thy chaste breast and quiet mind,
  To war and arms I fly.

True, a new mistress now I chase,
  The first foe in the field ;
And with a stronger faith embrace
  A sword, a horse, a shield.

Yet this inconstancy is such
  As you too shall adore ;
I could not love thee, Dear, so much,
  Loved I not Honour more.

R. LOVELACE.

246. THE SOLDIER GOING TO THE FIELD

PRESERVE thy sighs, unthrifty girl,
  To purify the air,
Thy tears to thread, instead of pearl,
  On bracelets of thy hair.

The trumpet makes the echo hoarse,
  And wakes the louder drum :
Expense of grief gains no remorse
  When sorrow should be dumb.

For I must go where lazy Peace
  Will hide her drowsy head,
And, for the sport of kings, increase
  The number of the dead.

But, first, I'll chide thy cruel theft :
  Can I in war delight,
Who (being of my heart bereft)
  Can have no heart to fight ?

Thou know'st, the sacred laws of old
  Ordained a thief should pay,
To quit him of his theft, sevenfold
  What he had stolen away.

Thy payment shall but double be ;
  O then with speed resign
My own seducèd heart to me,
  Accompanied with thine.

                              SIR W. DAVENANT.

247. A PARAPHRASE FROM THE FRENCH

IN grey-haired Celia's withered arms
  As mighty Louis lay,
She cried ' If I have any charms,
  My dearest, let's away !
For you, my love, is all my fear,
  Hark how the drums do rattle ;
Alas, sir ! what should you do here
  In dreadful day of battle ?
Let little Orange stay and fight,
  For danger 's his diversion ;
The wise will think you in the right,
  Not to expose your person :
Nor vex your thoughts how to repair
  The ruins of your glory :

You ought to leave so mean a care
    To those who pen your story.
Are not Boileau and Corneille paid
    For panegyric writing ?
They know how heroes may be made,
    Without the help of fighting.
When foes too saucily approach,
    'Tis best to leave them fairly ;
Put six good horses in your coach,
    And carry me to Marly.
Let Bouflers, to secure your fame,
    Go take some town, or buy it ;
Whilst you, great sir, at Notre Dame,
    Te Deum sing in quiet ! '

M. PRIOR.

248. THE GRAND QUESTION DEBATED

WHETHER HAMILTON'S BAWN SHOULD BE TURNED INTO A BARRACK
OR A MALT-HOUSE (1729)

THUS spoke to my lady the knight full of care :
' Let me have your advice in a weighty affair.
This Hamilton's Bawn, whilst it sticks on my hand,
I lose by the house what I get by the land ;
But how to dispose of it to the best bidder,
For a *barrack* or *malt-house*, we now must consider.
    ' First, let me suppose I make it a malt-house,
Here I have computed the profit will fall t 'us ;
There 's nine hundred pounds for labour and grain,
I increase it to twelve, so three hundred remain ;
A handsome addition for wine and good cheer,
Three dishes a day, and three hogsheads a year :
With a dozen large vessels my vault shall be stored,
No little scrub joint shall come on to my board :
And you and the dean no more shall combine
To stint me at night to one bottle of wine ;
Nor shall I, for his humour, permit you to purloin
A stone and a quarter of beef from my sirloin.
If I make it a barrack, the Crown is my tenant ;
My dear, I have pondered again and again on 't ;
In poundage and drawbacks I lose half my rent ;
Whatever they give me I must be content,
Or join with the Court in every debate ;
And rather than that I would lose my estate.'
    Thus ended the knight : thus began his meek wife ;
' It *must* and it *shall* be a barrack, my life.

I'm grown a mere mopus ; no company comes
But a rabble of tenants and rusty dull Rums.
With parsons what lady can keep herself clean ?
I'm all over daubed when I sit by the dean.
But if you will give us a barrack, my dear,
The captain, I'm sure, will always come here ;
I then shall not value his deanship a straw,
For the captain, I warrant, will keep him in awe ;
Or, should he pretend to be brisk and alert,
Will tell him that chaplains should not be so pert ;
That men of his coat should be minding their prayers,
And not among ladies to give themselves airs.'

　　Thus argued my lady, but argued in vain ;
The knight his opinion resolved to maintain.

　　But Hannah, who listened to all that was passed
And could not endure so vulgar a taste,
As soon as her ladyship called to be dressed,
Cried, ' Madam, why surely my master 's possessed,
Sir Arthur the maltster !　How fine it will sound !
I'd rather the bawn were sunk under ground.
But, madam, I guessed there would never come good,
When I saw him so often with Darby and Wood.
And now my dream 's out ; for I was a-dreamed
That I saw a huge rat ; O dear, how I screamed !
And after, methought I had lost my new shoes ;
And Molly, she said, I should hear some ill news.

　　' Dear madam, had you but the spirit to tease
You might have a barrack whenever you please ;
And, madam, I always believed you so stout
That for twenty denials you would not give out.
If I had a husband like him, I *pur*test,
Till he gave me my will, I would give him no rest ;
And rather than come in the same pair of sheets
With such a cross man, I would lie in the streets :
But, madam, I beg you, contrive and invent,
And worry him out, till he gives his consent.
Dear madam, whene'er of a barrack I think,
An I were to be hanged I can't sleep a wink :
For if a new crotchet comes into my brain,
I can't get it out, though I'd never so fain.
I fancy already a barrack contrived
At Hamilton's Bawn, and the troop is arrived ;
Of this, to be sure, Sir Arthur has warning,
And waits on the captain betimes the next morning.
Now see when they meet how their honours behave,
" Noble captain, your servant "—" Sir Arthur, your slave " ;
" You honour me much "—" the honour is mine "—
" 'Twas a sad rainy night "—" but the morning is fine."

" Pray how does my lady ? "—" My wife 's at your service."
" I think I have seen her picture by Jervis."
" Good morrow, good captain "—" I'll wait on you down "—
" You shan't stir a foot "—" you'll think me a clown "—
" For all the world, captain, not half an inch farther "—
" You must be obeyed—your servant, Sir Arthur ;
My humble respects to my lady unknown "—
" I hope you will use my house as your own."
    ' Go bring me my smock, and leave off your prate,
Thou hast certainly gotten a cup in thy pate.'
' Pray, madam, be quiet : what was it I said
You had like to have put quite out of my head.

    ' Next day, to be sure, the captain will come
At the head of his troop, with trumpet and drum ;
Now, madam, observe how he marches in state ;
The man with the kettle-drum enters the gate ;
Dub, dub, adub, dub.   The trumpeters follow,
Tantara, tantara ; while all the boys hallo.
See now comes the captain all daubed with gold lace ;
O, la ! the sweet gentleman, look in his face ;
And see how he rides like a lord of the land,
With the fine flaming sword that he holds in his hand ;
And his horse, the dear *creter*, it prances and rears,
With ribbons in knots at its tail and its ears ;
At last comes the troop, by the word of command,
Drawn up in our Court, when the captain cries, Stand !
Your ladyship lifts up the sash to be seen,
(For sure I had dizened you out like a queen) ;
The captain, to show he is proud of the favour,
Looks up to your window, and cocks up his beaver
(His beaver is cocked ; pray, madam, mark that,
For a captain of horse never takes off his hat ;
Because he has never a hand that is idle,
For the right holds the sword, and the left holds the bridle) ;
Then flourishes thrice his sword in the air,
As a compliment due to a lady so fair
(How I tremble to think of the blood it has spilt);
Then he lowers down the point, and kisses the hilt.
Your ladyship smiles, and thus you begin :
" Pray, captain, be pleased to alight and walk in."
The captain salutes you with congee profound,
And your ladyship curtsies halfway to the ground.
" Kit, run to your master, and bid him come to us ;
I'm sure he'll be proud of the honour you do us.
And, captain, you'll do us the favour to stay,
And take a short dinner here with us to-day ;
You're heartily welcome ; but as for good cheer,
You come in the very worst time of the year.

If I had expected so worthy a guest "——
" Lord, madam ! your ladyship sure is in jest ;
You banter me, madam, the kingdom must grant "——
" You officers, captain, are so complaisant." '
' Hist, hussy, I think I hear somebody coming ! '
' No, madam ! 'tis only Sir Arthur a-humming.
To shorten my tale (for I hate a long story)
The captain at dinner appears in his glory ;
The dean and the doctor have humbled their pride,
For the captain 's entreated to sit by your side ;
And, because he 's their betters, you carve for him first,
The parsons for envy are ready to burst ;
The servants amazed are scarce ever able
To keep off their eyes as they wait at the table ;
And Molly and I have thrust in our nose
To peep at the captain in all his fine clo'es ;
Dear madam, be sure he 's a fine-spoken man,
Do but hear on the clergy how glib his tongue ran :
And " Madam," says he, " if such dinners you give,
You'll ne'er want for parsons as long as you live ;
I ne'er knew a parson without a good nose,
But the devil 's as welcome wherever he goes ;
—— —— —— , they bid us reform and repent,
But z—s, by their looks they never keep Lent ;
Mister Curate, for all your grave looks, I'm afraid
You cast a sheep's eye on her ladyship's maid ;
I wish she would lend you her pretty white hand
In mending your cassock, and smoothing your band "
(For the dean was so shabby, and looked like a ninny,
That the captain supposed he was curate to Jinny),
" Whenever you see a cassock and gown,
A hundred to one but it covers a clown ;
Observe how a parson comes into a room,
—— —— —— , he hobbles as bad as my groom ;
A scholard, when just from his college broke loose,
Can hardly tell how to cry *Bo* to a goose ;
Your *Noveds*, and *Bluturks*, and *Omurs*, and stuff,
By ——, they don't signify this pinch of snuff.
To give a young gentleman right education,
The Army 's the only good school in the nation ;
My schoolmaster called me a dunce and a fool,
But at cuffs I was always the cock of the school ;
I never could take to my book for the blood o' me,
And the puppy confessed he expected no good of me.
He caught me one morning coquetting his wife,
And he mauled me ; I ne'er was so mauled in my life ;
So I took to the road, and, what 's very odd,
The first man I robbed was a parson, by G——.

Now, madam, you'll think it a strange thing to say,
But the sight of a book makes me sick to this day."
'Never since I was born did I hear so much wit,
And, madam, I laughed till I thought I should split.
So then you looked scornful, and sniffed at the dean,
As who should say, *Now, am I skinny and lean?*
But he durst not so much as once open his lips,
And the doctor was plaguily down in the hips.'
  Thus merciless Hannah ran on in her talk,
Till she heard the dean call 'Will your ladyship walk?'
Her ladyship answers, 'I'm just coming down,'
Then, turning to Hannah, and forcing a frown,
Although it was plain in her heart she was glad,
Cried, 'Hussy, why sure the wench has gone mad;
How could these chimeras get into your brains?
Come hither, and take this old gown for your pains.
But the dean, if this secret should come to his ears,
Will never have done with his jibes and his jeers.
For your life not a word of the matter, I charge ye,
Give me but a barrack; a fig for the clergy.'

J. SWIFT.

249. THE WAR SONG OF DINAS VAWR

THE mountain sheep are sweeter,
But the valley sheep are fatter;
We therefore deemed it meeter
To carry off the latter.
We made an expedition;
We met a host and quelled it;
We forced a strong position,
And killed the men who held it.

On Dyfed's richest valley,
Where herds of kine were browsing,
We made a mighty sally,
To furnish our carousing.
Fierce warriors rushed to meet us;
We met them, and o'erthrew them:
They struggled hard to beat us;
But we conquered them, and slew them.

As we drove our prize at leisure,
The king marched forth to catch us:
His rage surpassed all measure,
But his people could not match us.

He fled to his hall-pillars ;
And, ere our force we led off,
Some sacked his house and cellars,
While others cut his head off.

We there, in strife bewildering,
Spilt blood enough to swim in :
We orphaned many children,
And widowed many women.
The eagles and the ravens
We glutted with our foemen :
The heroes and the cravens,
The spearmen and the bowmen.

We brought away from battle,
And much their land bemoaned them,
Two thousand head of cattle,
And the head of him who owned them :
Ednyfed, King of Dyfed,
His head was borne before us ;
His wine and beasts supplied our feasts,
And his overthrow, our chorus.

                                    T. L. PEACOCK.

250. MARS DISARMED BY LOVE

AYE, bear it hence, thou blessèd child,
    Though dire the burthen be,
And hide it in the pathless wild,
    Or drown it in the sea :
The ruthless murderer prays and swears ;
    So let him swear and pray ;
Be deaf to all his oaths and prayers,
    And take the sword away.

We've had enough of fleets and camps,
    Guns, glories, odes, gazettes,
Triumphal arches, coloured lamps,
    Huzzas and epaulettes ;
We could not bear upon our head
    Another leaf of bay ;
That horrid Buonaparte 's dead ;—
    Yes, take the sword away.

We're weary of the noisy boasts
    That pleased our patriot throngs :
We've long been dull to Gooch's toasts,
    And tame to Dibdin's songs ;

We're quite content to rule the wave,
　　Without a great display ;
We're known to be extremely brave ;
　　But take the sword away.

We give a shrug, when fife and drum
　　Play up a favourite air ;
We think our barracks are become
　　More ugly than they were ;
We laugh to see the banners float ;
　　We loathe the charger's bray ;
We don't admire a scarlet coat ;
　　Do take the sword away.

Let Portugal have rulers twain ;
　　Let Greece go on with none ;
Let Popery sink or swim in Spain,
　　While we enjoy the fun ;
Let Turkey tremble at the knout ;
　　Let Algiers lose her Dey ;
Let Paris turn her Bourbons out ;—
　　Bah ! take the sword away.

Our honest friends in Parliament
　　Are looking vastly sad ;
Our farmers say with one consent
　　It 's all immensely bad ;
There was a time for borrowing,
　　But now it 's time to pay ;
A budget is a serious thing ;
　　So take the sword away.

And O, the bitter tears we wept,
　　In those our days of fame,—
The dread, that o'er our heart-strings crept
　　With every post that came,—
The home-affections, waged and lost
　　In every far-off fray,—
The price that British glory cost !
　　Ah ! take the sword away.

We've plenty left to hoist the sail,
　　Or mount the dangerous breach ;
And Freedom breathes in every gale,
　　That wanders round our beach.
When duty bids us dare or die,
　　We'll fight another day :
But till we know a reason why,
　　Take, take the sword away.

W. M. PRAED.

251. FAITHLESS NELLY GRAY

A Pathetic Ballad

Ben Battle was a soldier bold,
　And used to war's alarms ;
But a cannon-ball took off his legs,
　So he laid down his arms !

Now as they bore him off the field,
　Said he, ' Let others shoot,
For here I leave my second leg,
　And the Forty-second Foot ! '

The army-surgeons made him limbs :
　Said he :—' They're only pegs :
But there 's as wooden members quite
　As represent my legs ! '

Now Ben he loved a pretty maid,
　Her name was Nelly Gray ;
So he went to pay her his devours
　When he'd devoured his pay !

But when he called on Nelly Gray,
　She made him quite a scoff ;
And when she saw his wooden legs,
　Began to take them off !

' O, Nelly Gray ! O, Nelly Gray !
　Is this your love so warm ?
The love that loves a scarlet coat
　Should be more uniform ! '

Said she, ' I loved a soldier once,
　For he was blythe and brave ;
But I will never have a man
　With both legs in the grave !

' Before you had those timber toes,
　Your love I did allow,
But then, you know, you stand upon
　Another footing now ! '

' O, Nelly Gray ! O, Nelly Gray !
　For all your jeering speeches,
At duty's call, I left my legs
　In Badajos's *breaches !* '

' Why then,' said she, ' you've lost the feet
    Of legs in war's alarms,
And now you cannot wear your shoes
    Upon your feats of arms ! '

' O, false and fickle Nelly Gray ;
    I know why you refuse :—
Though I've no feet—some other man
    Is standing in my shoes !

' I wish I ne'er had seen your face ;
    But, now, a long farewell !
For you will be my death ;—alas !
    You will not be my *Nell !* '

Now when he went from Nelly Gray,
    His heart so heavy got—
And life was such a burthen grown,
    It made him take a knot !

So round his melancholy neck,
    A rope he did entwine,
And, for his second time in life,
    Enlisted in the Line !

One end he tied around a beam,
    And then removed his pegs,
And, as his legs were off,—of course,
    He soon was off his legs !

And there he hung, till he was dead
    As any nail in town,—
For though distress had cut him up,
    It could not cut him down !

A dozen men sat on his corpse,
    To find out why he died—
And they buried Ben in four cross-roads,
    With a *stake* in his inside !

                       T. HOOD.

252. THE SUPERIORITY OF MACHINERY

A MECHANIC his labour will often discard
    If the rate of his pay he dislikes ;
But a clock—and its *case* is uncommonly hard—
    Will continue to work though it *strikes*.

                       T. HOOD.

253. THE YANKEE VOLUNTEERS

Ye Yankee volunteers !
It makes my bosom bleed
When I your story read,
    Though oft 'tis told one.
So—in both hemispheres
The women are untrue,
And cruel in the New,
    As in the Old one !

What—in this company
Of sixty sons of Mars,
Who march 'neath Stripes and Stars,
    With fife and horn,
Nine-tenths of all we see
Along the warlike line
Had but one cause to join
    This Hope Forlorn ?

Deserters from the realm
Where tyrant Venus reigns,
You slipped her wicked chains,
    Fled and out-ran her.
And now, with sword and helm,
Together banded are
Beneath the Stripe and Star-
    Embroidered banner !

And is it so with all
The warriors ranged in line,
With lace bedizened fine
    And swords gold-hilted—
Yon lusty corporal,
Yon colour-man who gripes
The flag of Stars and Stripes—
    Has each been jilted ?

Come, each man of this line,
The privates strong and tall,
' The pioneers and all,'
    The fifer nimble—
Lieutenant and Ensign,
Captain with epaulets,
And Blacky there, who beats
    The clanging cymbal—

O cymbal-beating black,
Tell us, as thou canst feel,
Was it some Lucy Neal
    Who caused thy ruin ?

O nimble fifing Jack,
And drummer making din
So deftly on the skin,
    With thy rat-tattooing—

Confess, ye volunteers,
Lieutenant and Ensign,
And Captain of the line,
    As bold as Roman—
Confess, ye grenadiers,
However strong and tall,
The Conqueror of you all
    Is Woman, Woman !

No corslet is so proof
But through it from her bow
The shafts that she can throw
    Will pierce and rankle.
No champion e'er so tough,
But 's in the struggle thrown,
And tripped and trodden down
    By her slim ankle.

Thus always it was ruled :
And when a woman smiled,
The strong man was a child,
    The sage a noodle.
Alcides was befooled,
And silly Samson shorn,
Long, long ere you were born,
    Poor Yankee Doodle !

                            W. M. THACKERAY.

254. A BALLAD WHEN AT SEA

To you, fair ladies, now at land,
    We men at sea indite ;
But, first, would have you understand
    How hard it is to write.
The Muses now, and Neptune too,
We must implore, to write to you,
    With a fa, la, la, la, la !

But though the Muses should be kind,
    And fill our empty brain :
Yet if rough Neptune cause the wind
    To rouse the azure main,
Our paper, pens, and ink, and we
Roll up and down our ships at sea,
    With a fa, la, la, la, la !

Then if we write not by each post,
    Think not that we're unkind !
Nor yet conclude that we are lost
    By Dutch, by French, or wind.
Our griefs will find a speedier way :
The tide shall bring them twice a day,
        With a fa, la, la, la, la !

The King, with wonder and surprise,
    Will think the sea's grown bold,
For that the tide does higher rise
    Than e'er it did of old.
But let him know that 'tis our tears
Send floods of grief to Whitehall Stairs,
        With a fa, la, la, la, la !

Should Count Toulouse but come to know
    Our sad and dismal story,
The French would scorn so weak a foe,
    Where they can get no glory,
For what resistance can they find
From men, who've left their hearts behind,
        With a fa, la, la, la, la !

To pass our tedious time away
    We throw the merry Main,
Or else at serious Ombre play.
    But why should we in vain
Each other's ruin thus pursue ?
We were undone when we left you,
        With a fa, la, la, la, la !

When any mournful tune you hear,
    That dies in every note,
As if it sighed for each man's care,
    For being so remote,
Then think how often love we've made
To you, while all those tunes were played
        With a fa, la, la, la, la !

Let wind and weather do their worst
    Be you to us but kind,
Let Frenchmen vapour, Dutchmen curse,
    No sorrows we shall find.
'Tis then no matter how things go,
Nor who's our friend, nor who's our foe,
        With a fa, la, la, la, la !

Thus, having told you all our loves,
  And likewise all our fears,
In hopes this declaration moves
  Some pity to our tears,
Let's hear of no inconstancy ;
We have too much of that at sea,
  With a fa, la, la, la, la !

C. Sackville, Earl of Dorset.

255. BLACK-EYED SUSAN

All in the Downs the fleet was moored,
  The streamers waving in the wind,
When black-eyed Susan came aboard.
  ' Oh ! where shall I my true love find ?
Tell me, ye jovial sailors, tell me true,
If my sweet William sails among the crew.'

William, who high upon the yard
  Rocked with the billow to and fro,
Soon as her well-known voice he heard,
  He sighed, and cast his eyes below :
The cord slides swiftly through his glowing hands,
And (quick as lightning) on the deck he stands.

So the sweet lark, high poised in air,
  Shuts close his pinions to his breast,
If chance his mate's shrill call he hear,
  And drops at once into her nest :—
The noblest captain in the British fleet
Might envy William's lip those kisses sweet.

' O Susan, Susan, lovely dear,
  My vows shall ever true remain,
Let me kiss off that falling tear ;
  We only part to meet again.
Change, as ye list, ye winds ; my heart shall be
The faithful compass that still points to thee.

' Believe not what the landmen say,
  Who tempt with doubts thy constant mind.
They'll tell thee, sailors, when away,
  In every port a mistress find :
Yes, yes, believe them when they tell thee so,
For thou art present wheresoe'er I go.

' If to far India's coast we sail
  Thy eyes are seen in diamonds bright,
Thy breath is Afric's spicy gale,
  Thy skin is ivory so white.

Thus every beauteous object that I view
Wakes in my soul some charm of lovely Sue.

' Though battle call me from thy arms
    Let not my pretty Susan mourn ;
Though cannons roar, yet safe from harms
    William shall to his Dear return.
Love turns aside the balls that round me fly,
Lest precious tears should drop from Susan's eye.'

The boatswain gave the dreadful word,
    The sails their swelling bosom spread ;
No longer must she stay aboard ;
    They kissed, she sighed, he hung his head.
Her lessening boat unwilling rows to land ;
' Adieu ! ' she cries ; and waved her lily hand.

J. GAY.

256. A BALLAD UPON A WEDDING

I TELL thee, Dick, where I have been,
Where I the rarest things have seen,
        Oh, things beyond compare !
Such sights again cannot be found
In any place on English ground,
        Be it at wake or fair.

At Charing Cross, hard by the way
Where we (thou know'st) do sell our hay,
        There is a house with stairs ;
And there did I see coming down
Such folk as are not in our town,
        Forty at least, in pairs.

Amongst the rest, one pestilent fine
(His beard no bigger, though, than thine !)
        Walked on before the rest.
Our landlord looks like nothing to him ;
The king (God bless him !), 'twould undo him,
        Should he go still so dressed.

At Course-a-Park, without all doubt,
He should have first been taken out
        By all the maids i' th' town ;
Though lusty Roger there had been,
Or little George upon the green,
        Or Vincent of the Crown.

But wot you what ?   The youth was going
To make an end of all his wooing ;
    The Parson for him stayed.
Yet, by his leave, for all his haste,
He did not so much wish all passed,
    Perchance, as did the maid.

The maid (and thereby hangs a tale)
For such a maid no Whitsun ale
    Could ever yet produce ;
No grape that 's kindly ripe could be
So round, so plump, so soft, as she ;
    Nor half so full of juice !

Her finger was so small, the ring
Would not stay on ; which they did bring.
    It was too wide a peck !
And to say truth, for out it must,
It looked like the great collar (just)
    About our young colt's neck.

Her feet, beneath her petticoat,
Like little mice stole in and out,
    As if they feared the light :
But oh ! she dances such a way,
No sun, upon an Easter Day,
    Is half so fine a sight !

Her cheeks so rare a white was on ;
No daisy makes comparison,
    Who sees them is undone.
For streaks of red were mingled there,
Such as are on a Katherine pear
    (The side that 's next the sun).

Her lips were red, and one was thin
Compared to that was next her chin
    (Some bee had stung it newly).
But, Dick, her eyes so guard her face,
I durst no more upon them gaze,
    Than on the sun in July.

Her mouth so small, when she does speak
Thou'dst swear her teeth her words did break,
    That they might passage get :
But she so handled still the matter,
They came as good as ours or better,
    And are not spent a whit !

Passion o' me ! how I run on
There 's that that would be thought upon,
   I trow, besides the bride :
The business of the Kitchen's great,
For it is fit that men should eat ;
     Nor was it there denied.

Just in the nick, the cook knocked thrice,
And all the waiters, in a trice,
   His summons did obey.
Each serving-man, with dish in hand,
Marched boldly up like our trained band,
     Presented, and away !

When all the meat was on the table
What man of knife or teeth was able
   To stay to be entreated ?
And this the very reason was,
Before the Parson could say grace
     The company was seated.

Now hats fly off ; and youths carouse :
Healths first go round, and then the house.
   The bride's came thick and thick.
And when 'twas named another's health,
Perhaps he made it hers by stealth.
     (And who could help it, Dick ?)

O' th' sudden, up they rise and dance :
Then sit again and sigh and glance,
   Then dance again and kiss.
Thus several ways the time did pass ;
Whilst every woman wished her place,
     And every man wished his !

               Sir J. Suckling.

257. ON MARRIAGE

How happy a thing were a wedding,
   And a bedding,
If a man might purchase a wife
   For a twelvemonth and a day ;
But to live with her all a man's life,
   For ever and for aye,
Till she grow as grey as a cat,
Good faith, Mr. Parson, excuse me from that !

               T. Flatman.

258. MARRIAGE

A MAN may live thrice Nestor's life,
　　Thrice wander out Ulysses' race,
Yet never find Ulysses' wife ;—
　　Such change hath chancèd in this case !
Less age will serve than Paris had,
　　Small pain (if *none* be small enow)
To find good store of Helen's trade :
　　Such sap the root doth yield the bough !
For one good wife, Ulysses slew
　　A worthy knot of gentle blood :
For one ill wife, Greece overthrew
　　The town of Troy.—Sith bad and good
Bring mischief, Lord let be thy will
To keep me free from either ill.

UNKNOWN.

259. AGAINST MARRIAGE

To HIS MISTRESS

YES, all the world must sure agree,
He who 's secured of having thee,
　　Will be entirely blessed ;
But 'twere in me too great a wrong,
To make one who has been so long
　　My queen, my slave at last.

Nor ought those things to be confined,
That were for public good designed :
　　Could we, in foolish pride,
Make the sun always with us stay,
'Twould burn our corn and grass away,
　　To starve the world beside.

Let not the thoughts of parting fright
Two souls which passion does unite ;
　　For while our love does last,
Neither will strive to go away ;
And why the devil should we stay,
　　When once that love is past ?

W. WALSH.

260. DISAPPOINTMENT

' THE bliss which woman's charms bespeak,
　　I've sought in many, found in none ! '
' In many 'tis in vain you seek
　　What only can be found in one.'

COVENTRY PATMORE.

261. A REASONABLE AFFLICTION

On his death-bed poor Lubin lies ;
   His spouse is in despair :
With frequent sobs, and mutual cries,
   They both express their care.

' A different cause,' says parson Sly,
   ' The same effect may give :
Poor Lubin fears that he shall die ;
   His wife, that he may live.'

M. Prior

262. DUNCAN GRAY

Duncan Gray cam here to woo,
   Ha, ha, the wooing o't,
On blythe Yule night when we were fou,
   Ha, ha, the wooing o't.
Maggie coost her head fu' high,
Looked asklent and unco skeigh,
Gart poor Duncan stand abeigh ;
   Ha, ha, the wooing o't.

Duncan fleeched, and Duncan prayed ;
Meg was deaf as Ailsa Craig,
Duncan sighed baith out and in,
Grat his een baith bleer't and blin',
Spak o' lowpin o'er a linn !

Time and chance are but a tide,
Slighted love is sair to bide.
Shall I, like a fool, quoth he,
For a haughty hizzie die ?
She may gae to—France for me !

How it comes let doctors tell,
Meg grew sick as he grew haill.
Something in her bosom wrings,
For relief a sigh she brings,
And O, her een they spak sic things !

Duncan was a lad o' grace,
   Ha, ha, the wooing o't,
Maggie's was a piteous case.
   Ha, ha, the wooing o't.
Duncan couldna be her death,
Swelling pity smoored his wrath ;
Now they're crouse and canty baith !
   Ha, ha, the wooing o't.

R. Burns.

263. TO E. F.

No doubt thy little bosom beats
　　When sounds a wedding bell,
No doubt it pants to taste the sweets
　　That songs and stories tell.

Awhile in shade content to lie,
　　Prolong life's morning dream,
While others rise at the first fly
　　That glitters on the stream.

W. S. LANDOR.

264. NEW STYLE

I VERY much indeed approve
Of maidens moderating love
　　Until they've twenty pounds;
Then Prudence, with a poet's praise,
May loose the laces of their stays,
　　And let them quest like hounds.

Peggy, my theme, twelve years ago
(Or better) did precisely so:
　　She lived at farmer Spence's;
She scoured the pantry, milked the cows,
And answered every would-be spouse,
　　'D'ye think I've lost my senses?'

Until the twenty pounds were safe,
She tiffed at Tim, she ran from Ralph,
　　Squire nodded—deuce a curtsy!
Sam thought her mopish, Silas proud,
And Jedediah cried aloud,
　　'Pray who the devil hurts ye?'

But now the twenty pounds were got,
She knew the fire to boil the pot,
　　She knew the man to trust to.
I'm glad I gave this tidy lass
(Under my roof) a cheerful glass
　　(Of water) and a crust too.

Although the seventeenth of May,
It was a raw and misty day
　　When Ebenezer Smart,
(The miller's lad of Boxholm-mill)
Having obtained her right good-will
　　And prudent virgin heart,

Led her to church : and Joseph Stead
(The curate of said Boxholm) read
    The service ; and Will Sands
(The clerk) repeated the response
(They after him) which uttered once
    Holds fast two plighted hands.

And now they live aside the weir,
And (on my conscience) I declare
    As merrily as larks.
This I can vouch for : I went in
One day and sat upon the bin
    While Peggy hemmed two sarks.

I do not say two sarks entire,
Collar and wristband ; these require
    (I reckon) some time more ;
But mainly two stout sarks, the tail
And fore-flap, stiff as coat of mail
    On knight in days of yore.

I told my sister and our maid
(Anne Waddlewell) how long I stayed
    With Peggy : 'twas until her
Dinner-time : we expect, before
Eight or (at most) nine months are o'er,
    Another little miller.

                    W. S. LANDOR.

265. 'PLEASE TO RING THE BELLE'

I'LL tell you a story that's not in Tom Moore :—
Young Love likes to knock at a pretty girl's door :
So he called upon Lucy—'twas just ten o'clock—
Like a spruce single man, with a smart double knock.

Now a hand-maid, whatever her fingers be at,
Will run like a puss when she hears a *rat*-tat :
So Lucy ran up—and in two seconds more
Had questioned the stranger and answered the door.

The meeting was bliss ; but the parting was woe
For the moment will come when such comers must go :
So she kissed him, and whispered—poor innocent thing—
'The next time you come, love, pray come with a ring.'

                    T. HOOD.

266. ON THE MARRIAGE ACT

THE fools that are wealthy are sure of a bride ;
For riches like raiment their nakedness hide ;
The slave that is needy must starve all his life,
In a bachelor's plight, without mistress or wife.

In good days of yore they ne'er troubled their heads
In settling of jointures, or making of deeds ;
But Adam and Eve when they first entered course,
E'en took one another for better or worse.

Then prithee, dear Chloe, ne'er aim to be great,
Let love be the jointure, don't mind the estate ;
You can never be poor who have all of these charms ;
And I shall be rich when I've you in my arms.

UNKNOWN.

267. THE ROSY-BOSOMED HOURS

A FLORIN to the willing Guard
  Secured, for half the way
(He locked us in, ah, lucky starred),
  A curtained, front coupé.
The sparkling sun of August shone ;
  The wind was in the West ;
Your gown and all that you had on
  Was what became you best ;
And we were in that seldom mood
  When soul with soul agrees,
Mingling, like flood with equal flood,
  In agitated ease.
Far round, each blade of harvest bare
  Its little loaf of bread ;
Each furlong of that journey fair
  With separate sweetness sped.
The calm of use was coming o'er
  The wonder of our wealth,
And now, maybe, 'twas not much more
  Than Eden's common health.
We paced the sunny platform, while
  The train at Havant changed :
What made the people kindly smile,
  Or stare with looks estranged ?
Too radiant for a wife you seemed,
  Serener than a bride ;
Me happiest born of men I deemed,
  And showed perchance my pride.

I loved that girl, so gaunt and tall,
   Who whispered loud, ' Sweet Thing ! '
Scanning your figure, slight yet all
   Round as your own gold ring.
At Salisbury you strayed alone
   Within the shafted glooms,
Whilst I was by the Verger shown
   The brasses and the tombs.
At tea we talked of matters deep,
   Of joy that never dies ;
We laughed, till love was mixed with sleep
   Within your great sweet eyes.
The next day, sweet with luck no less
   And sense of sweetness past,
The full tide of our happiness
   Rose higher than the last.
At Dawlish, 'mid the pools of brine,
   You stepped from rock to rock,
One hand quick tightening upon mine,
   One holding up your frock.
On starfish and on weeds alone
   You seemed intent to be :
Flashed those great gleams of hope unknown
   From you, or from the sea ?
Ne'er came before, ah, when again
   Shall come two days like these :
Such quick delight within the brain,
   Within the heart such peace ?
I thought, indeed, by magic chance,
   A third from Heaven to win,
But as, at dusk, we reached Penzance,
   A drizzling rain set in.

                    COVENTRY PATMORE.

268. SYMPATHY

A KNIGHT and a lady once met in a grove,
While each was in quest of a fugitive love ;
A river ran mournfully murmuring by,
And they wept in its waters for sympathy.

' O, never was knight such a sorrow that bore ! '
' O, never was maid so deserted before ! '
' From life and its uses let us instantly fly,
And jump in together for company ! '

They searched for an eddy that suited the deed,
But here was a bramble, and there was a weed ;
' How tiresome it is ! ' said the fair with a sigh ;
So they sat down to rest them in company.

They gazed at each other, the maid and the knight :
How fair was her form, and how goodly his height !
' One mournful embrace ' ; sobbed the youth, ' ere we die ! '
So kissing and crying kept company.

' O, had I but loved such an angel as you ! '
' O, had but my swain been a quarter as true ! '
' To miss such perfection how blinded was I ! '
Sure now they were excellent company !

At length spoke the lass, 'twixt a smile and a tear,
' The weather is cold for a watery bier ;
When summer returns we may easily die,
Till then let us sorrow in company.'

R. HEBER.

269. TO HIS WIFE

With a Knife on the Fourteenth Anniversary
of her Wedding-day, which happened to be her
Birthday and New Year's Day

A KNIFE, dear girl, cuts love, they say—
Mere modish love perhaps it may ;
For any tool of any kind
Can separate what was never joined.
The knife that cuts our love in two
Will have much tougher work to do :
Must cut your softness, worth, and spirit
Down to the vulgar size of merit ;
To level yours with common taste,
Must cut a world of sense to waste ;
And from your single beauty's store,
Clip what would dizen out a score.
The self-same blade from me must sever
Sensation, judgement, sight—for ever !
All memory of endearments past,
All hope of comforts long to last,
All that makes fourteen years with you
A summer—and a short one too :
All that affection feels and fears,
When hours, without you, seem like years.

'Till that be done,—and I'd as soon
Believe this knife would clip the moon,—
Accept my present undeterred,
And leave their proverbs to the herd.
If in a kiss—delicious treat !
Your lips acknowledge the receipt ;
Love, fond of such substantial fare,
And proud to play the glutton there,
All thoughts of cutting will disdain,
Save only—' cut and come again.'

S. Bishop.

270. TO HIS WIFE

On the Sixteenth Anniversary of her Wedding-day,
with a Ring

' Thee, Mary, with this ring I wed,'
So sixteen years ago I said—
Behold another ring ! 'for what ?'
To wed thee o'er again—why not ?
  With the first ring I married youth,
Grace, beauty, innocence, and truth ;
Taste long admired, sense long revered,
And all my Molly then appeared.
  If she, by merit since disclosed,
Prove twice the woman I supposed,
I plead that double merit now,
To justify a double vow.
  Here then to-day, with faith as sure,
With ardour as intense and pure,
As when amidst the rites divine
I took thy troth, and plighted mine,
To thee, sweet girl, my second ring,
A token and a pledge I bring ;
With this I wed, till death us part,
Thy riper virtues to my heart ;
Those virtues which, before untried,
The wife has added to the bride—
Those virtues, whose progressive claim,
Endearing wedlock's very name,
My soul enjoys, my song approves,
For conscience' sake as well as love's.
  For why ? They teach me hour by hour
Honour's high thought, affection's power,
Discretion's deed. Sound judgement's sentence,
And teach me all things—but repentance.

S. Bishop.

271. THE GIFTS RETURNED

' You must give back,' her mother said,
To a poor sobbing little maid,
' All the young man has given you,
Hard as it now may seem to do.'
  ' 'Tis done already, mother dear ! '
Said the sweet girl, ' So, never fear.'
  Mother. Are you quite certain ? Come, recount
(There was not much) the whole amount.
  Girl. The locket : the kid gloves.
  Mother.   Go on.
  Girl. Of the kid gloves I found but one.
  Mother. Never mind that. What else ? Proceed.
You gave back all his trash ?
  Girl.   Indeed.
  Mother. And was there nothing you would save ?
  Girl. Everything I could give I gave.
  Mother. To the last tittle ?
  Girl.   Even to that.
  Mother. Freely ?
  Girl. My heart went *pit-a-pat*
At giving up . . . ah me ! ah me !
I cry so I can hardly see. . .
All the fond looks and words that passed,
And all the kisses, to the last.

                    W. S. LANDOR.

272. MOTHER, I CANNOT MIND MY WHEEL

MOTHER, I cannot mind my wheel ;
  My fingers ache, my lips are dry :
Oh ! if you felt the pain I feel !
  But oh ! who ever felt as I !
No longer could I doubt him true. . .
  All other men may use deceit ;
He always said my eyes were blue,
  And often swore my lips were sweet.

                    W. S. LANDOR.

273. MY MOTHER BIDS ME SPEND MY SMILES

My mother bids me spend my smiles
  On all who come and call me fair,
As crumbs are thrown upon the tiles,
  To all the sparrows of the air.

> But I've a darling of my own
>   For whom I hoard my little stock—
> What if I chirp him all alone,
>   And leave mamma to feed the flock !

T. Hood.

274. MY SECRET

I tell my secret ?   No indeed, not I :
Perhaps some day, who knows ?
But not to-day ; it froze, and blows, and snows,
And you're too curious : fie !
You want to hear it ? well :
Only, my secret 's mine, and I won't tell.

Or, after all, perhaps there 's none :
Suppose there is no secret after all,
But only just my fun.
To-day 's a nipping day, a biting day ;
In which one wants a shawl,
A veil, a cloak, and other wraps :
I cannot ope to every one who taps,
And let the draughts come whistling through my hall :
Come bounding and surrounding me,
Come buffeting, astounding me,
Nipping and clipping through my wraps and all.
I wear my mask for warmth : who ever shows
His nose to Russian snows
To be pecked at by every wind that blows ?
You would not peck ?   I thank you for good will,
Believe, but leave that truth untested still.

Spring 's an expansive time : yet I don't trust
March with its peck of dust,
Nor April with its rainbow-crowned brief showers,
Nor even May, whose flowers
One frost may wither through the sunless hours.

Perhaps some languid summer day,
When drowsy birds sing less and less,
And golden fruit is ripening to excess,
If there 's not too much sun nor too much cloud,
And the warm wind is neither still nor loud,
Perhaps my secret I may say,
Or you may guess.

C. G. Rossetti.

275. SONNET

A BOOK was writ of late called Tetrachordon ,
　And woven close, both matter, form and style ;
　The subject new : it walked the town awhile,
　Numbring good intellects ; now seldom pored on.
Cries the stall-reader, bless us ! what a word on
　A title page is this ! and some in file
　Stand spelling false, while one might walk to Mile-
　End Green.　Why is it harder, Sirs, than Gordon,
Colkitto, or Macdonnel, or Galasp ?
　Those rugged names to our like mouths grow sleek
　That would have made Quintilian stare and gasp.
Thy age, like ours, O soul of Sir John Cheek,
　Hated not learning worse than toad or asp ;
　When thou taught'st Cambridge, and King Edward Greek.

　　　　　　　　　　　　　　　　J. MILTON.

276. TO THE MUSES

WHETHER on Ida's shady brow,
　Or in the chambers of the East,
The chambers of the sun, that now
　From ancient melody have ceased ;

Whether in Heaven ye wander fair,
　Or the green corners of the earth,
Or the blue regions of the air
　Where the melodious winds have birth ;

Whether on crystal rocks ye rove,
　Beneath the bosom of the sea
Wandering in many a coral grove,
　Fair Nine, forsaking Poetry !

How have you left the ancient love
　That bards of old enjoyed in you !
The languid strings do scarcely move !
　The sound is forced, the notes are few !

　　　　　　　　　　　　　　　　W. BLAKE.

277. EPIGRAM

AUGUSTUS still survives in Maro's strain,
And Spenser's verse prolongs Eliza's reign ;
Great George's acts let tuneful Cibber sing ;
For Nature formed the poet for the king.

　　　　　　　　　　　　　　　　S. JOHNSON.

278. THE POET OF FASHION

His book is successful, he's steeped in renown,
His lyric effusions have tickled the town ;
Dukes, dowagers, dandies, are eager to trace
The fountain of verse in the verse-maker's face ;
While, proud as Apollo, with peers *tête-à-tête*,
From Monday till Saturday dining off plate,
His heart full of hope, and his head full of gain,
The Poet of Fashion dines out in Park Lane.

Now lean-jointured widows who seldom draw corks,
Whose tea-spoons do duty for knives and for forks,
Send forth, vellum-covered, a six o'clock card,
And get up a dinner to peep at the bard :
Veal, sweetbread, boiled chickens, and tongue, crown the cloth,
And soup *à la reine*, little better than broth ;
While, past his meridian, but still with some heat,
The Poet of Fashion dines out in Sloane Street.

Enrolled in the tribe who subsist by their wits,
Remembered by starts and forgotten by fits,
Now artists and actors, the bardling engage,
To squib in the journals, and write for the stage.
Now soup *à la reine* bends the knee to ox-cheek,
And chickens and tongue bow to bubble and squeak—
While, still in translation employed by ' The Row,'
The Poet of Fashion dines out in Soho.

Pushed down from Parnassus to Phlegethon's brink,
Tossed, torn, and trunk-lining, but still with some ink,
Now squab city misses their albums expand,
And woo the worn rhymer for ' something off-hand,'
No longer with stilted effrontery fraught,
Bucklersbury now seeks what St. James's once sought,
And (O what a classical haunt for a bard !)
The Poet of Fashion dines out in Barge Yard.

J. SMITH.

279. A NOVEL OF HIGH LIFE

Lord Harry has written a novel,
    A story of elegant life :
No stuff about love in a hovel,
    No sketch of a commoner's wife :
No trash, such as pathos and passion,
    Fine feelings, expression and wit ;
But all about people of fashion,
    Come look at his caps—how they fit !

O Radcliffe ! thou once wert the charmer
    Of girls who sat reading all night ;
Thy heroes were striplings in armour,
    Thy heroines damsels in white.
But past are thy terrible touches,
    Our lips in derision we curl,
Unless we are told how a Duchess
    Conversed with her cousin the Earl.

We now have each dialogue quite full
    Of titles—' I give you my word,
My lady, you're looking delightful.'
    ' O dear, do you think so, my lord ! '
' You've heard of the marquis's marriage,
    The bride with her jewels new set,
Four horses, new travelling carriage,
    And *déjeûner à la fourchette.*'

Haut Ton finds her privacy broken,
    We trace all her ins and her outs ;
The very small talk that is spoken
    By very great people at routs.
At Tenby Miss Jinks asks the loan of
    The book from the innkeeper's wife,
And reads till she dreams she is one of
    The leaders of elegant life.

                     T. H. BAYLY.

280. TO LEIGH HUNT, ON AN OMISSION IN HIS 'FEAST OF THE POETS'

LEIGH HUNT ! thou stingy man, Leigh Hunt !
May Charon swamp thee in his punt,
For having, in thy list, forgotten
So many poets scarce half rotten,
Who did expect of thee at least
A few cheese-parings from thy *Feast.*
Hast thou no pity on the men
Who suck (as babes their tongues) the pen,
Until it leaves no traces where
It lighted, and seems dipped in air.
At last be generous, Hunt ! and prithee
Refresh (and gratis too) in Lethe
Yonder sick Muse, surcharged with poppies
And heavier presentation-copies.
She *must* grow livelier, and the river
More potent in effect than ever.

                     W. S. LANDOR.

281. OUR MASTER, MELEAGER

OUR master, Meleager, he who framed
   The first Anthology and daintiest,
Mated each minstrel with a flower, and named
   For each the blossom that beseemed him best.
'Twas then as now; garlands were somewhat rare,
   Candidates many : one in doleful strain
Lamented thus, ' This is a sad affair ;
   How shall I face my publisher again ?
Lacking some emblem suitable for me,
   My book 's undone ; I shall not sell a copy.'
' Take courage, son,' quoth Phoebus, ' there must be
   Somewhere or other certainly a poppy.'

R. GARNETT.

282. HENDECASYLLABICS

O YOU chorus of indolent reviewers,
Irresponsible, indolent reviewers,
Look, I come to the test, a tiny poem
All composed in a metre of Catullus,
All in quantity, careful of my motion,
Like the skater on ice that hardly bears him,
Lest I fall unawares before the people,
Waking laughter in indolent reviewers.
Should I flounder awhile without a tumble
Through this metrification of Catullus,
They should speak to me not without a welcome,
All that chorus of indolent reviewers.
Hard, hard, hard is it, only not to tumble,
So fantastical is the dainty metre.
Wherefore slight me not wholly, nor believe me
Too presumptuous, indolent reviewers.
O blatant Magazines, regard me rather—
Since I blush to belaud myself a moment—
As some rare little rose, a piece of inmost
Horticultural art, or half coquette-like
Maiden, not to be greeted unbenignly.

ALFRED, LORD TENNYSON.

283. AGAINST WRITERS THAT CARP AT OTHER MEN'S BOOKS

THE readers and the hearers like my books,
   And yet some writers cannot them digest ;
But what care I ? for when I make a feast,
   I would my guests should praise it, not the cooks.

SIR J. HARINGTON.

284. TO MRS. THROCKMORTON

On her beautiful Transcript of Horace's Ode, *Ad Librum Suum*

Maria, could Horace have guessed
　　What honour awaited his ode
To his own little volume addressed,
　　The honour which you have bestowed,
Who have traced it in characters here,
　　So elegant, even, and neat ;
He had laughed at the critical sneer,
　　Which he seems to have trembled to meet.

And sneer, if you please, he had said,
　　Hereafter a nymph shall arise,
Who shall give me, when you are all dead,
　　The glory your malice denies ;
Shall dignity give to my lay,
　　Although but a mere bagatelle ;
And even a poet shall say,
　　Nothing ever was written so well.

W. Cowper.

285. ENIGMA ON THE LETTER H

'Twas whispered in Heaven, 'twas muttered in Hell,
And echo caught softly the sound as it fell ;
In the confines of earth 'twas permitted to rest,
And the depth of the ocean its presence confessed ;
'Twas seen in the lightning, 'twas heard in the thunder,
'Twill be found in the spheres when they're riven asunder ;
'Twas given to man with his earliest breath,
It assists at his birth and attends him in death,
Presides o'er his happiness, honour, and health,
'Tis the prop of his house and the end of his wealth ;
It begins every hope, every wish it must bound,
With the husbandman toils, and with monarchs is crowned ;
In the heaps of the miser 'tis hoarded with care,
But is sure to be lost in the prodigal heir ;
Without it the soldier and sailor may roam,
But woe to the wretch who expels it from home ;
In the whispers of conscience it there will be found,
Nor e'er in the whirlwind of passion be drowned ;
It softens the heart, and though deaf to the ear,
It will make it acutely and instantly hear ;
But in shades let it rest, like an elegant flower,
Oh ! breathe on it softly, it dies in an hour.

C. M. Fanshawe.

286. BLAME NOT MY LUTE

BLAME not my Lute ! for he must sound
   Of this or that as liketh me ;
For lack of wit the lute is bound
   To give such tunes as pleaseth me ;
Though my songs be somewhat strange,
And speak such words as touch thy change,
      Blame not my lute !

My lute, alas ! doth not offend,
   Though that perforce he must agree
To sound such tunes as I intend
   To sing to them that heareth me ;
Then though my songs be somewhat plain,
And toucheth some that use to feign,
      Blame not my lute !

My lute and strings may not deny,
   But as I strike they must obey ;
Break not them then so wrongfully,
   But wreak thyself some other way ;
And though the songs which I indite
Do quit thy change with rightful spite,
      Blame not my lute !

Spite asketh spite, and changing, change ;
   And falsèd faith must needs be known ;
The faults so great, the case so strange,
   Of right it must abroad be blown :
Then since that by thy own desert
My songs do tell how true thou art,
      Blame not my lute !

Blame but thyself that hast misdone,
   And well deservèd to have blame ;
Change thou thy way, so evil begun,
   And then my lute shall sound that same ;
But if till then my fingers play,
By thy desert their wonted way,
      Blame not my lute !

Farewell, unknown ! For though thou break
   My strings in spite with great disdain,
Yet have I found out, for thy sake,
   Strings for to string my lute again ;
And if perchance this silly rhyme
Do make thee blush at any time,
      Blame not my lute !

               SIR T. WYATT.

287. TO HIS LUTE

My Lute, awake ! Perform the last
Labour that thou and I shall waste,
   And end that I have now begun ;
For when this song is sung and past,
   My lute, be still, for I have done.

As to be heard where ear is none,
As lead to grave in marble stone,
   My song may pierce her heart as soon :
Should we then sing, or sigh, or moan ?
   No, no, my lute ! for I have done.

The rocks do not so cruelly
Repulse the waves continually,
   As she my suit and affection :
So that I am past remedy :
   Whereby my lute and I have done.

Proud of the spoil that thou hast got
Of simple hearts thorough Love's shot,
   By whom, unkind, thou hast them won ;
Think not he hath his bow forgot,
   Although my lute and I have done.

Vengeance shall fall on thy disdain,
That mak'st but game of earnest pain :
   Think not alone under the sun
Unquit to cause thy lover's plain,
   Although my lute and I have done.

May chance thee lie withered and old
The winter nights that are so cold,
   Plaining in vain unto the moon :
Thy wishes then dare not be told :
   Care then who list ! for I have done.

And then may chance thee to repent
The time that thou hast lost and spent
   To cause thy lover's sigh and swoon :
Then shalt thou know beauty but lent,
   And wish and want as I have done.

Now cease, my lute ! This is the last
Labour that thou and I shall waste,
   And ended is that we begun :
Now is this song both sung and past—
   My lute, be still, for I have done.

Sir T. Wyatt.

288. WHEN TO HER LUTE CORINNA SINGS

When to her lute Corinna sings,
Her voice revives the leaden strings,
And doth in highest notes appear,
As any challenged echo clear ;
But when she doth of mourning speak,
Even with her sighs the strings do break.

And as her lute doth live or die,
Led by her passion, so must I,
For when of pleasure she doth sing,
My thoughts enjoy a sudden spring,
But if she doth of sorrow speak,
Even from my heart the strings do break.

T. CAMPION.

289. TO A LADY SINGING

Chloris, yourself you so excel,
    When you vouchsafe to breathe my thought,
That like a spirit, with this spell
    Of my own teaching I am caught.

That eagle's fate and mine is one,
    Which, on the shaft that made him die,
Espied a feather of his own,
    Wherewith he wont to soar so high.

Had Echo, with so sweet a grace,
    Narcissus' loud complaints returned ;
Not for reflection of his face,
    But of his voice, the boy had mourned.

E. WALLER.

290. WITH A GUITAR, TO JANE

Ariel to Miranda :—Take
This slave of Music, for the sake
Of him who is the slave of thee,
And teach it all the harmony
In which thou canst, and only thou,
Make the delighted spirit glow,
Till joy denies itself again,
And, too intense, is turned to pain ;
For by permission and command
Of thine own Prince Ferdinand,
Poor Ariel sends this silent token
Of more than ever can be spoken ;

Your guardian spirit, Ariel, who
From life to life, must still pursue
Your happiness, for thus alone
Can Ariel ever find his own.
From Prospero's enchanted cell,
As the mighty verses tell,
To the throne of Naples, he
Lit you o'er the trackless sea,
Flitting on, your prow before,
Like a living meteor.
When you die, the silent Moon
In her interlunar swoon,
Is not sadder in her cell
Than deserted Ariel.
When you live again on earth,
Like an unseen star of birth
Ariel guides you o'er the sea
Of life from your nativity.
Many changes have been run
Since Ferdinand and you begun
Your course of love, and Ariel still
Has tracked your steps and served your will ;
Now, in humbler, happier lot,
This is all remembered not ;
And now, alas ! the poor sprite is
Imprisoned, for some fault of his,
In a body like a grave ;—
From you he only dares to crave,
For his service and his sorrow,
A smile to-day, a song to-morrow.

The artist who this idol wrought,
To echo all harmonious thought,
Felled a tree, while on the steep
The woods were in their winter sleep,
Rocked in that repose divine
On the wind-swept Apennine ;
And dreaming, some of Autumn past,
And some of Spring approaching fast,
And some of April buds and showers,
And some of songs in July bowers,
And all of love ; and so this tree,—
O that such our death may be !—
Died in sleep, and felt no pain,
To live in happier form again :
From which, beneath Heaven's fairest star,
The artist wrought this loved Guitar,
And taught it justly to reply,
To all who question skilfully,

In language gentle as thine own ;
Whispering in enamoured tone
Sweet oracles of woods and dells,
And summer winds in sylvan cells ;
For it had learned all harmonies
Of the plains and of the skies,
Of the forests and the mountains,
And the many-voicèd fountains ;
The clearest echoes of the hills,
The softest notes of falling rills,
The melodies of birds and bees,
The murmuring of summer seas,
And pattering rain, and breathing dew,
And airs of evening ; and it knew
That seldom-heard mysterious sound,
Which, driven on its diurnal round,
As it floats through boundless day,
Our world enkindles on its way.—
All this it knows, but will not tell
To those who cannot question well
The Spirit that inhabits it ;
It talks according to the wit
Of its companions ; and no more
Is heard than has been felt before,
By those who tempt it to betray
These secrets of an elder day :
But, sweetly as its answers will
Flatter hands of perfect skill,
It keeps its highest, holiest tone
For our belovèd Jane alone.

P. B. SHELLEY.

291. TO MR. HENRY LAWES

WHO HAD NEWLY SET A SONG OF MINE IN THE YEAR 1635

VERSES make heroic virtue live ;
But you can life to verses give.
As when in open air we blow,
The breath, though strained, sounds flat and low ;
But if a trumpet takes the blast,
It lifts it high and makes it last ;
So in your airs our numbers dressed
Make a shrill sally from the breast
Of nymphs, who, singing what we penned,
Our passions to themselves commend ;
While love, victorious with thy art,
Governs at once their voice and heart.

E. WALLER.

292. TO MR. H. LAWES, ON HIS AIRS

HARRY whose tuneful and well-measured song
 First taught our English music how to span
 Words with just note and accent, not to scan
 With Midas ears, committing short and long ;
Thy worth and skill exempts thee from the throng,
 With praise enough for Envy to look wan ;
 To after age thou shalt be writ the man,
 That with smooth air couldst humour best our tongue.
Thou honour'st verse, and verse must send her wing
 To honour thee, the priest of Phœbus' quire
 That tun'st their happiest lines in hymn, or story.
Dante shall give Fame leave to set thee higher
 Than his Casella, whom he wooed to sing
 Met in the milder shades of Purgatory.

J. MILTON.

293. A FAREWELL TO TOWN

SINCE secret Spite hath sworn my woe,
 And I am driven by Destiny
Against my will, God knows, to go
 From place of gallant company,
And, in the stead of sweet delight,
To reap the fruits of foul despite :

As it hath been a custom long,
 To bid farewell when men depart,
So will I sing this solemn song,
 Farewell, to some, with all my heart :
But those my friends : but to my foes,
I wish a nettle in their nose.

I wish my friends their hearts' content :
 My foes, again, the contrary :
I wish myself, the time were spent
 That I must spend in misery :
I wish my deadly foe, no worse
Than want of friends, and empty purse.

But, now my wishes thus are done,
 I must begin to bid farewell :
With friends and foes I have begun,
 And therefore, now I cannot tell
Which first to choose, or ere I part,
To write a farewell from my heart.

First, place of worldly Paradise,
   Thou gallant court, to thee farewell !
For froward Fortune me denies
   Now longer near to thee to dwell.
I must go live, I wot not where,
Nor how to live when I come there.

And next, adieu you gallant dames,
   The chief of noble youth's delight !
Untoward Fortune now so frames,
   That I am banished from your sight,
And, in your stead, against my will,
I must go live with country Jill.

Now next, my gallant youths farewell ;
   My lads that oft have cheered my heart !
My grief of mind no tongue can tell,
   To think that I must from you part.
I now must leave you all, alas,
And live with some odd lobcock ass !

And now farewell thou gallant lute,
   With instruments of music's sounds :
Recorder, cittern, harp and flute,
   And heavenly descants on sweet grounds ;
I now must leave you all indeed,
And make some music on a reed !

And now you stately stamping steeds
   And gallant geldings fair, adieu !
My heavy heart for sorrow bleeds,
   To think that I must part with you :
And on a strawen pannel sit,
And ride some country carting tit !

And now farewell both spear and shield,
   Caliver, pistol, arquebus,
See, see, what sighs my heart doth yield,
   To think that I must leave you thus ;
And lay aside my rapier blade,
And take in hand a ditching spade !

And you farewell, all gallant games,
   Primero and *Imperial,*
Wherewith I used, with courtly dames,
   To pass away the time withal :
I now must learn some country plays
For ale and cakes on holidays !

And now farewell each dainty dish,
　With sundry sorts of sugared wine '
Farewell, I say, fine flesh and fish,
　To please this dainty mouth of mine !
I now, alas, must leave all these,
And make good cheer with bread and cheese.

And now, all orders due, farewell !
　My table laid when it was noon ;
My heavy heart it irks to tell
　My dainty dinners all are done :
With leeks and onions, whig and whey,
I must content me as I may.

And farewell all gay garments now,
　With jewels rich, of rare device !
Like Robin Hood, I wot not how,
　I must go range in woodman's wise ;
Clad in a coat of green or grey,
And glad to get it if I may.

What shall I say, but bid adieu
　To every dram of sweet delight,
In place where pleasure never grew,
　In dungeon deep of foul despite,
I must, ah me ! wretch, as I may,
Go sing the song of welaway.

N. BRETON.

294. THE CONTRAST

IN London I never know what I'd be at,
Enraptured with this, and enchanted with that ;
I'm wild with the sweets of variety's plan,
And Life seems a blessing too happy for man.

But the country, Lord help me ! sets all matters right,
So calm and composing from morning to night ;
Oh ! it settles the spirits when nothing is seen
But an ass on a common, a goose on a green.

In town if it rain, why it damps not our hope,
The eye has her choice, and the fancy her scope ;
What harm though it pour whole nights or whole days ?
It spoils not our prospects, or stops not our ways.

In the country what bliss, when it rains in the fields,
To live on the transports that shuttlecock yields ;
Or go crawling from window to window, to see
A pig on a dunghill or crow on a tree.

In London, if folks ill together are put,
A bore may be dropped, and a quiz may be cut ;
We change without end ; and if lazy or ill,
All wants are at hand, and all wishes at will.

In the country you're nailed, like a pale in the park,
To some *stick* of a neighbour that 's crammed in the ark ;
And 'tis odd, if you're hurt, or in fits tumble down,
You reach death ere the doctor can reach you from town.

In London how easy we visit and meet,
Gay pleasure 's the theme, and sweet smiles are our treat :
Our morning 's a round of good-humoured delight,
And we rattle, in comfort, to pleasure at night.

In the country, how sprightly ! our visits we make
Through ten miles of mud, for Formality's sake ;
With the coachman in drink, and the moon in a fog,
And no thought in our head but a ditch or a bog.

In London the spirits are cheerful and light,
All places are gay and all faces are bright ;
We've ever new joys, and revived by each whim,
Each day on a fresh tide of pleasure we swim.

But how gay in the country ! what summer delight
To be waiting for winter from morning to night !
Then the fret of impatience gives exquisite glee
To relish the sweet rural subjects we see.

In town we've no use for the skies overhead,
For when the sun rises then go we to bed ;
And as to that old-fashioned virgin the moon,
She shines out of season, like satin in June.

In the country these planets delightfully glare
Just to show us the object we want isn't there ;
O, how cheering and gay, when their beauties arise,
To sit and gaze round with the tears in one's eyes !

But 'tis in the country alone we can find
That happy resource, that relief of the mind,
When, drove to despair, our last efforts we make,
And drag the old fish-pond, for novelty's sake :

Indeed I must own, 'tis a pleasure complete
To see ladies well draggled and wet in their feet ;
But what is all that to the transport we feel
When we capture, in triumph, two toads and an eel ?

I have heard, though, that love in a cottage is sweet,
When two hearts in one link of soft sympathy meet :
That 's to come—for as yet I, alas ! am a swain
Who require, I own it, more links to my chain.

Your magpies and stock-doves may flirt among trees,
And chatter their transports in groves, if they please :
But a house is much more to my taste than a tree,
And for groves, O ! a good grove of chimneys for me.

In the country, if Cupid should find a man out,
The poor tortured victim mopes hopeless about ;
But in London, thank Heaven ! our peace is secure,
Where for one eye to kill, there 's a thousand to cure.

I know love 's a devil, too subtle to spy,
That shoots through the soul, from the beam of an eye ;
But in London these devils so quick fly about,
That a new devil still drives an old devil out.

In town let me live then, in town let me die,
For in truth I can't relish the country, not I.
If one must have a villa in summer to dwell,
O, give me the sweet shady side of Pall Mall.

C. MORRIS.

295.   THE DAINTY YOUNG HEIRESS

THE dainty young heiress of Lincoln's Inn Fields,
   Brisk, beautiful, wealthy, and witty,
To the power of Love so unwillingly yields,
   That 'tis feared she'll unpeople the city.
The sparks and the beaus all languish and die,
   Yet, after the conquest of many,
One little good marksman, that aims with one eye,
   May wound her heart deeper than any.

C. SACKVILLE, EARL OF DORSET.

296.   TO CELIA

I HATE the town, and all its ways ;
Ridottos, operas, and plays ;
The ball, the ring, the mall, the Court,
Wherever the *beau monde* resort ;
Where beauties lie in ambush for folks,
Earl Straffords and the Dukes of Norfolks ;
All coffee-houses and their praters,
All courts of justice and debaters ;
All taverns, and the sots within 'em ;
All bubbles, and the rogues that skin 'em.

I hate all critics ; may they burn all,
From Bentley to the Grub Street Journal ;
All bards, as Dennis hates a pun ;
Those who have wit, and who have none.
All nobles of whatever station ;
And all the parsons in the nation.
I hate the world crammed altogether,
From beggars, up, the Lord knows whither !
Ask you then, Celia, if there be
The thing I love ? My charmer, thee.
Thee more than light, than life adore,
Thou dearest, sweetest creature, more
Than wildest raptures can express,
Than I can tell, or thou canst guess.
Then though I bear a gentle mind,
Let not my hatred of mankind
Wonder within my Celia move,
Since she possesses *all* I love.

H. FIELDING.

297.   NO !

No sun—no moon !
No morn—no noon—
No dawn—no dusk—no proper time of day—
No sky—no earthly view—
No distance looking blue—
No road—no street—no ' t'other side the way '—
No end to any Row—
No indications where the Crescents go—
No top to any steeple—
No recognitions of familiar people—
No courtesies for showing 'em—
No knowing 'em !—
No travelling at all—no locomotion,
No inkling of the way—no notion—
' No go '—by land or ocean—
No mail—no post—
No news from any foreign coast—
No Park—no Ring—no afternoon gentility—
No company—no nobility,—
No warmth, no cheerfulness, no healthful ease,
No comfortable feel in any member—
No shade, no shine, no butterflies, no bees,
No fruits, no flowers, no leaves, no birds—
November !

T. HOOD.

298. PICCADILLY

PICCADILLY !—shops, palaces, bustle, and breeze,
The whirring of wheels, and the murmur of trees,
By daylight, or nightlight,—or noisy, or stilly,—
Whatever my mood is—I love Piccadilly.

Wet nights, when the gas on the pavement is streaming,
And young Love is watching and old Love is dreaming,
And Beauty is whirled off to conquest, where shrilly
Cremona makes nimble thy toes, Piccadilly !

Bright days, when we leisurely pace to and fro,
And meet all the people we do or don't know,—
Here is jolly old Brown, and his fair daughter Lillie,—
No wonder, young pilgrim, you like Piccadilly !

See yonder pair riding, how fondly they saunter !
She smiles on her poet, whose heart 's in a canter :
Some envy her spouse, and some covet her filly,
He envies them both—he 's an ass, Piccadilly !

Now were I that gay bride, with a slave at my feet,
I would choose me a house in my favourite street ;
Yes or no—I would carry my point, willy, nilly,
If ' no ',—pick a quarrel, if ' yes ',—Piccadilly !

From Primrose balcony, long ages ago,
' Old Q ' sat at gaze,—who now passes below ?
A frolicsome Statesman, the Man of the Day,
A laughing philosopher, gallant and gay ;
No darling of Fortune more manfully trod,
Full of years, full of fame, and the world at his nod,
Heu, anni fugaces ! The wise and the silly,
Old P or old Q,—we must quit Piccadilly.

Life is chequered,—a patchwork of smiles and of frowns
We value its ups, let us muse on its downs ;
There 's a side that is bright, it will then turn us t'other,—
One turn, if a good one, deserves such another.
These downs are delightful, *these* ups are not hilly,—
Let us turn one more turn ere we quit Piccadilly.

F. LOCKER-LAMPSON.

299. EPIGRAM

To John I owed great obligation ;
    But John unhappily thought fit
To publish it to all the nation,
    Sure John and I are more than quit.

M. PRIOR.

300. ST. JAMES'S STREET

(A GRUMBLE)

St. James's Street, of classic fame!
  The finest people throng it!
St. James's Street? I know the name,
  I think I've passed along it.
Why, that's where Sacharissa sighed
  When Waller read his ditty;
Where Byron lived, and Gibbon died,
  And Alvanley was witty.

A noted street! It skirts the Park
  Where Pepys once took his pastime;
Come, gaze on fifty men of mark,
  And then recall the fast time!
The *plats* at White's, the play at Crock's,
  The bumpers to Miss Gunning;
The *bonhomie* of Charlie Fox,
  And Selwyn's ghastly funning.

The dear old street of clubs and cribs,
  As north and south it stretches,
Still seems to smack of Rolliad squibs,
  And Gillray's fiercer sketches;
The quaint old dress, the grand old style,
  The *mots*, the racy stories;
The wine, the dice, the wit, the bile,
  The hate of Whigs and Tories.

At dusk, when I am strolling there,
  Dim forms will rise around me;
Lepel flits past me in her chair,
  And Congreve's airs astound me!
And once Nell Gwyn, a frail young sprite,
  Looked kindly when I met her;
I shook my head, perhaps,—but quite
  Forgot to quite forget her.

The street is still a lively tomb
  For rich, and gay, and clever;
The crops of dandies bud, and bloom,
  And die as fast as ever.
Now gilded youth loves cutty pipes,
  And slang the worse for wearing:
It can't approach its prototypes
  In taste, or tone, or bearing.

In Brummell's day of buckle shoes,
  Lawn cravats, and roll collars,
They'd fight, and woo, and bet—and lose
  Like gentlemen and scholars:

I like young men to go the pace,
   I half forgive old Rapid ;
These louts disgrace their name and race,—
   So vicious and so vapid !

Worse times may come.   *Bon ton,* indeed,
   Will then be quite forgotten,
And all we much revere will speed
   From ripe to worse than rotten ;
Then grass will sprout between yon stones,
   And owls will roost at Boodle's,
For Echo will hurl back the tones
   Of screaming Yankee Doodles.

I love the haunts of old Cockaigne,
   Where wit and wealth were squandered ;
The halls that tell of hoop and train,
   Where grace and rank have wandered ;
Those halls where ladies fair and leal
   First ventured to adore me !—
And something of the like I feel
   For this old street before me.

F. LOCKER-LAMPSON.

301.   IN LONDON ON SATURDAY NIGHT

Is it not pleasant to wander
   In town on Saturday night,
While people go hither or thither,
   And shops shed cheerful light ?
And, arm in arm, while our shadows
   Chase us along the panes,
Are we not quite as cosy
   As down among country lanes ?

Nobody knows us, heeds us,
   Nobody hears or sees,
And the shop-lights gleam more gladly
   Than the moon on hedges and trees ;
And people coming and going,
   All upon ends of their own,
Though they work a spell on the spirit,
   Move it more finely alone.

The sound seems harmless and pleasant
   As the murmur of brook and wind ;
The shops with the fruit and the pictures
   Have sweetness to suit my mind ;

And nobody knows us, heeds us,
  And our loving none reproves,—
I, the poor figure-painter !
  You, the lady he loves !

And what if the world should scorn you,
  For now and again, as you do,
Assuming a country kirtle,
  And bonnet of straw thereto,
Or the robe of a vestal virgin,
  Or a nun's grey gabardine,
And keeping a brother and sister
  By standing and looking divine ?

And what if the world, moreover,
  Should silently pass me by,
Because, at the dawn of the struggle
  I labour some stories high !
Why, there 's comfort in waiting, working,
  And feeling one's heart beat right,—
And rambling alone, love-making,
  In London on Saturday night.

                              R. BUCHANAN.

302. CATHARINA

ADDRESSED TO MISS STAPLETON

SHE came—she is gone—we have met—
  And meet perhaps never again ;
The sun of that moment is set,
  And seems to have risen in vain.
Catharina has fled like a dream—
  (So vanishes pleasure, alas !)
But has left a regret and esteem,
  That will not so suddenly pass.

The last evening ramble we made,
  Catharina, Maria, and I,
Our progress was often delayed
  By the nightingale warbling nigh.
We paused under many a tree,
  And much she was charmed with a tone
Less sweet to Maria and me,
  Who had witnessed so lately her own.

My numbers that day she had sung,
   And gave them a grace so divine,
As only her musical tongue
   Could infuse into numbers of mine.
The longer I heard, I esteemed
   The work of my fancy the more,
And e'en to myself never seemed
   So tuneful a poet before.

Though the pleasures of London exceed
   In number the days of the year.
Catharina, did nothing impede,
   Would feel herself happier here ;
For the close-woven arches of limes
   On the banks of our river, I know.
Are sweeter to her many times
   Than all that the city can show.

So it is, when the mind is endued
   With a well-judging taste from above,
Then, whether embellished or rude,
   'Tis nature alone that we love.
The achievements of art may amuse,
   May even our wonder excite,
But groves, hills, and valleys diffuse
   A lasting, a sacred delight.

Since then in the rural recess
   Catharina alone can rejoice,
May it still be her lot to possess
   The scene of her sensible choice !
To inhabit a mansion remote
   From the clatter of street-pacing steeds,
And by Philomel's annual note
   To measure the life that she leads.

With her book, and her voice, and her lyre,
   To wing all her moments at home,
And with scenes that new rapture inspire
   As oft as it suits her to roam,
She will have just the life she prefers,
   With little to wish or to fear,
And ours will be pleasant as hers,
   Might we view her enjoying it here.

                             W. COWPER.

303. CORIDON'S SONG

OH, the sweet contentment
The countryman doth find.
　　High trolollie lollie loe,
　　High trolollie lee,
That quiet contemplation
Possesseth all my mind :
　　Then care away,
　　And wend along with me.

For courts are full of flattery,
As hath too oft been tried ;
　　High trolollie lollie loe,
　　High trolollie lee,
The city full of wantonness,
And both are full of pride.
　　Then care away,
　　And wend along with me.

But oh, the honest countryman
Speaks truly from his heart,
　　High trolollie lollie loe,
　　High trolollie lee,
His pride is in his tillage,
His horses and his cart :
　　Then care away,
　　And wend along with me.

Our clothing is good sheepskins,
Grey russet for our wives,
　　High trolollie lollie loe,
　　High trolollie lee.
'Tis warmth and not gay clothing
That doth prolong our lives ;
　　Then care away,
　　And wend along with me.

The ploughman, though he labour hard,
Yet on the holiday,
　　High trolollie lollie loe,
　　High trolollie lee,
No emperor so merrily
Does pass his time away ;
　　Then care away,
　　And wend along with me.

To recompense our tillage
The heavens afford us showers ;
　　High trolollie lollie loe,
　　High trolollie lee.

And for our sweet refreshments
The earth affords us bowers :
 Then care away,
 And wend along with me.

The cuckoo and the nightingale
Full merrily do sing,
 High trolollie lollie loe,
 High trolollie lee,
And with their pleasant roundelays,
Bid welcome to the spring :
 Then care away,
 And wend along with me.

This is not half the happiness
The countryman enjoys ;
 High trolollie lollie loe,
 High trolollie lee,
Though others think they have as much
Yet he that says so lies :
 Then come away,
 Turn countryman with me.

J. CHALKHILL.

304. JACK AND JOAN

JACK and Joan, they think no ill,
But loving live, and merry still ;
Do their weekday's work, and pray
Devoutly on the holy day ;
Skip and trip it on the green,
And help to choose the summer queen ;
Lash out, at a country feast,
Their silver penny with the best.

Well can they judge of nappy ale,
And tell at large a winter tale ;
Climb up to the apple loft,
And turn the crabs till they be soft.
Tib is all the father's joy,
And little Tom the mother's boy.
All their pleasure is content ;
And care, to pay their yearly rent.

Joan can call by name her cows,
And deck her windows with green boughs ;
She can wreaths and tutties make,
And trim with plums a bridal cake.

Jack knows what brings gain or loss;
And his long flail can stoutly toss;
Makes the hedge, which others break,
And ever thinks what he doth speak.

Now, you courtly dames and knights,
That study only strange delights;
Though you scorn the homespun grey
And revel in your rich array:
Though your tongues dissemble deep,
And can your heads from danger keep;
Yet, for all your pomp and train,
Securer lives the silly swain.

T. CAMPION.

305. OUR VILLAGE—BY A VILLAGER

'Sweet Auburn, loveliest village of the plain.'—*Goldsmith.*

OUR village, that 's to say not Miss Mitford's village, but our village of
    Bullock Smithy,
Is come into by an avenue of trees, three oak pollards, two elders, and
    a withy;
And in the middle, there 's a green of about not exceeding an acre and
    a half;
It 's common to all, and fed off by nineteen cows, six ponies, three horses,
    five asses, two foals, seven pigs, and a calf!
Besides a pond in the middle, as is held by a similar sort of common law
    lease,
And contains twenty ducks, six drakes, three ganders, two dead dogs,
    four drowned kittens, and twelve geese.
Of course the green 's cropt very close, and does famous for bowling
    when the little village boys play at cricket;
Only some horse, or pig, or cow, or great jackass, is sure to come and
    stand right before the wicket.
There 's fifty-five private houses, let alone barns and workshops, and
    pigstyes, and poultry huts, and such-like sheds;
With plenty of public-houses—two Foxes, one Green Man, three Bunch
    of Grapes, one Crown, and six King's Heads.
The Green Man is reckoned the best, as the only one that for love or
    money can raise
A postilion, a blue jacket, two deplorable lame white horses, and a ram-
    shackled 'neat postchaise'.
There 's one parish church for all the people, whatsoever may be their
    ranks in life or their degrees,
Except one very damp, small, dark, freezing-cold, little Methodist chapel
    of Ease;

And close by the church-yard there's a stone-mason's yard, that whe[...]
the time is seasonable
Will furnish with afflictions sore and marble urns and cherubims ver[...]
low and reasonable.
There's a cage, comfortable enough ; I've been in it with old Jac[...]
Jeffrey and Tom Pike ;
For the Green Man next door will send you in ale, gin, or anything els[...]
you like.
I can't speak of the stocks, as nothing remains of them but the uprigh[...]
post ;
But the pound is kept in repairs for the sake of Cob's horse, as is alway[...]
there almost.
There's a smithy of course, where that queer sort of a chap in his way
Old Joe Bradley,
Perpetually hammers and stammers, for he stutters and shoes horse[...]
very badly.
There's a shop of all sorts, that sells everything, kept by the widow o[...]
Mr. Task ;
But when you go there, it's ten to one she's out of everythin[...]
you ask.
You'll know her house by the swarm of boys, like flies, about the old
sugary cask :
There are six empty houses, and not so well papered inside as out,
For bill-stickers won't beware, but sticks notices of sales and electio[...]
placards all about.
That's the Doctor's with a green door, where the garden pots in th[...]
windows is seen ;
A weakly monthly rose that don't blow, and a dead geranium, and a tea[...]
plant with five black leaves and one green.
As for hollyoaks at the cottage doors, and honeysuckles and jasmines[...]
you may go and whistle ;
But the Tailor's front garden grows two cabbages, a dock, a ha'port[...]
of pennyroyal, two dandelions, and a thistle.
There are three small orchards—Mr. Busby's the schoolmaster's is th[...]
chief—
With two pear-trees that don't bear ; one plum and an apple, that every
year is stripped by a thief.
There's another small day-school too, kept by the respectable Mrs
Gaby.
A select establishment, for six little boys and one big, and four little girl[...]
and a baby ;
There's a rectory, with pointed gables and strange odd chimneys that
never smokes,
For the rector don't live on his living like other Christian sort o[...]
folks ;
There's a barber's, once a week well filled with rough black-bearded,
shock-headed churls,
And a window with two feminine men's heads, and two masculine ladies
in false curls ;

There 's a butcher's, and a carpenter's, and a plumber's, and a small
  greengrocer's and a baker,
But he won't bake on a Sunday, and there 's a sexton that 's a coal-
  merchant besides, and an undertaker ;
And a toyshop, but not a whole one, for a village can't compare with the
  London shops ;
One window sells drums, dolls, kites, carts, bats, Clout's balls, and the
  other sells malt and hops.
And Mrs. Brown, in domestic economy not to be a bit behind her betters,
Lets her house to a milliner, a watchmaker, a rat-catcher, a cobbler,
  lives in it herself, and it 's the post-office for letters.
Now I've gone through all the village—aye, from end to end, save and
  except one more house,
But I haven't come to that—and I hope I never shall—and that 's the
  Village Poor House !

T. Hood.

306. BLEÄKE'S HOUSE IN BLACKMWORE

John Bleäke he had a bit o' ground
Come to en by his mother's zide ;
An' after that, two hundred pound
His uncle left en when he died ;
' Well now,' cried John, ' it is my bent
To build a house, an' paÿ noo rent.'
An' Meäry gi'ed en her consent.
' Do, do,'—the maïdens cried.
' True, true,'—his wife replied.
' Done, done,—a house o' brick or stwone,'
Cried merry Bleäke o' Blackmwore.

Then John he call'd vor men o' skill,
An' builders answer'd to his call ;
An' met to reckon, each his bill,
Vor vloor an' windor, rwof an' wall.
An' woone did mark it on the groun',
An' woone did think, an' scratch his crown,
An' reckon work, an' write it down :
' Zoo, zoo,'—woone treädesman cried ;
' True, true,'—woone mwore replied.
' Aye, aye,—good work, an' have good paÿ,'
Cried merry Bleäke o' Blackmwore.

The work begun, an' trowels rung
An' up the brickèn wall did rise,
An' up the slantèn refters sprung,
Wi' busy blows, an' lusty cries ;

An woone brought planks to meäke a vloor,
An' woone did come wi' durns or door,
An' woone did zaw, an woone did bore.
' Brick, brick,—there down below.
Quick, quick,—why b'ye so slow ? '
' Lime, lime,—why we do wëaste the time,
Vor merry Bleäke o' Blackmwore.'

The house wer up vrom groun' to tun,
An' thatch'd ageän the raïny sky,
Wi' windors to the noonday zun,
Where rushy Stour do wander by.
In coo'se he had a pworch to screen
The inside door, when win's wer keen,
An' out avore the pworch, a green.
' Here ! here ! '—the childern cried ;
' Dear ! dear ! '—the wife replied ;
' There, there,—the house is perty feäir,'
Cried merry Bleäke o' Blackmwore.

Then John he ax'd his friends to warm
His house, an' they, a goodish batch,
Did come alwone, or eärm in eärm,
All roads, a-meäkèn vor his hatch :
An' there below the clavy beam
The kettle-spout did zing an' steam ;
An' there wer ceäkes, an' tea wi' cream.
' Lo ! lo ! '—the women cried ;
' Ho ! ho ! '—the men replied ;
' Health, health,—attend ye wi' your wealth,
Good merry Bleäke o' Blackmwore.'

Then John, a-praïsed, flung up his crown
All back, a-laughèn in a roar.
They praïs'd his wife, an' she looked down
A-simperèn towards the vloor.
Then up they sprung a-dancèn reels,
An' up went tooes, an' up went heels,
A-windèn roun' in knots an' wheels.
' Brisk, brisk,'—the maïdens cried ;
' Frisk, frisk,'—the men replied ;
' Quick, quick,—there wi' your fiddle-stick,'
Cried merry Bleäke o' Blackmwore.

An' when the morrow's zun did sheen
John Bleäke beheld, wi' jaÿ an' pride,
His brickèn house, an' pworch, an' green,
Above the Stour's rushy zide.

The zwallows left the lwonesome groves
To build below the thatchèn oves,
An' robins come vor crumb's o' lwoaves :
' Tweet, tweet,'—the birds all cried ;
' Sweet, sweet,'—John's wife replied ;
' Dad, dad,'—the childern cried so glad,
To merry Bleäke o' Blackmwore.

W. BARNES.

307. QUINCE

NEAR a small village in the West,
   Where many very worthy people,
Eat, drink, play whist, and do their best
   To guard from evil Church and steeple
There stood—alas ! it stands no more !—
   A tenement of brick and plaster,
Of which, for forty years and four,
   My good friend Quince was lord and master.

Welcome was he in hut and hall
   To maids and matrons, peers and peasants ;
He won the sympathies of all
   By making puns, and making presents.
Though all the parish were at strife,
   He kept his counsel, and his carriage,
And laughed, and loved a quiet life,
   And shrank from Chancery suits—and marriage.

Sound was his claret—and his head ;
   Warm was his double ale—and feelings ;
His partners at the whist club said
   That he was faultless in his dealings :
He went to church but once a week ;
   Yet Dr. Poundtext always found him
An upright man, who studied Greek,
   And liked to see his friends around him.

Asylums, hospitals and schools,
   He used to swear, were made to cozen ;
All who subscribed to them were fools,—
   And he subscribed to half a dozen :
It was his doctrine, that the poor
   Were always able, never willing ;
And so the beggar at his door
   Had first abuse, and then—a shilling.

Some public principles he had,
   But was no flatterer, nor fretter ;
He rapped his box when things were bad,
   And said ' I cannot make them better ! '

And much he loathed the patriot's snort,
    And much he scorned the placeman's snuffle ;
And cut the fiercest quarrels short
    With—'Patience, gentlemen—and shuffle ! '

For full ten years his pointer Speed
    Had couched beneath her master's table ;
For twice ten years his old white steed
    Had fattened in his master's stable ;
Old Quince averred, upon his troth,
    They were the ugliest beasts in Devon ;
And none knew why he fed them both,
    With his own hands, six days in seven.

Whene'er they heard his ring or knock,
    Quicker than thought, the village slatterns
Flung down the novel, smoothed the frock,
    And took up Mrs. Glasse, and patterns ;
Adine was studying baker's bills ;
    Louisa looked the queen of knitters ;
Jane happened to be hemming frills ;
    And Bell, by chance, was making fritters.

But all was vain ; and while decay
    Came, like a tranquil moonlight, o'er him,
And found him gouty still, and gay,
    With no fair nurse to bless or bore him,
His rugged smile and easy chair,
    His dread of matrimonial lectures,
His wig, his stick, his powdered hair,
    Were themes for very strange conjectures.

Some sages thought the stars above
    Had crazed him with excess of knowledge ;
Some heard he had been crossed in love
    Before he came away from College ;
Some darkly hinted that his Grace
    Did nothing, great or small, without him ;
Some whispered, with a solemn face,
    That there was 'something odd about him ! '

I found him, at threescore and ten,
    A single man, but bent quite double ;
Sickness was coming on him then
    To take him from a world of trouble :
He prosed of slipping down the hill,
    Discovered he grew older daily ;
One frosty day he made his will,—
    The next, he sent for Doctor Bailey.

And so he lived,—and so he died !—
   When last I sat beside his pillow
He shook my hand, and ' Ah ! ' he cried,
   ' Penelope must wear the willow.
Tell her I hugged her rosy chain
   While life was flickering in the socket ;
And say, that when I call again,
   I'll bring a licence in my pocket.

' I've left my house and grounds to Fag,—
   I hope his master's shoes will suit him ;
And I've bequeathed to you my nag,
   To feed him for my sake,—or shoot him.
The Vicar's wife will take old Fox,—
   She'll find him an uncommon mouser,—
And let her husband have my box,
   My Bible, and my Assmanshauser.

' Whether I ought to die or not,
   My Doctors cannot quite determine ;
It 's only clear that I shall rot,
   And be, like Priam, food for vermin.
My debts are paid :—but Nature's debt
   Almost escaped my recollection :
Tom !—we shall meet again ;—and yet
   I cannot leave you my direction ! '

W. M. PRAED.

308. THE TABLES TURNED

UP ! up ! my Friend, and quit your books ;
Or surely you'll grow double :
Up ! up ! my Friend, and clear your looks,
Why all this toil and trouble ?

The sun, above the mountain's head,
A freshening lustre mellow
Through all the long green fields has spread,
His first sweet evening yellow.

Books ! 'tis a dull and endless strife :
Come, hear the woodland linnet,
How sweet his music ! on my life,
There 's more of wisdom in it.

And hark ! how blithe the throstle sings !
He, too, is no mean preacher :
Come forth into the light of things,
Let Nature be your teacher.

She has a world of ready wealth,
Our minds and hearts to bless—
Spontaneous wisdom breathed by health,
Truth breathed by cheerfulness.

One impulse from a vernal wood
May teach you more of man,
Of moral evil and of good,
Than all the sages can.

Sweet is the lore which Nature brings ;
Our meddling intellect
Mis-shapes the beauteous forms of things :—
We murder to dissect.

Enough of Science and of Art ;
Close up those barren leaves ;
Come forth, and bring with you a heart
That watches and receives.

                                   W. WORDSWORTH.

309. CHERRY-RIPE

THERE is a garden in her face,
    Where roses and white lilies grow ;
A heavenly paradise is that place,
    Wherein all pleasant fruits do flow ;
There cherries grow, which none may buy,
Till cherry-ripe themselves do cry.

Those cherries fairly do enclose
    Of orient pearl a double row ;
Which when her lovely laughter shows,
    They look like rose-buds filled with snow.
Yet them nor peer nor prince can buy,
Till cherry-ripe themselves do cry.

Her eyes like angels watch them still ;
    Her brows like bended bows do stand,
Threatening with piercing frowns to kill
    All that attempt with eye or hand
These sacred cherries to come nigh—
Till cherry-ripe themselves do cry !

                                   T. CAMPION.

310. LIKE THE IDALIAN QUEEN

LIKE the Idalian Queen,
Her hair about her eyne
With neck and breast's ripe apples to be seen,
At first glance of the morn,
In Cyprus' gardens gathering those fair flowers
Which of her blood were born,
I saw, but fainting saw, my paramours.
The Graces naked danced about the place,
The winds and trees amazed
With silence on her gazed ;
The flowers did smile like those upon her face,
And as their aspen stalks those fingers band,
That she might read my case,
A hyacinth I wished me in her hand.

W. DRUMMOND.

311. THE PRIMROSE

ASK me why I send you here
This sweet Infanta of the year ;
Ask me why I send to you
This Primrose, thus bepearled with dew ;
I will whisper to your ears
The sweets of Love are mixed with tears.

Ask me why this flower does show
So yellow-green, and sickly too ;
Ask me why the stalk is weak
And bending, yet it doth not break ;
I will answer, These discover
What fainting hopes are in a lover.

R. HERRICK.

312. TO CARNATIONS

STAY while ye will, or go,
  And leave no scent behind ye :
Yet trust me, I shall know
  The place where I may find ye.

Within my Lucia's cheek,
  (Whose livery ye wear)
Play ye at hide or seek,
  I'm sure to find ye there.

R. HERRICK.

313.   ASK ME NO MORE WHERE JOVE BESTOWS

Ask me no more where Jove bestows,
When June is past, the fading rose ;
For in your beauty's orient deep
These flowers, as in their causes, sleep.

Ask me no more whither do stray
The golden atoms of the day ;
For in pure love heaven did prepare
Those powders to enrich your hair.

Ask me no more whither doth haste
The nightingale when May is past ;
For in your sweet dividing throat
She winters, and keeps warm her note.

Ask me no more where those stars 'light
That downwards fall in dead of night ;
For in your eyes they sit, and there
Fixèd become as in their sphere.

Ask me no more if east or west
The Phœnix builds her spicy nest ;
For unto you at last she flies,
And in your fragrant bosom dies.

T. Carew.

314.   TO ROSES, IN THE BOSOM OF CASTARA

Ye blushing Virgins happy are
  In the chaste nunnery of her breasts,
For he'd profane so chaste a fair,
  Whoe'er should call them Cupid's nests.

Transplanted thus, how bright ye grow,
  How rich a perfume do ye yield !
In some close garden, cowslips so
  Are sweeter than i' th' open field.

In those white cloisters, live secure
  From the rude blasts of wanton breath,
Each hour more innocent and pure,
  Till you shall wither into death.

Then that which, living, gave you room,
  Your glorious sepulchre shall be.
There wants no marble for a tomb,
  Whose breast hath marble been to me.

W. Habington.

315. A FRAGMENT

Go, rose, my Chloe's bosom grace.
　　How happy should I prove,
Might I supply that envied place
　　With never-fading love !
There, Phoenix-like, beneath her eye,
Involved in fragrance, burn and die.

Know, hapless flower, that thou shalt find
　　More fragrant roses there,
I see thy withering head reclined
　　With envy and despair ;
One common fate we both must prove ;
You die with envy, I with love.

J. GAY.

316. THE WHITE ROSE

SENT BY A YORKIST GENTLEMAN TO HIS LANCASTRIAN MISTRESS

　　If this fair rose offend thy sight,
　　　　Placed in thy bosom bare,
　　'Twill blush to find itself less white,
　　　　And turn Lancastrian there.

　　But if thy ruby lips it spy,—
　　　　As kiss it thou mayst deign,—
　　With envy pale 'twill lose its dye,
　　　　And Yorkist turn again.

UNKNOWN.

317. MARIAN'S COMPLAINT

SINCE truth ha' left the shepherd's tongue,
Adieu the cheerful pipe and song ;
Adieu the dance at closing day,
And, ah, the happy morn of May.

How oft he told me I was fair,
And wove the garland for my hair ;
How oft for Marian stripped the bower,
To fill my lap with every flower !

No more his gifts of guile I'll wear,
But from my brow the chaplet tear ;
The crook he gave in pieces break,
And rend his ribbons from my neck.

How oft he vowed a constant flame,
And carved on every oak my name !
Blush, Colin, that the wounded tree
Is all that will remember me.

J. WOLCOT.

318. THE POPLAR

AYE, here stands the Poplar, so tall and so stately,
  On whose tender rind—'twas a little one then—
We carved her initials ; though not very lately—
  We think in the year eighteen hundred and ten.

Yes, here is the G which proclaimed Georgiana ;
  Our heart's empress then ; see, 'tis grown all askew ;
And it 's not without grief we perforce entertain a
  Conviction, it now looks much more like a Q.

This should be the great D too, that once stood for Dobbin,
  Her loved patronymic—ah ! can it be so ?
Its once fair proportions, time, too, has been robbing ;
  A D ?—we'll be *Deed* if it isn't an O !

Alas ! how the soul sentimental it vexes,
  That thus on our labours stern *Chronos* should frown,
Should change our soft liquids to izzards and Xes,
  And turn true-love's alphabet all upside down !

R. H. BARHAM.

319. BOTANY

I HARDLY know one flower that grows
  On my small garden plot ;
Perhaps I may have seen a *Rose*,
  And said, *Forget-me-not.*

W. S. LANDOR.

320. TO E. ARUNDELL

NATURE ! thou mayest fume and fret,
There 's but one white violet ;
Scatter o'er the vernal ground
Faint resemblances around,
Nature ! I will tell thee yet
There 's but one white violet.

W. S. LANDOR.

321. THE CISTUS

CISTUS ! whose fragile flower
Waits but the vesper hour
  To droop and fall,
Smoothen thy petals now
The Floral Fates allow . . .
And why so ruffled in fresh youth are all ?

Thou breathest on my breast,
' We are but like the rest
  Of our whole family ;
Ruffled we are, 'tis true,
  Through life ; but are not *you ?* . . .
Without our privilege so soon to die.'

W. S. LANDOR.

322. GARDEN FANCIES

I. THE FLOWER'S NAME

HERE 's the garden she walked across,
  Arm in my arm, such a short while since :
Hark, now I push its wicket, the moss
  Hinders the hinges and makes them wince !
She must have reached this shrub ere she turned,
  As back with that murmur the wicket swung ;
For she laid the poor snail, my chance foot spurned,
  To feed and forget it the leaves among.

Down this side of the gravel-walk
  She went while her robe's edge brushed the box :
And here she paused in her gracious talk
  To point me a moth on the milk-white phlox.
Roses, ranged in valiant row,
  I will never think that she passed you by !
She loves you noble roses, I know ;
  But yonder, see, where the rock-plants lie !

This flower she stopped at, finger on lip,
  Stooped over, in doubt, as settling its claim ;
Till she gave me, with pride to make no slip,
  Its soft meandering Spanish name :
What a name ! was it love or praise ?
  Speech half-asleep, or song half-awake ?
I must learn Spanish, one of these days,
  Only for that slow sweet name's sake.

Roses, if I live and do well,
  I may bring her, one of these days,
To fix you fast with as fine a spell,
  Fit you each with his Spanish phrase ;

But do not detain me now ; for she lingers
   There; like sunshine over the ground,
And ever I see her soft white fingers
   Searching after the bud she found.

Flower, you Spaniard, look that you grow not,
   Stay as you are and be loved for ever !
Bud, if I kiss you 'tis that you blow not :
   Mind, the shut pink mouth opens never !
For while thus it pouts, her fingers wrestle,
   Twinkling the audacious leaves between,
Till round they turn and down they nestle—
   Is not the dear mark still to be seen ?

Where I find her not, beauties vanish ;
   Whither I follow her, beauties flee ;
Is there no method to tell her in Spanish
   June 's twice June since she breathed it with me ?
Come, bud, show me the least of her traces,
   Treasure my lady's lightest footfall
—Ah, you may flout and turn up your faces—
   Roses, you are not so fair after all !

R. BROWNING.

323.   GARDEN FANCIES

II. SIBRANDUS SCHAFNABURGENSIS

PLAGUE take all your pedants, say I !
   He who wrote what I hold in my hand,
Centuries back was so good as to die,
   Leaving this rubbish to cumber the land ;
This, that was a book in its time,
   Printed on paper and bound in leather,
Last month in the white of a matin-prime
   Just when the birds sang all together.

Into the garden I brought it to read,
   And under the arbute and laurustine
Read it, so help me grace in my need,
   From title-page to closing line.
Chapter on chapter did I count,
   As a curious traveller counts Stonehenge ;
Added up the mortal amount ;
   And then proceeded to my revenge.

Yonder 's a plum-tree with a crevice
   An owl would build in, were he but sage ;
For a lap of moss, like a fine pont-levis
   In a castle of the middle age,

Joins to a lip of gum, pure amber ;
  Where he'd be private, there might he spend
Hours alone in his lady's chamber :
  Into this crevice I dropped our friend.

Splash, went he, as under he ducked,
  —I knew at the bottom rain-drippings stagnate ;
Next a handful of blossoms I plucked
  To bury him with, my bookshelf's magnate ;
Then I went indoors, brought out a loaf,
  Half a cheese, and a bottle of Chablis ;
Lay on the grass and forgot the oaf
  Over a jolly chapter of Rabelais.

Now, this morning, betwixt the moss
  And gum that locked our friend in limbo,
A spider had spun his web across,
  And sat in the midst with arms akimbo :
So, I took pity, for learning's sake,
  And, *de profundis, accentibus laetis,*
Cantate ! quoth I, as I got a rake,
  And up I fished his delectable treatise.

Here you have it, dry in the sun,
  With all the binding all of a blister,
And great blue spots where the ink has run,
  And reddish streaks that wink and glister
O'er the page so beautifully yellow :
  Oh, well have the droppings played their tricks !
Did he guess how toadstools grow, this fellow ?
  Here 's one stuck in his chapter six !

How did he like it when the live creatures
  Tickled and toused and browsed him all over,
And worm, slug, eft, with serious features,
  Came in, each one, for his right of trover ?
—When the water-beetle with great blind deaf face
  Made of her eggs the stately deposit,
And the newt borrowed just so much of the preface
  As tiled in the top of his black wife's closet ?

All that life and fun and romping,
  All that frisking and twisting and coupling,
While slowly our poor friend's leaves were swamping
  And clasps were cracking and covers suppling !
As if you had carried sour John Knox
  To the play-house at Paris, Vienna or Munich,
Fastened him into a front-row box,
  And danced off the ballet with trousers and tunic.

Come, old martyr !   What, torment enough is it ?
  Back to my room shall you take your sweet self !
Good-bye, mother-beetle ; husband-eft, *sufficit* !
  See the snug niche I have made on my shelf.
A.'s book shall prop you up, B.'s shall cover you,
  Here 's C. to be grave with, or D. to be gay,
And with E. on each side, and F. right over you,
  Dry-rot at ease till the Judgement-day !

R. BROWNING.

324. BURNHAM BEECHES

A BARD, dear Muse, unapt to sing,
  Your friendly aid beseeches,
Help me to touch the lyric string,
  In praise of Burnham beeches.

What though my tributary lines
  Be less like Pope's than Creech's,
The theme, if not the poet, shines,
  So bright are Burnham beeches.

O'er many a dell and upland walk,
  Their sylvan beauty reaches,
Of Birnam wood let Scotland talk,
  While we've our Burnham beeches.

Oft do I linger, oft return
  (Say, who my taste impeaches),
Where holly, juniper, and fern,
  Spring up round Burnham beeches.

Though deep embowered their shades among,
  The owl at midnight screeches,
Birds of far merrier, sweeter song,
  Enliven Burnham beeches.

If ' sermons be in stones ', I'll bet
  Our vicar when he preaches,
He'll find it easier far to get
  A hint from Burnham beeches.

Their glossy rind here winter stains,
  Here the hot solstice bleaches.
Bow, stubborn oaks ! bow, graceful planes !
  Ye match not Burnham beeches.

Gardens may boast a tempting show
   Of nectarines, grapes, and peaches
But daintiest truffles lurk below
   The boughs of Burnham beeches.

Poets and painters, hither hie,
   Here ample room for each is
With pencil and with pen to try
   His hand at Burnham beeches.

When monks, by holy Church well schooled,
   Were lawyers, statesmen, leeches,
Cured souls and bodies, judged or ruled,
   Then flourished Burnham beeches,

Skirting the convent's walls of yore,
   As yonder ruin teaches.
But shaven crown and cowl no more
   Shall darken Burnham beeches.

Here bards have mused, here lovers true
   Have dealt in softest speeches,
While suns declined, and, parting, threw
   Their gold o'er Burnham beeches.

O ne'er may woodman's axe resound
   Nor tempest, making breaches
In the sweet shade that cools the ground
   Beneath our Burnham beeches.

Hold ! though I'd fain be jingling on,
   My power no further reaches—
Again that rhyme ? enough—I've done,
   Farewell to Burnham beeches.

H. LUTTRELL.

325. THE FLOWER

ALONE, across a foreign plain,
   The Exile slowly wanders,
And on his Isle beyond the main
   With saddened spirit ponders.

This lovely Isle beyond the sea,
   With all its household treasures ;
Its cottage homes, its merry birds,
   And all its rural pleasures :

Its leafy woods, its shady vales,
   Its moors, and purple heather ;
Its verdant fields bedecked with stars
   His childhood loves to gather.

When lo ! he starts, with glad surprise,
   Home-joys come rushing o'er him,
For ' modest, wee, and crimson-tipped ',
   He spies the flower before him !

With eager haste he stoops him down,
   His eyes with moisture hazy,
And as he plucks the simple bloom,
   He murmurs, ' Lawk-a-daisy ! '

                      T. HOOD.

326. TO MEADOWS

YE have been fresh and green,
   Ye have been filled with flowers :
And ye the walks have been
   Where maids have spent their hours.

You have beheld, how they
   With wicker arks did come
To kiss, and bear away
   The richer cowslips home.

Ye have heard them sweetly sing,
   And seen them in a round :
Each virgin, like a Spring,
   With honeysuckles crowned.

But now, we see none here
   Whose silvery feet did tread,
And with dishevelled hair
   Adorned this smoother mead.

Like unthrifts, having spent
   Your stock, and needy grown,
Ye are left here to lament
   Your poor estates alone.

                    R. HERRICK.

327. HOW SPRINGS CAME FIRST

THESE springs were maidens once that loved,
But, lost to that they most approved,
My story tells, by Love they were
Turned to these springs which we see here ;
The pretty whimpering that they make,
When of the banks their leave they take,
Tells ye but this, they are the same,
In nothing changed but in their name.

                    R. HERRICK.

328. AN ELEGY ON A LAP-DOG

Shock's fate I mourn ; poor Shock is now no more ;
Ye Muses, mourn ; ye chambermaids, deplore.
Unhappy Shock ! yet more unhappy Fair,
Doomed to survive thy joy and only care !
Thy wretched fingers now no more shall deck,
And tie the favourite riband round his neck ;
No more thy hand shall smooth his glossy hair,
And comb the wavings of his pendant ear.
Yet cease thy flowing grief, forsaken maid ;
All mortal pleasures in a moment fade ;
Our surest hope is in an hour destroyed,
And love, best gift of Heaven, not long enjoyed.

Methinks I see her frantic with despair,
Her streaming eyes, wrung hands, and flowing hair ;
Her Mechlin pinners, rent, the floor bestrow,
And her torn fan gives real signs of woe.
Hence Superstition, that tormenting guest,
That haunts with fancied fears the coward breast ;
No dread events upon this fate attend,
Stream, eyes, no more, no more thy tresses rend.
Though certain omens oft forewarn a state,
And dying lions show the monarch's fate ;
Why should such fears bid Celia's sorrow rise ?
For, when a lap-dog falls, no lover dies.

Cease, Celia, cease ; restrain thy flowing tears,
Some warmer passion will dispel thy cares.
In man you'll find a more substantial bliss,
More grateful toying, and a sweeter kiss.
He 's dead.   Oh lay him gently in the ground !
And may his tomb be by this verse renowned :
' Here Shock, the pride of all his kind, is laid,
Who fawned like man, but ne'er like man betrayed.'

J. Gay.

329. AN EPITAPH

Here lies one, who never drew
Blood himself, yet many slew ;
Gave the gun its aim, and figure
Made in field, yet ne'er pulled trigger.
Armèd men have gladly made
Him their guide, and him obeyed ;
At his signified desire,
Would advance, present, and fire—
Stout he was, and large of limb,
Scores have fled at sight of him ;

And to all this fame he rose
Only following his nose.
Neptune was he called, not he
Who controls the boisterous sea,
But of happier command,
Neptune of the furrowed land ;
And, your wonder vain to shorten,
Pointer to Sir John Throckmorton.

W. COWPER.

330. ODE ON THE DEATH OF A FAVOURITE CAT DROWNED IN A TUB OF GOLD FISHES

'TWAS on a lofty vase's side
Where China's gayest art had dyed
    The azure flowers, that blow ;
Demurest of the tabby kind,
The pensive Selima reclined,
    Gazed on the lake below.

Her conscious tail her joy declared ;
The fair round face, the snowy beard,
    The velvet of her paws,
Her coat, that with the tortoise vies,
Her ears of jet, and emerald eyes
    She saw ; and purred applause.

Still had she gazed ; but 'midst the tide
Two angel forms were seen to glide,
    The Genii of the stream :
Their scaly armour's Tyrian hue
Through richest purple to the view
    Betrayed a golden gleam.

The hapless Nymph with wonder saw :
A whisker first and then a claw
    With many an ardent wish,
She stretched in vain to reach the prize.
What female heart can gold despise ?
    What Cat 's averse to fish ?

Presumptuous Maid ! with looks intent
Again she stretched, again she bent,
    Nor knew the gulf between.
(Malignant Fate sàt by and smiled)
The slippery verge her feet beguiled,
    She tumbled headlong in.

Eight times emerging from the flood
She mewed to every watry God,
    Some speedy aid to send.
No Dolphin came, no Nereid stirred :
Nor cruel Tom, nor Susan heard.
    A Favourite has no friend !

From hence, ye Beauties, undeceived,
Know, one false step is ne'er retrieved,
    And be with caution bold.
Not all that tempts your wandering eyes
And heedless hearts, is lawful prize ;
    Nor all, that glisters, gold.

                        T. GRAY.

331. TO A KITTEN

WANTON droll, whose harmless play
Beguiles the rustics' closing day,
When, drawn the evening fire about,
Sit aged crone and thoughtless lout,
And child upon his three-foot stool,
Waiting till his supper cool ;
And maid, whose cheek outblooms the rose,
As bright the blazing faggot glows,
Who, bending to the friendly light,
Plies her task with busy sleight ;
Come, show thy tricks and sportive graces,
Thus circled round with many faces.

Backward coiled and crouching low,
With glaring eye-balls watch thy foe,—
The housewife's spindle whirling round,
Or thread or straw, that on the ground
Its shadow throws, by urchin sly
Held out to lure thy roving eye ;
Then onward stealing, fiercely spring
Upon the futile faithless thing.
Now, wheeling round with bootless skill,
Thy bo-peep tail provokes thee still,
As oft beyond thy curving side
Its jetty tip is seen to glide ;
And see !—the start, the jet, the bound,
The giddy scamper round and round
With leap and toss and high curvet,
And many a whirling somerset.

The featest tumbler, stage bedight,
To thee is but a clumsy wight,

Who every limb and sinew strains
To do what costs thee little pains ;
For which, I trow, the gaping crowd
Requite him oft with praises loud.
But, stopped awhile thy wanton play,
Applauses too thy pains repay,
For now, beneath some urchin's hand
With modest pride thou tak'st thy stand,
While many a stroke of kindness glides
Along thy back and tabby sides.
Dilated swells thy glossy fur
And loudly sings thy busy purr
As, timing well the equal sound,
Thy clutching feet bepat the ground,
And all their harmless claws disclose,
Like prickles of an early rose ;
While softly from thy whiskered cheek
Thy half-closed eyes peer mild and meek.

But not alone by cottage fire
Do rustics rude thy feats admire.
Even he, whose mood of gloomy bent,
In lonely tower or prison pent,
Reviews the coil of former days,
And loathes the world and all its ways,
What time the lamp's unsteady gleam
Hath roused him from his moody dream,
Feels, as thou gambol'st round his seat,
His heart of pride less fiercely beat,
And smiles, a link in thee to find,
That joins it still to living kind.

Whence hast thou, then, thou witless puss !
The magic power to charm us thus ?
Is it that in thy glaring eye
And rapid movements, we descry—
Whilst we at ease, secure from ill,
The chimney corner snugly fill,—
A lion darting on its prey,
A tiger at his ruthless play ?
Or is it that in thee we trace
With all thy varied wanton grace,
An emblem, view'd with kindred eye,
Of tricksy, restless infancy ?
Ah ! many a lightly sportive child,
Who hath like thee our wits beguiled,
To dull and sober manhood grown,
With strange recoil our hearts disown.

And so, poor kit ! must thou endure,
When thou becom'st a cat demure,
Full many a cuff and angry word,
Chased roughly from the tempting board.
But yet, for that thou hast, I ween,
So oft our favoured playmate been,
Soft be the change which thou shalt prove,
When time hath spoiled thee of our love.
Still be thou deemed by housewife fat
A comely, careful, mousing cat,
Whose dish is, for the public good,
Replenished oft with savoury food.
Nor, when thy span of life is past,
Be thou to pond or dunghill cast,
But gently borne on goodman's spade,
Beneath the decent sod be laid ;
And children show with glistening eyes
The place where poor old pussy lies.

JOANNA BAILLIE.

332. THE KITTEN AND FALLING LEAVES

THAT way look, my Infant, lo !
What a pretty baby-show !
See the Kitten on the wall,
Sporting with the leaves that fall,
Withered leaves—one—two—and three—
From the lofty elder-tree !
Through the calm and frosty air
Of this morning bright and fair,
Eddying round and round they sink
Softly, slowly ; one might think,
From the motions that are made,
Every little leaf conveyed
Sylph or Faery hither tending,—
To this lower world descending,
Each invisible and mute,
In his wavering parachute.
—But the Kitten, how she starts,
Crouches, stretches, paws, and darts !
First at one, and then its fellow,
Just as light and just as yellow ;
There are many now—now one—
Now they stop and there are none :
What intenseness of desire
In her upward eye of fire !

With a tiger-leap half-way
Now she meets the coming prey,
Lets it go as fast, and then
Has it in her power again :
Now she works with three or four,
Like an Indian conjurer ;
Quick as he in feats of art,
Far beyond in joy of heart.
Were her antics played in the eye
Of a thousand standers-by,
Clapping hands with shout and stare,
What would little Tabby care
For the plaudits of the crowd ?
Over happy to be proud,
Over wealthy in the treasure
Of her own exceeding pleasure !

'Tis a pretty baby-treat ;
Nor, I deem, for me unmeet ;
Here, for neither Babe nor me,
Other playmate can I see.
Of the countless living things,
That with stir of feet and wings
(In the sun or under shade,
Upon bough or grassy blade)
And with busy revellings,
Chirp and song, and murmurings,
Made this orchard's narrow space,
And this vale, so blithe a place ;
Multitudes are swept away
Never more to breathe the day :
Some are sleeping ; some in bands
Travelled into distant lands ;
Others slunk to moor and wood,
Far from human neighbourhood ;
And among the Kinds that keep
With us closer fellowship,
With us openly abide,
All have laid their mirth aside.

Where is he that giddy Sprite,
Blue-cap, with his colours bright,
Who was blest as bird could be,
Feeding in the apple-tree ;
Made such wanton spoil and rout,
Turning blossoms inside out ;
Hung—head pointing towards the ground—
Fluttered, perched, into a round
Bound himself, and then unbound ;

Lithest, gaudiest Harlequin !
Prettiest Tumbler ever seen !
Light of heart and light of limb ;
What is now become of Him ?
Lambs, that through the mountains went
Frisking, bleating merriment,
When the year was in its prime,
They are sobered by this time.
If you look to vale or hill,
If you listen, all is still,
Save a little neighbouring rill,
That from out the rocky ground
Strikes a solitary sound.
Vainly glitter hill and plain,
And the air is calm in vain ;
Vainly Morning spreads the lure
Of a sky serene and pure ;
Creature none can she decoy
Into open sign of joy :
Is it that they have a fear
Of the dreary season near ?
Or that other pleasures be
Sweeter even than gaiety ?

Yet, whate'er enjoyments dwell
In the impenetrable cell
Of the silent heart which Nature
Furnishes to every creature ;
Whatsoe'er we feel and know
Too sedate for outward show,
Such a light of gladness breaks,
Pretty Kitten ! from thy freaks, —
Spreads with such a living grace
O'er my little Dora's face ;
Yes, the sight so stirs and charms
Thee, Baby, laughing in my arms,
That almost I could repine
That your transports are not mine,
That I do not wholly fare
Even as ye do, thoughtless pair !
And I will have my careless season
Spite of melancholy reason,
Will walk through life in such a way
That, when time brings on decay,
Now and then I may possess
Hours of perfect gladsomeness.
—Pleased by any random toy ;
By a kitten's busy joy,

Or an infant's laughing eye
Sharing in the ecstasy ;
I would fare like that or this,
Find my wisdom in my bliss ;
Keep the sprightly soul awake
And have faculties to take,
Even from things by sorrow wrought,
Matter for a jocund thought,
Spite of care, and spite of grief,
To gambol with Life's falling Leaf.

W. WORDSWORTH.

333. TO A CAT

I

STATELY, kindly, lordly friend,
    Condescend
Here to sit by me, and turn
Glorious eyes that smile and burn,
Golden eyes, love's lustrous meed,
On the golden page I read.

All your wondrous wealth of hair,
    Dark and fair,
Silken-shaggy, soft and bright
As the clouds and beams of night,
Pays my reverent hand's caress
Back with friendlier gentleness.

Dogs may fawn on all and some
    As they come ;
You, a friend of loftier mind,
Answer friends alone in kind.
Just your foot upon my hand
Softly bids it understand.

Morning round this silent sweet
    Garden-seat
Sheds its wealth of gathering light,
Thrills the gradual clouds with might,
Changes woodland, orchard, heath,
Lawn, and garden there beneath.

Fair and dim they gleamed below :
    Now they glow
Deep as even your sunbright eyes,

Fair as even the wakening skies.
Can it not or can it be
Now that you give thanks to see ?

May not you rejoice as I,
    Seeing the sky
Change to heaven revealed, and bid
Earth reveal the heaven it hid
All night long from stars and moon,
Now the sun sets all in tune ?

What within you wakes with day
    Who can say ?
All too little may we tell,
Friends who like each other well,
What might haply, if we might,
Bid us read our lives aright.

II

Wild on woodland ways your sires
    Flashed like fires ;
Fair as flame and fierce and fleet
As with wings on wingless feet
Shone and sprang your mother, free,
Bright and brave as wind or sea.

Free and proud and glad as they,
    Here to-day
Rests or roams their radiant child,
Vanquished not, but reconciled,
Free from curb of aught above
Save the lovely curb of love.

Love through dreams of souls divine
    Fain would shine
Round a dawn whose light and song
Then should right our mutual wrong—
Speak, and seal the love-lit law
Sweet Assisi's seer foresaw.

Dreams were theirs ; yet haply may
    Dawn a day
When such friends and fellows born,
Seeing our earth as fair at morn,
May for wiser love's sake see
More of heaven's deep heart than we.

A. C. SWINBURNE.

334. FABLE

THE mountain and the squirrel
Had a quarrel ;
And the former called the latter
   ' Little Prig '.
Bun replied,
' You are doubtless very big ;
But all sorts of things and weather
Must be taken in together,
To make up a year
And a sphere.
And I think it no disgrace
To occupy my place.

' If I'm not so large as you,
You are not so small as I,
And not half so spry.
I'll not deny you make
A very pretty squirrel track ;
Talents differ : all is well and wisely put ;
If I cannot carry forests on my back,
Neither can you crack a nut.'

R. W. EMERSON

335. EPITAPH ON A HARE

HERE lies, whom hound did ne'er pursue,
   Nor swifter greyhound follow,
Whose foot ne'er tainted morning dew,
   Nor ear heard huntsman's hallo ',

Old Tiney, surliest of his kind,
   Who, nursed with tender care,
And to domestic bounds confined,
   Was still a wild Jack-hare.

Though duly from my hand he took
   His pittance every night,
He did it with a jealous look,
   And, when he could, would bite.

His diet was of wheaten bread,
   And milk, and oats, and straw,
Thistles, or lettuces instead,
   With sand to scour his maw.

On twigs of hawthorn he regaled,
   On pippins' russet peel ;
And, when his juicy salads failed,
   Sliced carrot pleased him well.

A Turkey carpet was his lawn,
  Whereon he loved to bound,
To skip and gambol like a fawn,
  And swing his rump around.

His frisking was at evening hours,
  For then he lost his fear ;
But most before approaching showers,
  Or when a storm drew near.

Eight years and five round-rolling moons
  He thus saw steal away,
Dozing out all his idle noons,
  And every night at play.

I kept him for his humour' sake,
  For he would oft beguile
My heart of thoughts that made it ache,
  And force me to a smile.

But now, beneath this walnut-shade
  He finds his long, last home,
And waits in snug concealment laid,
  Till gentler Puss shall come.

He, still more aged, feels the shocks
  From which no care can save,
And, partner once of Tiney's box,
  Must soon partake his grave.

                       W. COWPER.

336. THE MESSAGE

YE little birds that sit and sing
  Amidst the shady valleys,
And see how Phyllis sweetly walks
  Within her garden-alleys ;
Go, pretty birds, about her bower ;
Sing, pretty birds, she may not lower ;
Ah me ! methinks I see her frown !
  Ye pretty wantons, warble.

Go tell her through your chirping bills,
  As you by me are bidden,
To her is only known my love,
  Which from the world is hidden.
Go, pretty birds, and tell her so ;
See that your notes strain not too low,
For still methinks I see her frown ;
  Ye pretty wantons, warble.

Go tune your voices' harmony
   And sing, I am her lover ;
Strain loud and sweet, that every note
   With sweet content may move her :
And she that hath the sweetest voice,
Tell her I will not change my choice :
—Yet still methinks I see her frown !
   Ye pretty wantons, warble.

O fly ! make haste ! see, see, she falls
   Into a pretty slumber !
Sing round about her rosy bed
   That waking she may wonder.
Say to her, 'tis her lover true
That sendeth love to you, to you ;
And when you hear her kind reply
   Return with pleasant warblings.

T. HEYWOOD

337. SWEET SUFFOLK OWL

SWEET Suffolk owl, so trimly dight
With feathers, like a lady bright ;
Thou sing'st alone, sitting by night,
   ' Te whit ! Te whoo ! '

Thy note that forth so freely rolls
With shrill command the mouse controls ;
And sings a dirge for dying souls.
   ' Te whit ! Te whoo ! '

UNKNOWN.

338. THE JACKDAW

THERE is a bird, who by his coat,
And by the hoarseness of his note
   Might be supposed a crow ;
A great frequenter of the church,
Where, bishop-like, he finds a perch,
   And dormitory too.

Above the steeple shines a plate,
That turns and turns, to indicate
   From what point blows the weather.
Look up—your brains begin to swim,
'Tis in the clouds—that pleases him,
   He chooses it the rather.

Fond of the speculative height,
Thither he wings his airy flight,
   And thence securely sees

The bustle and the raree-show
That occupy mankind below,
   Secure and at his ease.

You think, no doubt, he sits and muses
On future broken bones and bruises,
   If he should chance to fall.
No ; not a single thought like that
Employs his philosophic pate,
   Or troubles it at all.

He sees, that this great roundabout——
The world, with all its motley rout,
   Church, army, physic, law,
Its customs, and its businesses,——
Is no concern at all of his,
   And says—what says he ?—Caw.

Thrice happy bird ! I too have seen
Much of the vanities of men ;
   And, sick of having seen 'em,
Would cheerfully these limbs resign
For such a pair of wings as thine,
   And such a head between 'em.

                       W. COWPER.

339. ON THE DEATH OF MRS. THROCKMORTON'S BULLFINCH

YE nymphs ! if e'er your eyes were red
With tears o'er hapless favourites shed,
   O share Maria's grief !
Her favourite, even in his cage,
(What will not hunger's cruel rage ?)
   Assassined by a thief.

Where Rhenus strays his vines among,
The egg was laid from which he sprung,
   And though by nature mute,
Or only with a whistle blest,
Well-taught, he all the sounds expressed
   Of flageolet or flute.

The honours of his ebon poll
Were brighter than the sleekest mole ;
   His bosom of the hue
With which Aurora decks the skies,
When piping winds shall soon arise
   To sweep up all the dew.

Above, below, in all the house,
Dire foe, alike to bird and mouse,
    No cat had leave to dwell ;
And Bully's cage supported stood,
On props of smoothest-shaven wood,
    Large-built and latticed well.

Well-latticed—but the grate, alas !
Not rough with wire of steel or brass,
    For Bully's plumage sake,
But smooth with wands from Ouse's side,
With which, when neatly peeled and dried,
    The swains their baskets make.

Night veiled the pole—all seemed secure—
When led by instinct sharp and sure,
    Subsistence to provide,
A beast forth-sallied on the scout,
Long-backed, long-tailed, with whiskered snout,
    And badger-coloured hide.

He, entering at the study-door,
Its ample area 'gan explore ;
    And something in the wind
Conjectured, sniffing round and round,
Better than all the books he found,
    Food, chiefly, for the mind.

Just then, by adverse fate impressed
A dream disturbed poor Bully's rest;
    In sleep he seemed to view
A rat, fast-clinging to the cage,
And, screaming at the sad presage,
    Awoke and found it true.

For, aided both by ear and scent,
Right to his mark the monster went—
    Ah, Muse ! forbear to speak
Minute the horrors that ensued ;
His teeth were strong, the cage was wood—
    He left poor Bully's beak.

He left it—but he should have ta'en
That beak, whence issued many a strain
    Of such mellifluous tone,
Might have repaid him well, I wote,
For silencing so sweet a throat,
    Fast set within his own.

Maria weeps—The Muses mourn—
So, when by Bacchanalians torn,
    On Thracian Hebrus' side
The tree-enchanter Orpheus fell ;
His head alone remained to tell
     The cruel death he died.

W. COWPER.

340. THE ROBIN'S GRAVE

TREAD lightly here, for here, 'tis said,
When piping winds are hushed around,
A small note wakes from underground,
Where now his tiny bones are laid.
No more in lone and leafless groves,
With ruffled wing and faded breast,
His friendless, homeless spirit roves ;
—Gone to the world where birds are blessed !
Where never cat glides o'er the green,
Or schoolboy's giant form is seen ;
But Love, and Joy, and smiling Spring
Inspire their little souls to sing.

S. ROGERS.

341. THE GOOSE

I KNEW an old wife lean and poor,
  Her rags scarce held together ;
There strode a stranger to the door,
  And it was windy weather.

He held a goose upon his arm,
  He uttered rhyme and reason,
' Here, take the goose, and keep you warm,
  It is a stormy season.'

She caught the white goose by the leg,
  A goose—'twas no great matter.
The goose let fall a golden egg
  With cackle and with clatter.

She dropped the goose, and caught the pelf,
  And ran to tell her neighbours ;
And blessed herself, and cursed herself,
  And rested from her labours.

And feeding high, and living soft,
　Grew plump and able-bodied ;
Until the grave churchwarden doffed,
　The parson smirked and nodded.

So sitting, served by man and maid,
　She felt her heart grow prouder :
But ah ! the more the white goose laid
　It clacked and cackled louder.

It cluttered here, it chuckled there ;
　It stirred the old wife's mettle :
She shifted in her elbow-chair,
　And hurled the pan and kettle.

' A quinsy choke thy cursèd note ! '
　Then waxed her anger stronger.
' Go, take the goose, and wring her throat,
　I will not bear it longer.'

Then yelped the cur, and yawled the cat ;
　Ran Gaffer, stumbled Gammer.
The goose flew this way and flew that,
　And filled the house with clamour.

As head and heels upon the floor
　They floundered all together,
There strode a stranger to the door,
　And it was windy weather :

He took the goose upon his arm,
　He uttered words of scorning ;
' So keep you cold, or keep you warm,
　It is a stormy morning.'

The wild wind rang from park and plain,
　And round the attics rumbled,
Till all the tables danced again,
　And half the chimneys tumbled.

The glass blew in, the fire blew out,
　The blast was hard and harder.
Her cap blew off, her gown blew up,
　And a whirlwind cleared the larder ;

And while on all sides breaking loose
　Her household fled the danger,
Quoth she, ' The Devil take the goose,
　And God forget the stranger ! '

ALFRED, LORD TENNYSON.

342.   THE BLACKBIRD

O BLACKBIRD ! sing me something well :
  While all the neighbours shoot thee round,
  I keep smooth plats of fruitful ground,
Where thou mayest warble, eat and dwell.

The espaliers and the standards all
  Are thine ; the range of lawn and park :
  The unnetted black-hearts ripen dark,
All thine, against the garden wall.

Yet, though I spared thee all the spring,
  Thy sole delight is, sitting still,
  With that gold dagger of thy bill
To fret the summer jenneting.

A golden bill ! the silver tongue,
  Cold February loved, is dry :
  Plenty corrupts the melody
That made thee famous once, when young :

And in the sultry garden-squares,
  Now thy flute-notes are changed to coarse,
  I hear thee not at all, or hoarse
As when a hawker hawks his wares.

Take warning ! he that will not sing
  While yon sun prospers in the blue,
  Shall sing for want, ere leaves are new,
Caught in the frozen palms of Spring.

                    ALFRED, LORD TENNYSON.

343.   BUSY, CURIOUS, THIRSTY FLY

  BUSY, curious, thirsty fly,
  Drink with me, and drink as I ;
  Freely welcome to my cup,
  Couldst thou sip and sip it up.
  Make the most of life you may,
  Life is short and wears away.

  Both alike are mine and thine
  Hastening quick to their decline ;
  Thine 's a summer, mine 's no more,
  Though repeated to threescore ;
  Threescore summers, when they're gone,
  Will appear as short as one.

                    W. OLDYS.

344. THE DRAGON-FLY

LIFE (priest and poet say) is but a dream ;
　I wish no happier one than to be laid
　Beneath a cool syringa's scented shade,
Or wavy willow, by the running stream,
　Brimful of moral, where the Dragon-fly
Wanders as careless and content as I.

Thanks for this fancy, insect king,
Of purple crest and filmy wing,
Who with indifference givest up
The water-lily's golden cup ;
To come again and overlook
What I am writing in my book.
Believe me, most who read the line
Will read with hornier eyes than thine ;
And yet their souls shall live for ever,
And thine drop dead into the river !
God pardon them, O insect king,
Who fancy so unjust a thing !

W. S. LANDOR.

345. TO AN INSECT

I LOVE to hear thine earnest voice,
　Wherever thou art hid,
Thou testy little dogmatist,
　Thou pretty Katydid !
Thou mindest me of gentlefolks,—
　Old gentlefolks are they,—
Thou say'st an undisputed thing
　In such a solemn way.

Thou art a female, Katydid !
　I know it by the trill
That quivers through thy piercing notes,
　So petulant and shrill ;
I think there is a knot of you
　Beneath the hollow tree,—
A knot of spinster Katydids,—
　Do Katydids drink tea ?

O tell me where did Katy live,
　And what did Katy do ?
And was she very fair and young,
　And yet so wicked, too ?

Did Katy love a naughty man,
  Or kiss more cheeks than one ?
I warrant Katy did no more
  Than many a Kate has done.

Dear me ! I'll tell you all about
  My fuss with little Jane,
And Ann, with whom I used to walk
  So often down the lane,
And all that tore their locks of black
  Or wet their eyes of blue,—
Pray tell me, sweetest Katydid,
  What did poor Katy do ?

Ah no ! the living oak shall crash,
  That stood for ages still,
The rock shall rend its mossy base
  And thunder down the hill,
Before the little Katydid
  Shall add one word, to tell
The mystic story of the maid
  Whose name she knows so well.

Peace to the ever-murmuring race
  And when the latest one
Shall fold in death her feeble wings
  Beneath the autumn sun,
Then shall she raise her fainting voice,
  And lift her drooping lid,
And then the child of future years
  Shall hear what Katy did.

O. W. HOLMES.

346.   THE BAIT

COME live with me, and be my love,
And we will some new pleasures prove
Of golden sands, and crystal brooks,
With silken lines and silver hooks.

There will the river whispering run
Warmed by thy eyes, more than the sun ;
And there the enamoured fish will stay,
Begging themselves they may betray.

When thou wilt swim in that live bath,
Each fish, which every channel hath,
Will amorously to thee swim,
Gladder to catch thee, than thou him.

If thou, to be so seen, beest loath,
By sun or moon, thou darkenest both,
And if myself have leave to see,
I need not their light, having thee.

Let others freeze with angling reeds,
And cut their legs with shells and weeds,
Or treacherously poor fish beset,
With strangling snare, or windowy net.

Let coarse bold hands from slimy nest
The bedded fish in banks out-wrest ;
Or curious traitors, sleeve-silk flies,
Bewitch poor fishes' wandering eyes.

For thee, thou need'st no such deceit,
For thou thyself art thine own bait :
That fish, that is not catched thereby,
Alas ! is wiser far than I.

J. DONNE.

347.　OH, THE BRAVE FISHER'S LIFE

OH, the brave fisher's life,
It is the best of any,
'Tis full of pleasure, void of strife,
And 'tis beloved of many :
　　　Other joys
　　　Are but toys,
　　　Only this
　　　Lawful is,
　　　For our skill
　　　Breeds no ill,
But content and pleasure.

In a morning up we rise
Ere Aurora's peeping,
Drink a cup to wash our eyes,
Leave the sluggard sleeping ;
　　　Then we go
　　　To and fro,
　　　With our knacks
　　　At our backs,
　　　To such streams
　　　As the Thames,
If we have the leisure.

When we please to walk abroad
For our recreation,
In the fields is our abode,
Full of delectation :
    Where in a brook
    With a hook,
    Or a lake
    Fish we take,
    There we sit
    For a bit,
Till we fish entangle.

We have gentles in a horn,
We have paste and worms too,
We can watch both night and morn,
Suffer rain and storms too :
    None do here
    Use to swear,
    Oaths do fray
    Fish away,
    We sit still,
    Watch our quill,
Fishers must not wrangle.

If the sun's excessive heat
Makes our bodies swelter,
To an osier hedge we get
For a friendly shelter,
    Where in a dike
    Perch or pike,
    Roach or dace
    We do chase,
    Bleak or gudgeon
    Without grudging,
We are still contented.

Or we sometimes pass an hour
Under a green willow,
That defends us from a shower,
Making earth our pillow ;
    There we may
    Think and pray
    Before death
    Stops our breath :
    Other joys
    Are but toys
And to be lamented.

J. CHALKHILL.

348. TO A FISH OF THE BROOKE

WHY flyest thou away with fear ?
Trust me there 's naught of danger near,
  I have no wicked hooke
All covered with a snaring bait,
Alas, to tempt thee to thy fate,
  And dragge thee from the brooke.

O harmless tenant of the flood,
I do not wish to spill thy blood,
  For Nature unto thee
Perchance hath given a tender wife,
And children dear, to charm thy life,
  As she hath done for me.

Enjoy thy stream, O harmless fish ;
And when an angler for his dish,
  Through gluttony's vile sin,
Attempts, a wretch, to pull thee *out*,
God give thee strength, O gentle trout,
  To pull the raskall *in* !

           J. WOLCOT.

349. TO THE IMMORTAL MEMORY OF THE HALIBUT ON WHICH I DINED THIS DAY

WHERE hast thou floated, in what seas pursued
Thy pastime ? when wast thou an egg new-spawned,
Lost in th' immensity of ocean's waste ?
Roar as they might, the overbearing winds
That rocked the deep, thy cradle, thou wast safe—
And in thy minikin and embryo state,
Attached to the firm leaf of some salt weed,
Didst outlive tempests, such as wrung and racked
The joints of many a stout and gallant bark,
And whelmed them in the unexplored abyss.
Indebted to no magnet and no chart,
Nor under guidance of the polar fire,
Thou wast a voyager on many coasts,
Grazing at large in meadows submarine,
Where flat Batavia just emerging peeps
Above the brine,—where Caledonia's rocks
Beat back the surge,—and where Hibernia shoots
Her wondrous causeway far into the main.
—Wherever thou hast fed, thou little thought'st,
And I not more, that I should feed on thee.

Peace therefore, and good health, and much good fish,
To him who sent thee ! and success, as oft
As it descends into the billowy gulf,
To the same drag that caught thee !—Fare thee well !
Thy lot thy brethren of the slimy fin
Would envy, could they know that thou wast doomed
To feed a bard, and to be praised in verse.

W. COWPER.

350. TO MISTRESS MARGARET HUSSEY

MERRY Margaret,
As midsummer flower,
Gentle as falcon,
Or hawk of the tower ;
With solace and gladness,
Much mirth and no madness,
All good and no badness ;
So joyously,
So maidenly,
So womanly
Her demeaning
In every thing,
Far, far passing
That I can indite,
Or suffice to write
Of Merry Margaret
As midsummer flower,
Gentle as falcon,
Or hawk of the tower.
As patient and as still
And as full of good will
As fair Isaphill,
Coliander,
Sweet pomander,
Good Cassander ;
Steadfast of thought,
Well made, well wrought,
Far may be sought,
Ere that ye can find
So courteous, so kind,
As merry Margaret,
This midsummer flower,
Gentle as falcon,
Or hawk of the tower.

J. SKELTON

351. HIS PRAYER TO BEN JONSON

WHEN I a verse shall make,
Know I have prayed thee,
For old religion's sake,
Saint Ben, to aid me.

Make the way smooth for me,
When I, thy Herrick,
Honouring thee, on my knee
Offer my lyric.

Candles I'll give to thee,
And a new altar ;
And thou, Saint Ben, shalt be
Writ in my psalter.

R. HERRICK.

352. TO CYRIACK SKINNER

CYRIACK, whose grandsire on the royal bench
  Of British Themis, with no mean applause
  Pronounced and in his volumes taught our laws,
  Which others at their bar so often wrench :
To-day deep thoughts resolve with me to drench
  In mirth, that after no repenting draws ;
  Let Euclid rest and Archimedes pause,
  And what the Swede intend, and what the French.
To measure life, learn thou betimes, and know
  Toward solid good what leads the nearest way ;
  For other things mild Heaven a time ordains,
And disapproves that care, though wise in show,
  That with superfluous burden loads the day,
  And when God sends a cheerful hour, refrains.

J. MILTON.

353. STANZAS TO AUGUSTA

THOUGH the day of my destiny 's over,
  And the star of my fate hath declined,
Thy soft heart refused to discover
  The faults which so many could find ;
Though thy soul with my grief was acquainted,
  It shrunk not to share it with me,
And the love which my spirit hath painted
  It never hath found but in *thee*.

Then when nature around me is smiling,
 The last smile which answers to mine,
I do not believe it beguiling,
 Because it reminds me of thine ;
And when winds are at war with the ocean,
 As the breasts I believed in with me,
If their billows excite an emotion,
 It is that they bear me from *thee*.

Though the rock of my last hope is shivered,
 And its fragments are sunk in the wave,
Though I feel that my soul is delivered
 To pain—it shall not be its slave.
There is many a pang to pursue me :
 They may crush, but they shall not contemn ;
They may torture, but shall not subdue me ;
 'Tis of *thee* that I think—not of them.

Though human, thou didst not deceive me,
 Though woman, thou didst not forsake,
Though loved, thou forborest to grieve me,
 Though slandered, thou never couldst shake ;
Though trusted, thou didst not disclaim me,
 Though parted, it was not to fly,
Though watchful, 'twas not to defame me,
 Nor, mute, that the world might belie.

Yet I blame not the world, nor despise it,
 Nor the war of the many with one ;
If my soul was not fitted to prize it,
 'Twas folly not sooner to shun :
And if dearly that error hath cost me,
 And more than I once could foresee,
I have found that, whatever it lost me,
 It could not deprive me of *thee*.

From the wreck of the past, which hath perished,
 Thus much I at least may recall,
It hath taught me that what I most cherished
 Deserved to be dearest of all :
In the desert a fountain is springing,
 In the wide waste there still is a tree,
And a bird in the solitude singing,
 Which speaks to my spirit of *thee*.

                    G. GORDON, LORD BYRON.

354. TO THOMAS MOORE

My boat is on the shore,
    And my bark is on the sea ;
But, before I go, Tom Moore,
    Here's a double health to thee !

Here's a sigh to those that love me,
    And a smile to those who hate ;
And, whatever sky's above me,
    Here's a heart for every fate.

Though the ocean roar around me,
    Yet it still shall bear me on ;
Though a desert should surround me,
    It hath springs that may be won.

Were 't the last drop in the well,
    As I gasped upon the brink,
Ere my fainting spirit fell,
    'Tis to thee that I would drink.

With that water, as this wine,
    The libation I would pour
Should be—peace with thine and mine,
    And a health to thee, Tom Moore.

G. Gordon, Lord Byron.

355. TO C. S. C.

Oh, when the grey courts of Christ's College glowed
With all the rapture of thy frequent lay,
When printers' devils chuckled as they strode,
And blithe compositors grew loudly gay :
Did Granta realize that here abode,
Here in the home of Milton, Wordsworth, Gray,
A poet not unfit to cope with any
That ever wore the bays or turned a penny ?

The wit of smooth delicious Matthew Prior,
The rhythmic grace which Hookham Frere displayed,
The summer lightning wreathing Byron's lyre,
The neat inevitable turns of Praed,
Rhymes to which Hudibras could scarce aspire,
Such metric pranks as Gilbert oft has played,
All these good gifts and others far sublimer
Are found in thee, belovèd Cambridge rhymer.

And scholarship as sound as his whose name
Matched thine (he lives to mourn, alas, thy death,
And now enjoys the plenitude of fame,
And oft to crowded audience lectureth,
Or writes to prove religion is the same
As science, unbelief a form of faith) :—
Ripe scholar ! Virgil's self would not be chary
Of praises for thy *Carmen Seculare.*

Whene'er I take my ' pint of beer ' a day,
I ' gaze into my glass ' and think of thee :
When smoking, after ' lunch is cleared away ',
Thy face amid the cloud I seem to see ;
When ' that sweet mite with whom I used to play ',
Or ' Araminta ', or ' the fair Miss P.'
Recur to me, I think upon thy verses,
Which still my beating heart and quench my curses.

Ah, Calverley ! if in these lays of mine
Some sparkle of thy radiant genius burned,
Or were in any poem—stanza—line
Some faint reflection of thy muse discerned :
If any critic would remark in fine
' Of C. S. C. this gentle art he learned ' ;
I should not then expect my book to fail,
Nor have my doubts about a decent sale.

J. K. STEPHEN.

356. TO ANDREW LANG

DEAR Andrew, with the brindled hair,
Who glory to have thrown in air,
High over arm, the trembling reed,
By Ale and Kail, by Till and Tweed :
An equal craft of hand you show
The pen to guide, the fly to throw :
I count you happy starred ; for God,
When he with inkpot and with rod
Endowed you, bade your fortune lead
Forever by the crooks of Tweed,
Forever by the woods of song
And lands that to the Muse belong ;
Or if in peopled streets, or in
The abhorred pedantic sanhedrim,
It should be yours to wander, still
Airs of the morn, airs of the hill,
The plovery Forest and the seas
That break about the Hebrides,

Should follow over field and plain
And find you at the window pane ;
And you again see hill and peel,
And the bright springs gush at your heel.
So went the fiat forth, and so
Garrulous like a brook you go,
With sound of happy mirth and sheen
Of daylight—whether by the green
You face that moment, or the grey ;
Whether you dwell in March or May ;
Or whether treat of reels and rods
Or of the old unhappy gods :
Still like a brook your page has shone,
And your ink sings of Helicon.

R. L. STEVENSON.

357.　MRS. FRANCES HARRIS'S PETITION

WRITTEN IN THE YEAR 1701

To their Excellencies the Lord Justices of Ireland
The Humble Petition of Frances Harris, who must
Starve, and die a Maid, if it Miscarries

Humbly showeth,

THAT I went to warm myself in Lady Betty's chamber, because I was cold,
And I had in a purse seven pounds, four shillings, and sixpence, besides farthings, in money and gold :
So, because I had been buying things for my lady last night,
I was resolved to tell my money, and see if it was right.
Now you must know, because my trunk has a very bad lock,
Therefore all the money I have, which God knows, is a very small stock,
I keep in my pocket, tied about my middle, next my smock.
So, when I went to put up my purse, as luck would have it, my smock was unripped,
And instead of putting it into my pocket, down it slipped :
Then the bell rung, and I went down to put my lady to bed :
And, God knows, I thought my money was as safe as my stupid head !
So, when I came up again, I found my pocket feel very light :
But when I searched, and missed my purse, law ! I thought I should have sunk outright.
' Lawk, madam,' says Mary, ' how d'ye do ? '　' Indeed,' says I, ' never worse :
But pray, Mary, can you tell what I've done with my purse ? '

'Lawk, help me!' said Mary, 'I never stirred out of this place:'
'Nay,' said I, 'I had it in Lady Betty's chamber, that's a plain case.'
So Mary got me to bed, and covered me up warm:
However, she stole away my garters, that I might do myself no harm.
So I tumbled and tossed all night, as you may very well think,
But hardly ever set my eyes together, or slept a wink.
So I was a-dreamed, methought, that I went and searched the folks round,
And in a corner of Mrs. Dukes's box, tied in a rag the money was found.
So next morning we told Whittle, and he fell a-swearing:
Then my dame Wadger came: and she, you know, is thick of hearing:
'Dame,' said I, as loud as I could bawl, 'do you know what a loss I have had?'
'Nay,' said she, 'my Lord Colway's folks are all very sad;
For my Lord Dromedary comes a Tuesday without fail.'
'Pugh!' said I, 'but that's not the business that I ail.'
Says Cary, says he, 'I've been a servant this five-and-twenty years come spring,
And in all the places I lived I never heard of such a thing.'
'Yes,' says the steward, 'I remember, when I was at my Lady Shrewsbury's,
Such a thing as this happened, just about the time of gooseberries.'
So I went to the party suspected, and I found her full of grief
(Now you must know, of all things in the world I hate a thief),
However, I was resolved to bring the discourse slily about:
'Mrs. Dukes,' said I, 'here's an ugly accident has happened out:
'Tis not that I value the money three skips of a mouse;
But the thing I stand upon is the credit of the house.
'Tis true, seven pounds, four shillings, and sixpence, makes a great hole in my wages:
Besides, as they say, service is no inheritance in these ages.
Now, Mrs. Dukes, you know, and everybody understands,
That though 'tis hard to judge, yet money can't go without hands.'
'The devil take me,' said she (blessing herself), 'if ever I saw 't!'
So she roared like a Bedlam, as though I had called her all to naught.
So you know, what could I say to her any more?
I e'en left her, and came away as wise as I was before.
Well: but then they would have had me gone to the cunning man.
'No,' said I, ''tis the same thing, the chaplain will be here anon.'
So the chaplain came in. Now the servants say he is my sweetheart,
Because he's always in my chamber, and I always take his part.
So, as the devil would have it, before I was aware, out I blundered,
'Parson,' said I, 'can you cast a nativity when a body's plundered?'
(Now you must know, he hates to be called parson, like the devil.)
'Truly,' says he, 'Mrs. Nab, it might become you to be more civil;
If your money be gone, as a learned divine says, d'ye see,
You are no text for my handling; so take that from me:

I was never taken for a conjurer before, I'd have you to know.'
' Law ! ' said I, ' don't be angry, I am sure I never thought you so ;
You know I honour the cloth ; I design to be a parson's wife,
I never took one in your coat for a conjurer in all my life.'
With that, he twisted his girdle at me like a rope, as who should say,
' Now you may hang yourself for me ! ' and so went away.
Well : I thought I should have swooned, ' Law ! ' said I, ' what shall
    I do ?
I have lost my money, and shall lose my true love too ! '
Then my lord called me : ' Harry,' said my lord, ' don't cry,
I'll give you something towards your loss ' ; and, says my lady, ' so
    will I.'
' O, but,' said I, ' what if, after all, the chaplain won't come to ? '
For that, he said (an't please your Excellencies), I must petition you.
The premises tenderly considered, I desire your Excellencies' protection,
And that I may have a share in next Sunday's collection ;
And, over and above, that I may have your Excellencies' letter,
With an order for the chaplain aforesaid, or, instead of him, a better :
And then your poor petitioner both night and day,
Or the chaplain (for 'tis his trade), as in duty bound, shall ever pray.

J. SWIFT.

358. MARY THE COOK-MAID'S LETTER
TO DOCTOR SHERIDAN

WRITTEN IN THE YEAR 1723

WELL ! if ever I saw such another man, since my mother bound my
    head !
You a gentleman ! Marry come up ! I wonder where you were bred ?
I am sure such words do not become a man of your cloth !
I would not give such language to a dog ! faith and troth !
Yes, you called my master a knave ! Fie ! Mr. Sheridan ! 'tis a shame
For a parson, who should know better things, to come out with such
    a name.
Knave in your teeth, Mr. Sheridan ! 'Tis both a shame and a sin ;
And the dean, my master, is an honester man than you and all your
    kin :
He has more goodness in his little finger, than you have in your whole
    body !
My master is a parsonable man, and not a spindle-shanked hoddy-
    doddy !
    And now whereby I find you would fain make an excuse,
Because my master, one day, in anger, called you goose !
Which, and I am sure I have been his servant four years since October,
And he never called me worse than sweetheart drunk or sober.

Not that I know that his Reverence was ever concerned, to my knowledge ;
Though you and your come-rogues keep him out so late, in your College.
You say you will eat grass on his grave : a Christian eat grass !
Whereby you now confess yourself to be a goose, or an ass.
But that 's as much as to say, that my master should die before ye.
Well ! Well ! That 's as God pleases, and I don't believe that 's a true story !
And so say I told you so, and you may go tell my master ! What care I ?
And I don't care who knows it, 'tis all one to Mary !
Everybody knows that I love to tell truth, and shame the Devil ;
I am but a poor servant ; but I think Gentlefolks should be civil !

Besides, you found fault with our vittels, one day that you were here :
I remember it was upon a Tuesday, of all days in the year !
And Saunders, the man, says you are always jesting and mocking.
' Mary,' said he, one day, as I was mending my master's stocking,
My master is so fond of that minister, that keeps the school !
I thought my master was a wise man ; but that man makes him a fool ! '
' Saunders,' says I, ' I would rather than a quart of ale,
He would come into our kitchen ; and I would pin a dish-clout to his tail ! '

And now I must go, and get Saunders to direct this letter,
For I write but a sad scrawl ; but my sister Marget, she writes better.
Well ! but I must run, and make the bed, before my master comes from prayers.
And see now, it strikes ten, and I hear him coming upstairs.
Whereof I could say more to your verses, if I could write written hand :
And so I remain, in a civil way, your servant to command,—Mary.

J. SWIFT.

359. TO SIR ROBERT WALPOLE

GREAT Sir, as on each levée day
I still attend you—still you say—
I'm busy now, to-morrow come ;
To-morrow, sir, you're not at home ;
So says your porter, and dare I
Give such a man as him the lie ?

In imitation, sir, of you,
I keep a mighty levée too :
Where my attendants, to their sorrow,
Are bid to come again to-morrow.
To-morrow they return, no doubt,
But then, like you, sir, I'm gone out.

So says my maid ; but they less civil
Give maid and master to the devil ;
And then with menaces depart,
Which could you hear would pierce your heart.
Good sir, do make my levée fly me,
Or lend your porter to deny me.

H. FIELDING.

360.   AN EPISTLE TO SIR ROBERT WALPOLE

WHILE at the helm of State you ride,
Our nation's envy, and its pride ;
While foreign Courts with wonder gaze,
And curse those counsels that they praise ;
Would you not wonder, sir, to view
Your bard a greater man than you ?
Which that he is, you cannot doubt,
When you have read the sequel out.

You know, great sir, that ancient fellows,
Philosophers, and such folks, tell us,
No great analogy between
Greatness and happiness is seen,
If then, as it might follow straight,
Wretched to be, is to be great ;
Forbid it, gods, that you should try
What 'tis to be so great as I !

The family that dines the latest
Is in our street esteemed the greatest ;
But latest hours must surely fall
'Fore him who never dines at all.
Your taste in architect, you know,
Hath been admired by friend and foe ;
But can your earthly domes compare
With all my castles—in the air ?
We're often taught, it doth behove us
To think those greater who're above us ;
Another instance of my glory,
Who live above you, twice two story ;
And from my garret can look down
On the whole street of Arlington.

Greatness by poets still is painted
With many followers acquainted ;
This, too, doth in my favour speak ;
Your levée is but twice a week ;
From mine I can exclude but one day,
My door is quiet on a Sunday.

Nor in the matter of attendance
Doth your great bard claim less ascendance.
Familiar you to admiration
May be approached by all the nation ;
While I, like the Mogul in Indo,
Am never seen but at the window.
If with my greatness you're offended,
The fault is easily amended ;
For I'll come down, with wondrous ease,
Into whatever *place* you please.
I'm not ambitious ; little matters
Will serve us great, but humble creatures.

Suppose a secretary o' this isle,
Just to be doing with a while ;
Admiral, general, judge, or bishop :
Or I can foreign treaties dish up.
If the good genius of the nation
Should call me to negotiation,
Tuscan and French are in my head,
Latin I write, and Greek—I read.
If you should ask, what pleases best ?
To get the most, and do the least ;
What fittest for ?—you know, I'm sure,
I'm fittest for—a sinecure.

H. FIELDING.

361. ON SEEING A PORTRAIT OF SIR ROBERT WALPOLE

SUCH were the lively eyes and rosy hue
Of Robin's face, when Robin first I knew,
The gay companion and the favourite guest,
Loved without awe, and without views caressed.
His cheerful smile and open honest look
Added new graces to the truth he spoke.
Then every man found something to commend,
The pleasant neighbour, and the worthy friend :
The generous master of a private house,
The tender father, and indulgent spouse.
The hardest censors at the worst believed,
His temper was too easily deceived
(A consequential ill good-nature draws,
A bad effect, but from a noble cause).
Whence then these clamours of a judging crowd,
' Suspicious, griping, insolent, and proud—
Rapacious, cruel, violent, and unjust ;
False to his friend, and traitor to his trust.'

LADY M. WORTLEY MONTAGU.

362.   TO MARIA GISBORNE

You are now
In London, that great sea, whose ebb and flow
At once is deaf and loud, and on the shore
Vomits its wrecks, and still howls on for more.
Yet in its depth what treasures !   You will see
That which was Godwin,—greater none than he
Though fallen—and fallen on evil times—to stand
Among the spirits of our age and land,
Before the dread tribunal of *to come*
The foremost,—while Rebuke cowers pale and dumb.
You will see Coleridge—he who sits obscure
In the exceeding lustre and the pure
Intense irradiation of a mind,
Which, with its own internal lightning blind,
Flags wearily through darkness and despair—
A cloud-encircled meteor of the air,
A hooded eagle among blinking owls.—
You will see Hunt—one of those happy souls
Which are the salt of the earth, and without whom
This world would smell like what it is—a tomb ;
Who is, what others seem ; his room no doubt
Is still adorned with many a cast from Shout,
With graceful flowers tastefully placed about ;
And coronals of bay from ribbons hung,
And brighter wreaths in neat disorder flung ;
The gifts of the most learned among some dozens
Of female friends, sisters-in-law, and cousins.
And there is he with his eternal puns,
Which beat the dullest brain for smiles, like duns
Thundering for money at a poet's door ;
Alas ! it is no use to say, ' I'm poor ! '
Or oft in graver mood, when he will look
Things wiser than were ever read in book,
Except in Shakespeare's wisest tenderness.—
You will see Hogg,—and I cannot express
His virtues,—though I know that they are great,
Because he locks, then barricades the gate
Within which they inhabit ;—of his wit
And wisdom, you'll cry out when you are bit.
He is a pearl within an oyster shell,
One of the richest of the deep ;—and there
Is English Peacock, with his mountain Fair,
Turned into a Flamingo ;—that shy bird
That gleams i' the Indian air—have you not heard
When a man marries, dies, or turns Hindoo,
His best friends hear no more of him ?—but you

Will see him, and will like him too, I hope,
With the milk-white Snowdonian Antelope
Matched with this cameleopard—his fine wit
Makes such a wound, the knife is lost in it ;
A strain too learnèd for a shallow age,
Too wise for selfish bigots ; let his page,
Which charms the chosen spirits of the time,
Fold itself up for the serener clime
Of years to come, and find its recompense
In that just expectation.—Wit and sense,
Virtue and human knowledge ; all that might
Make this dull world a business of delight,
Are all combined in Horace Smith.—And these,
With some exceptions, which I need not tease
Your patience by descanting on,—are all
You and I know in London.

P. B. SHELLEY.

363. EPISTLE TO JOHN HAMILTON REYNOLDS

DEAR Reynolds ! as last night I lay in bed,
There came before my eyes that wonted thread
Of shapes, and shadows, and remembrances,
That every other minute vex and please :
Things all disjointed come from north and south,—
Two Witch's eyes above a Cherub's mouth,
Voltaire with casque and shield and habergeon,
And Alexander with his nightcap on ;
Old Socrates a-tying his cravat,
And Hazlitt playing with Miss Edgeworth's cat ;
And Junius Brutus, pretty well so so,
Making the best of 's way towards Soho.

Few are there who escape these visitings,—
Perhaps one or two whose lives have patent wings,
And through whose curtains peeps no hellish nose,
No wild-boar tushes, and no Mermaid's toes ;
But flowers bursting out with lusty pride,
And young Aeolian harps personified ;
Some Titian colours touched into real life,—
The sacrifice goes on ; the pontiff knife
Gleams in the Sun, the milk-white heifer lows,
The pipes go shrilly, the libation flows :
A white sail shows above the green-head cliff,
Moves round the point, and throws her anchor stiff ;
The mariners join hymn with those on land.

You know the Enchanted Castle,—it doth stand
Upon a rock, on the border of a Lake,
Nested in trees, which all do seem to shake
From some old magic-like Urganda's Sword.
O Phoebus ! that I had thy sacred word
To show this Castle, in fair dreaming wise,
Unto my friend, while sick and ill he lies !

You know it well enough, where it doth seem
A mossy place, a Merlin's Hall, a dream ;
You know the clear Lake, and the little Isles,
The mountains blue, and cold near neighbour rills,
All which elsewhere are but half animate ;
There do they look alive to love and hate,
To smiles and frowns ; they seem a lifted mound
Above some giant, pulsing underground.

Part of the Building was a chosen See,
Built by a banished Santon of Chaldee ;
The other part, two thousand years from him,
Was built by Cuthbert de Saint Aldebrim ;
Then there 's a little wing, far from the Sun,
Built by a Lapland Witch turned maudlin Nun ;
And many other juts of agèd stone
Founded with many a mason-devil's groan.

The doors all look as if they oped themselves,
The windows as if latched by Fays and Elves,
And from them comes a silver flash of light,
As from the westward of a Summer's night ;
Or like a beauteous woman's large blue eyes
Gone mad through olden songs and poesies.

    See ! what is coming from the distance dim !
A Golden Galley all in silken trim !
Three rows of oars are lightening, moment whiles,
Into the verdurous bosoms of those isles ;
Towards the shade, under the Castle wall,
It comes in silence,—now 'tis hidden all.
The Clarion sounds and from a Postern-gate
An echo of sweet music doth create
A fear in the poor Herdsman, who doth bring
His beasts to trouble the enchanted spring,—
He tells of the sweet music, and the spot,
To all his friends, and they believe him not.

    O, that our dreamings all, of sleep or wake,
Would all their colours from the sunset take :
From something of material sublime,
Rather than shadow our own soul's day-time

In the dark void of night.   For in the world
We jostle,—but my flag is not unfurled
On the Admiral-staff,—and so philosophize
I dare not yet !   Oh, never will the prize,
High reason, and the love of good and ill,
Be my award !   Things cannot to the will
Be settled, but they tease us out of thought ;
Or is it that imagination brought
Beyond its proper bound, yet still confined,
Lost in a sort of Purgatory blind,
Cannot refer to any standard law
Of either earth or heaven ?   It is a flaw
In happiness, to see beyond our bourn,—
It forces us in summer skies to mourn,
It spoils the singing of the Nightingale.

   Dear Reynolds ! I have a mysterious tale,
And cannot speak it : the first page I read
Upon a Lampit rock of green sea-weed
Among the breakers ; 'twas a quiet eve,
The rocks were silent, the wide sea did weave
An untumultuous fringe of silver foam
Along the flat brown sand ; I was at home
And should have been most happy,—but I saw
Too far into the sea, where every maw
The greater on the less feeds evermore.—
But I saw too distinct into the core
Of an eternal fierce destruction,
And so from happiness I far was gone.
Still am I sick of it, and though, to-day,
I've gathered young spring-leaves, and flowers gay
Of periwinkle and wild strawberry,
Still do I that most fierce destruction see,—
The Shark at savage prey,—the Hawk at pounce,—
The gentle Robin, like a Pard or Ounce,
Ravening a worm,—Away, ye horrid moods !
Moods of one's mind !   You know I hate them well.
You know I'd sooner be a clapping Bell
To some Kamschatkan Missionary Church,
Than with these horrid moods be left i' the lurch.

                                J. KEATS.

364. A LETTER OF ADVICE

*(From Miss Medora Trevilian, at Padua, to Miss Araminta
Vavasour, in London)*

You tell me you're promised a lover,
    My own Araminta, next week ;
Why cannot my fancy discover
    The hue of his coat and his cheek ?
Alas ! if he look like another,
    A vicar, a banker, a beau,
Be deaf to your father and mother,
    My own Araminta, say ' No ! '

Miss Lane, at her Temple of Fashion,
    Taught us both how to sing and to speak,
And we loved one another with passion,
    Before we had been there a week :
You gave me a ring for a token ;
    I wear it wherever I go ;
I gave you a chain—is it broken ?
    My own Araminta, say ' No ! '

O think of our favourite cottage,
    And think of our dear Lalla Rookh !
How we shared with the milkmaids their pottage,
    And drank of the stream from the brook ;
How fondly our loving lips faltered,
    ' What further can grandeur bestow ? '
My heart is the same ;—is yours altered ?
    My own Araminta, say ' No ! '

Remember the thrilling romances
    We read on the bank in the glen ;
Remember the suitors our fancies
    Would picture for both of us then.
They wore the red cross on their shoulder,
    They had vanquished and pardoned their foe—
Sweet friend, are you wiser or colder ?
    My own Araminta, say ' No ! '

You know, when Lord Rigmarole's carriage
    Drove off with your cousin Justine,
You wept, dearest girl, at the marriage,
    And whispered, ' How base she has been ! '
You said you were sure it would kill you,
    If ever your husband looked so ;
And you will not apostatize,—will you ?
    My own Araminta, say ' No ! '

When I heard I was going abroad, love,
  I thought I was going to die ;
We walked arm-in-arm to the road, love,
  We looked arm-in-arm to the sky ;
And I said, ' When a foreign postilion
  Has hurried me off to the Po,
Forget not Medora Trevilian :
  My own Araminta, say " No ! " '

We parted ! but sympathy's fetters
  Reach far over valley and hill ;
I muse o'er your exquisite letters,
  And feel that your heart is mine still ;
And he who would share it with me, love,—
  The richest of treasures below,—
If he 's not what Orlando should be, love,
  My own Araminta, say ' No ! '

If he wears a top-boot in his wooing,
  If he comes to you riding a cob,
If he talks of his baking or brewing,
  If he puts up his feet on the hob,
If he ever drinks port after dinner,
  If his brow or his breeding is low,
If he calls himself ' Thompson ' or ' Skinner ',—
  My own Araminta, say ' No ! '

If he studies the news in the papers
  While you are preparing the tea,
If he talks of the damps or the vapours
  While moonlight lies soft on the sea,
If he 's sleepy while you are capricious,
  If he has not a musical ' Oh ! '
If he does not call *Werther* delicious,—
  My own Araminta, say ' No ! '

If he ever sets foot in the City
  Among the stockbrokers and Jews,
If he has not a heart full of pity,
  If he don't stand six feet in his shoes,
If his lips are not redder than roses,
  If his hands are not whiter than snow,
If he has not the model of noses,—
  My own Araminta, say ' No ! '

If he speaks of a tax or a duty,
  If he does not look grand on his knees,
If he 's blind to a landscape of beauty,
  Hills, valleys, rocks, waters, and trees,

If he dotes not on desolate towers,
  If he likes not to hear the blast blow,
If he knows not the language of flowers,—
  My own Araminta, say ' No ! '

He must walk—like a god of old story
  Come down from the home of his rest ;
He must smile—like the sun in his glory
  On the bud he loves ever the best ;
And oh ! from its ivory portal
  Like music his soft speech must flow !
If he speak, smile, or walk like a mortal,
  My own Araminta, say ' No ! '

Don't listen to tales of his bounty,
  Don't hear what they say of his birth,
Don't look at his seat in the county,
  Don't calculate what he is worth ;
But give him a theme to write verse on,
  And see if he turns out his toe ;
If he 's only an excellent person,—
  My own Araminta, say ' No ! '

                                        W. M. PRAED.

365. THE TALENTED MAN

A LETTER FROM A LADY IN LONDON TO A LADY AT LAUSANNE

DEAR Alice ! you'll laugh when you know it,—
  Last week, at the Duchess's ball,
I danced with the clever new poet,—
  You've heard of him,—Tully St. Paul.
Miss Jonquil was perfectly frantic ;
  I wish you had seen Lady Anne !
It really was very romantic,
  He *is* such a talented man !

He came up from Brazen nose College,
  Just caught, as they call it, this spring ;
And his head, love, is stuffed full of knowledge
  Of every conceivable thing.
Of science and logic he chatters,
  As fine and as fast as he can ;
Though I am no judge of such matters,
  I'm sure he 's a talented man.

His stories and jests are delightful ;—
  Not stories or jests, dear, for you ;
The jests are exceedingly spiteful,
  The stories not always *quite* true.

Perhaps to be kind and veracious
   May do pretty well at Lausanne ;
But it never would answer,—good gracious !
   Chez nous—in a talented man.

He sneers,—how my Alice would scold him !—
   At the bliss of a sigh or a tear ;
He laughed—only think !—when I told him
   How we cried o'er Trevelyan last year ;
I vow I was quite in a passion ;
   I broke all the sticks of my fan ;
But sentiment 's quite out of fashion,
   It seems, in a talented man.

Lady Bab, who is terribly moral,
   Has told me that Tully is vain,
And apt—which is silly—to quarrel,
   And fond—which is sad—of champagne.
I listened and doubted, dear Alice,
   For I saw, when my Lady began,
It was only the Dowager's malice ;—
   She *does* hate a talented man !

He's hideous, I own it. But fame, love,
   Is all that these eyes can adore ;
He's lame,—but Lord Byron was lame, love,
   And dumpy,—but so is Tom Moore.
Then his voice,—*such* a voice ! my sweet creature,
   It 's like your Aunt Lucy's toucan :
But oh ! what 's a tone or a feature,
   When once one 's a talented man ?

My mother, you know, all the season,
   Has talked of Sir Geoffrey's estate ;
And truly, to do the fool reason,
   He *has* been less horrid of late.
But to-day, when we drive in the carriage,
   I'll tell her to lay down her plan ;—
If ever I venture on marriage,
   It must be a talented man !

P.S.—I have found, on reflection,
   One fault in my friend,—*entre nous ;*
Without it, he'd just be perfection ;—
   Poor fellow, he has not a *sou !*
And so, when he comes in September
   To shoot with my uncle, Sir Dan,
I've promised mamma to remember
   He 's *only* a talented man !

W. M. PRAED.

366. A NICE CORRESPONDENT

' The glow and the glory are plighted
   To darkness, for evening is come ;
The lamp in Glebe Cottage is lighted,
   The birds and the sheep-bells are dumb ;
I'm alone at my casement, for Pappy
   Is summoned to dinner at Kew ;
I'm alone, my dear Fred, but I'm happy,—
   I'm thinking of you.

' I wish you were here ; were I duller
   Than dull, you'd be dearer than dear,—
I am dressed in your favourite colour,—
   Dear Fred, how I wish you were here !
I am wearing my lazuli necklace,
   The necklace you fastened askew !
Was there ever so rude or so reckless
   A darling as you ?

' I want you to come and pass sentence
   On two or three books with a plot :
Of course you know " Janet's Repentance " :
   I'm reading Sir Waverley Scott,
The story of Edgar and Lucy,—
   How thrilling, romantic, and true !
The Master,—his bride was a goosey,—
   Reminds me of you.

' To-day, in my ride, I've been crowning
   The Beacon whose magic still lures,
For up there you discoursed about Browning,—
   That stupid old Browning of yours :
His verve and his vogue are alarming,
   I'm anxious to give him his due ;
But, Fred, he 's not nearly so charming
   A poet as you.

' I have heard how you shot at the Beeches,
   I saw how you rode Chanticleer,
I have read the reports of your speeches,
   And echoed the echoing cheer :
There 's a whisper of hearts you are breaking,—
   I envy their owners.   I do !—
Small marvel that fashion is making
   Her idol of you.

' Alas for the world, and its dearly
   Bought triumph, and fugitive bliss ;
Sometimes I half wish I was merely
   A plain or a penniless Miss :

But, perhaps, one is best with a measure
   Of pelf ; and I'm not sorry, too,
That I'm pretty, because it 's a pleasure,
         My dearest, to you.

' Your whim is for frolic and fashion,
   Your taste is for letters and art ;—
This rhyme is the common-place passion
   That glows in a fond woman's heart :
Put it by in a dainty deposit
   For relics,—we all have a few !
Some day, love, they'll print it, because it
         Was written to you.'

                  F. Locker-Lampson.

367. MY LETTERS

   ' Litera scripta manet '—*Old Saw.*

Another mizzling, drizzling day !
   Of clearing up there 's no appearance ;
So I'll sit down without delay,
   And here, at least, I'll make a clearance.

Oh, ne'er ' on such a day as this ',
   Would Dido with her woes oppressèd
Have wooed Aeneas back to bliss,
   Or Troilus gone to hunt for Cressid !

No, they'd have stayed at home, like me,
   And popped their toes up on the fender,
And drunk a quiet cup of tea :—
   On days like this one can't be tender.

So, Molly, draw that basket nigher,
   And put my desk upon the table—
Bring that Portfolio—stir the fire—
   Now off as fast as you are able !

First, here 's a card from Mrs. Grimes,
   ' A ball ! '—she knows that I'm no dancer—
That woman 's asked me fifty times,
   And yet I never send an answer.

' Dear Jack,—Just lend me twenty pounds
   Till Monday next, when I'll return it.
Yours truly, Henry Gibbs.' Why, Z—ds !
   I've seen the man but twice—here, burn it.

One from my Cousin Sophy Daw—
   Full of Aunt Margery's distresses ;
' The Cat has kittened in " the *draw* ",
   And ruined two bran-new silk dresses.'

From Sam, ' The Chancellor's motto,'—nay,
   Confound his puns, he knows I hate 'em ;
' Pro Rege, Lege, Grege,'—Aye,
    ' For King read Mob ! '   Brougham's old *erratum*.

From Seraphina Price—' At two '—
   ' Till then I can't, my dearest John, stir ' ;
Two more because I did not go,
   Beginning ' Wretch ' and ' Faithless Monster ! '

' DEAR SIR,—This morning Mrs. P——,
   Who's doing quite as well as may be,
Presented me at half-past three,
   Precisely, with another baby.

' We'll name it John, and know with pleasure
   You'll stand '—Five guineas more, confound it !—
I wish they'd called it Nebuchadnezzar,
   Or thrown it in the Thames and drowned it.

What have we next ?   A civil Dun :
   ' John Brown would take it as a favour '—
Another, and a surlier one,
   ' I can't put up with *sich* behaviour.'

' Bill so long standing,'—' quite tired out,'—
   ' Must sit down to insist on payment,'
' Called ten times,'—Here's a fuss about
   A few coats, waistcoats, and small raiment !

For once I'll send an answer, and in-
   form Mr. Snip he needn't ' call ' so ;
But when his bill's as ' tired of standing '
   As he is, beg 'twill ' sit down also '.

This from my rich old Uncle Ned,
   Thanking me for my annual present ;
And saying he last Tuesday wed
   His cook-maid, Molly—vastly pleasant !

An ill-spelt note from Tom at school,
   Begging I'll let him learn the fiddle ;
Another from that precious fool,
   Miss Pyefinch, with this stupid riddle.

' D'ye give it up ? '   Indeed I do !
   Confound these antiquated minxes ;
I won't play ' *Billy Black* ' to a ' *Blue* '
   Or Oedipus to such old sphinxes.

A note sent up from Kent to show me,
   Left with my bailiff, Peter King ;

' I'll burn them precious stacks down, blow me !
   ' Yours most sincerely, CAPTAIN SWING.'

Four begging letters with petitions,
   One from my sister Jane, to pray
I'll ' execute a few commissions '
   In Bond Street, ' when I go that way.'

' And buy at Pearsal's in the city
   Twelve skeins of silk for netting purses ;
Colour no matter, so it's pretty ;—
   Two hundred pens '—two hundred curses !

From Mistress Jones : ' My little Billy
   Goes up his schooling to begin,
Will you just step to Piccadilly,
   And meet him when the coach comes in ?

' And then, perhaps, you will as well see
   The poor dear fellow safe to school
At Dr. Smith's in Little Chelsea ! '
   Heaven send he flog the little fool !

From Lady Snooks : ' Dear Sir, you know
   You promised me last week a Rebus ;
A something smart and *apropos*,
   For my new Album ? '—Aid me, Phoebus !

' My first is followed by my second ;
   Yet should my first my second see,
A dire mishap it would be reckoned,
   And sadly shocked my first would be.

' Were I but what my whole implies,
   And passed by chance across your portal,
You'd cry, " Can I believe my eyes ?
   I never saw so queer a mortal ! "

' For then my head would not be on,
   My arms their shoulders must abandon ;
My very body would be gone,
   I should not have a leg to stand on.'

Come, that's dispatched—what follows ?—Stay,
   ' Reform demanded by the nation—
Vote for Tagrag and Bobtail ! '   Aye,
   By Jove, a blessed *Reformation !*

Jack, clap the saddle upon Rose—
   Or, no !—the filly—she's the fleeter ;
The devil take the rain—here goes,
   I'm off—a plumper for St. Peter !

                R. H. BARHAM.

368. TO THE REV. F. D. MAURICE

COME, when no graver cares employ,
Godfather, come and see your boy :
   Your presence will be sun in winter,
Making the little one leap for joy.

For, being of that honest few,
Who give the Fiend himself his due,
   Should eighty thousand college-councils
Thunder ' Anathema ', friend, at you ;

Should all our churchmen foam in spite
At you, so careful of the right,
   Yet one lay-hearth would give you welcome
(Take it and come) to the Isle of Wight ;

Where, far from noise and smoke of town,
I watch the twilight falling brown
   All round a careless-ordered garden
Close to the ridge of a noble down.

You'll have no scandal while you dine,
But honest talk and wholesome wine,
   And only hear the magpie gossip
Garrulous under a roof of pine :

For groves of pine on either hand,
To break the blast of winter, stand ;
   And further on, the hoary Channel
Tumbles a breaker on chalk and sand ;

Where, if below the milky steep
Some ship of battle slowly creep,
   And on through zones of light and shadow
Glimmer away to the lonely deep,

We might discuss the Northern sin
Which made a selfish war begin ;
   Dispute the claims, arrange the chances ;
Emperor, Ottoman, which shall win :

Or whether war's avenging rod
Shall lash all Europe into blood
   Till you should turn to dearer matters,
Dear to the man that is dear to God ;

How best to help the slender store,
How mend the dwellings, of the poor ;
   How gain in life, as life advances,
Valour and charity more and more.

Come, Maurice, come : the lawn as yet
Is hoar with rime, or spongy-wet ;
  But when the wreath of March has blossomed,
Crocus, anemone, violet,

Or later, pay one visit here,
For those are few we hold as dear ;
  Nor pay but one, but come for many,
Many and many a happy year.

ALFRED, LORD TENNYSON.

January, 1854.

369. THE INVITATION

TO TOM HUGHES

COME away with me, Tom,
Term and talk are done ;
My poor lads are reaping,
Busy every one.
Curates mind the parish,
Sweepers mind the court ;
We'll away to Snowdon
For our ten days' sport :
Fish the August evening
Till the eve is past,
Whoop like boys, at pounders
Fairly played and grassed.
When they cease to dimple,
Lunge, and swerve, and leap,
Then up over Siabod,
Choose our nest, and sleep.
Up a thousand feet, Tom,
Round the lion's head,
Find soft stones to leeward
And make up our bed.
Eat our bread and bacon,
Smoke the pipe of peace,
And, ere we be drowsy,
Give our boots a grease.
Homer's heroes did so,
Why not such as we ?
What are sheets and servants ?
Superfluity !
Pray for wives and children
Safe in slumber curled,
Then to chat till midnight
O'er this babbling world—

Of the workmen's college,
Of the price of grain,
Of the tree of knowledge,
Of the chance of rain ;
If Sir A. goes Romeward,
If Miss B. sings true,
If the fleet comes homeward,
If the mare will do,—
Anything and everything—
Up there in the sky
Angels understand us,
And no ' saints ' are by.
Down, and bathe at day-dawn,
Tramp from lake to lake,
Washing brain and heart clean
Every step we take.
Leave to Robert Browning
Beggars, fleas, and vines ;
Leave to mournful Ruskin
Popish Apennines,
Dirty Stones of Venice
And his Gas-lamps Seven—
We've the stones of Snowdon
And the lamps of heaven.
Where 's the mighty credit
In admiring Alps ?
Any goose sees ' glory '
In their ' snowy scalps '.
Leave such signs and wonders
For the dullard brain,
As aesthetic brandy,
Opium and cayenne.
Give me Bramshill common
(St. John's harriers by),
Or the vale of Windsor,
England's golden eye.
Show me life and progress,
Beauty, health, and man ;
Houses fair, trim gardens,
Turn where'er I can.
Or, if bored with ' High Art '
And such popish stuff,
One's poor ears need airing,
Snowdon's high enough.
While we find God's signet
Fresh on English ground,
Why go gallivanting
With the nations round ?
Though we try no ventures

Desperate or strange ;
Feed on commonplaces
In a narrow range ;
Never sought for Franklin
Round the frozen Capes ;
Even, with Macdougall,
Bagged our brace of apes ;
Never had our chance, Tom,
In that black Redan ;
Can't avenge poor Brereton
Out in Sakarran ;
Though we earn our bread, Tom,
By the dirty pen,
What we can we will be,
Honest Englishmen.
Do the work that 's nearest,
Though it's dull at whiles,
Helping, when we meet them,
Lame dogs over stiles ;
See in every hedgerow
Marks of angels' feet,
Epics in each pebble
Underneath our feet ;
Once a year, like schoolboys,
Robin-Hooding go,
Leaving fops and fogies
A thousand feet below.

                         C. Kingsley.

370. TO ALFRED TENNYSON

I entreat you, Alfred Tennyson,
Come and share my haunch of venison.
I have too a bin of claret,
Good, but better when you share it.
Though 'tis only a small bin,
There 's a stock of it within.
And as sure as I'm a rhymer
Half a butt of Rudesheimer.
Come : among the sons of men is one
Welcomer than Alfred Tennyson ?

                         W. S. Landor.

371. INVITING A FRIEND TO SUPPER

To-night, grave sir, both my poor house and I
Do equally desire your company:
Not that we think us worthy such a guest,
But that your worth will dignify our feast,
With those that come; whose grace may make that seem
Something, which else, could hope for no esteem.
It is the fair acceptance, sir, creates
The entertainment perfect, not the cates.
Yet shall you have, to rectify your palate,
An olive, capers, or some better salad
Ushering the mutton, with a short-legged hen
If we can get her, full of eggs, and then
Lemons, and wine for sauce; to these, a coney
Is not to be despaired of for our money;
And though fowl now be scarce, yet there are clerks,
The sky not falling, think we may have larks.
I'll tell you of more, and lie, so you will come:
Of partridge, pheasant, woodcock, of which some
May yet be there; and godwit if we can,
Knat, rail and ruff too. Howsoe'er, my man
Shall read a piece of Virgil, Tacitus,
Livy, or of some better book to us,
Of which we'll speak our minds, amidst our meat,
And I'll profess no verses to repeat:
To this if aught appear, which I not know of,
That will the pastry, not the paper, show of.
Digestive cheese and fruit there sure will be,
But that which most doth take my Muse and me,
Is a pure cup of rich Canary wine,
Which is the Mermaid's now, but shall be mine:
Of which had Horace or Anacreon tasted,
Their lives, as do their lines, till now had lasted.
Tobacco, nectar, or the Thespian spring,
Are all but Luther's beer, to this I sing.
Of this we will sup free, but moderately,
And we will have no Pooly or Parrot by;
Nor shall our cups make any guilty men
But, at our parting, we will be as when
We innocently met. No simple word,
That shall be uttered at our mirthful board,
Shall make us sad next morning; or affright
The liberty that we'll enjoy to-night.

BEN. JONSON.

372.   AN ODE FOR BEN JONSON

Ah Ben !
Say how, or when
Shall we, thy guests,
Meet at those lyric feasts,
Made at the Sun,
The Dog, the Triple Tun ;
Where we such clusters had,
As made us nobly wild, not mad ?
And yet each verse of thine
Out-did the meat, out-did the frolic wine.

My Ben !
Or come agen,
Or send to us
Thy wit's great over-plus ;
But teach us yet
Wisely to husband it,
Lest we that talent spend ;
And having once brought to an end
That precious stock, the store
Of such a wit the world should have no more.

R. HERRICK,

373.   TO HIS PECULIAR FRIEND, MR. JOHN WICKS

Since shed or cottage I have none,
I sing the more that thou hast one,
To whose glad threshold and free door
I may a poet come, though poor,
And eat with thee a savoury bit,
Paying but common thanks for it.
Yet should I chance, my Wicks, to see
An over-leaven look in thee,
To sour the bread, and turn the beer
To an exalted vinegar ;
Or shouldst thou prize me as a dish
Of thrice boiled worts, or third day's fish,
I'd rather hungry go and come
Than to thy house be burdensome :
Yet in my depth of grief I'd be
One that should drop his beads for thee.

R. HERRICK.

374. THE HAUNCH OF VENISON

A Poetical Epistle to Lord Clare

Thanks, my Lord, for your venison, for finer or fatter
Never ranged in a forest, or smoked in a platter ;
The haunch was a picture for painters to study,
The fat was so white, and the lean was so ruddy.
Though my stomach was sharp, I could scarce help regretting
To spoil such a delicate picture by eating ;
I had thoughts, in my chambers, to place it in view,
To be shown to my friends as a piece of *virtù* ;
As in some Irish houses, where things are so so,
One gammon of bacon hangs up for a show :
But for eating a rasher of what they take pride in,
They'd as soon think of eating the pan it is fried in.
But hold—let me pause—Don't I hear you pronounce
This tale of the bacon a damnable bounce ?
Well, suppose it a bounce—sure a poet may try,
By a bounce now and then, to get courage to fly.

But, my Lord, it 's no bounce : I protest in my turn,
It 's a truth—and your Lordship may ask Mr. Byrne.
To go on with my tale—as I gazed on the haunch,
I thought of a friend that was trusty and staunch ;
So I cut it, and sent it to Reynolds undressed,
To paint it, or eat it, just as he liked best.
Of the neck and the breast I had next to dispose ;
'Twas a neck and a breast—that might rival M—r—'s :
But in parting with these I was puzzled again,
With the how, and the who, and the where, and the when.
There 's H—d, and C—y, and H—rth, and H—ff,
I think they love venison—I know they love beef ;
There 's my countryman H—gg—ns—Oh ! let him alone,
For making a blunder, or picking a bone.
But hang it—to poets who seldom can eat,
Your very good mutton 's a very good treat ;
Such dainties to them, their health it might hurt,
It 's like sending them ruffles, when wanting a shirt.
While thus I debated, in reverie centred,
An acquaintance, a friend as he called himself, entered ;
An under-bred, fine-spoken fellow was he,
And he smiled as he looked at the venison and me.
' What have we got here ?—Why, this is good eating !
Your own, I suppose—or is it in waiting ? '
' Why, whose should it be ? ' cried I with a flounce,
' I get these things often ; '—but that was a bounce :
' Some lords, my acquaintance, that settle the nation,
Are pleased to be kind—but I hate ostentation.'

'If that be the case, then,' cried he, very gay,
'I'm glad I have taken this house in my way.
To-morrow you take a poor dinner with me;
No words—I insist on 't—precisely at three:
We'll have Johnson, and Burke; all the wits will be there;
My acquaintance is slight, or I'd ask my Lord Clare.
And now that I think on't, as I am a sinner!
We wanted this venison to make out the dinner.
What say you—a pasty? it shall, and it must,
And my wife, little Kitty, is famous for crust.
Here, porter!—this venison with me to Mile-end;
No stirring—I beg—my dear friend—my dear friend!'
Thus snatching his hat, he brushed off like the wind,
And the porter and eatables followed behind.

Left alone to reflect, having emptied my shelf,
'And nobody with me at sea but myself';
Though I could not help thinking my gentleman hasty,
Yet Johnson, and Burke, and a good venison pasty,
Were things that I never disliked in my life,
Though clogged with a coxcomb, and Kitty his wife.
So next day, in due splendour to make my approach,
I drove to his door in my own hackney coach.

When come to the place where we all were to dine,
(A chair-lumbered closet just twelve feet by nine :)
My friend bade me welcome, but struck me quite dumb,
With tidings that Johnson and Burke would not come;
'For I knew it,' he cried, 'both eternally fail,
The one with his speeches, and t'other with Thrale;
But no matter, I'll warrant we'll make up the party
With two full as clever, and ten times as hearty.
The one is a Scotchman, the other a Jew,
They're both of them merry and authors like you;
The one writes the *Snarler*, the other the *Scourge*;
Some think he writes *Cinna*—he owns to *Panurge.*'
While thus he described them by trade, and by name,
They entered, and dinner was served as they came.

At the top a fried liver and bacon were seen,
At the bottom was tripe in a swinging tureen;
At the sides there was spinach and pudding made hot;
In the middle a place where the pasty—was not.
Now, my Lord, as for tripe, it 's my utter aversion,
And your bacon I hate like a Turk or a Persian;
So there I sat stuck, like a horse in a pound,
While the bacon and liver went merrily round.
But what vexed me most was that d—'d Scottish rogue,
With his long-winded speeches, his smiles and his brogue.

And, ' Madam,' quoth he, ' may this bit be my poison,
A prettier dinner I never set eyes on ;
Pray a slice of your liver, though may I be cursed,
But I've eat of your tripe till I'm ready to burst.'
' The tripe,' quoth the Jew, with his chocolate cheek,
' I could dine on this tripe seven days in the week :
I like these here dinners so pretty and small ;
But your friend there, the Doctor, eats nothing at all.'
' O—Oh ! ' quoth my friend, ' he'll come on in a trice,
He 's keeping a corner for something that 's nice :
There 's a pasty '—' A pasty ! ' repeated the Jew,
' I don't care if I keep a corner for 't too.'
' What the de'il, mon, a pasty ! ' re-echoed the Scot,
' Though splitting, I'll still keep a corner for thot.'
' We'll all keep a corner,' the lady cried out ;
' We'll all keep a corner,' was echoed about.
While thus we resolved, and the pasty delayed,
With looks that quite petrified, entered the maid ;
A visage so sad, and so pale with affright,
Waked Priam in drawing his curtains by night.
But we quickly found out, for who could mistake her ?
That she came with some terrible news from the baker :
And so it fell out, for that negligent sloven
Had shut out the pasty on shutting his oven.
Sad Philomel thus—but let similes drop—
And now that I think on 't, the story may stop.
To be plain, my good Lord, it 's but labour misplaced
To send such good verses to one of your taste ;
You've got an odd something—a kind of discerning—
A relish—a taste—sickened over by learning ;
At least, it 's your temper, as very well known,
That you think very slightly of all that 's your own :
So, perhaps, in your habits of thinking amiss,
You may make a mistake, and think slightly of this.

                                        O. GOLDSMITH.

375.   RETALIATION

OF old, when Scarron his companions invited,
Each guest brought his dish, and the feast was united ;
If our landlord supplies us with beef, and with fish,
Let each guest bring himself, and he brings the best dish :
Our Dean shall be venison, just fresh from the plains ;
Our Burke shall be tongue, with a garnish of brains ;
Our Will shall be wild-fowl, of excellent flavour,
And Dick with his pepper shall heighten their savour :
Our Cumberland's sweet-bread its place shall obtain,
And Douglas is pudding, substantial and plain :

Our Garrick 's a salad ; for in him we see
Oil, vinegar, sugar, and saltness agree :
To make out the dinner, full certain I am,
That Ridge is anchovy, and Reynolds is lamb ;
That Mickey 's a capon, and by the same rule,
Magnanimous Goldsmith a gooseberry fool.
At a dinner so various, at such a repast,
Who'd not be a glutton, and stick to the last ?
Here, waiter ! more wine, let me sit while I'm able,
Till all my companions sink under the table ;
Then, with chaos and blunders encircling my head,
Let me ponder, and tell what I think of the dead.

Here lies the good Dean, re-united to earth,
Who mixed reason with pleasure, and wisdom with mirth :
If he had any faults, he has left us in doubt,
At least, in six weeks, I could not find 'em out ;
Yet some have declared, and it can't be denied 'em,
That sly-boots was cursedly cunning to hide 'em.

Here lies our good Edmund, whose genius was such,
We scarcely can praise it, or blame it too much ;
Who, born for the Universe, narrowed his mind,
And to party gave up what was meant for mankind.
Though fraught with all learning, yet straining his throat
To persuade Tommy Townshend to lend him a vote ;
Who, too deep for his hearers, still went on refining,
And thought of convincing, while they thought of dining ;
Though equal to all things, for all things unfit,
Too nice for a statesman, too proud for a wit :
For a patriot, too cool ; for a drudge, disobedient ;
And too fond of the *right* to pursue the *expedient.*
In short, 'twas his fate, unemployed, or in place, Sir,
To eat mutton cold, and cut blocks with a razor.

Here lies honest William, whose heart was a mint,
While the owner ne'er knew half the good that was in 't ;
The pupil of impulse, it forced him along,
His conduct still right, with his argument wrong ;
Still aiming at honour, yet fearing to roam,
The coachman was tipsy, the chariot drove home ;
Would you ask for his merits ? alas ! he had none ;
What was good was spontaneous, his faults were his own.

Here lies honest Richard, whose fate I must sigh at ;
Alas, that such frolic should now be so quiet !
What spirits were his ! what wit and what whim !
Now breaking a jest, and now breaking a limb ;
Now wrangling and grumbling to keep up the ball,
Now teasing and vexing, yet laughing at all !

In short, so provoking a devil was Dick,
That we wished him full ten times a day at Old Nick ;
But, missing his mirth and agreeable vein,
As often we wished to have Dick back again.

Here Cumberland lies, having acted his parts,
The Terence of England, the mender of hearts ;
A flattering painter, who made it his care
To draw men as they ought to be, not as they are.
His gallants are all faultless, his women divine,
And comedy wonders at being so fine ;
Like a tragedy queen he has dizened her out,
Or rather like tragedy giving a rout.
His fools have their follies so lost in a crowd
Of virtues and feelings, that folly grows proud ;
And coxcombs, alike in their failings alone,
Adopting his portraits, are pleased with their own.
Say, where has our poet this malady caught ?
Or, wherefore his characters thus without fault ?
Say, was it that vainly directing his view
To find out men's virtues, and finding them few,
Quite sick of pursuing each troublesome elf,
He grew lazy at last, and drew from himself ?

Here Douglas retires, from his toils to relax,
The scourge of impostors, the terror of quacks :
Come, all ye quack bards, and ye quacking divines,
Come, and dance on the spot where your tyrant reclines :
When Satire and Censure encircled his throne,
I feared for your safety, I feared for my own ;
But now he is gone, and we want a detector,
Our Dodds shall be pious, our Kenricks shall lecture ;
Macpherson write bombast, and call it a style,
Our Townshend make speeches, and I shall compile ;
New Lauders and Bowers the Tweed shall cross over,
No countryman living their tricks to discover ;
Detection her taper shall quench to a spark,
And Scotchman meet Scotchman, and cheat in the dark.

Here lies David Garrick, describe me, who can,
An abridgement of all that was pleasant in man ;
As an actor, confessed without rival to shine :
As a wit, if not first, in the very first line :
Yet, with talents like these, and an excellent heart,
The man had his failings, a dupe to his art.
Like an ill-judging beauty, his colours he spread,
And beplastered with rouge his own natural red.
On the stage he was natural, simple, affecting ;
'Twas only that when he was off he was acting.

With no reason on earth to go out of his way,
He turned and he varied full ten times a day.
Though secure of our hearts, yet confoundedly sick
If they were not his own by finessing and trick,
He cast off his friends, as a huntsman his pack,
For he knew when he pleased he could whistle them back.
Of praise a mere glutton, he swallowed what came,
And the puff of a dunce he mistook it for fame ;
Till his relish grown callous, almost to disease,
Who peppered the highest was surest to please.
But let us be candid, and speak out our mind,
If dunces applauded, he paid them in kind.
Ye Kenricks, ye Kellys, and Woodfalls so grave,
What a commerce was yours, while you got and you gave !
How did Grub Street re-echo the shouts that you raised,
While he was be-Rosciused, and you were be-praised !
But peace to his spirit, wherever it flies,
To act as an angel, and mix with the skies :
Those poets, who owe their best fame to his skill,
Shall still be his flatterers, go where he will.
Old Shakespeare, receive him, with praise and with love,
And Beaumonts and Bens be his Kellys above.

Here Mickey reclines, a most blunt, pleasant creature,
And slander itself must allow him good nature :
He cherished his friend, and he relished a bumper ;
Yet one fault he had, and that one was a thumper.
Perhaps you may ask if the man was a miser ?
I answer, no, no, for he always was wiser :
Too courteous, perhaps, or obligingly flat ?
His very worst foe can't accuse him of that :
Perhaps he confided in men as they go,
And so was too foolishly honest ?   Ah no !
Then what was his failing ? come, tell it, and, burn ye !
He was, could he help it ?—a special attorney.

Here Reynolds is laid, and, to tell you my mind,
He has not left a better or wiser behind :
His pencil was striking, resistless, and grand ;
His manners were gentle, complying, and bland ;
Still born to improve us in every part,
His pencil our faces, his manners our heart :
To coxcombs averse, yet most civilly steering,
When they judged without skill he was still hard of hearing :
When they talked of their Raphaels, Correggios, and stuff,
He shifted his trumpet, and only took snuff.

O. GOLDSMITH.

376. THE MAHOGANY TREE

CHRISTMAS is here ;
Winds whistle shrill,
Icy and chill,
Little care we :
Little we fear
Weather without,
Sheltered about
The Mahogany Tree.

Commoner greens,
Ivy and oaks,
Poets, in jokes,
Sing, do ye see ?
Good fellows' shins
Here, boys, are found,
Twisting around
The Mahogany Tree.

Once on the boughs,
Birds of rare plume
Sang, in its bloom ;
Night-birds are we :
Here we carouse,
Singing, like them,
Perched round the stem
Of the jolly old tree.

Here let us sport,
Boys, as we sit ;
Laughter and wit
Flashing so free.
Life is but short—
When we are gone,
Let them sing on,
Round the old tree.

Evenings we knew,
Happy as this ;
Faces we miss,
Pleasant to see.
Kind hearts and true,
Gentle and just,
Peace to your dust !
We sing round the tree.

Care, like a dun,
Lurks at the gate :
Let the dog wait ;
Happy we'll be !
Drink every one ;
Pile up the coals,
Fill the red bowls,
Round the old tree !

Drain we the cup.—
Friend, art afraid ?
Spirits are laid
In the Red Sea.
Mantle it up ;
Empty it yet ;
Let us forget,
Round the old tree.

Sorrows, begone !
Life and its ills,
Duns and their bills,
Bid we to flee.
Come with the dawn,
Blue-devil sprite,
Leave us to night,
Round the old tree.

W. M. THACKERAY.

377. AD MINISTRAM

DEAR Lucy, you know what my wish is,—
    I hate all your Frenchified fuss :
Your silly entrées and made dishes
    Were never intended for us.
No footman in lace and in ruffles
    Need dangle behind my arm-chair ;
And never mind seeking for truffles,
    Although they be ever so rare.

But a plain leg of mutton, my Lucy,
    I prithee get ready at three :
Have it smoking, and tender and juicy,
    And what better meat can there be ?
And when it has feasted the master,
    'Twill amply suffice for the maid ;
Meanwhile I will smoke my canaster,
    And tipple my ale in the shade.

W. M. THACKERAY

378. OLD STYLE

AURELIUS, Sire of Hungrinesses !
Thee thy old friend Catullus blesses,
And sends thee six fine watercresses.
There are who would not think me quite
(Unless we were old friends) polite
To mention whom you should invite.
Look at them well ; and turn it o'er
In your own mind . . . I'd have but four . .
Lucullus, Caesar, and two more.

W. S. LANDOR.

379. HANS BREITMANN'S BARTY

HANS BREITMANN gif a barty ;
    Dey hat biano-blayin',
I felled in luf mit a 'Merican frau,
    Her name vas Madilda Yane.
She hat haar ash prown ash a pretzel,
    Her eyes vas himmel-plue,
Und ven dey looket indo mine,
    Dey shplit mine heart in doo.

Hans Breitmann gif a barty,
    I vent dere, you'll be pound ;
I valtz't mit Madilda Yane,
    Und vent shpinnen' roundt und roundt.
Der pootiest Fraulein in der hause,
    She vayed 'pout doo hoondred poundt,
Und efery dime she gif a shoomp
    She make der vinders sound.

Hans Breitmann gif a barty,
    I dells you, it cosht him dear ;
Dey rolled in more ash sefen kecks
    Of foost-rate lager-peer.
Und venefer dey knocks der sphicket in
    Der Deutschers gifs a cheer.
I dinks dat so vine a barty
    Nefer coom to a het dis year.

Hans Breitmann gif a barty ;
    Dere all vash Souse undt Brouse,
Ven der sooper comed in, de gompany
    Did make demselfs to house ;
Dey ate das Brot und Gensy-broost,
  – Der Bratwurst und Braten vine,
Undt vash der Abendessen down
    Mit vour parrels ov Neckarwein.

Hans Breitmann gif a barty ;
   Ve all cot troonk ash bigs.
I poot mine mout' to a parrel of peer
   Undt emptied it oop mit a schwigs ;
Und den I gissed Madilda Yane
   Und she schlog me on der kop,
Und der gompany vighted mit daple-lecks
   Dill der coonshtable mate oos shtop.

Hans Breitmann gif a barty—
   Vhere ish dat barty now ?
Vhere ish der lufly colden gloud
   Dat float on der moundain's prow ?
Vhere ish de himmelstrahlende stern—
   De shtar of de shpirit's light ?
All goned afay mit der lager-peer—
   Afay in de ewigkeit !

C. G. LELAND.

380. STELLA'S BIRTHDAY, 1718

STELLA this day is thirty-four,
(We shan't dispute a year or more :)
However, Stella, be not troubled ;
Although thy size and years are doubled
Since first I saw thee at sixteen,
The brightest virgin on the green ;
So little is thy form declined ;
Made up so largely in thy mind.

  O, would it please the gods to split
Thy beauty, size, and years, and wit !
No age could furnish out a pair
Of nymphs so graceful, wise, and fair ;
With half the lustre of your eyes,
With half your wit, your years, and size.
And then, before it grew too late,
How should I beg of gentle fate
(That either nymph might have her swain)
To split my worship too in twain.

J. SWIFT.

381. STELLA'S BIRTHDAY, 1720

ALL travellers at first incline
Where'er they see the fairest sign ;
And, if they find the chamber neat,
And like the liquor and the meat,
Will call again, and recommend
The Angel Inn to every friend.
What though the painting grows decayed,
The House will never lose its trade :
Nay, though the treacherous tapster, *Thomas*,
Hangs a new angel two doors from us,
As fine as dauber's hands can make it,
In hopes that strangers may mistake it,
We think it both a shame and sin
To quit the true old Angel Inn.

Now this is Stella's case in fact ;
An angel's face, a little cracked ;
(Could poets, or could painters fix
How angels look at thirty-six :)
This drew us in at first to find
In such a form an angel's mind ;
And every virtue now supplies
The fainting rays of Stella's eyes.
See at her levée crowding swains,
Whom Stella freely entertains
With breeding, humour, wit, and sense,
And puts them but to small expense ;
Their mind so plentifully fills,
And makes such reasonable bills,
So little gets for what she gives,
We really wonder how she lives !
And had her stock been less, no doubt
She must have long ago run out.

Then who can think we'll quit the place,
When Doll hangs out a newer face ;
Or stop and light at Chloe's Head,
With scraps and leavings to be fed ?

Then, Chloe, still go on to prate
Of thirty-six, and thirty-eight ;
Pursue your trade of scandal-picking,
Your hints, that Stella is no chicken ;
Your innuendoes, when you tell us
That Stella loves to talk with fellows :
And let me warn you to believe
A truth, for which your soul should grieve ;

That should you live to see the day
When Stella's locks must all be grey,
When age must print a furrowed trace
On every feature of her face ;
That you, and all your senseless tribe,
Could art, or time, or nature bribe
To make you look like beauty's queen,
And hold for ever at fifteen ;
No bloom of youth can ever blind
The cracks and wrinkles of your mind ;
All men of sense will pass your door,
And crowd to Stella's at four score.

J. SWIFT.

382. STELLA'S BIRTHDAY, 1724

As, when a beauteous nymph decays,
We say, she 's past her dancing days ;
So poets lose their feet by time,
And can no longer dance in rhyme.
Your annual bard had rather chose
To celebrate your birth in prose :
Yet merry folks, who want by chance
A pair to make a country dance,
Call the old housekeeper, and get her
To fill a place, for want of better :
While Sheridan is off the hooks,
And friend Delany at his books,
That Stella may avoid disgrace,
Once more the Dean supplies their place.
    Beauty and wit, too sad a truth !
Have always been confined to youth ;
The god of wit, and beauty's queen,
He twenty-one, and she fifteen.
No poet ever sweetly sung,
Unless he were, like Phoebus, young ;
Nor ever nymph inspired to rhyme,
Unless, like Venus, in her prime.
At fifty-six, if this be true,
Am I a poet fit for you ?
Or, at the age of forty-three,
Are you a subject fit for me ?
Adieu ! bright wit, and radiant eyes,
You must be grave, and I be wise.
Our fate in vain we would oppose :
But I'll be still your friend in prose ;
Esteem and friendship to express,
Will not require poetic dress ;

And, if the Muse deny her aid
To have them sung, they may be said.
　But, Stella, say, what evil tongue
Reports you are no longer young ;
That Time sits, with his scythe to mow
Where erst sat Cupid with his bow ;
That half your locks are turned to grey ?
I'll ne'er believe a word they say.
'Tis true, but let it not be known,
My eyes are somewhat dimmish grown :
For Nature, always in the right,
To your decay adapts my sight ;
And wrinkles undistinguished pass,
For I'm ashamed to use a glass ;
And till I see them with these eyes,
Whoever says you have them, lies.
　No length of time can make you quit
Honour and virtue, sense and wit ;
Thus you may still be young to me,
While I can better hear than see.
O ne'er may Fortune show her spite,
To make me deaf and mend my sight.

J. Swift.

383.　STELLA'S BIRTHDAY, 1726

This day, whate'er the Fates decree,
Shall still be kept with joy by me :
This day then let us not be told
That you are sick, and I grown old ;
Nor think on our approaching ills,
And talk of spectacles and pills :
To-morrow will be time enough
To hear such mortifying stuff.
Yet, since from reason may be brought
A better and more pleasing thought,
Which can in spite of all decays
Support a few remaining days,
From not the gravest of divines
Accept for once some serious lines.
　Although we now can form no more
Long schemes of life, as heretofore ;
Yet you, while time is running fast,
Can look with joy on what is past.
　Were future happiness and pain
A mere contrivance of the brain,
As atheists argue, to entice
And fit their proselytes for vice

(The only comfort they propose,
To have companions in their woes),
Grant this the case ; yet sure 'tis hard
That virtue, styled its own reward
And by all sages understood
To be the chief of human good,
Should acting die, nor leave behind
Some lasting pleasure in the mind,
Which, by remembrance, will assuage
Grief, sickness, poverty, and age ;
And strongly shoot a radiant dart
To shine through life's declining part.

Say, Stella, feel you no content,
Reflecting on a life well spent ?
Your skilful hand employed to save
Despairing wretches from the grave ;
And then supporting with your store
Those whom you dragged from death before :
So Providence on mortals waits,
Preserving what it first creates :
Your generous boldness to defend
An innocent and absent friend ;
That courage which can make you just
To merit humbled in the dust ;
The detestation you express
For vice in all its glittering dress ;
That patience under torturing pain,
Where stubborn stoics would complain :
Must these like empty shadows pass,
Or forms reflected from a glass ?
Or mere chimeras in the mind,
That fly, and leave no marks behind ?
Does not the body thrive and grow
By food of twenty years ago ?
And, had it not been still supplied,
It must a thousand times have died.
Then who with reason can maintain
That no effects of food remain ?
And is not virtue in mankind
The nutriment that feeds the mind ;
Upheld by each good action past,
And still continued by the last ?
Then who with reason can pretend
That all effects of virtue end ?
Believe me, Stella, when you show
That true contempt for things below,
Nor prize your life for other ends
Than merely to oblige your friends ;

Your former actions claim their part,
And join to fortify your heart.
For virtue in her daily race,
Like Janus, bears a double face;
Looks back with joy where she has gone,
And therefore goes with courage on.
She at your sickly couch will wait,
And guide you to a better state.
    O then, whatever Heaven intends,
Take pity on your pitying friends!
Nor let your ills affect your mind,
To fancy they can be unkind.
Me, surely me, you ought to spare,
Who gladly would your suffering share,
Or give my scrap of life to you,
And think it far beneath your due;
You, to whose care so oft I owe
That I'm alive to tell you so.

J. SWIFT.

384. TO MRS. MARTHA BLOUNT

SENT ON HER BIRTHDAY

O BE thou blest with all that Heaven can send,
Long health, long youth, long pleasure and a friend!
Not with those toys the female race admire,
Riches that vex, and vanities that tire.
Not as the world its petty slaves rewards,
A youth of frolics, an old age of cards;
Fair to no purpose, artful to no end;
Young without lovers, old without a friend;
A fop their passion, but their prize a sot;
Alive, ridiculous,—and dead, forgot!

    Let joy or ease, let affluence or content,
And the gay conscience of a life well spent,
Calm every thought, inspirit every grace,
Glow in thy heart and smile upon thy face;
Let day improve on day, and year on year,
Without a pain, a trouble, or a fear;
Till death unfelt that tender frame destroy,
In some soft dream, or ecstasy of joy;
Peaceful sleep out the Sabbath of the tomb,
And wake to raptures in a life to come.

A. POPE.

385. TO MR. THOMAS SOUTHERNE

ON HIS BIRTHDAY, 1742

RESIGNED to live, prepared to die,
With not one sin,—but poetry,
This day Tom's fair account has run
(Without a blot) to eighty-one.
Kind Boyle, before his poet, lays
A table, with a cloth of bays ;
And Ireland, mother of sweet singers,
Presents her harp still to his fingers.
The feast his towering genius marks
In yonder wild goose and the larks !
The mushrooms show his wit was sudden !
And for his judgement, lo, a pudden !
Roast beef, though old, proclaims him stout,
And grace, although a bard, devout.
May Tom, whom Heaven sent down to raise
The price of prologues and of plays,
Be every birthday more a winner,
Digest his thirty-thousandth dinner;
Walk to his grave without reproach,
And scorn a rascal and a coach.

A. POPE.

6. TO MRS. THRALE ON HER COMPLETING HER
THIRTY-FIFTH YEAR

OFT in danger, yet alive,
We are come to thirty-five ;
Long may better years arrive,
Better years than thirty-five !
Could philosophers contrive
Life to stop at thirty-five,
Time his hours should never drive
O'er the bounds of thirty-five,
High to soar and deep to dive,
Nature gives at thirty-five,
Ladies, stock and tend your hive,
Trifle not at thirty-five ;
For, howe'er we boast and strive,
Life declines from thirty-five,
He that ever hopes to thrive
Must begin by thirty-five ;
And all who wisely wish to wive
Must look on Thrale at thirty-five.

S. JOHNSON.

387. ROSE'S BIRTHDAY

TELL me, perverse young year !
Why is the morn so drear ?
   Is there no flower to twine ?
Away, thou churl, away !
'Tis Rose's natal day,
   Reserve thy frowns for mine.

W. S. LANDOR.

388. A BIRTHDAY

MY heart is like a singing bird
   Whose nest is in a watered shoot ;
My heart is like an apple-tree
   Whose boughs are bent with thickset fruit ;
My heart is like a rainbow shell
   That paddles in a halcyon sea ;
My heart is gladder than all these,
   Because my love is come to me.

Raise me a dais of silk and down ;
   Hang it with vair and purple dyes ;
Carve it in doves, and pomegranates,
   And peacocks with a hundred eyes ;
Work it in gold and silver grapes,
   In leaves, and silver fleurs-de-lys ;
Because the birthday of my life
   Is come, my love is come to me.

C. G. ROSSETTI.

389. IMPROVEMENT IN THE FORTIES

I LATELY thought no man alive
Could e'er improve past forty-five,
   And ventured to assert it.
The observation was not new,
But seemed to me so just and true
   That none could controvert it.

' No, sir,' said Johnson, ' 'tis not so ;
'Tis your mistake, and I can show
   An instance, if you doubt it.
You, who perhaps are forty-eight,
May still improve, 'tis not too late ;
   I wish you'd set about it.'

Encouraged thus to mend my faults,
I turned his counsel in my thoughts
   Which way I could apply it ;

Genius I knew was past my reach,
For who can learn what none can teach ?
   And wit—I could not buy it.

Then come, my friends, and try your skill ;
You may improve me if you will,
   (My books are at a distance) :
With you I'll live and learn, and then
Instead of books I shall read men,
   So lend me your assistance.

Dear Knight of Plympton, teach me how
To suffer with unclouded brow,
   And smile serene as thine,
The jest uncouth and truth severe ;
Like thee to turn my deafest ear,
   And calmly drink my wine.

Thou say'st not only skill is gained,
But genius, too, may be attained,
   By studious imitation ;
Thy temper mild, thy genius fine,
I'll study till I make them mine
   By constant meditation.

The art of pleasing teach me, Garrick,
Thou who reversest odes Pindaric
   A second time read o'er ;
O could we read thee backwards too,
Last thirty years thou shouldst review,
   And charm us thirty more.

If I have thoughts and can't express 'em,
Gibbon shall teach me how to dress 'em
   In terms select and terse ;
Jones, teach me modesty and Greek ;
Smith, how to think ; Burke, how to speak ;
   And Beauclerk, to converse.

Let Johnson teach me how to place
In fairest light each borrowed grace,
   From him I'll learn to write :
Copy his free and easy style,
And from the roughness of his file
   Grow, like himself, polite.

                      T. BARNARD.

390. OH SAY NOT, MY LOVE

Oh say not, my love, with that mortified air,
  That your spring-time of pleasure is flown,
Nor bid me to maids that are younger repair
  For those raptures that still are thine own.

Though April his temples may wreathe with the vine,
  Its tendrils in infancy curled,
'Tis the ardour of August matures us the wine,
  Whose life-blood enlivens the world.

Though thy form, that was fashioned as light as a fay's,
  Has assumed a proportion more round,
And thy glance, that was bright as a falcon's at gaze,
  Looks soberly now on the ground;

Enough, after absence to meet me again,
  Thy steps still with ecstasy move;
Enough, that those dear sober glances retain
  For me the kind language of love.

Sir W. Scott.

391. THE AGE OF WISDOM

Ho, pretty page, with the dimpled chin,
  That never has known the barber's shear,
All your wish is woman to win,
This is the way that boys begin,—
  Wait till you come to Forty Year.

Curly gold locks cover foolish brains,
  Billing and cooing is all your cheer;
Sighing and singing of midnight strains,
Under Bonnybell's window panes,—
  Wait till you come to Forty Year.

Forty times over let Michaelmas pass,
  Grizzling hair the brain doth clear—
Then you know a boy is an ass,
Then you know the worth of a lass,
  Once you have come to Forty Year.

Pledge me round, I bid ye declare,
  All good fellows whose beards are grey,
Did not the fairest of the fair
Common grow and wearisome ere
  Ever a month was passed away?

The reddest lips that ever have kissed,
    The brightest eyes that ever have shone,
May pray and whisper, and we not list,
Or look away, and never be missed,
    Ere yet ever a month is gone.

Gillian 's dead, God rest her bier,
    How I loved her twenty years syne !
Marian 's married, but I sit here
Alone and merry at Forty Year,
    Dipping my nose in the Gascon wine.

W. M. THACKERAY.

392.   REASONS FOR DRINKING

IF all be true that I do think,
There are five reasons we should drink ;
Good wine—a friend—or being dry—
Or lest we should be by and by—
Or any other reason why.

H. ALDRICH.

393.   DRINKING

THE thirsty earth soaks up the rain,
And drinks, and gapes for drink again.
The plants suck in the earth, and are
With constant drinking fresh and fair ;
The sea itself—which one would think
Should have but little need of drink—
Drinks ten thousand rivers up,
So filled that they o'erflow the cup.
The busy sun—and one would guess
By 's drunken fiery face no less—
Drinks up the sea, and when he 's done,
The moon and stars drink up the sun :
They drink and dance by their own light
They drink and revel all the night.
Nothing in nature 's sober found,
But an eternal health goes round.
Fill up the bowl then, fill it high,
Fill up the glasses there ; for why
Should every creature drink but I ;
Why, man of morals, tell me why ?

A. COWLEY.

394. A TOAST

She 's pretty to walk with,
And witty to talk with,
And pleasant too to think on:
But the best use of all
Is, her health is a stale,
And helps to make us drink on.

SIR J. SUCKLING.

395. TO CELIA

Drink to me only with thine eyes,
And I will pledge with mine ;
Or leave a kiss but in the cup,
And I'll not look for wine.
The thirst that from the soul doth rise,
Doth ask a drink divine :
But might I of Jove's nectar sup,
I would not change for thine.

I sent thee late a rosy wreath,
Not so much honouring thee,
As giving it a hope that there
It could not withered be.
But thou thereon didst only breathe,
And sent'st it back to me :
Since when it grows, and smells, I swear,
Not of itself, but thee.

BEN. JONSON

396. FILL THE GOBLET AGAIN

Fill the goblet again ! for I never before
Felt the glow which now gladdens my heart to its core ;
Let us drink !—who would not ?—since, through life's varied round,
In the goblet alone no deception is found.

I have tried in its turn all that life can supply ;
I have basked in the beam of a dark rolling eye ;
I have loved !—who has not ?—but what heart can declare
That pleasure existed while passion was there ?

In the days of my youth, when the heart 's in its spring,
And dreams that affection can never take wing,
I had friends !—who has not ?—but what tongue will avow,
That friends, rosy wine ! are so faithful as thou ?

The heart of a mistress some boy may estrange,
Friendship shifts with the sunbeam—thou never canst change ;
Thou growest old—who does not ?—but on earth what appears,
Whose virtues, like thine, still increase with its years ?

Yet if blest to the utmost that love can bestow,
Should a rival bow down to our idol below,
We are jealous !—who 's not ?—thou hast no such alloy ;
For the more that enjoy thee, the more we enjoy.

Then the season of youth and its vanities past,
For refuge we fly to the goblet at last ;
There we find—do we not ?—in the flow of the soul,
That truth, as of yore, is confined to the bowl.

When the box of Pandora was opened on earth,
And Misery's triumph commenced over Mirth,
Hope was left,—was she not ?—but the goblet we kiss,
And care not for Hope, who are certain of bliss.

Long life to the grape ! for when summer is flown
The age of our nectar shall gladden our own :
We must die—who shall not ?—May our sins be forgiven,
And Hebe shall never be idle in heaven.

G. GORDON, LORD BYRON.

397. IN HIS LAST BINN SIR PETER LIES

In his last binn Sir Peter lies,
  Who knew not what it was to frown :
Death took him mellow, by surprise,
  And in his cellar stopped him down.
Through all our land we could not boast
  A knight more gay, more prompt than he,
To rise and fill a bumper toast,
  And pass it round with three times three.

None better knew the feast to sway,
  Or keep mirth's boat in better trim ;
For Nature had but little clay
  Like that of which she moulded him.
The meanest guest that graced his board
  Was there the freest of the free,
His bumper toast when Peter poured,
  And passed it round with three times three.

He kept at true good humour's mark
  The social flow of pleasure's tide :
He never made a brow look dark,
  Nor caused a tear, but when he died.
No sorrow round his tomb should dwell :
  More pleased his gay old ghost would be,
For funeral song, and passing bell,
  To hear no sound but three times three.

T. L. PEACOCK.

398.   THE CUP

A Paraphrase of Anacreon

Make me a bowl, a mighty bowl,
Large as my capacious soul,
Vast as my thirst is.   Let it have
Depth enough to be my grave.
I mean the grave of all my care,
For I intend to bury 't there.
Let it of silver fashioned be,
Worthy of wine ! worthy of me !
Worthy to adorn the spheres
As that bright Cup among the stars !

Yet draw no shapes of armour there,
No casque nor shield nor sword nor spear,
Nor wars of Thebes nor wars of Troy,
Nor any other martial toy.
For what do I vain armour prize,
Who mind not such rough exercise ?
But gentle sieges, softer wars,
Fights that cause no wounds or scars.
I'll have no battles on my plate,
Lest sight of them should brawls create,
Lest that provoke to quarrels too,
Which wine itself enough can do.

J. Oldham.

399.   UPON HIS DRINKING IN A BOWL

Vulcan, contrive me such a cup
　As Nestor used of old ;
Show all thy skill to trim it up,
　Damask it round with gold.

Make it so large that, filled with sack
　Up to the swelling brim,
Vast toasts on the delicious lake
　Like ships at sea may swim.

Engrave not battle on his cheek :
　With war I've naught to do.
I'm none of those that took Maestrich,
　Nor Yarmouth leaguer knew.

Let it no name of planets tell,
　Fixed stars or constellations,
For I am no Sir Sidrophel,
　Nor none of his relations.

But carve thereon a spreading vine,
　　Then add two lovely boys ;
Their limbs in amorous folds entwine,
　　The type of future joys.

Cupid and Bacchus my saints are ;
　　May drink and love still reign !
With wine I wash away my cares
　　And then to love again.

J. WILMOT, EARL OF ROCHESTER.

400.　ON LENDING A PUNCH BOWL

THIS ancient silver bowl of mine,— it tells of good old times,
Of joyous days, and jolly nights, and merry Christmas chimes ;
They were a free and jovial race, but honest, brave, and true,
That dipped their ladle in the punch when this old bowl was new.

A Spanish galleon brought the bar ; so runs the ancient tale ;
'Twas hammered by an Antwerp smith, whose arm was like a flail ;
And now and then between the strokes, for fear his strength should fail,
He wiped his brow, and quaffed a cup of good old Flemish ale.

'Twas purchased by an English squire to please his loving dame,
Who saw the cherubs, and conceived a longing for the same ;
And oft, as on the ancient stock another twig was found,
'Twas filled with caudle spiced and hot, and handed smoking round.

But, changing hands, it reached at length a Puritan divine,
Who used to follow Timothy, and take a little wine,
But hated punch and prelacy ; and so it was, perhaps,
He went to Leyden, where he found conventicles and schnaps.

And then, of course, you know what 's next,—it left the Dutchman's
　　shore
With those that in the *Mayflower* came,—a hundred souls and more,—
Along with all the furniture, to fill their new abodes,—
To judge by what is still on hand, at least a hundred loads.

'Twas on a dreary winter's eve, the night was closing dim,
When brave Miles Standish took the bowl, and filled it to the brim ;
The little Captain stood and stirred the posset with his sword,
And all his sturdy men-at-arms were ranged about the board.

He poured the fiery Hollands in,—the man that never feared,—
He took a long and solemn draught, and wiped his yellow beard ;
And one by one the musketeers—the men that fought and prayed—
All drank as 'twere their mother's milk, and not a man afraid.

That night, affrighted from his nest, the screaming eagle flew,
He heard the Pequot's ringing whoop, the soldier's wild halloo ;
And there the sachem learned the rule he taught to kith and kin,
' Run from the white man when you find he smells of Hollands gin ! '

A hundred years, and fifty more, had spread their leaves and snows,
A thousand rubs had flattened down each little cherub's nose,
When once again the bowl was filled, but not in mirth or joy,
'Twas mingled by a mother's hand to cheer her parting boy.

' Drink, John,' she said, ' 'twill do you good,—poor child, you'll never
     bear
This working in the dismal trench, out in the midnight air ;
And if—God bless me !—you were hurt, 'twould keep away the chill.'
So John *did* drink,—and well he wrought that night at Bunker's Hill !

I tell you, there was generous warmth in good old English cheer ;
I tell you, 'twas a pleasant thought to bring its symbol here.
'Tis but the fool that loves excess ;—hast thou a drunken soul ?
Thy bane is in thy shallow skull, not in my silver bowl !

I love the memory of the past,—its pressed yet fragrant flowers,—
The moss that clothes its broken walls,—the ivy on its towers ;—
Nay, this poor bauble it bequeathed,—my eyes grow moist and dim,
To think of all the vanished joys that danced around its brim.

Then fill a fair and honest cup, and bear it straight to me ;
The goblet hallows all it holds, whate'er the liquid be ;
And may the cherubs on its face protect me from the sin,
That dooms me to those dreadful words,—' My dear, where *have* you
     been ? '

O. W. Holmes.

401. CATAWBA WINE

This song of mine
Is a Song of the Vine,
To be sung by the glowing embers
Of wayside inns,
When the rain begins
To darken the drear Novembers.

It is not a song
Of the Scuppernong,
From warm Carolinian valleys,
Nor the Isabel
And the Muscadel
That bask in our garden alleys.

Nor the red Mustang,
Whose clusters hang
O'er the waves of the Colorado,
And the fiery flood
Of whose purple blood
Has a dash of Spanish bravado.

For richest and best
Is the wine of the West,
That grows by the Beautiful River ;
Whose sweet perfume
Fills all the room
With a benison on the giver.

And as hollow trees
Are the haunts of bees,
For ever going and coming ;
So this crystal hive
Is all alive
With a swarming and buzzing and humming.

Very good in its way
Is the Verzenay,
Or the Sillery soft and creamy ;
But Catawba wine
Has a taste more divine,
More dulcet, delicious, and dreamy.

There grows no vine
By the haunted Rhine,
By Danube or Guadalquivir,
Nor on island or cape,
That bears such a grape
As grows by the Beautiful River.

Drugged is their juice
For foreign use,
When shipped o'er the reeling Atlantic,
To rack our brains
With the fever pains,
That have driven the Old World frantic.

To the sewers and sinks
With all such drinks,
And after them tumble the mixer ;
For a poison malign
Is such Borgia wine,
Or at best but a Devil's Elixir.

While pure as a spring
    Is the wine I sing,
And to praise it, one needs but name it ;
    For Catawba wine
    Has need of no sign,
No tavern-bush to proclaim it.

And this Song of the Vine,
    This greeting of mine,
The winds and the birds shall deliver
    To the Queen of the West,
    In her garlands dressed,
On the banks of the Beautiful River.

H. W. LONGFELLOW

402. NATIONALITY IN DRINKS

My heart sank with our Claret-flask,
    Just now, beneath the heavy sedges
That serves this pond's black face for mask ;
    And still at yonder broken edges
Of the hole, where up the bubbles glisten,
After my heart I look and listen.

Our laughing little flask, compelled
    Through depth to depth more bleak and shady ;
As when, both arms beside her held,
    Feet straightened out, some gay French lady
Is caught up from life's light and motion,
And dropped into death's silent ocean !

———————

Up jumped Tokay on our table,
Like a pygmy castle-warder,
Dwarfish to see, but stout and able,
Arms and accoutrements all in order ;
And fierce he looked North, then, wheeling South,
Blew with his bugle a challenge to Drouth,
Cocked his flap-hat with the tosspot-feather,
Twisted his thumb in his red moustache,
Jingled his huge brass spurs together,
Tightened his waist with its Buda sash,
And then, with an impudence naught could abash,
Shrugged his hump-shoulder, to tell the beholder,
For twenty such knaves he should laugh but the bolder :

And so, with his sword-hilt gallantly jutting,
And dexter-hand on his haunch abutting,
Went the little man, Sir Ausbruch, strutting !

Here 's to Nelson's memory !
'Tis the second time that I, at sea,
Right off Cape Trafalgar here,
Have drunk it deep in British Beer.
Nelson for ever—any time
Am I his to command in prose or rhyme !
Give me of Nelson only a touch,
And I save it, be it little or much :
Here 's one our Captain gives, and so
Down at the word, by George, shall it go !
He says that at Greenwich they point the beholder
To Nelson's coat, ' still with tar on the shoulder,
For he used to lean with one shoulder digging,
Jigging, as it were, and zig-zag-zigging
Up against the mizen-rigging ! '

R. BROWNING.

403. ALE

I CANNOT eat but little meat,
   My stomach is not good ;
But sure, I think that I can drink
   With him that wears a hood.
Though I go bare, take ye no care,
   I am nothing a-cold ;
I stuff my skin so full within
   Of jolly good ale and old.
Back and side go bare, go bare,
   Both foot and hand go cold ;
But, belly, God send thee good ale enough,
   Whether it be new or old.

I love no roast but a nut-brown toast,
   And a crab laid in the fire ;
A little bread shall do me stead ;
   Much bread I not desire.
No frost, nor snow, no wind, I trow,
   Can hurt me if I would ;
I am so wrapped, and throughly lapped
   Of jolly good ale and old.
Back and side go bare, go bare, &c.

And Tyb my wife, that as her life
　　Loveth well good ale to seek,
Full oft drinks she, till ye may see
　　The tears run down her cheek ;
Then doth she troll to me the bowl,
　　Even as a malt-worm should ;
And saith, ' Sweetheart, I took my part
　　Of this jolly good ale and old ! '
Back and side go bare, go bare, &c.

Now let them drink till they nod and wink,
　　Even as good fellows should do ;
They shall not miss to have the bliss
　　Good ale doth bring men to ;
And all poor souls that have scoured bowls
　　Or have them lustily trolled,
God save the lives of them and their wives,
　　Whether they be young or old.
Back and side go bare, go bare,
　　Both foot and hand go cold ;
But, belly, God send thee good ale enough,
　　Whether it be new or old.

　　　　　　　　　　　　　　J. STILL.

404.　BEER

IN those old days which poets say were golden—
　　(Perhaps they laid the gilding on themselves :
And, if they did, I'm all the more beholden
　　To those brown dwellers in my dusty shelves,
Who talk to me ' in language quaint and olden '
　　Of gods and demigods and fauns and elves,
Pan with his pipes, and Bacchus with his leopards,
And staid young goddesses who flirt with shepherds :)

In those old days, the Nymph called Etiquette
　　(Appalling thought to dwell on) was not born.
They had their May, but no Mayfair as yet,
　　No fashions varying as the hues of morn.
Just as they pleased they dressed and drank and ate,
　　Sang hymns to Ceres (their John Barleycorn)
And danced unchaperoned, and laughed unchecked,
And were no doubt extremely incorrect.

Yet do I think their theory was pleasant :
　　And oft, I own, my ' wayward fancy roams '
Back to those times, so different from the present ;
　　When no one smoked cigars, nor gave At-homes,

Nor smote a billiard-ball, nor winged a pheasant,
   Nor ' did ' her hair by means of long-tailed combs,
Nor migrated to Brighton once a year,
   Nor—most astonishing of all—drank Beer.

No, they did not drink Beer, ' which brings me to '
   (As Gilpin said) ' the middle of my song.'
Not that ' the middle ' is precisely true,
   Or else I should not tax your patience long :
If I had said ' beginning ' it might do ;
   But I have a dislike to quoting wrong :
I was unlucky—sinned against, not sinning—
When Cowper wrote down ' middle ' for ' beginning.'

So to proceed.   That abstinence from Malt
   Has always struck me as extremely curious.
The Greek mind must have had some vital fault,
   That they should stick to liquors so injurious—
(Wine, water, tempered p'raps with Attic salt)—
   And not at once invent that mild, luxurious,
And artful beverage, Beer.   How the digestion
Got on without it, is a startling question.

Had they digestions ? and an actual body
   Such as dyspepsia might make attacks on ?
Were they abstract ideas—(like Tom Noddy
   And Mr. Briggs)—or men, like Jones and Jackson ?
Then nectar—was that beer, or whisky-toddy ?
   Some say the Gaelic mixture, I the Saxon :
I think a strict adherence to the latter
Might make some Scots less pigheaded, and fatter.

Besides, Bon Gaultier definitely shows
   That the real beverage for feasting gods on
Is a soft compound, grateful to the nose
   And also to the palate, known as ' Hodgson '.
I know a man—a tailor's son—who rose
   To be a peer : and this I would lay odds on,
(Though in his Memoirs it may not appear),
That that man owed his rise to copious Beer.

O Beer ! O Hodgson, Guinness, Allsop, Bass !
   Names that should be on every infant's tongue !
Shall days and months and years and centuries pass,
   And still your merits be unrecked, unsung ?
Oh ! I have gazed into my foaming glass,
   And wished that lyre could yet again be strung
Which once rang prophet-like through Greece, and taught her
Misguided sons that ' the best drink was water '.

How would he now recant that wild opinion,
  And sing—as would that I could sing—of you !
I was not born (alas !) the ' Muses' minion ',
  I'm not poetical, not even blue :
And he, we know, but strives with waxen pinion,
  Whoe'er he is that entertains the view
Of emulating Pindar, and will be
Sponsor at last to some now nameless sea.

Oh ! when the green slopes of Arcadia burned
  With all the lustre of the dying day,
And on Cithaeron's brow the reaper turned,
  (Humming, of course, in his delightful way,
How Lycidas was dead, and how concerned
  The Nymphs were when they saw his lifeless clay ;
And how rock told to rock the dreadful story
That poor young Lycidas was gone to glory :)

What would that lone and labouring soul have given,
  At that soft moment for a pewter pot !
How had the mists that dimmed his eye been riven,
  And Lycidas and sorrow all forgot !
If his own grandmother had died unshriven,
  In two short seconds he'd have recked it not ;
Such power hath Beer.   The heart which Grief hath cankered
Hath one unfailing remedy—the Tankard.

Coffee is good, and so no doubt is cocoa ;
  Tea did for Johnson and the Chinamen :
When ' Dulce est desipere in loco '
  Was written, real Falernian winged the pen.
When a rapt audience has encored ' Fra Poco '
  Or ' Casta Diva ', I have heard that then
The Prima Donna, smiling herself out,
Recruits her flagging powers with bottled stout.

But what is coffee, but a noxious berry,
  Born to keep used-up Londoners awake ?
What is Falernian, what is Port or Sherry,
  But vile concoctions to make dull heads ache ?
Nay stout itself—(though good with oysters, very)—
  Is not a thing your reading man should take.
He that would shine, and petrify his tutor,
Should drink draught Allsop in its ' native pewter '.

But hark ! a sound is stealing on my ear—
  A soft and silvery sound—I know it well
Its tinkling tells me that a time is near
  Precious to me—it is the Dinner Bell.

O blessed Bell ! Thou bringest beef and beer,
   Thou bringest good things more than tongue may tell :
Seared is, of course, my heart—but unsubdued
Is, and shall be, my appetite for food.

I go.   Untaught and feeble is my pen :
   But on one statement I may safely venture :
That few of our most highly gifted men
   Have more appreciation of the trencher.
I go.   One pound of British beef, and then
   What Mr. Swiveller called a ' modest quencher ' ;
That, home-returning, I may ' soothly say ',
' Fate cannot touch me : I have dined to-day.'

                         C. S. CALVERLEY.

405. WRITTEN AT AN INN AT HENLEY

To thee, fair freedom ! I retire
   From flattery, cards, and dice, and din ;
Nor art thou found in mansions higher
   Than the low cot, or humble inn.

'Tis here with boundless power I reign ;
   And every health which I begin,
Converts dull port to bright champagne ;
   Such freedom crowns it, at an inn.

I fly from pomp, I fly from plate !
   I fly from falsehood's specious grin ;
Freedom I love, and form I hate,
   And choose my lodgings at an inn.

Here, waiter ! take my sordid ore,
   Which lackeys else might hope to win ;
It buys, what courts have not in store ;
   It buys me freedom at an inn.

Whoe'er has travelled life's dull round,
   Where'er his stages may have been,
May sigh to think he still has found
   The warmest welcome at an inn.
                     W. SHENSTONE.

406. THE MERMAID TAVERN

Souls of Poets dead and gone,
What Elysium have ye known,
Happy field or mossy cavern,
Choicer than the Mermaid Tavern ?
Have ye tippled drink more fine
Than mine host's Canary wine ?
Or are fruits of Paradise
Sweeter than those dainty pies
Of venison ? O generous food !
Dressed as though bold Robin Hood
Would, with his maid Marian,
Sup and bowse from horn and can.

I have heard that on a day
Mine host's sign-board flew away,
Nobody knew whither, till
An astrologer's old quill
To a sheepskin gave the story,
Said he saw you in your glory,
Underneath a new old sign
Sipping beverage divine,
And pledging with contented smack
The Mermaid in the Zodiac !

Souls of Poets dead and gone,
What Elysium have ye known,
Happy field or mossy cavern,
Choicer than the Mermaid Tavern ?

J. Keats.

407. MADE AT THE COCK

O plump head-waiter at the Cock,
    To which I most resort,
How goes the time ? 'Tis five o'clock.
    Go fetch a pint of port:
But let it not be such as that
    You set before chance comers,
But such whose father-grape grew fat
    On Lusitanian summers.

No vain libation to the Muse,
    But may she still be kind,
And whisper lovely words, and use
    Her influence on the mind,

To make me write my random rhymes,
    Ere they be half-forgotten;
Nor add and alter, many times,
    Till all be ripe and rotten,
       .   .   .   .   .

Head-waiter, honoured by the guest
    Half-mused, or reeling-ripe,
The pint, you brought me, was the best
    That ever came from pipe.
But though the port surpasses praise,
    My nerves have dealt with stiffer.
Is there some magic in the place?
    Or do my peptics differ?

For since I came to live and learn,
    No pint of white or red
Had ever half the power to turn
    This wheel within my head,
Which bears a seasoned brain about,
    Unsubject to confusion,
Though soaked and saturate, out and out,
    Through every convolution.

For I am of a numerous house,
    With many kinsmen gay,
Where long and largely we carouse
    As who shall say me nay:
Each month, a birth-day coming on,
    We drink, defying trouble,
Or sometimes two would meet in one,
    And then we drank it double;

Whether the vintage, yet unkept,
    Had relish fiery-new,
Or, elbow-deep in sawdust, slept,
    As old as Waterloo;
Or stowed (when classic Canning died)
    In musty bins and chambers,
Had cast upon its crusty side
    The gloom of ten Decembers.

The Muse, the jolly Muse, it is!
    She answered to my call,
She changes with that mood or this,
    Is all-in-all to all:
She lit the spark within my throat,
    To make my blood run quicker,
Used all her fiery will, and smote
    Her life into the liquor.

And hence this halo lives about
   The waiter's hands, that reach
To each his perfect pint of stout,
   His proper chop to each.
He looks not like the common breed
   That with the napkin dally ;
I think he came like Ganymede,
   From some delightful valley.

The Cock was of a larger egg
   Than modern poultry drop,
Stepped forward on a firmer leg,
   And crammed a plumper crop ;
Upon an ampler dunghill trod,
   Crowed lustier late and early,
Sipped wine from silver, praising God,
   And raked in golden barley.

A private life was all his joy,
   Till in a court he saw
A something-pottle-bodied boy
   That knuckled at the taw :
He stooped and clutched him, fair and good,
   Flew over roof and casement :
His brothers of the weather stood
   Stock-still for sheer amazement.

But he, by farmstead, thorpe and spire,
   And followed with acclaims,
A sign to many a staring shire,
   Came crowing over Thames,
Right down by smoky Paul's they bore,
   Till, where the street grows straiter,
One fixed for ever at the door,
   And one became head-waiter.

                  ALFRED, LORD TENNYSON.

408. A JACOBITE TOAST

GOD bless the king !—I mean the Faith's Defender ;
God bless (no harm in blessing) the Pretender !
But who Pretender is, or who is King,
God bless us all !—that 's quite another thing.

                        J. BYROM.

409. A BALLAD OF BOUILLABAISSE

A STREET there is in Paris famous,
  For which no rhyme our language yields,
Rue Neuve des Petits Champs its name is—
  The New Street of the Little Fields ;
And here 's an inn, not rich and splendid,
  But still in comfortable case ;
The which in youth I oft attended,
  To eat a bowl of Bouillabaisse.

This Bouillabaisse a noble dish is—
  A sort of soup, or broth, or brew,
Or hotchpotch of all sorts of fishes,
  That Greenwich never could outdo ;
Green herbs, red peppers, mussels, saffern,
  Soles, onions, garlic, roach, and dace ;
All these you eat at Terré's tavern,
  In that one dish of Bouillabaisse.

Indeed, a rich and savoury stew 'tis ;
  And true philosophers, methinks,
Who love all sorts of natural beauties,
  Should love good victuals and good drinks.
And Cordelier or Benedictine
  Might gladly, sure, his lot embrace,
Nor find a fast-day too afflicting
  Which served him up a Bouillabaisse.

I wonder if the house still there is ?
  Yes, here the lamp is, as before ;
The smiling red-cheeked écaillère is
  Still opening oysters at the door.
Is Terré still alive and able ?
  I recollect his droll grimace ;
He'd come and smile before your table,
  And hope you liked your Bouillabaisse.

We enter—nothing's changed or older.
  ' How 's Monsieur Terré, waiter, pray ? '
The waiter stares and shrugs his shoulder—
  ' Monsieur is dead this many a day.'
' It is the lot of saint and sinner,
  So honest Terré 's run his race.'
' What will Monsieur require for dinner ? '
  ' Say, do you still cook Bouillabaisse ? '

' Oh, oui, Monsieur,' 's the waiter's answer ;
  ' Quel vin Monsieur désire-t-il ? '
' Tell me a good one.'—' That I can, Sir :
  The Chambertin with yellow seal.'

' So Terré 's gone,' I say, and sink in
  My old accustomed corner-place ;
' He's done with feasting and with drinking,
  With Burgundy and Bouillabaisse.'

My old accustomed corner here is,
  The table still is in the nook ;
Ah ! vanished many a busy year is,
  This well-known chair since last I took.
When first I saw ye, *cari luoghi*,
  I'd scarce a beard upon my face,
And now a grizzled, grim old fogy,
  I sit and wait for Bouillabaisse.

Where are you, old companions trusty,
  Of early days, here met to dine ?
Come, waiter ! quick, a flagon crusty—
  I'll pledge them in the good old wine.
The kind old voices and old faces
  My memory can quick retrace ;
Around the board they take their places,
  And share the wine and Bouillabaisse.

There's Jack has made a wondrous marriage
  There's laughing Tom is laughing yet ;
There's brave Augustus drives his carriage ;
  There's poor old Fred in the Gazette ;
On James's head the grass is growing :
  Good Lord ! the world has wagged apace
Since here we set the Claret flowing,
  And drank, and ate the Bouillabaisse.

Ah me ! how quick the days are flitting !
  I mind me of a time that 's gone,
When here I'd sit, as now I'm sitting,
  In this same place—but not alone.
A fair young form was nestled near me,
  A dear, dear face looked fondly up,
And sweetly spoke and smiled to cheer me
  —There's no one now to share my cup.

I drink it as the Fates ordain it.
  Come, fill it, and have done with rhymes :
Fill up the lonely glass, and drain it
  In memory of dear old times.
Welcome the wine, whate'er the seal is ;
  And sit you down and say your grace
With thankful heart, whate'er the meal is.
  —Here comes the smoking Bouillabaisse !

                              W. M. THACKERAY.

410. SPECTATOR AB EXTRA

I

As I sat at the Café I said to myself,
They may talk as they please about what they call pelf,
They may sneer as they like about eating and drinking,
But help it I cannot, I cannot help thinking
    How pleasant it is to have money, heigh-ho !
    How pleasant it is to have money.

I sit at my table *en grand seigneur,*
And when I have done, throw a crust to the poor ;
Not only the pleasure itself of good living,
But also the pleasure of now and then giving :
    So pleasant it is to have money, heigh-ho !
    So pleasant it is to have money.

They may talk as they please about what they call pelf,
And how one ought never to think of one's self,
How pleasures of thought surpass eating and drinking,—
My pleasure of thought is the pleasure of thinking
    How pleasant it is to have money, heigh-ho !
    How pleasant it is to have money.

II

Le Diner

Come along, 'tis the time, ten or more minutes past,
And he who came first had to wait for the last ;
The oysters ere this had been in and been out ;
Whilst I have been sitting and thinking about
    How pleasant it is to have money, heigh-ho !
    How pleasant it is to have money.

A clear soup with eggs ; *voilà tout* ; of the fish
The *filets de sole* are a moderate dish
A là Orly, but you're for red mullet, you say :
By the gods of good fare, who can question to-day
    How pleasant it is to have money, heigh-ho !
    How pleasant it is to have money.

After oysters, sauterne ; then sherry ; champagne,
Ere one bottle goes, comes another again ;
Fly up, thou bold cork, to the ceiling above,
And tell to our ears in the sound that they love
    How pleasant it is to have money, heigh-ho !
    How pleasant it is to have money.

I've the simplest of palates ; absurd it may be,
But I almost could dine on a *poulet-au-riz,*

Fish and soup and omelette and that—but the deuce—
There were to be woodcocks, and not *Charlotte Russe!*
　　So pleasant it is to have money, heigh-ho !
　　So pleasant it is to have money.

Your chablis is acid, away with the hock,
Give me the pure juice of the purple médoc :
St. Peray is exquisite ; but, if you please,
Some burgundy just before tasting the cheese.
　　So pleasant it is to have money, heigh-ho !
　　So pleasant it is to have money.

As for that, pass the bottle, and d—n the expense,
I've seen it observed by a writer of sense,
That the labouring classes could scarce live a day,
If people like us didn't eat, drink, and pay.
　　So useful it is to have money, heigh-ho !
　　So useful it is to have money.

One ought to be grateful, I quite apprehend,
Having dinner and supper and plenty to spend,
And so suppose now, while the things go away,
By way of a grace we all stand up and say
　　How pleasant it is to have money, heigh-ho !
　　How pleasant it is to have money.

III

Parvenant

I cannot but ask, in the park and the streets
When I look at the number of persons one meets,
What e'er in the world the poor devils can do
Whose fathers and mothers can't give them a *sou.*
　　So needful it is to have money, heigh-ho !
　　So needful it is to have money.

I ride, and I drive, and I care not a d—n,
The people look up and they ask who I am ;
And if I should chance to run over a cad,
I can pay for the damage, if ever so bad.
　　So useful it is to have money, heigh-ho !
　　So useful it is to have money.

It was but this winter I came up to town,
And already I'm gaining a sort of renown ;
Find my way to good houses without much ado,
Am beginning to see the nobility too.
　　So useful it is to have money, heigh-ho !
　　So useful it is to have money.

O dear what a pity they ever should lose it,
Since they are the people that know how to use it ;
So easy, so stately, such manners, such dinners,
And yet, after all, it is we are the winners.
  So needful it is to have money, heigh-ho !
  So needful it is to have money.

It 's all very well to be handsome and tall,
Which certainly makes you look well at a ball ;
It 's all very well to be clever and witty,
But if you are poor, why it 's only a pity.
  So needful it is to have money, heigh-ho !
  So needful it is to have money.

There 's something undoubtedly in a fine air,
To know how to smile and be able to stare,
High breeding is something, but well-bred or not,
In the end the one question is, what have you got.
  So needful it is to have money, heigh-ho !
  So needful it is to have money.

And the angels in pink and the angels in blue,
In muslins and moirés so lovely and new,
What is it they want, and so wish you to guess,
But if you have money, the answer is Yes.
  So needful, they tell you, is money, heigh-ho !
  So needful it is to have money.

         A. H. CLOUGH.

411. NEW-MADE HONOUR

A FRIEND I met some half-hour since—
 ' *Good-morrow, Jack !* ' quoth I ;
The new-made Knight, like any Prince,
 Frowned, nodded, and passed by ;
When up came Jem—' *Sir John, your slave !* '
 ' Ah, James ; we dine at eight—
Fail not—'(low bows the supple knave)
 ' Don't make my lady wait.'
The King can do no wrong ?   As I 'm a sinner,
He 's spoilt an honest tradesman and my dinner.

        R. H. BARHAM.

412. A PIPE OF TOBACCO

I. Mr. Phillips's style imitated

Little tube of mighty power,
Charmer of an idle hour,
Object of my warm desire,
Lip of wax and eye of fire:
And thy snowy taper waist,
With my finger gently braced;
And thy swelling ashy crest,
With my little stopper pressed;
And the sweetest bliss of blisses,
Breathing from thy balmy kisses.
Happy thrice and thrice agen—
Happiest he of happy men!
Who, when agen the night returns,
When agen the taper burns;
When agen the cricket's gay
(Little cricket) full of play,
Can afford his tube to feed,
With the fragrant Indian weed;
Pleasure for a nose divine,
Incense of the god of wine:
Happy thrice and thrice agen—
Happiest he of happy men!

I. H. Browne.

413. A PIPE OF TOBACCO

II. Mr. Pope's style imitated

Blest leaf! whose aromatic gales dispense
To templars modesty, to parsons sense:
So raptured priests, at famed Dodona's shrine
Drank inspiration from the steam divine.
Poison that cures, a vapour that affords
Content, more solid than the smile of lords:
Rest to the weary, to the hungry food,
The last kind refuge of the wise and good.
Inspired by thee, dull cits adjust the scale
Of Europe's peace, when other statesmen fail.
By thee protected, and thy sister, beer,
Poets rejoice, nor think the bailiff near.
Nor less the critic owns thy genial aid,
While supperless he plies the piddling trade.
What, though to love and soft delights a foe,
By ladies hated, hated by the beau,
Yet social freedom, long to court unknown,
Fair health, fair truth, and virtue are thy own.
Come to thy poet, come with healing wings,
And let me taste thee unexcised by kings.

I. H. Browne.

414. TO THE REV. WILLIAM BULL

June 22, 1782.

MY DEAR FRIEND,

If reading verse be your delight,
'Tis mine as much, or more, to write ;
But what we would, so weak is man,
Lies oft remote from what we can.
For instance, at this very time
I feel a wish, by cheerful rhyme
To soothe my friend, and, had I power,
To cheat him of an anxious hour ;
Not meaning (for I must confess,
It were but folly to suppress)
His pleasure, or his good alone,
But squinting partly at my own.
But though the sun is flaming high
I' th' centre of yon arch, the sky,
And he had once (and who but he ?)
The name for setting genius free,
Yet whether poets of past days
Yielded him undeserved praise,
And he by no uncommon lot
Was famed for virtues he had not ;
Or whether, which is like enough,
His Highness may have taken huff,
So seldom sought with invocation,
Since it has been the reigning fashion
To disregard his inspiration,
I seem no brighter in my wits
For all the radiance he emits,
Than if I saw, through midnight vapour,
The glimmering of a farthing taper.
Oh for a succedaneum, then,
To accelerate a creeping pen !
Oh for a ready succedaneum,
Quod caput, cerebrum, et cranium
Pondere liberet exoso,
Et morbo jam caliginoso !
'Tis here ; this oval box well filled
With best tobacco, finely milled,
Beats all Anticyra's pretences
To disengage the encumbered senses.
    Oh Nymph of Transatlantic fame,
Where'er thine haunt, whate'er thy name,
Whether reposing on the side
Of Oroonoquo's spacious tide,
Or listening with delight not small
To Niagara's distant fall,

'Tis thine to cherish and to feed
The pungent nose-refreshing weed,
Which, whether pulverized it gain
A speedy passage to the brain,
Or whether, touched with fire, it rise
In circling eddies to the skies,
Does thought more quicken and refine
Than all the breath of all the Nine—
Forgive the Bard, if Bard he be,
Who once too wantonly made free,
To touch with a satiric wipe
That symbol of thy power, the pipe ;
So may no blight infest thy plains,
And no unseasonable rains,
And so may smiling Peace once more
Visit America's sad shore ;
And thou, secure from all alarms
Of thundering drums and glittering arms,
Rove unconfined beneath the shade
Thy wide-expanded leaves have made ;
So may thy votaries increase,
And fumigation never cease.
May Newton with renewed delights
Perform thy odoriferous rites,
While clouds of incense half divine
Involve thy disappearing shrine ;
And so may smoke-inhaling Bull
Be always filling, never full.

W. COWPER.

415. SUBLIME TOBACCO

SUBLIME tobacco ! which from east to west
Cheers the tar's labour or the Turkman's rest ;
Which on the Moslem's ottoman divides
His hours, and rivals opium and his brides ;
Magnificent in Stamboul, but less grand,
Though not less loved, in Wapping or the Strand
Divine in hookas, glorious in a pipe,
When tipped with amber, mellow, rich, and ripe ;
Like other charmers, wooing the caress,
More dazzlingly when daring in full dress ;
Yet thy true lovers more admire by far
Thy naked beauties—Give me a cigar !

G. GORDON, LORD BYRON.

416. A FAREWELL TO TOBACCO

MAY the Babylonish curse
Strait confound my stammering verse,
If I can a passage see
In this word-perplexity,
Or a fit expression find,
Or a language to my mind,
(Still the phrase is wide or scant)
To take leave of thee, GREAT PLANT
Or in any terms relate
Half my love, or half my hate :
For I hate, yet love, thee so,
That, whichever thing I show,
The plain truth will seem to be
A constrained hyperbole,
And the passion to proceed
More from a mistress than a weed.

Sooty retainer to the vine,
Bacchus' black servant, negro fine ;
Sorcerer, that mak'st us dote upon
Thy begrimed complexion,
And, for thy pernicious sake,
More and greater oaths to break
Than reclaimèd lovers take
'Gainst women : thou thy siege dost lay
Much too in the female way,
While thou suck'st the labouring breath
Faster than kisses or than death.

Thou in such a cloud dost bind us,
That our worst foes cannot find us,
And ill-fortune, that would thwart us,
Shoots at lovers, shooting at us ;
While each man, through thy heightening steam,
Does like a smoking Etna seem,
And all about us does express
(Fancy and wit in richest dress)
A Sicilian fruitfulness.

Thou through such a mist dost show us,
That our best friends do not know us,
And, for those allowed features,
Due to reasonable creatures,
Liken'st us to fell Chimeras,
Monsters that, who see us, fear us ;
Worse than Cerberus or Geryon,
Or, who first loved a cloud, Ixion.

Bacchus we know, and we allow
His tipsy rites.   But what art thou
That but by reflex canst show
What his deity can do,
As the false Egyptian spell
Aped the true Hebrew miracle?
Some few vapours thou may'st raise,
The weak brain may serve to amaze,
But to the reins and nobler heart
Canst nor life nor heat impart.

Brother of Bacchus, later born,
The old world was sure forlorn,
Wanting thee, that aidest more
The god's victories than before
All his panthers, and the brawls
Of his piping Bacchanals.
These, as stale, we disallow,
Or judge of *thee* meant: only thou
His true Indian conquest art;
And, for ivy round his dart,
The reformed god now weaves
A finer thyrsus of thy leaves.

Scent to match thy rich perfume
Chemic art did ne'er presume
Through her quaint alembic strain,
None so sovereign to the brain.
Nature, that did in thee excel,
Framed again no second smell.
Roses, violets, but toys
For the smaller sort of boys,
Or for greener damsels meant;
Thou art the only manly scent.

Stinking'st of the stinking kind,
Filth of the mouth and fog of the mind.
Africa, that brags her foyson,
Breeds no such prodigious poison,
Henbane, nightshade, both together,
Hemlock, aconite—
                    Nay, rather,
Plant divine, of rarest virtue;
Blisters on the tongue would hurt you.
'Twas but in a sort I blamed thee;
None e'er prospered who defamed thee;
Irony all, and feigned abuse,
Such as perplexed lovers use,

At a need, when, in despair
To paint forth their fairest fair,
Or in part but to express
That exceeding comeliness
Which their fancies doth so strike,
They borrow language of dislike ;
And, instead of Dearest Miss,
Jewel, Honey, Sweetheart, Bliss,
And those forms of old admiring,
Call her Cockatrice and Siren,
Basilisk, and all that 's evil,
Witch, Hyena, Mermaid, Devil,
Ethiop, Wench, and Blackamoor,
Monkey, Ape, and twenty more ;
Friendly Trait'ress, loving Foe,—
Not that she is truly so,
But no other way they know
A contentment to express,
Borders so upon excess,
That they do not rightly wot
Whether it be pain or not.

Or as men, constrained to part
With what 's nearest to their heart,
While their sorrow 's at the height,
Lose discrimination quite,
And their hasty wrath let fall,
To appease their frantic gall,
On the darling thing whatever
Whence they feel it death to sever,
Though it be, as they, perforce,
Guiltless of the sad divorce.

For I must (nor let it grieve thee,
Friendliest of plants, that I must) leave thee.
For thy sake, Tobacco, I
Would do any thing but die,
And but seek to extend my days
Long enough to sing thy praise.
But as she, who once hath been
A king's consort, is a queen
Ever after, nor will bate
Any tittle of her state,
Though a widow, or divorced,
So I, from thy converse forced,
The old name and style retain,
A right Katherine of Spain ;
And a seat, too, 'mongst the joys
Of the blest Tobacco boys ;

Where, though I, by sour physician,
Am debarred the full fruition
Of thy favours, I may catch
Some collateral sweets, and snatch
Sidelong odours, that give life
Like glances from a neighbour's wife;
And still live in the by-places
And the suburbs of thy graces;
And in thy borders take delight,
An unconquered Canaanite.

C. LAMB.

417. ODE TO TOBACCO

THOU who, when fears attack,
Bid'st them avaunt, and Black
Care, at the horseman's back
    Perching, unseatest;
Sweet when the morn is grey;
Sweet, when they've cleared away
Lunch; and at close of day
    Possibly sweetest:

I have a liking old
For thee, though manifold
Stories, I know, are told,
    Not to thy credit;
How one (or two at most)
Drops make a cat a ghost—
Useless, except to roast—
    Doctors have said it:

How they who use fusees
All grow by slow degrees
Brainless as chimpanzees,
    Meagre as lizards;
Go mad, and beat their wives;
Plunge (after shocking lives)
Razors and carving knives
    Into their gizzards.

Confound such knavish tricks!
Yet know I five or six
Smokers who freely mix
    Still with their neighbours;
Jones—(who, I'm glad to say,
Asked leave of Mrs. J——)—
Daily absorbs a clay
    After his labours.

Cats may have had their goose
Cooked by tobacco-juice ;
Still why deny its use
    Thoughtfully taken ?
We're not as tabbies are :
Smith, take a fresh cigar !
Jones, the tobacco-jar !
    Here 's to thee, Bacon !

C. S. CALVERLEY.

418. THE HEADACHE

My head doth ache,
O Sappho ! take
    Thy fillet,
And bind the pain ;
Or bring some bane
    To kill it.

But less that part,
Than my poor heart,
    Now is sick :
One kiss from thee
Will counsel be,
    And physic.

R. HERRICK.

419. TO MINERVA

(FROM THE GREEK)

My temples throb, my pulses boil,
    I'm sick of Song, and Ode, and Ballad—
So, Thyrsis, take the Midnight Oil,
    And pour it on a lobster salad.

My brain is dull, my sight is foul,
    I cannot write a verse, or read,—
Then, Pallas, take away thine Owl,
    And let us have a lark instead.

T. HOOD.

420. THE REMEDY WORSE THAN THE DISEASE

I SENT for Ratcliffe ; was so ill,
   That other doctors gave me over :
He felt my pulse, prescribed his pill,
   And I was likely to recover.

But when the wit began to wheeze,
   And wine had warmed the politician,
Cured yesterday of my disease,
   I died last night of my physician.

M. PRIOR.

421. ADVICE TO A LADY IN AUTUMN

ASSES' milk, half a pint, take at seven, or before,
Then sleep for an hour or two, and no more.
At nine stretch your arms, and, oh ! think when alone
There 's no pleasure in bed.—Mary, bring me my gown.
Slip on that ere you rise ; let your caution be such ;
Keep all cold from your breast, there 's already too much ;
Your pinners set right, your twitcher tied on,
Your prayers at an end, and your breakfast quite done,
Retire to some author improving and gay,
And with sense like your own, set your mind for the day.
At twelve you may walk, for at this time o' the year,
The sun, like your wit, is as mild as 'tis clear :
But mark in the meadows the ruin of time ;
Take the hint, and let life be improved in its prime.
Return not in haste, nor of dressing take heed ;
For beauty like yours no assistance can need.
With an appetite thus down to dinner you sit,
Where the chief of the feast is the flow of your wit :
Let this be indulged, and let laughter go round ;
As it pleases your mind to your health 'twill redound.
After dinner two glasses at least, I approve ;
Name the first to the King, and the last to your love :
Thus cheerful, with wisdom, with innocence, gay,
And calm with your joys, gently glide through the day.
The dews of the evening most carefully shun ;
Those tears of the sky for the loss of the sun.
Then in chat, or at play, with a dance or a song,
Let the night, like the day, pass with pleasure along.
All cares, but of love, banish far from your mind ;
And those you may end, when you please to be kind.

P. STANHOPE, EARL OF CHESTERFIELD.

422. THE SECRETARY

WHILE with labour assiduous due pleasure I mix,
And in one day atone for the business of six,
In a little Dutch chaise, on a Saturday night,
On my left hand my Horace, a nymph on my right ;
No memoirs to compose, and no post-boy to move,
That on Sunday may hinder the softness of love.
For her neither visits nor parties at tea,
Nor the long-winded cant of a dull refugee.
This night and the next shall be hers, shall be mine,
To good or ill fortune the third we resign.
Thus scorning the world, and superior to fate,
I drive in my car in professional state.
So with Phia through Athens Pisistratus rode ;
Men thought her Minerva, and him a new god.
But why should I stories of Athens rehearse
Where people knew love, and were partial to verse,
Since none can with justice my pleasures oppose
In Holland half-drownèd in interest and prose ?
By Greece and past ages what need I be tried
When The Hague and the present are both on my side ;
And is it enough for the joys of the day
To think what Anacreon or Sappho would say ?
When good Vandergoes and his provident vrow,
As they gaze on my triumph do freely allow,
That, search all the province, you'll find no man dar is
So blest as the Englishen Heer Secretar' is.

The Hague, 1696.   M. PRIOR.

423. TO ——

COMPOSED AT ROTTERDAM

I GAZE upon a city,
A city new and strange ;
Down many a watery vista
My fancy takes a range ;
From side to side I saunter,
And wonder where I am ;—
And can *you* be in England,
And *I* at Rotterdam !

Before me lie dark waters,
In broad canals and deep,
Whereon the silver moonbeams
Sleep, restless in their sleep :

A sort of vulgar Venice
Reminds me where I am,—
Yes, yes, you are in England,
And I'm at Rotterdam.

Tall houses with quaint gables,
Where frequent windows shine,
And quays that lead to bridges,
And trees in formal line,
And masts of spicy vessels,
From distant Surinam,
All tell me you're in England,
And I'm in Rotterdam.

Those sailors—how outlandish
The face and garb of each !
They deal in foreign gestures,
And use a foreign speech ;
A tongue not learned near Isis,
Or studied by the Cam,
Declares that you're in England,
But I'm at Rotterdam.

And now across a market
My doubtful way I trace,
Where stands a solemn statue,
The Genius of the place ;
And to the great Erasmus
I offer my salaam,—
Who tells me you're in England,
And I'm at Rotterdam.

The coffee-room is open,
I mingle in its crowd ;
The dominoes are rattling,
The hookahs raise a cloud ;
A flavour, none of Fearon's,
That mingles with my dram,
Reminds me you're in England,
But I'm in Rotterdam.

Then here it goes, a bumper,—
The toast it shall be mine,
In schiedam, or in sherry,
Tokay, or hock of Rhine,—
It well deserves the brightest,
Where sunbeam ever swam—
' The girl I love in England ',
I drink at Rotterdam !

T. Hood.

424. TO SALLY

THE man in righteousness arrayed,
  A pure and blameless liver,
Needs not the keen Toledo blade,
  Nor venom-freighted quiver.
What though he wind his toilsome way
  O'er regions wild and weary—
Through Zara's burning desert stray,
  Or Asia's jungles dreary :

What though he plough the billowy deep
  By lunar light, or solar,
Meet the resistless Simoon's sweep,
  Or iceberg circumpolar !
In bog or quagmire deep and dank
  His foot shall never settle ;
He mounts the summit of Mont Blanc,
  Or Popocatapetl.

On Chimborazo's breathless height
  He treads o'er burning lava ;
Or snuffs the Bohan Upas blight,
  The deathful plant of Java.
Through every peril he shall pass,
  By Virtue's shield protected ;
And still by Truth's unerring glass
  His path shall be directed.

Else wherefore was it, Thursday last,
  While strolling down the valley,
Defenceless, musing as I passed
  A canzonet to Sally,
A wolf, with mouth-protruding snout,
  Forth from the thicket bounded—
I clapped my hands and raised a shout—
  He heard—and fled—confounded.

Tangier nor Tunis never bred
  An animal more crabbèd ;
Nor Fez, dry-nurse of lions, fed
  A monster half so rabid ;
Nor Ararat so fierce a beast
  Has seen since days of Noah ;
Nor stronger, eager for a feast,
  The fell constrictor boa.

J. Q. ADAMS.

425. FAREWELL TO MALTA

ADIEU, ye joys of La Valette !
Adieu, sirocco, sun, and sweat !
Adieu, thou palace rarely entered !
Adieu, ye mansions where—I've ventured !
Adieu, ye cursèd streets of stairs !
(How surely he who mounts you swears !)
Adieu, ye merchants often failing !
Adieu, thou mob for ever railing !
Adieu, ye packets—without letters !
Adieu, ye fools—who ape your betters !
Adieu, thou damned'st quarantine,
That gave me fever, and the spleen !
Adieu, that stage which makes us yawn, Sirs,
Adieu, his Excellency's dancers !
Adieu to Peter—whom no fault 's in,
But could not teach a colonel waltzing ;
Adieu, ye females fraught with graces !
Adieu, red coats, and redder faces !
Adieu, the supercilious air
Of all that strut ' en militaire ! '
I go—but God knows when, or why,
To smoky towns and cloudy sky,
To things (the honest truth to say)
As bad—but in a different way.

Farewell to these, but not adieu,
Triumphant sons of truest blue !
While either Adriatic shore,
And fallen chiefs, and fleets no more,
And nightly smiles, and daily dinners,
Proclaim you war and woman's winners.
Pardon my Muse, who apt to prate is,
And take my rhyme—because 'tis ' gratis '.

And now, O Malta ! since thou'st got us,
Thou little military hothouse !
I'll not offend with words uncivil,
And wish thee rudely at the Devil,
But only stare from out my casement,
And ask, for what is such a place meant ?
Then, in my solitary nook,
Return to scribbling, or a book,
Or take my physic while I'm able
(Two spoonfuls hourly by the label),
Prefer my nightcap to my beaver,
And bless the gods I've got a fever.

                              G. GORDON, LORD BYRON.

426. LINES TO MR. HODGSON

WRITTEN ON BOARD THE LISBON PACKET

HUZZA ! Hodgson, we are going,
   Our embargo's off at last ;
Favourable breezes blowing
   Bend the canvas o'er the mast.
From aloft the signal's streaming,
   Hark ! the farewell gun is fired ;
Women screeching, tars blaspheming,
   Tell us that our time's expired.
      Here 's a rascal
      Come to task all,
   Prying from the custom-house
      Trunks unpacking,
      Cases cracking,
Not a corner for a mouse
'Scapes unsearched amid the racket,
Ere we sail on board the Packet.

Now our boatmen quit their mooring,
   And all hands must ply the oar ;
Baggage from the quay is lowering,
   We're impatient, push from shore.
' Have a care ! that case holds liquor—
   Stop the boat—I'm sick—oh Lord ! '
' Sick, ma'am, hang it, you'll be sicker
   Ere you've been an hour on board.'
      Thus are screaming
      Men and women,
   Gemmen, ladies, servants, Jacks ;
      Here entangling,
      All are wrangling,
Stuck together close as wax.—
Such the general noise and racket,
Ere we reach the Lisbon Packet.

Now we've reached her, Io ! the captain,
   Gallant Kidd, commands the crew ;
Passengers their berths are clapped in,
   Some to grumble, some to spew.
' Heyday ! call you that a cabin ?
   Why 'tis hardly three feet square :
Not enough to stow Queen Mab in—
   Who the deuce can harbour there ? '
      ' Who, sir ? plenty—
      Nobles twenty
Did at once my vessel fill.'—

'Did they ? Bacchus,
    How you pack us !
  Would to Heaven they did so still :
Then I'd scape the heat and racket
Of the good ship, Lisbon Packet.'

Fletcher ! Murray ! Bob ! where are you ?
    Stretched along the deck like logs—
  Bear a hand, you jolly tar, you !
    Here 's a rope's end for the dogs.
Hobhouse muttering fearful curses,
    As the hatchway down he rolls
Now his breakfast, now his verses,
    Vomits forth—and d—s our souls.
        ' Here 's a stanza
        On Braganza—
  Help ! '—' A couplet ? '—' No, a cup
    Of warm water—'
    ' What 's the matter ? '
  ' Zounds ! my liver 's coming up ;
I shall not survive the racket
Of this brutal Lisbon Packet.'

Now at length we're off for Turkey,
    Lord knows when we shall come back !
Breezes foul and tempests murky
    May unship us in a crack.
But, since life at most a jest is,
    As philosophers allow,
Still to laugh by far the best is,
    Then laugh on—as I do now.
        Laugh at all things,
        Great and small things,
  Sick or well, at sea or shore ;
        While we're quaffing,
        Let's have laughing—
  Who the devil cares for more ?—
Some good wine ! and who would lack it,
Ev'n on board the Lisbon Packet ?
                    G. Gordon, Lord Byron.

427. HAD CAIN BEEN SCOT

Had Cain been Scot, God would have changed his doom,—
Not forced him wander, but confined him home.
                                    J. Cleveland.

428. EPISTLE FROM ALGIERS

To Horace Smith

Dear Horace ! be melted to tears,
   For I'm melting with heat as I rime ;
Though the name of the place is Algiers
   'Tis no joke to fall in with its clime.

With a shaver from France who came o'er,
   To an African inn I ascend ;
I am cast on a barbarous shore,
   Where a barber alone is my friend.

Do you ask me the sights and the news
   Of this wonderful city to sing ?
Alas ! my hotel has its mews,
   But no muse of the Helicon's spring.

My windows afford me the sight
   Of a people all diverse in hue ;
They are black, yellow, olive, and white,
   Whilst I in my sorrow look blue.

Here are groups for the painter to take,
   Whose fingers jocosely combine,—
The Arab disguised in his haik,
   And the Frenchman disguised in his wine.

In his breeches of petticoat size
   You may say, as the Mussulman goes,
That his garb is a fair compromise
   'Twixt a kilt and a pair of small-clothes.

The Mooresses, shrouded in white,
   Save two holes for their eyes to give room,
Seem like corpses in sport or in spite
   That have slily whipped out of their tomb.

The old Jewish dames make me sick :
   If I were the devil—I declare
Such hags should not mount a broom-stick
   In my service to ride through the air.

But hipped and undined as I am,
   My hippogriff's course I must rein—
For the pain of my thirst is no sham,
   Though I'm bawling aloud for Champagne.

Dinner 's brought ; but their wines have no pith—
  They are flat as the statutes at law ;
And for all that they bring me, dear Smith !
  Would a glass of brown stout they could draw !

O'er each French trashy dish as I bend,
  My heart feels a patriot's grief !
And the round tears, O England ! descend
  When I think on a round of thy beef.

Yes, my soul sentimentally craves
  British beer.—Hail, Britannia, hail !
To thy flag on the foam of the waves,
  And the foam on thy flagons of ale.

Yet I own, in this hour of my drought,
  A dessert has most welcomely come ;
Here are peaches that melt in the mouth,
  And grapes blue and big as a plum.

There are melons too, luscious and great,
  But the slices I eat shall be few,
For from melons incautiously eat
  Melancholic effects may ensue.

Horrid pun ! you'll exclaim ; but be calm,
  Though my letter bears date, as you view,
From the land of the date-bearing palm,
  I will palm no more puns upon you.

T. CAMPBELL.

429. COLOGNE

In Köln, a town of monks and bones,
And pavements fanged with murderous stones,
And rags, and hags, and hideous wenches ;
I counted two and seventy stenches,
All well defined, and several stinks !
Ye Nymphs that reign o'er sewers and sinks,
The river Rhine, it is well known,
Doth wash your city of Cologne ;
But tell me, Nymphs ! what power divine
Shall henceforth wash the river Rhine ?

S. T. COLERIDGE.

430. THE VENETIAN SERENADE

WHEN along the light ripple the far serenade
Has accosted the ear of each passionate maid,
She may open the window that looks on the stream,—
She may smile on her pillow and blend it in dream ;
Half in words, half in music, it pierces the gloom,
' I am coming—Stalì—but you know not for whom !
      Stalì—not for whom ! '

Now the tones become clearer—you hear more and more
How the water divided returns on the oar,—
Does the prow of the gondola strike on the stair ?
Do the voices and instruments pause and prepare ?
Oh ! they faint on the ear as the lamp on the view,
' I am coming—Premì—but I stay not for you !
      Premì—not for you ! '

Then return to your couch, you who stifle a tear,
Then awake not, fair sleeper—believe he is here ;
For the young and the loving no sorrow endures,
If to-day be another's, to-morrow is yours ;—
May, the next time you listen, your fancy be true,
' I am coming—Sciàr—and for you and to you !
      Sciàr—and to you ! '

R. M. MILNES, LORD HOUGHTON.

431. OCCASIONED BY READING THE TRAVELS OF CAPTAIN LEMUEL GULLIVER

TO QUINBUS FLESTRIN, THE MAN-MOUNTAIN

An ode by Tilly-tit, poet-laureate to his Majesty of Lilliput

Translated into English

    IN amaze,
    Lost I gaze,
    Can our eyes
    Reach thy size ?
    May my lays
    Swell with praise,
    Worthy thee !
    Worthy me !

Muse, inspire,
All thy fire !
Bards of old
Of him told,
When they said
Atlas' head
Propped the skies :
See ! and believe your eyes !

See him stride
Valleys wide,
Over woods,
Over floods !
When he treads
Mountains' heads
Groan and shake :
Armies quake :
Lest his spurn
Overturn
Man and steed :
Troops, take heed !
Left and right,
Speed your flight !
Lest an host
Beneath his foot be lost.

Turned aside,
From his hide,
Safe from wound,
Darts rebound.
From his nose
Clouds he blows :
When he speaks,
Thunder breaks !
When he eats,
Famine threats !
When he drinks,
Neptune shrinks !
Nigh thy ear
In mid air,
On thy hand
Let me stand ;
So shall I,
Lofty poet, touch the sky.

A. POPE.

432. TO MADAME DE DAMAS LEARNING ENGLISH

Though British accents your attention fire,
  You cannot learn so fast as we admire,
Scholars like you can slowly but improve,
  For who would teach you but the verb ' I love ' ?

H. Walpole, Earl of Orford.

433. THE GROVES OF BLARNEY

The groves of Blarney,
They look so charming,
Down by the purlings
Of sweet silent brooks,
All decked by posies
That spontaneous grew there,
Planted in order
In the rocky nooks.
'Tis there the daisy,
And the sweet carnation,
The blooming pink,
And the rose so fair ;
Likewise the lily,
And the daffodilly—
All flowers that scent
The sweet open air.

'Tis Lady Jeffers
Owns this plantation ;
Like Alexander,
Or like Helen fair,
There 's no commander
In all the nation,
For regulation,
Can with her compare.
Such walls surround her,
That no nine-pounder
Could ever plunder
Her place of strength ;
But Oliver Cromwell,
Her he did pommel,
And made a breach
In her battlement.

There is a cave where
No daylight enters,
But cats and badgers

Are for ever bred ;
And mossed by nature
Makes it completer
Than a coach-and-six,
Or a downy bed.
'Tis there the lake is
Well stored with fishes,
And comely eels in
The verdant mud ;
Besides the leeches,
And groves of beeches,
Standing in order
To guard the flood.

There gravel walks are
For recreation,
And meditation
In sweet solitude.
'Tis there the lover
May hear the dove, or
The gentle plover,
In the afternoon ;
And if a lady
Would be so engaging
As for to walk in
Those shady groves,
'Tis there the courtier
Might soon transport her
Into some fort, or
The ' sweet rock-close '.

There are statues gracing
This noble place in—
All heathen gods,
And nymphs so fair ;
Bold Neptune, Caesar,
And Nebuchadnezzar,
All standing naked
In the open air !
There is a boat on
The lake to float on,
And lots of beauties
Which I can't entwine ;
But were I a preacher,
Or a classic teacher,
In every feature
I'd make 'em shine !

There is a stone there
That whoever kisses,
Oh ! he never misses
To grow eloquent.
'Tis he may clamber
To a lady's chamber,
Or become a member
Of Parliament :
A clever spouter
He'll sure turn out, or
An out-and-outer,
' To be let alone.'
Don't hope to hinder him,
Or to bewilder him ;
Sure he 's a pilgrim
From the Blarney stone !

R. A. MILLIKIN.

434. THE SHANDON BELLS

WITH deep affection,
And recollection,
I often think of
    Those Shandon bells,
Whose sounds so wild would,
In the days of childhood,
Fling around my cradle
    Their magic spells.
On this I ponder
Where'er I wander,
And thus grow fonder,
    Sweet Cork, of thee ;
With thy bells of Shandon,
That sound so grand on
The pleasant waters
    Of the River Lee.

I've heard bells chiming
Full many a clime in,
Tolling sublime in
    Cathedral shrine,
While at a glib rate
Brass tongues would vibrate—
But all the music
    Spoke naught like thine ;
For memory, dwelling
On each proud swelling

Of the belfry knelling
　　Its bold notes free,
Made the bells of Shandon
Sound far more grand on
The pleasant waters
　　Of the River Lee.

I've heard bells tolling
Old Adrian's Mole in,
Their thunder rolling
　　From the Vatican,
And cymbals glorious
Swinging uproarious
In the glorious turrets
　　Of Notre Dame ;
But thy sounds were sweeter
Than the dome of Peter
Flings o'er the Tiber,
　　Pealing solemnly ;—
O, the bells of Shandon
Sound far more grand on
The pleasant waters
　　Of the River Lee.

There's a bell in Moscow,
While in tower and kiosk O
In Saint Sophia
　　The Turkman gets ;
And loud in air
Calls men to prayer
From the tapering summits
　　Of tall minarets.
Such empty phantom
I freely grant them ;
But there's an anthem
　　More dear to me,—
'Tis the bells of Shandon
That sound so grand on
The pleasant waters
　　Of the River Lee.
　　　　　　　F. S. MAHONY (FATHER PROUT).

435. KITTY OF COLERAINE

As beautiful Kitty one morning was tripping,
  With a pitcher of milk from the fair of Coleraine,
When she saw me she stumbled, the pitcher it tumbled,
  And all the sweet butter-milk watered the plain.

O, what shall I do now, 'twas looking at you now,
  Sure, sure, such a pitcher I'll ne'er meet again,
'Twas the pride of my dairy, O, Barney M'Leary,
  You're sent as a plague to the girls of Coleraine.

I sat down beside her,—and gently did chide her,
  That such a misfortune should give her such pain,
A kiss then I gave her,—before I did leave her,
  She vowed for such pleasure she'd break it again.

'Twas hay-making season, I can't tell the reason,
  Misfortunes will never come single,—that's plain,
For, very soon after poor Kitty's disaster,
  The devil a pitcher was whole in Coleraine.

E. LYSAGHT.

436. PEG OF LIMAVADDY

RIDING from Coleraine
  (Famed for lovely Kitty),
Came a Cockney bound
  Unto Derry city ;
Weary was his soul,
  Shivering and sad, he
Bumped along the road
  Leads to Limavaddy.

Mountains stretched around,
  Gloomy was their tinting,
And the horse's hoofs
  Made a dismal clinting ;
Wind upon the heath
  Howling was and piping,
On the heath and bog,
  Black with many a snipe in,
'Mid the bogs of black,
  Silver pools were flashing,
Crows upon their sides
  Picking were and splashing.

Cockney on the car
　　Closer folds his plaidy,
Grumbling at the road
　　Leads to Limavaddy.

Through the crashing woods
　　Autumn brawled and blustered,
Tossing round about
　　Leaves the hue of mustard ;
Yonder lay Lough Foyle,
　　Which a storm was whipping,
Covering with mist
　　Lake, and shores, and shipping.
Up and down the hill
　　(Nothing could be bolder),
Horse went with a raw
　　Bleeding on his shoulder.
' Where are horses changed ? '
　　Said I to the laddy
Driving on the box :
　　' Sir, at Limavaddy.'

Limavaddy inn 's
　　But a humble baithouse,
Where you may procure
　　Whisky and potatoes ;
Landlord at the door
　　Gives a smiling welcome
To the shivering wights
　　Who to his hotel come.
Landlady within
　　Sits and knits a stocking,
With a wary foot
　　Baby's cradle rocking.

To the chimney nook
　　Having found admittance,
There I watch a pup
　　Playing with two kittens
(Playing round the fire,
　　Which of blazing turf is,
Roaring to the pot
　　Which bubbles with the murphies);
And the cradled babe
　　Fond the mother nursed it,
Singing it a song
　　As she twists the worsted !

Up and down the stair
　　Two more young ones patter

(Twins were never seen
  Dirtier nor fatter) ;
Both have mottled legs,
  Both have snubby noses,
Both have—Here the host
  Kindly interposes :
' Sure you must be froze
  With the sleet and hail, sir,
So will you have some punch,
  Or will you have some ale, sir ?

Presently a maid
  Enters with the liquor
(Half a pint of ale
  Frothing in a beaker).
Gads ! I didn't know
  What my beating heart meant,
Hebe's self, I thought,
  Entered the apartment.
As she came she smiled,
  And the smile bewitching,
On my word and honour,
  Lighted all the kitchen !

With a curtsy neat
  Greeting the new-comer
Lovely, smiling Peg
  Offers me the rummer ;
But my trembling hand
  Up the beaker tilted,
And the glass of ale
  Every drop I spilt it :
Spilt it every drop
  (Dames, who read my volumes,
Pardon such a word)
  On my what-d'ye-call-'ems

Witnessing the sight
  Of that dire disaster,
Out began to laugh
  Missis, maid, and master ;
Such a merry peal,
  'Specially Miss Peg's was
(As the glass of ale
  Trickling down my legs was),
That the joyful sound
  Of that mingling laughter
Echoed in my ears
  Many a long day after.

Such a silver peal !
　In the meadows listening,
You who've heard the bells
　Ringing to a christening ;
You who ever heard
　Caradori pretty,
Smiling like an angel,
　Singing Giovinetti ;
Fancy Peggy's laugh,
　Sweet, and clear, and cheerful,
At my pantaloons
　With half a pint of beer full !

When the laugh was done,
　Peg, the pretty hussy,
Moved about the room
　Wonderfully busy ;
Now she looks to see
　If the kettle keep hot ;
Now she rubs the spoons,
　Now she cleans the tea-pot ;
Now she sets the cups
　Trimly and secure ;
Now she scours a pot,
　And so it was I drew her.

Thus it was I drew her
　Scouring of a kettle
(Faith ! her blushing cheeks
　Reddened on the metal).
Ah ! but 'tis in vain
　That I try to sketch it ;
The pot perhaps is like,
　But Peggy's face is wretched.
No : the best of lead
　And of indiarubber,
Never could depict
　That sweet kettle-scrubber !

See her as she moves !
　Scarce the ground she touches,
Airy as a fay,
　Graceful as a duchess ;
Bare her rounded arm,
　Bare her little leg is,
Vestris never showed
　Ankles like to Peggy's ;

Braided is her hair,
  Soft her look and modest,
Slim her little waist
  Comfortably bodiced.

This I do declare,
  Happy is the laddy
Who the heart can share
  Of Peg of Limavaddy;
Married if she were,
  Blest would be the daddy
Of the children fair
  Of Peg of Limavaddy.
Beauty is not rare
  In the land of Paddy,
Fair beyond compare
  Is Peg of Limavaddy.

Citizen or Squire,
  Tory, Whig, or Radi-
cal would all desire
  Peg of Limavaddy.
Had I Homer's fire,
  Or that of Serjeant Taddy,
Meetly I'd admire
  Peg of Limavaddy.
And till I expire,
  Or till I grow mad, I
Will sing unto my lyre
  Peg of Limavaddy!

                        W. M. THACKERAY.

437. IRELAND NEVER WAS CONTENTED

IRELAND never was contented.
Say you so? You are demented.
Ireland was contented when
All could use the sword and pen,
And when Tara rose so high
That her turrets split the sky,
And about her courts were seen
Liveried angels robed in green,
Wearing, by St. Patrick's bounty,
Emeralds big as half the county.

                        W. S. LANDOR.

438. THE BATTLE OF LIMERICK

YE Genii of the nation,
  Who look with veneration,
And Ireland's desolation onsaysingly deplore;
  Ye sons of General Jackson,
  Who thrample on the Saxon,
Attend to the thransaction upon Shannon shore

  When William, Duke of Schumbug,
  A tyrant and a humbug,
With cannon and with thunder on our city bore,
  Our fortitude and valliance
  Insthructed his battalions
To rispict the galliant Irish upon Shannon shore.

  Since that capitulation,
  No city in this nation
So grand a reputation could boast before,
  As Limerick prodigious,
  That stands with quays and bridges,
And the ships up to the windies of the Shannon shore.

  A chief of ancient line,
  'Tis William Smith O'Brine,
Reprisints this darling Limerick, this ten years or more:
  Oh, the Saxons can't endure
  To see him on the flure,
And thrimble at the Cicero from Shannon shore !

  This valliant son of Mars
  Had been to visit Par's,
That land of Revolution, that grows the tricolor ;
  And to welcome his returrn
  From pilgrimages furren,
We invited him to tay on the Shannon shore.

  Then we summoned to our board
  Young Meagher of the Sword :
'Tis he will sheath that battle-axe in Saxon gore ;
  And Mitchil of Belfast
  We bade to our repast,
To dthrink a dish of coffee on the Shannon shore.

  Convaniently to hould
  These patriots so bould,
We tuck the opportunity of Tim Doolan's store ;
  And with ornamints and banners
  (As becomes gintale good manners)
We made the loveliest tay-room upon Shannon shore.

'Twould binifit your sowls
To see the butthered rowls,
The sugar-tongs and sangwidges and craim galyore,
And the muffins and the crumpets,
And the band of harps and thrumpets,
To celebrate the sworry upon Shannon shore.

Sure the Imperor of Bohay
Would be proud to dthrink the tay
That Misthress Biddy Rooney for O'Brine did pour ;
And, since the days of Strongbow,
There never was such Congo—
Mitchil dthrank six quarts of it—by Shannon shore.

But Clarndon and Corry
Connellan beheld this sworry
With rage and imulation in their black hearts' core ;
And they hired a gang of ruffins
To interrupt the muffins
And the fragrance of the Congo on the Shannon shore.

When full of tay and cake,
O'Brine began to spake,
But juice a one could hear him, for a sudden roar
Of a ragamuffin rout
Began to yell and shout,
And frighten the propriety of Shannon shore.

As Smith O'Brine harangued,
They batthered and they banged :
Tim Doolan's doors and windies down they tore ;
They smashed the lovely windies
(Hung with muslin from the Indies),
Purshuing of their shindies upon Shannon shore.

With throwing of brickbats,
Drowned puppies, and dead rats,
These ruffin democrats themselves did lower ;
Tin kettles, rotten eggs,
Cabbage-stalks, and wooden legs,
They flung among the patriots of Shannon shore.

Oh, the girls began to scrame
And upset the milk and crame ;
And the honourable gintlemin, they cursed and swore :
And Mitchil of Belfast,
'Twas he that looked aghast,
When they roasted him in effigy by Shannon shore.

Oh, the lovely tay was spilt
On that day of Ireland's guilt ;
Says Jack Mitchil, ' I am kilt ! Boys, where 's the back door ?
'Tis a national disgrace ;
Let me go and veil me face ; '
And he boulted with quick pace from the Shannon shore.

' Cut down the bloody horde ! '
Says Meagher of the Sword,
' This conduct would disgrace any blackamore ' ;
But the best use Tommy made
Of his famous battle blade
Was to cut his own stick from the Shannon shore.

Immortal Smith O'Brine
Was raging like a line ;
'Twould have done your sowl good to have heard him roar ;
In his glory he arose,
And he rushed upon his foes,
But they hit him on the nose by the Shannon shore.

Then the Futt and the Dthragoons
In squadthrons and platoons,
With their music playing chunes, down upon us bore ;
And they bate the rattatoo,
But the Peelers came in view,
And ended the shaloo on the Shannon shore.

W. M. THACKERAY.

439. WOMEN'S LONGING

TELL me what is that only thing
For which all women long ;
Yet having what they most desire,
To have it does them wrong ?

'Tis not to be chaste nor fair,
(Such gifts malice may impair),
Richly trimmed, to walk or ride,
Or to wanton unespied,
To preserve an honest name
And so to give it up to fame—
These are toys.   In good or ill
They desire to have their will :
Yet when they have it, they abuse it,
For they know not how to use it.

J. FLETCHER.

440. THE WISH

WELL then, I now do plainly see
This busy world and I shall ne'er agree.
The very honey of all earthly joy
Does, of all meats, the soonest cloy ;
   And they, methinks, deserve my pity
Who for it can endure the stings,
The crowd and buzz and murmurings
   Of this great hive, the city !

Ah yet, ere I descend to the grave,
May I a small house and large garden have ;
And a few friends, and many books, both true,
Both wise, and both delightful too !
   And since Love ne'er will from me flee,—
A Mistress moderately fair,
And good as guardian angels are,
   Only beloved, and loving me !

O founts ! Oh, when in you shall I
Myself eased of unpeaceful thoughts espy ?
O fields ! O woods ! when, when shall I be made
The happy tenant of your shade ?
   Here 's the spring-head of Pleasure's flood !
Here 's wealthy Nature's treasury,
Where all the riches lie that she
   Has coined and stamped for good.

Pride and ambition here
Only in far-fetched metaphors appear ;
Here naught but winds can hurtful murmurs scatter,
And naught but echo flatter.
   The gods, when they descended, hither
From heaven did always choose their way ;
And therefore we may boldly say
   That 'tis the way too thither.

How happy here should I
And one dear She live, and embracing die !
She who is all the world, and can exclude
In deserts solitude.
   I should have then this only fear :
Lest men, when they my pleasures see,
Should hither throng to live like me,
   And so make a city here.

A. COWLEY.

441. THE OLD MAN'S WISH

If I live to grow old (for I find I go down !)
Let this be my fate in a country town :
Let me have a warm house, with a stone at the gate ;
And a cleanly young girl to rub my bald pate :
    May I govern my passions with an absolute sway,
      And grow wiser and better as my strength wears away,
    Without gout or stone, by a gentle decay.

In a country town, by a murmuring brook,
The ocean at distance, on which I may look ,
With a spacious plain, without hedge or stile,
And an easy pad-nag to ride out a mile ;

With a pudding on Sunday, and stout humming liquor,
And remnants of Latin to puzzle the vicar ;
With a hidden reserve of Burgundy wine
To drink the King's health as oft as I dine :

With Plutarch and Horace and one or two more
Of the best wits that lived in the ages before ;
With a dish of roast mutton, not venison nor teal,
And clean, though coarse, linen at every meal :

And if I should have guests I must add to my wish,
On Fridays, a mess of good buttered fish ;
For full well I do know, and the truth I reveal,
I had better do so than come short of a meal :

With breeches and jerkin of good country grey ;
And live without working, now my strength doth decay ;
With a hogshead of sherry, for to drink when I please,
With friends to be merry, and to live at my ease.

Without molestation, may I spend my last days
In sweet recreation ; and sound forth the praise
Of all those that are true to the King and his laws ;
Since it be their due, they shall have my applause.

When the days are grown short and it freezes and snows,
May I have a coal fire as high as my nose !
A fire which, once stirred up with a prong,
Will keep the room temperate all the night long.

With courage undaunted, may I face my last day ;
And when I am dead may the better sort say,
' In the morning, when sober ; in the evening, when mellow,
He is gone, and has left not behind him his fellow.
    For he governed his passions with an absolute sway,
      And grew wiser and better, as his strength wore away,
    Without gout or stone, by a gentle decay.'

W. POPE.

442. TO-MORROW

In the downhill of life when I find I'm declining,
  May my fate no less fortunate be,
Than a snug elbow-chair will afford for reclining,
  And a cot that o'erlooks the wide sea ;
With an ambling pad-pony to pace o'er the lawn,
  While I carol away idle sorrow ;
And, blythe as the lark that each day hails the dawn,
  Look forward with hope to To-morrow.

With a porch at my door, both for shelter and shade, too,
  As the sunshine or rain may prevail ;
And a small spot of ground for the use of the spade, too,
  With a barn for the use of the flail :
A cow for my dairy, a dog for my game,
  And a purse when a man wants to borrow,
I'll envy no nabob his riches or fame,
  Or what honours may wait him To-morrow.

From the bleak northern blast may my cot be completely
  Secured, by a neighbouring hill ;
And at night may repose steal upon me more sweetly,
  By the sound of a murmuring rill :
And while peace and plenty I find at my board,
  With a heart free from sickness and sorrow,
With my friends let me share what to-day may afford,
  And let them spread the table To-morrow.

And when I, at last, must throw off this frail covering,
  Which I've worn for three-score years and ten,
On the brink of the grave I'll not seek to keep hovering,
  Nor my thread wish to spin o'er again ;
But my face in the glass I'll serenely survey,
  And with smiles count each wrinkle and furrow,
As this old worn-out stuff, which is threadbare to-day,
  May become everlasting To-morrow.

J. Collins.

443. THE LADY WHO OFFERS HER LOOKING-GLASS TO VENUS

Venus, take my votive glass ;
Since I am not what I was,
What from this day I shall be,
Venus, let me never see.

M. Prior.

444. CONTENTMENT

'Man wants but little here below.'—*Goldsmith.*

LITTLE I ask ; my wants are few ;
 I only wish a hut of stone
(A *very plain* brown stone will do),
  That I may call my own ;—
And close at hand is such a one,
In yonder street that fronts the sun.

Plain food is quite enough for me ;
 Three courses are as good as ten ;—
If Nature can subsist on three,
  Thank Heaven for three. Amen !
I always thought cold victual nice ;—
My *choice* would be vanilla-ice.

I care not much for gold or land ;—
 Give me a mortgage here and there,—
Some good bank-stock,—some note of hand,
  Or trifling railroad share ;—
I only ask that Fortune send
A *little* more than I shall spend.

Honours are silly toys, I know,
 And titles are but empty names ;—
I would, *perhaps*, be Plenipo,—
  But only near St. James ;
I'm very sure I should not care
To fill the Gubernator's chair.

Jewels are baubles ; 'tis a sin
 To care for such unfruitful things ;—
One good-sized diamond in a pin,—
  Some, *not so large*, in rings,—
A ruby, and a pearl, or so,
Will do for me ;—I laugh at show.

My dame shall dress in cheap attire
 (Good, heavy silks are never dear) ;—
I own perhaps I *might* desire
  Some shawls of true Cashmere,—
Some marrowy crapes of China silk,
Like wrinkled skins on scalded milk.

I would not have the horse I drive
 So fast that folks must stop and stare ;
An easy gait,—two, forty-five—
  Suits me ; I do not care ;—
Perhaps, for just a *single spurt*,
Some seconds less would do no hurt.

Of pictures I should like to own
 Titians and Raphaels three or four,—
I love so much their style and tone,—
 One Turner, and no more,—
(A landscape,—foreground golden dirt,—
The sunshine painted with a squirt.)

Of books but few,—some fifty score
 For daily use, and bound for wear ;
The rest upon an upper floor ;—
 Some *little* luxury *there*
Of red morocco's gilded gleam,
And vellum rich as country cream.

Busts, cameos, gems,—such things as these,
 Which others often show for pride,
I value for their power to please,
 And selfish churls deride ;
One Stradivarius, I confess,
Two Meerschaums, I would fain possess.

Wealth's wasteful tricks I will not learn,
 Nor ape the glittering upstart fool ;—
Shall not carved tables serve my turn,
 But *all* must be of buhl ?
Give grasping pomp its double share,—
I ask but *one* recumbent chair.

Thus humble let me live and die,
 Nor long for Midas' golden touch,
If Heaven more generous gifts deny,
 I shall not miss them *much*,—
Too grateful for the blessing lent
Of simple tastes and mind content !

O. W. Holmes.

445. EHEU FUGACES

What Horace says is,
Eheu fugaces
Anni labuntur, Postume, Postume !
Years glide away, and are lost to me, lost to me !
Now, when the folks in the dance sport their merry toes,
Taglionis and Ellslers, Duvernays and Ceritos,
Sighing I murmur, ' *O mihi praeteritos !* '

R. H. Barham.

446. WRITTEN IN A YOUNG LADY'S ALBUM

A PRETTY task, Miss S——, to ask
    A Benedictine pen,
That cannot quite at freedom write
    Like those of other men.
No lover's plaint my Muse must paint
    To fill this page's span,
But be correct and recollect
    I'm not a single man.

Pray only think for pen and ink
    How hard to get along,
That may not turn on words that burn
    Or Love, the life of song !
Nine Muses, if I chooses, I
    May woo all in a clan,
But one Miss S—— I daren't address—
    I'm not a single man.

Scribbles unwed, with little head
    May eke it out with heart,
And in their lays it often plays
    A rare first-fiddle part.
They make a kiss to rhyme with bliss,
    But if *I* so began,
I have my fears about my ears—
    I'm not a single man.

Upon your cheek I may not speak,
    Nor on your lip be warm,
I must be wise about your eyes,
    And formal with your form,
Of all that sort of thing, in short,
    On T. H. Bayly's plan,
I must not twine a single line—
    I'm not a single man.

A watchman's part compels my heart
    To keep you off its *beat*,
And I might dare as soon to swear
    At *you*, as at your feet.
I can't expire in passion's fire
    As other poets can—
My life (she 's by) won't let me die—
    I'm not a single man.

Shut out from love, denied a dove,
　　Forbidden bow and dart,
Without a groan to call my own,
　　With neither hand nor heart,
To Hymen vowed, and not allowed
　　To flirt e'en with your fan,
Here end, as just a friend, I must—
　　I'm not a single man.

T. HOOD.

447.　WHY WRITE *MY* NAME

WHY write *my* name 'midst songs and flowers,
　　To meet the eye of lady gay ?
I have no voice for lady's bowers—
　　For page like this no fitting lay.

Yet though my heart no more must bound
　　At witching call of sprightly joys,
Mine is the brow that never frowned
　　On laughing lips, or sparkling eyes.

No—though behind me now is closed
　　The youthful paradise of Love,
Yet can I bless, with soul composed,
　　The lingerers in that happy grove !

Take, then, fair girls, my blessing take !
　　Where'er amid its charms you roam ;
Or where, by western hill or lake,
　　You brighten a serener home.

And while the youthful lover's name,
　　Here with the sister beauty's blends,
Laugh not to scorn the humbler aim,
　　That to their list would add a friend's !

FRANCIS, LORD JEFFREY.

448.　SENEX TO MATT. PRIOR

AH ! Matt. : old age has brought to me
Thy wisdom, less thy certainty :
The world 's a jest, and joy 's a trinket :
I knew that once : but now—I think it.

J. K. STEPHEN.

449. 'TIS LATE, AND I MUST HASTE AWAY

'Tis late, and I must haste away,
  My usual hour of rest is near—
And do you press me, youths, to stay—
  To stay and revel longer here ?

Then give me back the scorn of care
  Which spirits light in health allow,
And give me back the dark brown hair
  Which curled upon my even brow.

And give me back the sportive jest
  Which once could midnight hours beguile ;
The life that bounded in my breast,
  And joyous youth's becoming smile :

And give me back the fervid soul
  Which love inflamed with strange delight,
When erst I sorrowed o'er the bowl
  At Chloe's coy and wanton flight.

'Tis late, and I must haste away,
  My usual hour of rest is near—
But give me these, and I will stay—
  Will stay till noon, and revel here !

W. LAMB, VISCOUNT MELBOURNE.

450. ON THE DOWAGER LADY E. H——D

VAIN are the charms of white and red,
  Which divide the blooming fair ;
Give me the nymph whose snow is spread
  Not o'er her breast, but hair.

Of smoother cheeks, the winning grace,
  As open forces I defy ;
But in the wrinkles of her face
  Cupids, as in ambush, lie.

If naked eyes set hearts on blaze,
  And amorous warmth inspire ;
Through glass who darts her pointed rays,
  Lights up a fiercer fire !

W. PULTENEY, EARL OF BATH.

451. AN ANCIENT RHYME

THE burden of an ancient rhyme
Is, 'By the forelock seize on Time.
Time in some corner heard it said;
Pricking his ears, away he fled;
And, seeing me upon the road,
A hearty curse on me bestowed.
' What if I do the same by thee ?
How wouldst thou like it ?' thundered he,
And, without answer thereupon,
Seizing *my* forelock . . . it was gone.

W. S. LANDOR.

452. NO, MY OWN LOVE OF OTHER YEARS

No, my own love of other years !
  No, it must never be.
Much rests with you that yet endears,
  Alas ! but what with me ?

Could those bright years o'er me revolve
  So gay, o'er you so fair,
The pearl of life we would dissolve,
  And each the cup might share.

You show that truth can ne'er decay,
  Whatever fate befalls ;
I, that the myrtle and the bay
  Shoot fresh on ruined walls.

W. S. LANDOR.

453. THE VESSEL THAT RESTS HERE

THE vessel that rests here at last
Had once stout ribs and topping mast,
And, whate'er wind there might prevail,
Was ready for a row or sail.
It now lies idle on its side,
Forgetful o'er the stream to glide.
And yet there have been days of yore,
When pretty maids their posies bore
To crown its prow, its deck to trim,
And freighted a whole world of whim.
A thousand stories it could tell,
But it loves secrecy too well.
Come closer, my sweet girl, pray do !
There may be still one left for you.

W. S. LANDOR.

454. I REMEMBER THE TIME

I REMEMBER the time ere his temples were grey,
And I frowned at the things he'd the boldness to say,
But now he 's grown old he may say what he will,
I laugh at his nonsense and take nothing ill.

Indeed I must say he 's a little improved,
For he watches no longer the slily beloved,
No longer as once he awakens my fears,
Not a glance he perceives, not a whisper he hears.

If he heard one of late, it has never transpired,
For his only delight is to see me admired ;
And now pray what better return can I make
Than to flirt and be always admired . . . for his sake.

W. S. LANDOR.

455. THERE ARE SOME WISHES

THERE are some wishes that may start
Nor cloud the brow nor sting the heart.
Gladly then would I see how smiled
One who now fondles with her child ;
How smiled she but six years ago,
Herself a child, or nearly so.
Yes, let me bring before my sight
The silken tresses chained up tight,
The tiny fingers tipt with red
By tossing up the strawberry-bed ;
Half-open lips, long violet eyes,
A little rounder with surprise,
And then (her chin against the knee)
'Mama ! who can that stranger be ?
How grave the smile he smiles on me !'

W. S. LANDOR.

456. THE LAST LEAF

I SAW him once before,
As he passed by the door,
    And again
The pavement stones resound,
As he totters o'er the ground
    With his cane.

They say that in his prime,
Ere the pruning-knife of Time
    Cut him down,

Not a better man was found
By the Crier on his round
  Through the town.

But now he walks the streets,
And he looks at all he meets
  Sad and wan,
And he shakes his feeble head,
That it seems as if he said,
  ' They are gone.'

The mossy marbles rest
On the lips that he has prest
  In their bloom,
And the names he loved to hear
Have been carved for many a year
  On the tomb.

My grandmamma has said,—
Poor old lady, she is dead
  Long ago,—
That he had a Roman nose,
And his cheek was like a rose
  In the snow.

But now his nose is thin,
And it rests upon his chin
  Like a staff,
And a crook is in his back,
And a melancholy crack
  In his laugh.

I know it is a sin
For me to sit and grin
  At him here ;
But the old three-cornered hat,
And the breeches, and all that,
  Are so queer !

And if I should live to be
The last leaf upon the tree
  In the spring,—
Let them smile, as I do now,
At the old forsaken bough
  Where I cling.

              O. W. HOLMES.

457. TO MY GRANDMOTHER

(SUGGESTED BY A PICTURE BY MR. ROMNEY)

THIS relative of mine
Was she seventy and nine
   When she died ?
By the canvas may be seen
How she looked at seventeen,—
   As a bride.

Beneath a summer tree
As she sits, her reverie
   Has a charm ;
Her ringlets are in taste,—
What an arm ! and what a waist
   For an arm !

In bridal coronet,
Lace, ribbons, and *coquette*
   Falbala ;
Were Romney's limning true,
What a lucky dog were you,
   Grandpapa !

Her lips are sweet as love,—
They are parting !   Do they move ?
   Are they dumb ?—
Her eyes are blue, and beam
Beseechingly, and seem
   To say, ' Come.'

What funny fancy slips
From atween these cherry lips ?
   Whisper me,
Sweet deity, in paint,
What canon says I mayn't
   Marry thee ?

That good-for-nothing Time
Has a confidence sublime !
   When I first
Saw this lady, in my youth,
Her winters had, forsooth,
   Done their worst.

Her locks (as white as snow)
Once shamed the swarthy crow
   By and by
That fowl's avenging sprite
Set his cloven foot for spite
   In her eye.

Her rounded form was lean,
And her silk was bombazine :—
    Well I wot,
With her needles would she sit,
And for hours would she knit,—
    Would she not ?

Ah, perishable clay !
Her charms had dropped away
    One by one.
But if she heaved a sigh
With a burthen, it was ' Thy
    Will be done.'

In travail, as in tears,
With the fardel of her years
    Overprest,—
In mercy was she borne
Where the weary ones and worn
    Are at rest.

I'm fain to meet you there,—
If as witching as you were,
    Grandmamma !
This nether world agrees
That the better it must please
    Grandpapa.

F. LOCKER-LAMPSON.

458. LOVE AND AGE

I PLAYED with you 'mid cowslips blowing,
    When I was six and you were four ;
When garlands weaving, flower-balls throwing,
    Were pleasures soon to please no more.
Through groves and meads, o'er grass and heather,
    With little playmates, to and fro,
We wandered hand in hand together ;
    But that was sixty years ago.

You grew a lovely roseate maiden,
    And still our early love was strong ;
Still with no care our days were laden,
    They glided joyously along ;
And I did love you very dearly,
    How dearly words want power to show ;
I thought your heart was touched as nearly ;
    But that was fifty years ago.

Then other lovers came around you,
  Your beauty grew from year to year,
And many a splendid circle found you
  The centre of its glittering sphere.
I saw you then, first vows forsaking,
  On rank and wealth your hand bestow;
Oh, then I thought my heart was breaking,—
  But that was forty years ago.

And I lived on, to wed another:
  No cause she gave me to repine;
And when I heard you were a mother,
  I did not wish the children mine.
My own young flock, in fair progression,
  Made up a pleasant Christmas row:
My joy in them was past expression;—
  But that was thirty years ago.

You grew a matron plump and comely,
  You dwelt in fashion's brightest blaze;
My earthly lot was far more homely;
  But I too had my festal days.
No merrier eyes have ever glistened
  Around the hearth-stone's wintry glow,
Than when my youngest child was christened,—
  But that was twenty years ago.

Time passed. My eldest girl was married,
  And I am now a grandsire grey;
One pet of four years old I've carried
  Among the wild-flowered meads to play.
In our old fields of childish pleasure,
  Where now, as then, the cowslips blow,
She fills her basket's ample measure;—
  And that is not ten years ago.

But though love's first impassioned blindness
  Has passed away in colder light,
I still have thought of you with kindness,
  And shall do, till our last good-night.
The ever-rolling silent hours
  Will bring a time we shall not know,
When our young days of gathering flowers
  Will be an hundred years ago.

                                    T. L. PEACOCK.

459. AN EPITAPH ON SALATHIEL PAVY

A Child of Queen Elizabeth's Chapel

Weep with me, all you that read
    This little story ;
And know, for whom a tear you shed,
    Death's self is sorry.
'Twas a child, that so did thrive
    In grace and feature,
As heaven and nature seemed to strive
    Which owned the creature.

Years he numbered scarce thirteen,
    When Fates turned cruel ;
Yet three filled zodiacs had he been
    The stage's jewel ;
And did act, what now we moan,
    Old men so duly,
As, sooth, the Parcae thought him one,
    He played so truly.

So, by error, to his fate
    They all consented ;
But, viewing him since (alas, too late !),
    They have repented ;
And have sought, to give new birth,
    In baths to steep him :
But, being so much too good for earth,
    Heaven vows to keep him.

Ben. Jonson.

460. TWENTY YEARS HENCE

Twenty years hence my eyes may grow
If not quite dim, yet rather so,
Still yours from others they shall know
      Twenty years hence.

Twenty years hence though it may hap
That I be called to take a nap
In a cool cell where thunder-clap
      Was never heard,

There breathe but o'er my arch of grass
A not too sadly sighed *Alas*,
And I shall catch, ere you can pass,
      That wingèd word.

W. S. Landor.

461. HESTER

WHEN maidens such as Hester die,
Their place ye may not well supply,
Though ye among a thousand try,
    With vain endeavour.

A month or more hath she been dead,
Yet cannot I by force be led
To think upon the wormy bed,
    And her together.

A springy motion in her gait,
A rising step, did indicate
Of pride and joy no common rate,
    That flushed her spirit.

I know not by what name beside
I shall it call :—if 'twas not pride,
It was a joy to that allied,
    She did inherit.

Her parents held the Quaker rule,
Which doth the human feeling cool,
But she was trained in Nature's school,
    Nature had blest her.

A waking eye, a prying mind,
A heart that stirs, is hard to bind,
A hawk's keen sight ye cannot blind,
    Ye could not Hester.

My sprightly neighbour, gone before
To that unknown and silent shore,
Shall we not meet, as heretofore,
    Some summer morning,

When from thy cheerful eyes a ray
Hath struck a bliss upon the day,
A bliss that would not go away,
    A sweet fore-warning ?

C. LAMB.

462. DIRCE

STAND close around, ye Stygian set,
    With Dirce in one boat conveyed !
Or Charon, seeing, may forget
    That he is old and she a shade.

W. S. LANDOR.

463. MY KATE

SHE was not as pretty as women I know,
And yet all your best made of sunshine and snow
Drop to shade, melt to naught in the long-trodden ways,
While she's still remembered on warm and cold days—
My Kate.

Her air had a meaning, her movements a grace;
You turned from the fairest to gaze on her face:
And when you had once seen her forehead and mouth,
You saw as distinctly her soul and her truth—
My Kate.

Such a blue inner light from her eyelids outbroke,
You looked at her silence and fancied she spoke:
When she did, so peculiar yet soft was the tone,
Though the loudest spoke also, you heard her alone—
My Kate.

I doubt if she said to you much that could act
As a thought or suggestion: she did not attract
In the sense of the brilliant or wise: I infer
'Twas her thinking of others, made you think of her—
My Kate.

She never found fault with you, never implied
Your wrong by her right; and yet men at her side
Grew nobler, girls purer, as through the whole town
The children were gladder that pulled at her gown—
My Kate.

None knelt at her feet confessed lovers in thrall;
They knelt more to God than they used,—that was all:
If you praised her as charming, some asked what you meant,
But the charm of her presence was felt when she went—
My Kate.

The weak and the gentle, the ribald and rude,
She took them as she found them, and did them all good;
It was always so with her—see what you have!
She has made the grass greener even here .. with her grave—
My Kate.

My dear one!—when thou wast alive with the rest,
I held thee the sweetest and loved thee the best:
And now thou art dead, shall I not take thy part
As thy smiles used to do for thyself, my sweet Heart—
My Kate ?

E. B. BROWNING.

464. THE GARLAND

THE pride of every grove I chose,
　　The violet sweet, and lily fair,
The dappled pink, and blushing rose,
　　To deck my charming Chloe's hair.

At morn the nymph vouchsafed to place
　　Upon her brow the various wreath ;
The flowers less blooming than her face,
　　The scent less fragrant than her breath.

The flowers she wore along the day ;
　　And every nymph and shepherd said,
That in her hair they looked more gay,
　　Than glowing in their native bed.

Undrest at evening, when she found
　　Their odours lost,　their colours past ;
She changed her look, and on the ground
　　Her garland and her eye she cast.

That eye dropt sense distinct and clear,
　　As any muse's tongue could speak ;
When from its lid a pearly tear
　　Ran trickling down her beauteous cheek.

Dissembling what I knew too well,
　　' My love, my life,' said I, ' explain
This change of humour : pr'ythee tell :
　　That falling tear—what does it mean ? '

She sighed : she smiled : and to the flowers
　　Pointing, the lovely moralist said :
' See ! friend, in some few fleeting hours,
　　See yonder, what a change is made.

' Ah me, the blooming pride of May,
　　And that of Beauty are but one ;
At morn both flourish bright and gay,
　　Both fade at evening, pale, and gone.

' At morn poor Stella danced and sung ;
　　The amorous youth around her bowed ;
At night her fatal knell was rung ;
　　I saw and kissed her in her shroud.

' Such as she is, who died to-day ;
　　Such I, alas ! may be to-morrow :
Go, Damon, bid thy muse display
　　The justice of thy Chloe's sorrow.'

M. PRIOR.

465. FOR MY OWN MONUMENT

As doctors give physic by way of prevention,
  Mat, alive and in health, of his tombstone took care ;
For delays are unsafe, and his pious intention
  May haply be never fulfilled by his heir.

Then take Mat's word for it, the sculptor is paid ;
  That the figure is fine, pray believe your own eye ;
Yet credit but lightly what more may be said,
  For we flatter ourselves, and teach marble to lie.

Yet counting as far as to fifty his years,
  His virtues and vices were as other men's are ;
High hopes he conceived, and he smothered great fears,
  In a life parti-coloured, half pleasure, half care.

Nor to business a drudge, nor to faction a slave,
  He strove to make interest and freedom agree ;
In public employments industrious and grave,
  And alone with his friends, Lord ! how merry was he !

Now in equipage stately, now humble on foot,
  Both fortunes he tried, but to neither would trust ;
And whirled in the round as the wheel turned about,
  He found riches had wings, and knew man was but dust.

This verse, little polished, though mighty sincere,
  Sets neither his titles nor merit to view ;
It says that his relics collected lie here,
  And no mortal yet knows too if this may be true.

Fierce robbers there are that infest the highway,
  So Mat may be killed, and his bones never found ;
False witness at court, and fierce tempests at sea,
  So Mat may yet chance to be hanged or be drowned.

If his bones lie in earth, roll in sea, fly in air,
  To Fate we must yield, and the thing is the same ;
And if passing thou giv'st him a smile or a tear,
  He cares not—yet, prithee, be kind to his fame.

M. PRIOR.

466. EPITAPH ON HIMSELF

NOBLES and heralds, by your leave,
  Here lies what once was Matthew Prior,
The son of Adam and of Eve ;
  Can Bourbon or Nassau claim higher ?

M. PRIOR.

467.   EPITAPH FOR ONE WHO WOULD NOT BE BURIED IN
WESTMINSTER ABBEY

HEROES and kings ! your distance keep,
    In peace let one poor poet sleep,
    Who never flattered folks like you :
    Let Horace blush, and Virgil too.

A. POPE.

468.   DIRGE FOR FIDELE

To fair Fidele's grassy tomb
    Soft maids and village hinds shall bring
Each opening sweet of earliest bloom,
    And rifle all the breathing Spring.

No wailing ghost shall dare appear
    To vex with shrieks this quiet grove :
But shepherd lads assemble here,
    And melting virgins own their love.

No withered witch shall here be seen ;
    No goblins lead their nightly crew :
The female fays shall haunt the green,
    And dress thy grave with pearly dew !

The red-breast oft at evening hours
    Shall kindly lend his little aid ;
With hoary moss, and gathered flowers,
    To deck the ground where thou art laid.

When howling winds, and beating rain,
    In tempests shake the sylvan cell ;
Or 'midst the chase on every plain,
    The tender thought on thee shall dwell.

Each lonely scene shall thee restore,
    For thee the tear be duly shed ;
Beloved till life can charm no more,
    And mourned, till Pity's self be dead.

W. COLLINS.

469. THE MOURNER À LA MODE

I saw her last night at a party
  (The elegant party at Mead's),
And looking remarkably hearty
  For a widow so young in her weeds;
Yet I know she was suffering sorrow
  Too deep for the tongue to express,—
Or why had she chosen to borrow
  So much from the language of dress?

Her shawl was as sable as night;
  And her gloves were as dark as her shawl;
And her jewels—that flashed in the light—
  Were black as a funeral pall;
Her robe had the hue of the rest
  (How nicely it fitted her shape!),
And the grief that was heaving her breast
  Boiled over in billows of crape!

What tears of vicarious woe,
  That else might have sullied her face,
Were kindly permitted to flow
  In ripples of ebony lace!
While even her fan, in its play,
  Had quite a lugubrious scope,
And seemed to be waving away
  The ghost of the angel of Hope!

Yet rich as the robes of a queen
  Was the sombre apparel she wore;
I'm certain I never had seen
  Such a sumptuous sorrow before;
And I couldn't help thinking the beauty
  In mourning the loved and the lost,
Was doing her conjugal duty
  Altogether regardless of cost!

One surely would say a devotion
  Performed at so vast an expense
Betrayed an excess of emotion
  That was really something immense;
And yet as I viewed, at my leisure,
  Those tokens of tender regard,
I thought:—It is scarce without measure—
  The sorrow that goes by the yard!

Ah! grief is a curious passion;
  And yours—I am sorely afraid
The very next phase of the fashion
  Will find it beginning to fade;

Though dark are the shadows of grief,
  The morning will follow the night,
Half-tints will betoken relief,
  Till joy shall be symboled in white !

Ah well ! it were idle to quarrel
  With Fashion, or aught she may do ;
And so I conclude with a moral
  And metaphor—warranted new :—
When *measles* come handsomely out,
  The patient is safest, they say ;
And the *Sorrow* is mildest, no doubt,
  That works in a similar way !

J. G. SAXE.

470.   AN ADDRESS TO THE MUMMY IN BELZONI'S EXHIBITION

AND thou hast walked about (how strange a story !)
  In Thebes's streets three thousand years ago,
When the Memnonium was in all its glory,
  And time had not begun to overthrow
Those temples, palaces, and piles stupendous,
Of which the very ruins are tremendous !

Speak ! for thou long enough hast acted dummy ;
  Thou hast a tongue, come, let us hear its tune ;
Thou'rt standing on thy legs above ground, mummy !
  Revisiting the glimpses of the moon,
Not like thin ghosts or disembodied creatures,
But with thy bones and flesh, and limbs and features.

Tell us—for doubtless thou canst recollect—
  To whom we should assign the Sphinx's fame ?
Was Cheops or Cephrenes architect
  Of either Pyramid that bears his name ?
Is Pompey's Pillar really a misnomer ?
Had Thebes a hundred gates, as sung by Homer ?

Perhaps thou wert a mason, and forbidden
  By oath to tell the secrets of thy trade—
Then say, what secret melody was hidden
  In Memnon's statue, which at sunrise played ?
Perhaps thou wert a priest—if so, my struggles
Are vain, for priestcraft never owns its juggles.

Perchance that very hand, now pinioned flat,
  Has hob-a-nobbed with Pharaoh, glass to glass ;
Or dropped a halfpenny in Homer's hat,
  Or doffed thine own to let Queen Dido pass,
Or held, by Solomon's own invitation,
A torch at the great Temple's dedication.

I need not ask thee if that hand, when armed,
  Has any Roman soldier mauled and knuckled,
For thou wert dead and buried and embalmed,
  Ere Romulus and Remus had been suckled :
Antiquity appears to have begun
Long after thy primaeval race was run.

Thou couldst develop, if that withered tongue
  Might tell us what those sightless orbs have seen,
How the world looked when it was fresh and young,
  And the great Deluge still had left it green—
Or was it then so old, that History's pages
Contained no record of its early ages ?

Still silent ! incommunicative elf !
  Art sworn to secrecy ? then keep thy vows ;
But prythee tell us something of thyself—
  Reveal the secrets of thy prison-house ;
Since in the world of spirits thou hast slumbered,
What hast thou seen—what strange adventures numbered ?

Since first thy form was in this box extended,
  We have, above-ground, seen some strange mutations.
The Roman empire has begun and ended,
  New worlds have risen—we have lost old nations,
And countless Kings have into dust been humbled,
While not a fragment of thy flesh has crumbled.

Didst thou not hear the pother o'er thy head,
  When the great Persian conqueror, Cambyses,
Marched armies o'er thy tomb with thundering tread,
  O'erthrew Osiris, Orus, Apis, Isis,
And shook the Pyramids with fear and wonder,
When the gigantic Memnon fell asunder ?

If the tomb's secrets may not be confessed,
  The nature of thy private life unfold :—
A heart has throbbed beneath that leathern breast,
  And tears adown that dusty cheek have rolled :—
Have children climbed those knees, and kissed that face ?
What was thy name and station, age and race ? . . .

H. SMITH.

471. AN ELEGY ON THAT GLORY OF HER SEX, MRS. MARY BLAIZE

Good people all, with one accord,
　　Lament for Madam Blaize,
Who never wanted a good word—
　　From those who spoke her praise.

The needy seldom passed her door,
　　And always found her kind ;
She freely lent to all the poor,—
　　Who left a pledge behind.

She strove the neighbourhood to please,
　　With manners wonderous winning,
And never followed wicked ways,—
　　Unless when she was sinning.

At church, in silks and satins new,
　　With hoop of monstrous size,
She never slumbered in her pew,—
　　But when she shut her eyes.

Her love was sought, I do aver,
　　By twenty beaux and more ;
The king himself has followed her,—
　　When she has walked before.

But now her wealth and finery fled,
　　Her hangers-on cut short all ;
The doctors found, when she was dead,—
　　Her last disorder mortal.

Let us lament, in sorrow sore,
　　For Kent Street well may say,
That had she lived a twelve-month more,—
　　She had not died to-day.

　　　　　　　　　　　　　　O. Goldsmith.

472. IF THE MAN WHO TURNIPS CRIES

If the man who turnips cries,
Cry not when his father dies,
'Tis a proof that he had rather
Have a turnip than his father.

　　　　　　　　　　　　　　S. Johnson.

473.   THE CARELESS GALLANT

OR

A FAREWELL TO SORROW

LET us drink and be merry, dance, joke, and rejoice,
With claret and sherry, theorbo and voice,
The changeable world to our joy is unjust,
All treasures uncertain, then down with your dust ;
In frolics dispose your pounds, shillings, and pence,
For we shall be nothing a hundred years hence.

We'll sport and be free with Frank, Betty, and Dolly,
Have lobsters and oysters to cure melancholy,
Fish dinners will make a man spring like a flea,
Dame Venus, love's lady, was born of the sea,
With her and with Bacchus we'll tickle the sense,
For we shall be past it a hundred years hence.

Your beautiful bit who hath all eyes upon her,
That her honesty sells for a hogo of honour,
Whose lightness and brightness doth cast such a splendour,
That none are thought fit but the stars to attend her,
Though now she seems pleasant and sweet to the sense,
Will be damnable mouldy a hundred years hence.

Your usurer that in the hundred takes twenty,
Who wants in his wealth and pines in his plenty,
Lays up for a season which he shall ne'er see ;
The year of one thousand eight hundred and three
Shall have changed all his bags, his houses and rents,
For a worm-eaten coffin a hundred years hence.

Your Chancery-lawyer who by conscience thrives,
In spinning a suit to the length of three lives,
A suit which the client doth wear out in slavery,
While pleader makes conscience a cloak for his knavery,
Can boast of his cunning but i' th' present tense,
For *non est inventus* a hundred years hence.

Then why should we turmoil in cares and in fears,
And turn our tranquillity to sighs and tears,
Let 's eat, drink and play ere the worms do corrupt us,
For I say that, *Post mortem nulla voluptas*,
Let 's deal with our chances that so we may thence,
Be held in remembrance a hundred years hence.

I never could gain satisfaction upon
Your dreams of a bliss when we're cold as a stone ;
Though sages may say we're to Bacchus a debtor,
By Venus ! are sages themselves so much better ?
And Abigail, Hannah, and sister Prudence,
Will simper to nothing a hundred years hence.

The butterfly courtier, that pageant of state,
The mouse-trap of honour and May-game of Fate,
With all his ambitions, intrigues, and his tricks,
Must die like a clown, and then drops into Styx,
His plots against death are too slender a fence,
For he'll be out of place a hundred years hence.

Yea, the poet himself that so loftily sings,
As he scorns any subjects but heroes or kings,
Must to the capriccios of fortune submit,
And often be counted a fool for his wit ;
Thus beauty, wit, wealth, law, learning and sense,
All comes to nothing a hundred years hence.

T. JORDAN.

474. DOMESTIC DIDACTICS BY AN OLD SERVANT
THE BROKEN DISH

WHAT's life but full of care and doubt,
    With all its fine humanities,
With parasols we walk about,
    Long pigtails and such vanities.

We plant pomegranate trees and things,
    And go in gardens sporting,
With toys and fans of peacock's wings,
    To painted ladies courting.

We gather flowers of every hue,
    And fish in boats for fishes,
Build summer-houses painted blue,
    But life's as frail as dishes.

Walking about their groves of trees,
    Blue bridges and blue rivers,
How little thought them two Chinese,
    They'd both be smashed to shivers.

T. HOOD.

475. SINCERE FLATTERY

Of W. S. (Mr.)

For Greek Iambics

Pe. Not so, my liege, for even now the town
   Splits with sedition, and the incensed mob
   Rush hither roaring.
Olc.   Let them roar their fill,
   Bluster and bellow till the enormous wings
   Of gusty Boreas flap with less ado.
   Ask they my treacherous nephew's wretched life,
   As if that order were a thing of nought
   Which I did publish ?   Let them beg or threaten,
   I'll not regard them.   Oh my trusty friend,
   There is no rock defies the elements,
   With half the constancy that kinglike men
   Shut up their breasts against such routs as these.
Pe. O my most valiant lord, I feel 'tis so,
   Permit me to advance against the foe.

                    (*Olcis and Terranea*, Act iv. Sc. iii.)

                                    J. K. Stephen.

476. SORROWS OF WERTHER

Werther had a love for Charlotte
   Such as words could never utter ;
Would you know how first he met her ?
   She was cutting bread-and-butter.

Charlotte was a married lady,
   And a moral man was Werther,
And, for all the wealth of Indies,
   Would do nothing for to hurt her.

So he sighed and pined and ogled,
   And his passion boiled and bubbled,
Till he blew his silly brains out,
   And no more was by it troubled.

Charlotte, having seen his body
   Borne before her on a shutter,
Like a well-conducted person,
   Went on cutting bread-and butter.

                                    W. M. Thackeray.

477. SONG BY ROGERO

WHENE'ER with haggard eyes I view
  This dungeon, that I'm rotting in,
I think of those companions true
Who studied with me in the U-
    -niversity of Gottingen—
    -niversity of Gottingen.

> (*Weeps, and pulls out a blue 'kerchief, with which he
> wipes his eyes; gazing tenderly at it, he proceeds.*)

Sweet 'kerchief checked with heavenly blue,
  Which once my love sat knotting in,
Alas, Matilda then was true,
At least I thought so at the U-
    -niversity of Gottingen—
    -niversity of Gottingen.

> (*At the repetition of this line Rogero clanks his chains
> in cadence.*)

Barbs! barbs! alas! how swift ye flew,
  Her neat post-wagon trotting in!
Ye bore Matilda from my view;
Forlorn I languished at the U-
    -niversity of Gottingen—
    -niversity of Gottingen.

This faded form! this pallid hue!
  This blood my veins is clotting in,
My years are many—they were few
When first I entered at the U-
    -niversity of Gottingen—
    -niversity of Gottingen.

There first for thee my passion grew,
  Sweet! sweet Matilda Pottingen!
Thou wast the daughter of my tu-
-tor, Law Professor at the U-
    -niversity of Gottingen—
    -niversity of Gottingen.

Sun, moon, and thou vain world, adieu,
  That kings and priests are plotting in;
Here, doomed to starve on water-gru-
-el, never shall I see the U-
    -niversity of Gottingen!—
    -niversity of Gottingen!

> (*During the last stanza Rogero dashes his head repeat-
> edly against the walls of his prison; and, finally, so
> hard as to produce a visible contusion. He then throws
> himself on the floor in an agony. The curtain drops—the
> music still continuing to play till it is wholly fallen.*)

G. CANNING.

478. A PORTRAIT IN DELIA'S PARLOUR

I WOULD I were that portly gentleman,
With gold-laced hat and golden-headed cane,
Who hangs in Delia's parlour ! For whene'er
From books or needlework her looks arise,
On him CONVERGE THE SUNBEAMS OF HER EYES,
And he UNBLAMED may gaze upon MY FAIR,
And oft MY FAIR his FAVOURED form surveys.
O HAPPY PICTURE ! still on HER to gaze !
I envy him ! and jealous fear alarms,
Lest the STRONG *glance* of those *divinest* charms
WARM HIM TO LIFE, as in the ancient days,
When MARBLE MELTED in Pygmalion's arms.
I would I were that portly gentleman
With gold-laced hat and golden-headed cane.

R. SOUTHEY.

479. IMITATION OF SOUTHEY

INSCRIPTION

FOR THE DOOR OF THE CELL IN NEWGATE, WHERE MRS. BROWNRIGG, THE
PRENTICE-CIDE, WAS CONFINED PREVIOUS TO HER EXECUTION

FOR one long term, or e'er her trial came,
Here Brownrigg lingered. Often have these cells
Echoed her blasphemies, as with shrill voice
She screamed for fresh Geneva. Not to her
Did the blithe fields of Tothill, or thy street,
St. Giles, its fair varieties expand ;
Till at the last, in slow-drawn cart, she went
To execution. Dost thou ask her crime ?
SHE WHIPPED TWO FEMALE PRENTICES TO DEATH,
AND HID THEM IN THE COAL-HOLE. For her mind
Shaped strictest plans of discipline. Sage schemes !
Such as Lycurgus taught, when at the shrine
Of the Orthyan Goddess he bade flog
The little Spartans ; such as erst chastised .
Our Milton, when at college. For this act
Did Brownrigg swing. Harsh laws ! But time shall come,
When France shall reign, and laws be all repealed !

G. CANNING and J. H. FRERE.

480. YOU ARE OLD, FATHER WILLIAM

'You are old, Father William,' the young man said,
  'And your hair has become very white;
And yet you incessantly stand on your head—
  Do you think, at your age, it is right?'

'In my youth,' Father William replied to his son,
  'I feared it might injure the brain;
But, now that I'm perfectly sure I have none,
  Why, I do it again and again.'

'You are old,' said the youth, 'as I mentioned before,
  And have grown most uncommonly fat;
Yet you turned a back-somersault in at the door—
  Pray, what is the reason of that?'

'In my youth,' said the sage, as he shook his grey locks,
  'I kept all my limbs very supple
By the use of this ointment—one shilling the box—
  Allow me to sell you a couple?'

'You are old,' said the youth, 'and your jaws are too weak
  For anything tougher than suet;
Yet you finished the goose, with the bones and the beak—
  Pray how did you manage to do it?

'In my youth,' said his father, 'I took to the law,
  And argued each case with my wife;
And the muscular strength, which it gave to my jaw,
  Has lasted the rest of my life.'

'You are old,' said the youth, 'one would hardly suppose
  That your eye was as steady as ever;
Yet you balanced an eel on the end of your nose—
  What made you so awfully clever?'

'I have answered three questions, and that is enough,'
  Said his father; 'don't give yourself airs!
Do you think I can listen all day to such stuff?
  Be off, or I'll kick you downstairs!'

                              C. L. DODGSON (LEWIS CARROLL).

481. A SONNET

Two voices are there: one is of the deep;
  It learns the storm-cloud's thunderous melody,
  Now roars, now murmurs with the changing sea,
Now bird-like pipes, now closes soft in sleep:
  And one is of an old half-witted sheep
Which bleats articulate monotony,

And indicates that two and one are three,
That grass is green, lakes damp, and mountains steep :
And, Wordsworth, both are thine : at certain times
Forth from the heart of thy melodious rhymes,
The form and pressure of high thoughts will burst :
At other times—good Lord ! I'd rather be
Quite unacquainted with the ABC
Than write such hopeless rubbish as thy worst.

                                    J. K. STEPHEN

482. THE BABY'S DEBUT

[SPOKEN IN THE CHARACTER OF NANCY LAKE, A GIRL
    EIGHT YEARS OF AGE, WHO IS DRAWN UPON THE
    STAGE IN A CHILD'S CHAISE BY SAMUEL HUGHES,
    HER UNCLE'S PORTER]

My brother Jack was nine in May,
And I was eight on New Year's day ;
        So in Kate Wilson's shop
Papa (he 's my papa and Jack's)
Bought me, last week, a doll of wax,
        And brother Jack a top.

Jack 's in the pouts, and this it is,—
He thinks mine came to more than his ;
        So to my drawer he goes,
Takes out the doll, and, O, my stars!
He pokes her head between the bars,
        And melts off half her nose !

Quite cross, a bit of string I beg,
And tie it to his peg-top's peg,
        And bang, with might and main,
Its head against the parlour-door ;
Off flies the head, and hits the floor,
        And breaks a window-pane.

This made him cry with rage and spite :
Well, let him cry, it serves him right.
        A pretty thing, forsooth !
If he 's to melt, all scalding hot,
Half my doll's nose, and I am not
        To draw his peg-top's tooth !

Aunt Hannah heard the window break,
And cried, ' O naughty Nancy Lake,
    Thus to distress your aunt:
No Drury Lane for you to-day ! '
And while papa said, ' Pooh, she may ! '
    Mamma said, ' No, she shan't ! '

Well, after many a sad reproach,
They got into a hackney coach,
    And trotted down the street.
I saw them go : one horse was blind,
The tails of both hung down behind,
    Their shoes were on their feet.

The chaise in which poor brother Bill
Used to be drawn to Pentonville,
    Stood in the lumber-room :
I wiped the dust from off the top,
While Molly mopped it with a mop,
    And brushed it with a broom.

My uncle's porter, Samuel Hughes,
Came in at six to black the shoes,
    (I always talk to Sam :)
So what does he, but takes, and drags
Me in the chaise along the flags,
    And leaves me where I am.

My father's walls are made of brick,
But not so tall and not so thick
    As these ; and, goodness me !
My father's beams are made of wood,
But never, never half so good
    As those that now I see.

What a large floor ! 'tis like a town !
The carpet, when they lay it down,
    Won't hide it, I'll be bound ;
And there 's a row of lamps !—my eye
How they do blaze ! I wonder why
    They keep them on the ground.

At first I caught hold of the wing,
And kept away ; but Mr. Thing-
    umbob, the prompter man,
Gave with his hand my chaise a shove,
And said, ' Go on, my pretty love ;
    Speak to 'em, little Nan.

'You've only got to curtsey, whisp-
er, hold your chin up, laugh, and lisp,
    And you are sure to take :
I've known the day when brats, not quite
Thirteen, got fifty pounds a-night ;
    Then why not Nancy Lake ?'

But while I'm speaking, where 's papa ?
And where 's my aunt ? and where 's mamma ?
    Where 's Jack ?   O, there they sit !
They smile, they nod, I'll go my ways,
And order round poor Billy's chaise,
    To join them in the pit.

And now, good gentlefolk, I go
To join mamma, and see the show :
    So, bidding you adieu,
I curtsey like a pretty miss,
And if you'll blow to me a kiss,
    I'll blow a kiss to you.

                                    J. SMITH.

483.   SONG BY MR. CYPRESS

THERE is a fever of the spirit,
    The brand of Cain's unresting doom,
Which in the lone dark souls that bear it
    Glows like the lamp in Tullia's tomb.
Unlike the lamp, its subtle fire
    Burns, blasts, consumes its cell, the heart.
Till, one by one, hope, joy, desire,
    Like dreams of shadowy smoke depart.

When hope, love, life itself, are only
    Dust—spectral memories—dead and cold—
The unfed fire burns bright and lonely,
    Like that undying lamp of old ;
And by that drear illumination,
    Till time its clay-built home has rent,
Thought broods on feeling's desolation—
    The soul is its own monument.

                                T. L. PEACOCK.

484. THE LAY OF THE LOVELORN

COMRADES, you may pass the rosy. With permission of the chair,
I shall leave you for a little, for I'd like to take the air.

Whether 'twas the sauce at dinner, or that glass of ginger-beer,
Or these strong cheroots, I know not, but I feel a little queer.

Let me go. Nay, Chuckster, blow me, 'pon my soul, this is too bad
When you want me, ask the waiter ; he knows where I'm to be had.

Whew ! This is a great relief now ! Let me but undo my stock,
Resting here beneath the porch, my nerves will steady like a rock.

In my ears I hear the singing of a lot of favourite tunes—
Bless my heart, how very odd ! Why, surely there 's a brace of moons !

See ! the stars ! how bright they twinkle, winking with a frosty glare,
Like my faithless cousin Amy when she drove me to despair.

O my cousin, spider-hearted ! O my Amy ! No, confound it !
I must wear the mournful willow,—all around my hat I've bound it.

Falser than the Bank of Fancy, frailer than a shilling glove,
Puppet to a father's anger, minion to a·nabob's love !

Is it well to wish thee happy ? Having known me, could you ever
Stoop to marry half a heart, and little more than half a liver ?

Happy ! Damme ! Thou shalt lower to his level day by day,
Changing from the best of china to the commonest of clay.

As the husband is, the wife is,—he is stomach-plagued and old ;
And his curry soups will make thy cheek the colour of his gold.

When his feeble love is sated, he will hold thee surely then
Something lower than his hookah,—something less than his cayenne.

What is this ? His eyes are pinky. Was 't the claret ? Oh, no, no,
Bless your soul ! it was the salmon,—salmon always makes him so.

Take him to thy dainty chamber—soothe him with thy lightest fancies,
He will understand thee, won't he ?—pay thee with a lover's glances ?

Louder than the loudest trumpet, harsh as harshest ophicleide,
Nasal respirations answer the endearments of his bride.

Sweet response, delightful music ! Gaze upon thy noble charge,
Till the spirit fill thy bosom that inspired the meek Laffarge.

Better thou wert dead before me,—better, better that I stood,
Looking on thy murdered body, like the injured Daniel Good !

Better, thou and I were lying, cold and timber-stiff and dead,
With a pan of burning charcoal underneath our nuptial bed !

Cursèd be the Bank of England's notes, that tempt the soul to sin !
Cursèd be the want of acres,—doubly cursed the want of tin !

Cursèd be the marriage contract, that enslaved thy soul to greed !
Cursèd be the sallow lawyer, that prepared and drew the deed !

Cursèd be his foul apprentice, who the loathsome fees did earn !
Cursèd be the clerk and parson, cursèd be the whole concern !

   .   .   .   .

Oh, 'tis well that I should bluster,—much I'm like to make of that ;
Better comfort have I found in singing ' All Around my Hat '

But that song, so wildly plaintive, palls upon my British ears.
'Twill not do to pine for ever,—I am getting up in years.

Can't I turn the honest penny, scribbling for the weekly press,
And in writing Sunday libels drown my private wretchedness ?

Oh, to feel the wild pulsation that in manhood's dawn I knew,
When my days were all before me, and my years were twenty-two !

When I smoked my independent pipe along the Quadrant wide,
With the many larks of London flaring up on every side ;

When I went the pace so wildly, caring little what might come ;
Coffee-milling care and sorrow, with a nose-adapted thumb ;

Felt the exquisite enjoyment, tossing nightly off, oh heavens !
Brandy at the Cider Cellars, kidneys smoking-hot at Evans' !

Or in the Adelphi sitting, half in rapture, half in tears,
Saw the glorious melodrama conjure up the shades of years !

Saw Jack Sheppard, noble stripling, act his wondrous feats again,
Snapping Newgate's bars of iron, like an infant's daisy chain.

Might was right, and all the terrors, which had held the world in awe,
Were despised, and prigging prospered, spite of Laurie, spite of law.

In such scenes as these I triumphed, ere my passion's edge was rusted
And my cousin's cold refusal left me very much disgusted !

Since, my heart is sere and withered, and I do not care a curse,
Whether worse shall be the better, or the better be the worse.

Hark ! my merry comrades call me, bawling for another jorum ;
They would mock me in derision, should I thus appear before 'em.

Womankind no more shall vex me, such at least as go arrayed
In the most expensive satins and the newest silk brocade.

I'll to Afric, lion-haunted, where the giant forest yields
Rarer robes and finer tissue than are sold at Spitalfields.

Or to burst all chains of habit, flinging habit's self aside,
I shall walk the tangled jungle in mankind's primeval pride ;

Feeding on the luscious berries and the rich cassava root,
Lots of dates and lots of guavas, clusters of forbidden fruit.

Never comes the trader thither, never o'er the purple main
Sounds the oath of British commerce, or the accents of Cockaigne.

There, methinks, would be enjoyment, where no envious rule prevents ;
Sink the steamboats ! cuss the railways ! rot, O rot the Three per Cents.

There the passions, cramped no longer, shall have space to breathe, my
          cousin !
I will wed some savage woman—nay, I'll wed at least a dozen.

There I'll rear my young mulattoes, as no Bond Street brats are reared :
They shall dive for alligators, catch the wild goats by the beard—

Whistle to the cockatoos, and mock the hairy-faced baboon,
Worship mighty Mumbo Jumbo in the Mountains of the Moon.

I myself, in far Timbuctoo, leopard's blood will daily quaff,
Ride a tiger-hunting, mounted on a thorough-bred giraffe.

Fiercely shall I shout the war-whoop, as some sullen stream he crosses,
Startling from their noonday slumbers iron-bound rhinoceroses.

Fool ! again the dream, the fancy ! But I know my words are mad,
For I hold the grey barbarian lower than the Christian cad.

I the swell—the city dandy ! I to seek such horrid places,—
I to haunt with squalid negroes, blubber-lips, and monkey-faces.

I to wed with Coromantees ! I, who managed—very near—
To secure the heart and fortune of the widow Shillibeer !

Stuff and nonsense ! let me never fling a single chance away,
Maids ere now, I know, have loved me, and another maiden may.

' Morning Post ' (' The Times ' won't trust me), help me, as I know you
          can ;
I will pen an advertisement,—that 's a never-failing plan.

' WANTED—By a bard in wedlock, some young interesting woman :
Looks are not so much an object, if the shiners be forthcoming !

' Hymen's chains the advertiser vows shall be but silken fetters,
Please address to A. T., Chelsea. N.B.—You must pay the letters.'

That 's the sort of thing to do it. Now I'll go and taste the balmy,—
Rest thee with thy yellow nabob, spider-hearted Cousin Amy !

                                        SIR T. MARTIN.

485. PROVERBIAL PHILOSOPHY

OF PROPRIETY

STUDY first Propriety : for she is indeed the Pole-star
Which shall guide the artless maiden through the mazes of Vanity Fair ;
Nay, she is the golden chain which holdeth together Society ;
The lamp by whose light young Psyche shall approach unblamed her
    Eros.
Verily Truth is as Eve, which was ashamed being naked ;
Wherefore doth Propriety dress her with the fair foliage of artifice :
And when she is dressed, behold ! she knoweth not herself again.—
I walked in the Forest ; and above me stood the Yew,
Stood like a slumbering giant, shrouded in impenetrable shade ;
Then I passed into the citizen's garden, and marked a tree clipped into
    shape,
(The giant's locks had been shorn by the Dalilah-shears of Decorum ;)
And I said, 'Surely nature is goodly ; but how much goodlier
    is Art !'
I heard the wild notes of the lark floating far over the blue sky,
And my foolish heart went after him, and, lo ! I blessed him as
    he rose ;
Foolish ! for far better is the trained boudoir bullfinch,
Which pipeth the semblance of a tune, and mechanically draweth up
    water :
And the reinless steed of the desert, though his neck be clothed with
    thunder,
Must yield to him that danceth and 'moveth in the circles' at Astley's.

For verily, O my daughter, the world is a masquerade,
And God made thee one thing, that thou mightest make thyself another :
A maiden's heart is as champagne, ever aspiring and struggling upwards,
And it needed that its motions be checked by the silvered cork of Pro-
    priety :
He that can afford the price, his be the precious treasure,
Let him drink deeply of its sweetness, nor grumble if it tasteth of the
    cork.

C. S. CALVERLEY.

486. POETS AND LINNETS

WHERE'ER there 's a thistle to feed a linnet
And linnets are plenty, thistles rife—
Or an acorn-cup to catch dew-drops in it
There 's ample promise of further life.
Now, mark how we begin it.

For linnets will follow, if linnets are minded,
As blows the white-feather parachute ;
And ships will reel by the tempest blinded—
Aye, ships and shiploads of men to boot !
How deep whole fleets you'll find hid.

And we blow the thistle-down hither and thither
Forgetful of linnets, and men, and God.
The dew ! for its want an oak will wither—
By the dull hoof into the dust is trod,
And then who strikes the cither ?

But thistles were only for donkeys intended,
And that donkeys are common enough is clear,
And that drop ! what a vessel it might have befriended,
Does it add any flavour to Glugabib's beer ?
Well, there's my musing ended.

                                T. Hood, the Younger.

487.   SINCERE FLATTERY OF R. B.
To A. S.

Birthdays ? yes, in a general way ;
For the most if not for the best of men :
You were born (I suppose) on a certain day :
So was I : or perhaps in the night : what then ?

Only this : or at least, if more,
You must know, not think it, and learn, not speak :
There is truth to be found on the unknown shore,
And many will find where few will seek.

For many are called and few are chosen,
And the few grow many as ages lapse :
But when will the many grow few : what dozen
Is fused into one by Time's hammer-taps ?

A bare brown stone in a babbling brook :—
It was wanton to hurl it there, you say :
And the moss, which clung in the sheltered nook
(Yet the stream runs cooler), is washed away.

That begs the question : many a prater
Thinks such a suggestion a sound ' stop thief ! '
Which, may I ask, do you think the greater
Sergeant-at-arms or a Robber Chief ?

And if it were not so ? still you doubt ?
Ah ! yours is a birthday indeed if so.
That were something to write a poem about,
If one thought a little.   I only know.

P.S.

There 's a Me Society down at Cambridge,
Where my works, *cum notis variorum*,
Are talked about ; well, I require the same bridge
That Euclid took toll at as *Asinorum* :

And, as they have got through several ditties
I thought were as stiff as a brick-built wall,
I've composed the above, and a stiff one *it* is,
A bridge to stop asses at, once for all.

J. K. STEPHEN.

488.   BALLAD

THE auld wife sat at her ivied door,
  (*Butter and eggs and a pound of cheese*)
A thing she had frequently done before ;
  And her spectacles lay on her aproned knees.

The piper he piped on the hill-top high,
  (*Butter and eggs and a pound of cheese*)
Till the cow said ' I die,' and the goose asked ' Why ? '
  And the dog said nothing, but searched for fleas.

The farmer he strove through the square farmyard ;
  (*Butter and eggs and a pound of cheese*)
His last brew of ale was a trifle hard—
  The connexion of which with the plot one sees

The farmer's daughter hath frank blue eyes ;
  (*Butter and eggs and a pound of cheese*)
She hears the rooks caw in the windy skies,
  As she sits at her lattice and shells her peas.

The farmer's daughter hath ripe red lips ;
  (*Butter and eggs and a pound of cheese*)
If you try to approach her, away she skips
  Over tables and chairs with apparent ease.

The farmer's daughter hath soft brown hair ;
  (*Butter and eggs and a pound of cheese*)
And I met with a ballad, I can't say where,
  Which wholly consisted of lines like these.

Part II

She sat, with her hands 'neath her dimpled cheeks,
  (*Butter and eggs and a pound of cheese*)
And spake not a word.   While a lady speaks
  There is hope, but she didn't even sneeze.

She sat, with her hands 'neath her crimson cheeks,
  (*Butter and eggs and a pound of cheese*)
She gave up mending her father's breeks,
  And let the cat roll in her new chemise.

She sat, with her hands 'neath her burning cheeks,
  (*Butter and eggs and a pound of cheese*)
And gazed at the piper for thirteen weeks;
  Then she followed him out o'er the misty leas.

Her sheep followed her, as their tails did them.
  (*Butter and eggs and a pound of cheese*)
And this song is considered a perfect gem,
  And as to the meaning, it 's what you please.

C. S. CALVERLEY.

489. LOVERS, AND A REFLECTION

In moss-prankt dells which the sunbeams flatter
  (And heaven it knoweth what that may mean ;
Meaning, however, is no great matter)
  Where woods are a-tremble, with rifts atween ;

Through God's own heather we wonned together,
  I and my Willie (O love my love) :
I need hardly remark it was glorious weather,
  And flitterbats wavered alow, above :

Boats were curtseying, rising, bowing,
  (Boats in that climate are so polite),
And sands were a ribbon of green endowing,
  And O the sundazzle on bark and bight !

Through the rare red heather we danced together,
  (O love my Willie !) and smelt for flowers :
I must mention again it was gorgeous weather,
  Rhymes are so scarce in this world of ours :—

By rises that flushed with their purple favours,
  Through becks that brattled o'er grasses sheen,
We walked and waded, we two young shavers,
  Thanking our stars we were both so green.

We journeyed in parallels, I and Willie,
   In fortunate parallels ! Butterflies,
Hid in weltering shadows of daffodilly
   Or marjoram, kept making peacock eyes :

Songbirds darted about, some inky
   As coal, some snowy (I ween) as curds ;
Or rosy as pinks, or as roses pinky—
   They reck of no eerie To-come, those birds !

But they skim over bents which the millstream washes,
   Or hang in the lift 'neath a white cloud's hem ;
They need no parasols, no goloshes ;
   And good Mrs. Trimmer she feedeth them.

Then we thrid God's cowslips (as erst His heather)
   That endowed the wan grass with their golden blooms
And snapped—(it was perfectly charming weather)—
   Our fingers at Fate and her goddess-glooms :

And Willie 'gan sing (O, his notes were fluty ;
   Wafts fluttered them out to the white-winged sea)—
Something made up of rhymes that have done much duty
   Rhymes (better to put it) of ' ancientry ' :

Bowers of flowers encountered showers
   In William's carol—(O love my Willie !)
Then he bade sorrow borrow from blithe to-morrow
   I quite forget what—say a daffodilly :

A nest in a hollow, ' with buds to follow,'
   I think occurred next in his nimble strain ;
And clay that was ' kneaden ' of course in Eden—
   A rhyme most novel, I do maintain :

Mists, bones, the singer himself, love-stories,
   And all least furlable things got ' furled ' ;
Not with any design to conceal their ' glories ',
   But simply and solely to rhyme with ' world '.

  .   .   .   .   .   .

O if billows and pillows and hours and flowers,
   And all the brave rhymes of an elder day,
Could be furled together, this genial weather,
   And carted, or carried on ' wafts ' away,
Nor ever again trotted out—ah me !
How much fewer volumes of verse there 'd be !

C. S. CALVERLEY.

490. SINCERE FLATTERY

Of W. W. (Americanus)

THE clear cool note of the cuckoo which has ousted the legitimate nest-
 holder,
The whistle of the railway guard dispatching the train to the inevitable
 collision,
The maiden's monosyllabic reply to a polysyllabic proposal,
The fundamental note of the last trump, which is presumably D natural ;
All of these are sounds to rejoice in, yea to let your very ribs re-echo with :
But better than all of them is the absolutely last chord of the apparently
 inexhaustible pianoforte player.

J. K. Stephen.

491. CIMABUELLA

FAIR-TINTED cheeks, clear eyelids drawn
 In crescent curves above the light
Of eyes, whose dim, uncertain dawn
 Becomes not day : a forehead white
Beneath long yellow heaps of hair :
She is so strange she must be fair.

Had she sharp, slant-wise wings outspread,
 She were an angel ; but she stands
With flat dead gold behind her head,
 And lilies in her long thin hands :
Her folded mantle, gathered in,
Falls to her feet as it were tin.

Her nose is keen as pointed flame ;
 Her crimson lips no thing express ;
And never dread of saintly blame
 Held down her heavy eyelashes :
To guess what she were thinking of,
Precludeth any meaner love.

An azure carpet, fringed with gold,
 Sprinkled with scarlet spots, I laid
Before her straight, cool feet unrolled :
 But she nor sound nor movement made
(Albeit I heard a soft, shy smile,
Printing her neck a moment's while) ;

And I was shamed through all my mind
 For that she spake not, neither kissed,
But stared right past me. Lo ! behind
 Me stood, in pink and amethyst,
Sword-girt and velvet-doubleted,
A tall, gaunt youth, with frowzy head.

Wide nostrils in the air, dull eyes,
    Thick lips that simpered, but, ah me !
I saw, with most forlorn surprise,
    He was the Thirteenth Century,
I but the Nineteenth : then despair
Curdled beneath my curling hair.

O Love and Fate !   How could she choose
    My rounded outlines, broader brain,
And my resuscitated Muse ?
    Some tears she shed, but whether pain
Or joy in him unlocked their source,
I could not fathom which, of course.

But I from missals, quaintly bound,
    With cither and with clavichord
Will sing her songs of sovran sound :
    Belike her pity will afford
Such faint return as suits a saint
So sweetly done in verse and paint.

                              BAYARD TAYLOR

492.   AFTER DILETTANTE CONCETTI

' Why do you wear your hair like a man,
                    Sister Helen ?
This week is the third since you began.'
' I'm writing a ballad ; be still if you can,
                    Little brother.
        (*O Mother Carey, mother !*
What chickens are these between sea and heaven ?) '

But why does your figure appear so lean,
                    Sister Helen ?
And why do you dress in sage, sage green ? '
' Children should never be heard, if seen,
                    Little brother ?
        (*O Mother Carey, mother !*
What fowls are a-wing in the stormy heaven !) '

' But why is your face so yellowy white,
                    Sister Helen ?
And why are your skirts so funnily tight ? '
' Be quiet, you torment, or how can I write,
                    Little brother ?
        (*O Mother Carey, mother !*
How gathers thy train to the sea from the heaven !) '

And who's Mother Carey, and what is her train,
    Sister Helen?
And why do you call her again and again?'
     'You troublesome boy, why that's the refrain,
      Little brother.
    (O Mother Carey, mother!
What work is toward in the startled heaven?)'

'And what's a refrain? What a curious word,
    Sister Helen!
Is the ballad you're writing about a sea-bird?'
'Not at all; why should it be? Don't be absurd,
     Little brother.
    (O Mother Carey, mother!
Thy brood flies lower as lowers the heaven.)'

    (A big brother speaketh :)
'The refrain you've studied a meaning had,
    Sister Helen!
It gave strange force to a weird ballàd.
But refrains have become a ridiculous 'fad'
     Little brother.
    And *Mother Carey, mother,*
Has a bearing on nothing in earth or heaven.

'But the finical fashion has had its day,
    Sister Helen.
And let's try in the style of a different lay
To bid it adieu in poetical way,
     Little brother.
    So, Mother Carey, mother!
Collect your chickens and go to—heaven.'
 (A pause. Then the big brother singeth, accompanying him-
     self in a plaintive wise on the triangle :

'Look in my face. My name is Used-to-was,
 I am also called Played-out and Done-to-death,
  And It-will-wash-no more. Awakeneth
Slowly, but sure awakening it has,
The common-sense of man; and I, alas!
 The ballad-burden trick, now known too well,
 Am turned to scorn, and grown contemptible—
A too transparent artifice to pass.

'What a cheap dodge I am! The cats who dart
 Tin-kettled through the streets in wild surprise
  Assail judicious ears not otherwise;
And yet no critics praise the urchin's 'art',
Who to the wretched creature's caudal part
 Its foolish empty-jingling 'burden' ties.'
         H. D. TRAILL.

493.   THE PERSON OF THE HOUSE
Idyl ccclxvi.   The Kid

My spirit, in the doorway's pause,
  Fluttered with fancies in my breast;
Obsequious to all decent laws,
  I felt exceedingly distressed.
I knew it rude to enter there
  With Mrs. V. in such a state;
And, 'neath a magisterial air,
  Felt actually indelicate.
I knew the nurse began to grin;
  I turned to greet my Love. Said she—
'Confound your modesty, come in!
  —What shall we call the darling, V. ?'
(There are so many charming names!
  Girls'—Peg, Moll, Doll, Fan, Kate, Blanche, Bab:
Boys'—Mahershahal-hashbaz, James,
  Luke, Nick, Dick, Mark, Aminadab.)

Lo, as the acorn to the oak,
  As well-heads to the river's height,
As to the chicken the moist yolk,
  As to high noon the day's first white—
Such is the baby to the man.
  There, straddling one red arm and leg,
Lay my last work, in length a span,
  Half hatched, and conscious of the egg.
A creditable child, I hoped;
  And half a score of joys to be
Through sunny lengths of prospect sloped
  Smooth to the bland futurity.
O, fate surpassing other dooms,
  O, hope above all wrecks of time!
O, light that fills all vanquished glooms,
  O, silent song o'ermastering rhyme!
I covered either little foot,
  I drew the strings about its waist;
Pink as the unshelled inner fruit,
  But barely decent, hardly chaste,
Its nudity had startled me;
  But when the petticoats were on,
'I know,' I said; 'its name shall be
  Paul Cyril Athanasius John.'
'Why,' said my wife, 'the child's a girl.'
  My brain swooned, sick with failing sense;
With all perception in a whirl,
  How could I tell the difference?

' Nay,' smiled the nurse, ' the child 's a boy.'
  And all my soul was soothed to hear
That so it was : then startled Joy
  Mocked Sorrow with a doubtful tear
And I was glad as one who sees
  For sensual optics things unmeet :
As purity makes passion freeze,
  So faith warns science off her beat.
Blessed are they that have not seen,
  And yet, not seeing, have believed :
To walk by faith, as preached the Dean,
  And not by sight, have I achieved.
Let love, that does not look, believe ;
  Let knowledge, that believes not, look :
Truth pins her trust on falsehood's sleeve,
  While reason blunders by the book.
Then Mrs. Prig addressed me thus ;
  ' Sir, if you'll be advised by me,
You'll leave the blessed babe to us ;
  It 's my belief he wants his tea.'

                                 A. C. SWINBURNE.

494. SONNET FOR A PICTURE

THAT nose is out of drawing. With a gasp,
  She pants upon the passionate lips that ache
  With the red drain of her own mouth, and make
A monochord of colour. Like an asp,
One lithe lock wriggles in his rutilant grasp.
  Her bosom is an oven of myrrh, to bake
  Love's white warm shewbread to a browner cake.
The lock his fingers clench has burst its hasp.
The legs are absolutely abominable.
  Ah ! what keen overgust of wild-eyed woes
  Flags in that bosom, flushes in that nose ?
Nay ! Death sets riddles for desire to spell,
  Responsive. What red hem earth's passion sews,
But may be ravenously unripped in hell ?

                                 A. C. SWINBURNE.

495. NEPHELIDIA

FROM the depth of the dreamy decline of the dawn through a notable
  nimbus of nebulous noonshine,
  Pallid and pink as the palm of the flag-flower that flickers with fear of
  the flies as they float,
Are they looks of our lovers that lustrously lean from a marvel of mystic
  miraculous moonshine,
  These that we feel in the blood of our blushes that thicken and threaten
  with throbs through the throat ?
Thicken and thrill as a theatre thronged at appeal of an actor's appalled
  agitation,
  Fainter with fear of the fires of the future than pale with the promise
  of pride in the past ;
Flushed with the famishing fullness of fever that reddens with radiance
  of rathe recreation,
  Gaunt as the ghastliest of glimpses that gleam through the gloom of
  the gloaming when ghosts go aghast ?
Nay, for the nick of the tick of the time is a tremulous touch on the
  temples of terror,
  Strained as the sinews yet strenuous with strife of the dead who is
  dumb as the dust-heaps of death :
Surely no soul is it, sweet as the spasm of erotic emotional exquisite error,
  Bathed in the balms of beatified bliss, beatific itself by beatitude's
  breath.
Surely no spirit or sense of a soul that was soft to the spirit and soul of
  our senses
  Sweetens the stress of suspiring suspicion that sobs in the semblance
  and sound of a sigh ;
Only this oracle opens Olympian, in mystical moods and triangular
  tenses—
  ' Life is the lust of a lamp for the light that is dark till the dawn of the
  day when we die.'
Mild is the mirk and monotonous music of memory, melodiously mute as
  it may be,
  While the hope in the heart of a hero is bruised by the breach of men's
  rapiers, resigned to the rod ;
Made meek as a mother whose bosom-beats bound with the bliss-bringing
  bulk of a balm-breathing baby,
  As they grope through the graveyard of creeds, under skies growing
  green at a groan for the grimness of God.
Blank is the book of his bounty beholden of old, and its binding is blacker
  than bluer :
  Out of blue into black is the scheme of the skies, and their dews are
  the wine of the bloodshed of things ;
Till the darkling desire of delight shall be free as a fawn that is freed
  from the fangs that pursue her,
  Till the heart-beats of hell shall be hushed by a hymn from the hunt
  that has harried the kennel of kings.

A. C. SWINBURNE.

496. GOOD-NIGHT

GOOD-NIGHT ? ah ! no ; the hour is ill
  Which severs those it should unite ;
Let us remain together still,
  Then it will be *good* night.

How can I call the lone night good,
  Though thy sweet wishes wing its flight ?
Be it not said, thought, understood,
  Then it will be—*good* night.

To hearts which near each other move
  From evening close to morning light,
The night *is* good ; because, my love,
  They never *say* good-night.

P. B. SHELLEY.

497. AUF WIEDERSEHEN

SUMMER

THE little gate was reached at last,
  Half hid in lilacs down the lane ;
She pushed it wide, and, as she past,
A wistful look she backward cast,
  And said,—' *Auf wiedersehen !* '

With hand on latch, a vision white
  Lingered reluctant, and again
Half doubting if she did aright,
Soft as the dews that fell that night,
  She said,—' *Auf wiedersehen !* '

The lamp's clear gleam flits up the stair ;
  I linger in delicious pain ;
Ah, in that chamber, whose rich air
To breathe in thought I scarcely dare,
  Thinks she,—' *Auf wiedersehen !* '

'Tis thirteen years ; once more I press
  The turf that silences the lane ;
I hear the rustle of her dress,
I smell the lilacs, and—ah, yes,
  I hear ' *Auf wiedersehen !* '

Sweet piece of bashful maiden art !
  The English words had seemed too fain,
But these—they drew us heart to heart,
Yet held us tenderly apart ;
  She said, ' *Auf wiedersehen !* '

J. R. LOWELL.

NOTES

[The notes marked F. L.-L. are those of Mr. Locker-Lampson in the 'new and revised edition' of *Lyra Elegantiarum*, published in 1867.]

PAGE 1. No. 1.—Cowper, the poet, says, ' Every man conversant with verse-making knows, and knows by painful experience, that the familiar style is of all styles the most difficult to succeed in. To make verse speak the language of prose, without being prosaic, to marshal the words of it in such an order as they might naturally take in falling from the lips of an extemporary speaker, yet without meanness, harmoniously, elegantly, and without seeming to displace a syllable for the sake of the rhyme, is one of the most arduous tasks a poet can undertake. He that could accomplish this task was Prior : many have imitated his excellence in this particular, but the best copies have fallen short of the original.'—F. L.-L.

PAGE 6. Nos. 9 and 10.—Mr. Swinburne says : ' There are loftier sonnets in the language, there is no lovelier sonnet in the world, than the late Lord Rosslyn's " Bedtime ". "It gives a very echo to the seat where love is throned "—the painless and stainless love of little children. Landor might and would, for all his fantastic and factitious abhorrence of their form, have given a place to this divine sonnet and its coequal companion in a truly blessed immortality, Mr. Tennyson Turner's on "Letty's Globe", in his list of exceptions to the common rule or the conventional axiom which denies that any work of man's can ever be absolutely perfect.'

PAGE 11. No. 18.—'Among the happiest of Praed's efforts.'—F. L.-L.

PAGE 14. No. 22.—For the guidance of the reader more familiar with Gray's ' On a distant prospect of Eton College', Hood notes that this has ' no connexion with any other ode '.

PAGE 20. No. 25.—Mr. Swinburne disliked Calverley—' the monstrously overrated and preposterously overpraised.' ' A jester, graduate, or under-graduate,' he wrote, ' may be fit enough to hop, skip, and tumble before university audiences, without capacity to claim an enduring or even a passing station among even the humblest of English humorists.'
Calverley quotes the lines of Gray :—

> Poor moralist, and what art thou ?
> A solitary fly

a : a footnote to ' poor moralist' in the last stanza.

PAGE 22. No. 26.—This parody appeared in *The Light Green*, reprints of Parts I and II of which can be obtained of Messrs. Metcalfe, Cambridge. It is, of course, a parody of Bret Harte's poem which will be found on page 145.

PAGE 24. No. 27.—' It is rather difficult to make a selection from Thomas Moore : nearly everything that he has written might be claimed as *vers de société*, whether it be epitaph, epigram, ballad, or sacred song. He could not help being witty and sparkling, and perhaps a little artificial.'—F. L.-L.

Moore suppressed two verses—the third and sixth as originally printed, i.e.

> Young Sappho, for want of employments,
>   Alone o'er her Ovid may melt,
> Condemned but to read of enjoyments
>   Which wiser Corinna had felt.
>
> . . . .
>
> In Ethics—'tis you that can check,
>   In a minute, their doubts and their quarrels ;
> Oh! show but that mole on your neck,
>   And 'twill soon put an end to their morals.

PAGE 26. No. 29.—The young gentleman was Mr. Thrale's nephew, Sir John Lade, who made an ' unfortunate marriage ' and contrived to waste the whole of a fine fortune before he died. Boswell remarks that ' these improviso lines' show ' a mind of surprising activity and warmth; the more so as he [Johnson] was past seventy years of age when he composed them.' Johnson sent to Mrs. Piozzi the ' song, which you must not show to anybody '.

PAGE 28. No. 34.—This and the next are based on Catullus's ' Vivamus mea Lesbia, atque amamus '.

PAGE 29. No. 36.—From *Occasional Verses* (1665), where the poem, which contains two more verses than here, is called ' Ditty in imitation of the Spanish Entre tantoque L'Avril.'

PAGE 32. No. 42.—Compare Matthew Arnold's ' Horatian Echo ' :—

> The day approaches, when we must
> Be crumbling bones and windy dust ;
> And scorn us as our mistress may,
> Her beauty will no better be
> Than the poor face she slights in thee,
>   When dawns that day, that day.

PAGE 33. No. 45.—Mr. Swinburne would rule this out as not a sample of social verse : ' it is an echo from the place of conscious or unconscious torment which is paved with penitence and roofed with despair. Its quiet note of commonplace resignation is more bitter and more impressive in the self-scornful sadness of its retrospect than any shriek of rebellion or any imprecation of appeal.'

PAGE 39. No. 54.—From ' Don Juan ', Canto I, stanzas 123 to 127.

PAGE 42. No. 61.—A well, attended by a nymph, Aganippe, at the foot of Mount Helicon, sacred to the Muses, the water of which gave inspiration to the drinker.

PAGE 43. No. 64.—Compare No. 171, page 112.

PAGE 46. No. 71.—From the German by Lessing.

PAGE 63. No. 100.—One of the ' Love Songs by the Fat Contributor' in *Punch*. 'Articles of furniture are deservedly favourite subjects with domestic poets; witness those celebrated verses, "My Uncle's Old Hat," 'My Grandmother's Muff," "My Ancestor's Coal-scuttle," &c., by Miss Bunion and other poetesses, who have taken such a strong hold on the affections of the public.'—W. M. T.

PAGE 68. No. 107.—Mr. Swinburne asserts that, ' If Skelton's and Wyatt's orthography may be modified or modernized, as assuredly it may be without protest from any but the most horny-eyed and beetle-headed of pedants, so assuredly may Chaucer's.' By permission of the Rev. Professor Skeat the following modern version by him is appended :—

> My lady, ye of beauty are the shrine,
> As far as stretches earth's remotest bound ;
> For as the crystal glorious ye shine,
> And like the ruby are your cheeks so round.
> Beside, your jocund mirth doth so redound,
> That, at a revel when I see you dance,
> 'Tis like an ointment to my inward wound
> Though ye vouchsafe to me no cómplaisance.
>
> For though my tears should fill a tun for wine,
> Yet e'en that woe will not my heart confound ;
> The charming notes ye sing, so clear and fine,
> Can make my thoughts with joy and bliss abound.
> So courteously I move, by love so crowned,
> That to myself I say, in my sad chance,
> Content am I to love you, Rosamound,
> Though ye vouchsafe to me no cómplaisance.
>
> Was never pike so soused in galantine
> As I by love am wrapped and compassed round ;
> And therefore of myself I oft divine,
> A second Tristram is in me renowned.
> My love can ne'er be chilled, nor yet be drowned ;
> I burn for ever in an amorous trance.
> Do what ye will, your thrall will I be found,
> Though ye vouchsafe to me no cómplaisance.

G. CHAUCER (trans. by REV. PROF. SKEAT).

Dr. Skeat, in his Oxford edition of Chaucer, gives the following explanations:—mappemonde is French, Latin mappa mundi—' as far as the map of the world extends ' ; tyne = a large tub ; seemly = pleasing ; smal =

fine in tone, delicate, perhaps treble ; out-twyne = twist out, force out. Verse iii ' never was pike so involved in galantine-sauce as I am completely involved in love,' a humorous allusion to a manner of serving up pikes which is well illustrated in the fifteenth-century cookery-books ; refreyd = refrigerated ; afounde = sink, be submerged. The *Oxford English Dictionary* defines galantine ' as a kind of sauce for fish and fowl ' : this use of the word being obsolete.

Compare Sam Weller's description of Mr. Winkle : ' He 's in a horrid state o' love ; reg'larly comfoozled, and done over with it.'

PAGE 69. No. 110.—Elizabeth, daughter of James I and wife of the Elector Palatine, Frederick V, chosen King of Bohemia in 1619. Howell, in *Familiar Letters*, says she was not only Queen of Bohemia, but also ' for her winning princely comportment the Queen of Hearts '.

PAGE 74. No. 119.—Bonnie Lesley was Miss Lesley Baillie. Mr. Baillie, of Ayrshire, with his two daughters, called on Burns at Dumfries, and he accompanied his visitors for fifteen miles on their way to England, composing the song on his ride homeward.

PAGE 78. No. 126.—' Has things in it vivid and subtle as anything in Shelley at his best ; and I affirm this deliberately ' !—GROSART.

PAGE 84. No. 129.—Margaret was a servant girl employed by the poet's cousin, Gray.

PAGE 86. No. 132.—Mr. F. T. Palgrave says (*Golden Treasury*) :—' A little masterpiece in a very difficult style : Catullus himself could hardly have bettered it. In grace, tenderness, simplicity, and humour, it is worthy of the Ancients ; and even more so, from the completeness and unity of the picture presented.' It is rejected by Mr. Locker-Lampson as ' too homely, and too entirely simple and natural ' for the *Lyra Elegantiarum*.

PAGE 91. No. 138.—In Mr. Godley's Oxford Edition of Moore there is the following note, which explains the reference in the second verse :— ' This alludes to a kind of Irish fairy, which is to be met with, they say, in the fields at dusk. As long as you keep your eyes upon him, he is fixed, and in your power ;—but the moment you look away (and he is ingenious in furnishing some inducement) he vanishes. I had thought that this was the sprite which we call the Leprechaun ; but a high authority upon such subjects, Lady Morgan (in a note upon her national and interesting novel, *O'Donnel*), has given a very different account of that goblin.'

PAGE 103. No. 160.—This reply to Marlowe's ' Come live with me ' (excluded by Mr. Locker-Lampson as ' too highly poetical ', though the reply is admitted ' because it is depressed to the requisite level by the tinge of worldly satire which runs through it ') is attributed to Ralegh ' in his younger days', on the authority of Isaak Walton in *The Compleat Angler*. Compare Donne's poem (p. 261).

PAGE 121. No. 190.—From 'Cadenus and Vanessa', 'thought to be', Goldsmith says, 'one of Dr. Swift's correctest pieces'. Vanessa was Miss Vanhomrigh ; Cadenus, of course, Dean (' Decanus') Swift himself.

PAGE 122. No. 194.—' Kitty was Lady Katherine Hyde, afterwards Duchess of Queensberry. Lady Jenny was Lady Jane Hyde, then Countess of Essex.'—F. L.-L.

PAGES 122 and 123. Nos. 195 and 196.—Miss Lepel was maid of honour to Queen Caroline. She afterwards married Lord Hervey.

PAGE 124. No. 198.—A humorous account of the poet's acquaintance with Lady Cobham, who lived at Stoke Pogis. This lady sent her relative, Miss Harriet Speed, and Lady Schaub to invite the poet to call upon her, so impressed was she by the Elegy. ' My grave Lord Keeper' is Sir Christopher Hatton; Sir Luke Schaub, 'cap à pie from France,' had been Ambassador in Paris ; ' the other Amazon', Miss Speed, afterwards wife of Count de Viry ; the Rev. Mr. Purt was tutor to the Duke of Bridgewater ; Tyacke was the housekeeper; Squib, groom of the chamber; Groom, steward ; Macleane, a highwayman, just hanged.

PAGE 137. No. 209.—With regard to the last word in verse four, Moore's early poems were published in the name of Thomas Little, and his later judgement suppressed them for being too erotic.

PAGE 139. No. 210.—Another version, signed Phi, appeared in the *Court Journal* in 1832. I am able to give Sir George Young's conclusion, viz. :— ' That (1) the *idea* of this piece, with a hint or two as to how it should be worked out, was given by Praed to his friend E. Marlborough Fitzgerald ; who thereupon (2) produced the piece, substantially as in the *Court Journal* ; which again (3) was probably corrected and enriched by Praed ; (4) Praed afterwards rewriting it as in the MSS., which recently came into my possession, according to his own original idea.

PAGE 145. No. 215.—*See* p. 22 for Hilton's parody of this.

PAGE 150. No. 222.—Coleridge wrote that he had no particular General in mind. Several verses have been omitted.

PAGE 151. No. 223.—This was suggested by a speech in which Mr. Wilberforce, replying to an observation of Dr. Lushington, that ' the Society for the Suppression of Vice meddled with the poor alone ', said that ' the offences of the poor came more under observation than those of the rich'. Mr. Swinburne considers 'the riper and richer humour of Peacock as superior to Praed's as dry champagne to sweet, or a sultana grape to a green gooseberry '.

PAGE 152. No. 224.—This appeared in the first number of *The Brazen Head*, a short-lived periodical started by Praed and others in 1826, and was thus introduced : ' Brazen companion of my solitary hours ! do you, while I recline, pronounce a prologue to those sentiments of Wisdom and Virtue, which are hereafter to be the oracles of statesmen, and the guides of philosophers. Give me to-night a proem of our essay, an opening of our case, a division of our subject. Speak ! ' (*Slow music. The Friar falls asleep. The head chaunts as follows.*)

PAGE 154. No. 225.—Published anonymously at first in *An Offering to Lancashire* issued for the benefit of the sufferers from the cotton famine.

PAGE 155. No. 226.—This is only a fragment from a long poem.

PAGE 168. No. 238.—' Even more out of place in such good company [than Calverley : see note to No. 25 on p. 413] is the weary and wearisome laureate of Oxonicules and Bostonicules, Mr. Lowell's realized and chosen representative of English poetry at its highest in the generation of Tennyson and Browning ; whose message to his generation may be summed up as follows :

> We've got no faith, and we don't know what to do :
> To think one can't believe a creed because it isn't true ! *

> (* Et certamen erat, Corydon cum Thyrside, parvum.)

Literary history will hardly care to remember or to register the fact that there was a bad poet named Clough, whom his friends found it useless to puff : for the public, if dull, has not quite such a skull as belongs to believers in Clough.'—A. C. SWINBURNE.

PAGE 169. No. 240.—Mr. Swinburne also condemned Mr. Locker-Lampson for including poems from the *Anti-Jacobin*. ' It is something above and beyond all realized conceptions of incongruity,' he wrote, ' to hoist the flag of " no politics " and pass the watchword of " no parodies ", and then to salute the reader with a broadside of brutality and burlesque, a discharge of mildewed mockery and fly-blown caricature, from the social and political battery of Messrs. Canning and Frere.'

Southey's essay in sapphics, of which this is a parody, was entitled ' The Widow ' and began :

> Cold was the night wind, drifting fast the snow fell ;
> Wide were the downs and shelterless and naked,
> When a poor wanderer struggled on her journey,
> Weary and way-sore.

The ' Friend of Humanity ' signified George Tierney, who fought a duel with Pitt, and held several offices, being finally Master of the Mint, under Canning. Canning's copy of the *Anti-Jacobin* credits Frere and himself with this poem, and with ' Mrs. Brownrigg ', which is given on p. 393.

PAGE 170. No. 241.—'Mr. Falck, the Dutch Minister in 1826, having made a proposition by which a considerable advantage would have accrued to Holland, this poetical dispatch was actually sent by Canning to Sir Charles Bagot, the English Ambassador at the Hague, and soon afterwards an Order in Council was issued to put into effect the intention so announced.'—F. L.-L. The dispatch was sent in cypher: this version, of several, is the correct one.

PAGE 170. No. 242.—Moore says that this 'squib' was wrung from him by the Irish Coercion Act of his friends, the Whigs.

PAGE 172. No. 244.—These lines are extremely characteristic of the author's extraordinary fluency and mastery of rhyme. They appeared originally in the book of the 'Cambridge Lotus Club'. The fifteenth line from the end was printed, by a lapsus calami, incorrectly in *Lapsus Calami*.

PAGE 176. No. 248.—Hamilton's Bawn was an old house belonging to Sir Arthur Acheson, Bart., whose wife, Anne Savage, was daughter of an Irish Chancellor of the Exchequer. Rums = Irish for poor country clergymen; Darby and Wood = two of Sir Arthur's managers; Dr. Jinny: a local clergyman; Noveds, &c. = Ovids, Plutarchs, and Homers. *See* note to No. 357, pp. 421 and 422.

PAGE 181. No. 250.—'These verses express, with much force and humour, the feelings of the British nation on military affairs after the close of the long struggle with France. Five-and-twenty years of almost incessant fighting had made people heartily weary of soldiers and soldiering. But at the present era of non-intervention the poem has a satirical application which Praed probably did not intend.'—F. L.-L.

PAGE 185. No. 253.—This poem is prefaced by the following extract from the *Morning Post* :—'A surgeon of the United States army says that, on inquiring of the Captain of his company, he found that *nine-tenths* of the men had enlisted on account of some female difficulty.'

PAGE 186. No. 254.—The Higher Criticism has sought to deprive these lines of their impromptu character. Instead of having been written on the night before the engagement, in which the Dutch admiral was blown up with all his crew, the composition is said to have cost its author time and trouble.

PAGE 188. No. 255.—In the marriage register of Warlingham, for 1724, is this entry :—'Sweet William and Black-eyed Susan, alias William Blackman and Susan Humfrey, both of this parish of Warlingham, were married by banns, Dec. 26th, 1724. D. Price, Vicar.'

PAGE 189. No. 256.—'Suckling is remarkable for a careless natural grace. This is one of his best poems, and, as Leigh Hunt says, "his fancy is so full of gusto as to border on imagination." The bridegroom is said to have been Lord Broghill, and the bride Lady Margaret Howard, daughter of the Earl of Suffolk. Three [several] stanzas of this poem have been necessarily omitted.'—F. L.-L.

PAGE 193. No. 262.—' That kind of horse-gallop of an air which precludes sentiment. The ludicrous is its ruling feature.'—BURNS.

PAGE 195. No. 265.—This poem, when first published in the *London Magazine*, was thus introduced :—

' We have received the following letter :

" SIR,—After reading the other day that Pope could have extracted poetry out of a warming pan, it occurred to me that I could, perhaps, wring a verse of two out of a bell, or strike a few stanzas out of a brass knocker." '

PAGE 196. No. 267.—From the volume entitled *Amelia*, published in 1878.

PAGE 200. No. 272.—' Low as is the key of these tenderer verses in comparison with the fiery and faultless music, the subtle and simple intensity of the four transcendent lines which suggested them, it seems to me,' Mr. Swinburne observes, 'that Sappho's very self might have smiled approval, or at least condonation of their gentler loveliness and less passionate melody than her own.'

PAGE 209. No. 290.—Jane = Mrs. Williams. ' All the verses Shelley addressed to her passed through her husband's hands without the slightest interruption to their intercourse ; and Mrs. Shelley, who was not unpardonably jealous of her Ariel, continued to be Mrs. Williams's warm friend.'— J. ADDINGTON SYMONDS. Trelawny says the MS. ' was a frightful scrawl ; words smeared out with his finger, and one upon the other, over and over in tiers, and all run together in " most admired disorder ".'

PAGES 211, 212. Nos. 291, 292.—Herrick also wrote some lines to Lawes : ' Touch but thy lyre, my Harry.'

PAGE 219. No. 300.—In later editions the author was at pains to explain that the remark in the seventh stanza was that of a habitué of St. James's, but that he himself had a sincere admiration for the American people. *See* the note on Lepel, p. 417.

PAGE 220. No. 301.—An excerpt from ' Artist and Model '.

PAGE 224. No. 304.—Tutties = nosegays.

PAGE 227. No. 306.—Verse 3, line 6, durns=doorposts ; verse 4, line 1, tun = chimney ; verse 5, line 4, hatch = gate, line 5, clavy = mantel.

PAGE 235. No. 316.—The authorship of these lines is uncertain, but they are obviously based on an inferior poem of four verses written by William Somerville (1675-1742), who wrote ' The Chase '.

PAGE 236. No. 318.—'The flexibility and variety of Barham's rhythm is quite wonderful. Tom Moore, Praed, and Prior could not have produced a more graceful piece of drollery than these lines.'—F. L. L.

PAGE 236. No. 320.—'This gracefullest and sweetest of all compliments ever offered to a sweet and graceful English girl,' is Mr. Swinburne's comment.

PAGE 237. No. 321.—'The lovely song (as of a graver and more thoughtful Herrick).'—A. C. SWINBURNE.

PAGE 240. No. 324.—' Creech's :—

> Plain truth, dear Murray, needs no flowers of speech,
> To take it in the very words of Creech.'—A. POPE.

PAGE 244. No. 330.—Walpole, after the death of Gray, preserved the China vase on a pedestal at Strawberry Hill, with an inscription from the ode.

PAGE 245. No. 331.—'This has been cut down to bring it within the scope of the collection. I think it has not suffered in consequence.'— F. L.-L.

PAGE 261. No. 346.—See Ralegh's poem on p. 103, and the note on p. 416.

PAGE 266. No. 352.—Themis was the goddess of justice. Skinner's mother was Sir E. Coke's daughter. Sweden was at the time of writing at war with Poland, and France with the Spanish Netherlands.

PAGE 266. No. 353.—Mr. Swinburne's remarks on this poem must be given in full :—

' The melodious stanzas to Augusta might surely have found a place— with or without the closing verses (unaccountably omitted from the current editions of Byron) which are hardly necessary to explain and justify the enthusiastic admiration of that most exquisite critic, Edgar Poe, for the metrical perfection of that most mellifluous poem—usually and prematurely broken off short after the fourth of the following sweet lines:

> In the desert a fountain is springing,
> *In the wide waste there still is a tree,*
> And a bird in the solitude singing
> Which speaks to my spirit of thee.
>
> Thou thought'st verses like these could be scanned—which
> Was absurd, but uncommonly kind :
> Thou said'st each stanza was not a sandwich
> Of blank prose and rank doggerel combined :
> Thou found'st out some strange sort of sweet fitness
> In the rhythms mauled and mangled by me ;
> And such ears, I take Midas to witness,
> Belong but to donkeys and thee.'

PAGE 268. No. 354.—' This brave affectionate lyric—(surely its second stanza embodies as good and sound a philosophy of life as Protestant could desire ?)—was meant as the writer's farewell ere he went into exile in the April of 1816.'—W. E. HENLEY.

PAGE 269. No. 356.—Mr. Lang has also been immortalized in the ' Ballade of Andrew Lang ', published in the *Oxford Magazine* :

> You ask me, Fresher, who it is
>   Who rhymes, researches, and reviews,
> Who sometimes writes like Genesis,
>   And sometimes for the *Daily News* :
> Who jests in words that angels use,
>   And is most solemn with most slang :
> Who 's who—who 's which—and which is whose ?
>   Who can it be but Andrew Lang ?

PAGE 270. No. 357.—' Perhaps this is the most humorous piece of verse in the English language, and yet it is essentially *vers de société*. One or two slight expressions have been softened down, both here and in other pieces, to suit the taste of the day. " Whittle " was the Earl of Berkeley's valet ; " Dame Wadger " was the deaf old housekeeper ; " Lord Colway " means Galway ; " Lord Dromedary " means Drogheda ; " Cary " was clerk of the kitchen ; " Mrs. Dukes " was a servant, and wife to one of the footmen. " The Chaplain " refers to Swift himself.'—F. L.-L.

With regard to this, Mr. Swinburne notes : ' The perfection of taste and tact displayed in the discharge of such a task as the presentation of Swift at his best, and of Swift in the fullness of his powers, to the modern reader of either sex and any possible age—and this without hint or suspicion of offence—is notable alike for simplicity, for dexterity, and for daring. Two poems in which the genius of Aristophanes shakes hands with the genius of Dickens—for Swift has revived the one and anticipated the other in his exquisite abuse of language, and his delicious perversion of proper names—" Hamilton's Bawn " and " Mrs. Harris's Petition ", are now, by the slightest and most delicate of touches, made accessible to all lovers of the rarest humour and the most resplendent wit : we only miss Mary the cookmaid's not less wonderful and delightful letter to Dr. Sheridan.'

The last mentioned has been included in this volume, and it has the merit of not needing any excision: *see* page 272. ' Hamilton's Bawn ' will be found on page 176.

PAGE 275. No. 361.—' Lady Mary W. Montagu wrote very smartly. Lord Lyttelton once sent her some highly didactic and sentimental lines, beginning, " The councils of a friend, Belinda, hear," of which Lady Mary made the following concise summary :

> " Be plain in dress, and sober in your diet,
>   In short, my deary, kiss me, and be quiet."

Her verses on Sir Robert Walpole are happy, but they inevitably recall the exquisite couplets of Pope :

> "Seen him I have, but in his happier hour
> Of social pleasure, ill-exchanged for power ;
> Seen him, uncumbered with the venal tribe,
> Smile without art, and win without a bribe." '—F. L.-L.

PAGE 276. No. 362.—This poem, of which only a part is here printed, was written at Pisa in 1820, and, Mr. J. Addington Symonds says, might be mentioned as a pendant to ' Julian and Maddalo for its treatment of familiar things ; one of Shelley's most genial poems '.

Byron in ' Don Juan ' wrote :

> And Coleridge, too, has lately taken wing,
> But like a hawk encumbered with his hood.

PAGE 289. No. 369.—At the conclusion of a prefatory memoir of Kingsley, contributed by T. Hughes to the 1876 edition of *Alton Locke*, the writer states : ' A few weeks later [in the summer of 1856] I received the following invitation to Snowdon, and to Snowdon we went in the autumn of 1856,' Macdougall was the Bishop of Labuan.

PAGE 292. No. 371, l. 20.—Knat, also gnat, now obsolete except in dialect, was a kind of sandpiper ; ruff was also the male of a bird of the sandpiper family ; rail, a bird of the family *Rallidae*, especially of the genus *Rallus* : compare land-rail, water-rail

PAGE 294. No. 374.—' That it represents the actual thanks of the poet to Lord Clare [afterwards Earl Nugent, *see* p. 117] for an actual present of venison, part of which he promptly transferred to Reynolds, is probably the fact. But it is also clear that Goldsmith borrowed, if not his entire fable, at least some of its details, from Boileau's third satire ; and that, in certain of the lines, he had in memory Swift's " Grand Question Debated " [*see* p. 176], the measure of which he adopts.'—Mr. AUSTIN DOBSON (Oxford edition of Goldsmith's Poems).

In the second paragraph : Mr. Byrne was a relative of Lord Clare. M—r—'s=Dorothy Monroe's. The line, ' There's H—d,' &c., originally was : ' There's Coley, and Williams, and Howard, and Hiff ' (i. e. Hiffernan) ; ' my countryman ' was Higgins.

PAGE 296. No. 375.—' Dr. Goldsmith and some of his friends occasionally dined at the St. James's Coffee-house, where one day it was proposed to write epitaphs on him. He was challenged to retaliate, and these lines were the result. " Our Dean," Dr. Barnard, Dean of Derry [then, finally Bishop of Limerick ; *see* p. 310] ; Edmund Burke ; Mr. William Burke, M.P. for Bedwin ; Mr. Richard Burke, Collector of Grenada ; Cumberland the dramatist ; Dr. Douglas, Canon of Windsor [afterwards Bishop of Salisbury] ; Counsellor John Ridge, an Irish barrister ; Hickey, an eminent

attorney; Townshend, M.P. for Whitchurch; Dr. Dodd, the popular
preacher; Dr. Kenrick lectured at the Devil's Tavern; Macpherson, of
"Ossian" celebrity; Mr. Woodfall was printer of the *Morning Chronicle*.'—
F. L.-L.

Scarron (1610–60), whose works Goldsmith had been translating.

Mr. Austin Dobson points out that this poem was composed and circulated
in detached fragments, and that Goldsmith was still working on it when he
was seized with his last illness.

PAGE 301. No. 377.—From 'Memories of Gormandizing', in which it is
printed side by side with the Latin. 'Who knew or studied this cheap
philosophy of life better than old Horace ? . . . How affecting (Thackeray
wrote) is the last ode of the first book :

> To his serving-boy—*Persicos odi,*
> > *Puer, apparatur,*' &c.

PAGE 302. No. 379.—Pretzel—bretzel, bread ; Souse undt Brouse, i. e.
Saus und Braus, riot and bustle ; Gensy-broost, i. e. Gänsebust, goose meat ;
Bratwurst und Braten, sausages and roast meats ; Abendessen, supper ;
himmelstrahlende stern, heavenly shining star ; ewigkeit, eternity.

PAGE 310. No. 389.—'Dr. Barnard had asserted, in Dr. Johnson's
presence, that men did not improve after the age of forty-five. "That is
not true, sir," said Johnson. "You, who perhaps are forty-eight, may still
improve, if you will try ; I wish you would set about it. And I am afraid,"
he added, "there is great room for it." Johnson afterwards greatly regretted
his rudeness to the bishop, who took the insult in good part, wrote the
following verses next day, and sent them to Sir Joshua Reynolds.'—F. L.-L.

'I know not,' Boswell writes, 'whether Johnson ever saw the poem, but I
had occasion to find that as Dr. Barnard and he knew each other better,
their mutual regard increased.' Boswell also gives with peculiar pleasure
to the world, 'a just and elegant compliment' paid to the Bishop by Johnson
in the form of a charade :

> My first shuts out thieves from your house or your room,
> My second expresses a Syrian perfume.
> My whole is a man in whose converse is shar'd,
> The strength of a Bar and the sweetness of Nard.

PAGE 314. No. 394.—Stale=an excuse, or snare. Shakespeare uses the
same word—'for stale to catch these thieves'—in *The Tempest*, IV. i. 187.

PAGE 314. No. 395.—'It is one of Ben Jonson's distinctions among
English poets that he contrives to be most spontaneous when most imitative.
This immortally careless rapture is meticulously pieced together from scraps
of the Love Letters of Philostratus, a Greek rhetorician of the second century
A.D.' (Sir A. T. Quiller-Couch in *The Golden Pomp*). Jonson's 'Still to be

Neat' (p. 52), and 'Come, my Celia' (p. 29), are also imitated from the classics.

PAGE 321.   No. 403.—Bishop Still's poem is from 'Gammer Gurton's Needle' (1575).

PAGE 322.   No. 404.—The allusion in verse 7 is to ' Jupiter and the Indian Ale ' :

> 'Bring it!' quoth the Cloud-compeller;
> And the wine-god brought the beer—
> 'Port and Claret are like water
> To the noble stuff that 's here.'

PAGE 326.   No. 407.—From ' Will Waterproof's Lyrical Monologue made at the Cock,' addressed to 'the plump head-waiter ', and ending :

> No carved cross-bones, the types of Death,
> Shall show thee passed to Heaven :
> But carved cross-pipes, and, underneath,
> A pint-pot, neatly graven.'

PAGE 334.   Nos. 412, 413.—These are two of a series, *A Pipe of To-bacco: in imitation of six several authors* (1768)—Cibber, Ambrose Philips, Thomson, Young, Pope, and Swift.

The imitation of Philips (*see* page 5 for the original) is prefaced by the line from Virgil :

> Tenues fugit ceu fumus in auras.

Lucan is quoted at the beginning of the imitation of Pope's style :

> Solis ad ortus
> Vanescit fumus.

PAGE 336.   No. 415.—Taken from ' The Island ', Canto II, stanza xix.

PAGE 349.   No. 428.—This was written in 1835, ' a composition,' Campbell wrote, ' which will remain in the English language until it is forgotten.' The poet was sea-sick, and received kindness from a person whom he took for a doctor, but who proved to be an Algerian barber.

PAGE 353.   No. 433.—Mr. Arthur Symons in *A Book of Parodies* states that ' The Groves of Blarney ' is a parody of a doggerel ballad ' Castle Hyde ' written by an itinerant poet named Barrett about 1790.   ' The Groves ' was translated into French, Latin, and Greek by Father Prout, who composed ' The Shandon Bells ' (No. 434) to its tune.

PAGE 370.   No. 446.—This was written in the album of Horace Smith's daughter.

PAGE 371.   No. 448.—Gay :   ' my own epitaph.'
> Life is a jest, and all things show it;
> I thought so once, but now I know it.

PAGE 380. No. 462.—Mr. Swinburne asserts that there is nothing in our language comparable with this quatrain.

PAGE 381. No. 463.—Mr. Swinburne also testifies to the beauty of these lines : ' The beautiful and simple memorial stanzas, so light and soft in movement, so grave and tender in emotion, which give so perfect and so sweet a picture of the typical English girl whom Mrs. Browning has made lovable and memorable for ever.'

PAGE 388. No. 471.—Based on a very long popular French song on Monsieur de la Palisse, the work originally of Bernard de la Monnoye, born 1641.

PAGE 389. No. 473.—Mr. Swinburne pleaded for the inclusion of at least part of this, especially the verse beginning ' Your most beautiful bit '. Bit=girl ; hogo (French, *haut goût*) = a savoury dish. One or two verses have been omitted, and certain lines modified.

PAGE 392. No. 477.—From ' The Rovers,' a farce ridiculing the German drama of Schiller, Kotzebue, and Goethe. It was played at the Haymarket Theatre in 1811. Sir Robert Adair, the friend of Fox, was educated at Gottingen, and was frequently burlesqued in the *Anti-Jacobin*. The last stanza is ascribed by some to Pitt. It is not published in the first edition, and there is a story that Canning showed the lament to Pitt in MS., and the Prime Minister was so delighted with it that he dashed off, impromptu, an ending. But, as Mr. Lloyd Sanders suggests, in *Selections from ' The Anti-Jacobin'*, even Gifford would not have dared to knock out a contribution by Pitt.

PAGE 393. No. 478.—Southey wrote several ' Sonnets and Elegies of Abel Shufflebottom', inspired by Coleridge's ' Higginbottom ' sonnets. The poetry that Southey made fun of was that of the Della Cruscan school, composed by English residents in Florence, who at the end of the eighteenth century became notorious for the rubbishy verses which they printed. The brotherhood found many admiring imitators : to quote Gifford, ' the epidemic malady spread from fool to fool.'

PAGE 393. No. 479.—Mrs. Brownrigg, the wife of a house-painter, was a real person, and was hanged at Tyburn in 1767. The poem parodied, written in 1795, when Southey was still in sympathy with the French Revolution, was an ' inscription for the apartment in Chepstow Castle, where Henry Martin, the regicide, was imprisoned thirty years '. It was excluded from later editions of Southey's works. *See* the parody on p. 169, and the note thereto.

PAGE 394. No. 480.—From *Alice in Wonderland*. This is a parody of Southey's ' The Old Man's Comforts, and how he gained them,' beginning :

You are old, Father William, the young man cried,
 The few locks that are left you are grey ;
You are hale, Father William, a hearty old man,
 Now tell me the reason I pray.

The poem ends :

 In the days of my youth I remembered my God !
  And he hath not forgotten my age.

PAGE 395. No. 482.—*Author's Note.* 'Jack and Nancy, as it was afterwards remarked to the Authors, are here made to come into the world at periods not sufficiently remote. The writers were then bachelors. One of them, unfortunately, still continues so, as he has thus recorded in his niece's album :

  Should I seek Hymen's tie,
  As a poet I die—
  Ye Benedicks, mourn my distresses ;
  For what little fame
  Is annexed to my name
 Is derived from *Rejected Addresses.*

The blunder, notwithstanding, remains unrectified. The reader of poetry is always dissatisfied with emendations ; they sound discordantly upon the ear, like a modern song, by Bishop or Braham, introduced in *Love in a Village.*' James Smith alone is credited with the authorship of this parody.

PAGE 397. No. 483.—The quintessence of Byron as distilled by Peacock into what Mr. Swinburne calls 'the two consummate stanzas which utter or exhale the lyric agony of Mr. Cypress.' It occurs in *Nightmare Abbey.*

Peacock's son-in-law, George Meredith, wrote some very contemptuous lines on Byron, entitled ' Manfred '.

PAGE 398. No. 484.—From the *Book of Ballads edited by Bon Gaultier,* i.e. Sir Theodore Martin and W. E. Aytoun. This parody of ' Locksley Hall ', by Sir T. Martin only, was considered by the author (in a letter to the present editor) his best contribution to the collection.

PAGE 403. No. 488.—Calverley is said to have had in mind William Morris's ' Two Red Roses across the Moon ', but probably the source of his inspiration was Jean Ingelow's ' The Apple Woman's Song ', from *Mopsa the Fairy,* which has for a recurring second line, ' Feathers, and moss, and a wisp of hay.'

PAGE 404. No. 489.—This is, of course, an imitation of the poetry of Miss Ingelow, who retaliated in *Fated to be Free* with satirical lines at the expense of ' Gifford Crayshaw '.

PAGE 406. No. 491.—From *The Diversions of the Echo Club,* in which a score of poets are parodied.

PAGE 407.   No. 492.—Compare D. G. Rossetti's 'Sister Helen', which begins :

> 'Why did you melt your waxen man,
>   Sister Helen ?
> To-day is the third since you began.'
> 'The time was long, yet the time ran,
>   Little brother.'
>   (*O Mother, Mary Mother,*
>   *Three days to-day, between Hell and Heaven !*)

PAGE 409.   No. 493.—This and the two following parodies are from *Specimens of Modern Poets | The Heptalogia | or | The Seven against Sense | A Cap with Seven Bells*, originally published anonymously.   The poets parodied include Tennyson, Robert and Mrs. Browning, Coventry Patmore, 'Owen Meredith', D. G. Rossetti, and Swinburne himself.   The first is the third part of a parody of Coventry Patmore's *The Angel in the House* ; No. 494 is a Rossetti ; No. 495 is, of course, a Swinburne, and shows that no one, gifted with a sense of humour, can more successfully parody a poet's style than the poet himself.

INDEX OF FIRST LINES AND TITLES

[The titles are printed in italics where differing from the first lines.]

OXFORD: HORACE HART
PRINTER TO THE UNIVERSITY